MI5 IN THE GREAT WAR

# MI5

## IN THE GREAT WAR

EDITED BY NIGEL WEST

Biteback Publishing

First published in Great Britain in 2014 by
Biteback Publishing Ltd
Westminster Tower
3 Albert Embankment
London SE1 7SP
Copyright © Nigel West 2014

ISBN 978-1-84954-670-6

10 9 8 7 6 5 4 3 2 1

A CIP catalogue record for this book is available from the British Library.

Set in Bembo by Soapbox

Printed and bound in Great Britain by
CPI Group (UK) Ltd, Croydon CR0 4Y

# CONTENTS

# ACKNOWLEDGEMENTS

THE editor is grateful for the advice of Judy Nokes of the National Archive at Kew for permission to reproduce the MI5 files KV 1/39 to KV 1/44.

# ABBREVIATIONS

| | |
|---|---|
| AOIC | Air Officer in Command |
| ARO | Aliens Restriction Order |
| BCI | Bureau Central Interallié |
| BEF | British Expeditionary Force |
| CGS | Chief of the General Staff |
| CSIS | Chief of the Secret Intelligence Service |
| DMI | Director of Military Intelligence |
| DMO | Director of Military Operations |
| DNI | Director of Naval Intelligence |
| DRR | Defence of the Realm Regulations |
| DSI | Defence Security Intelligence |
| GSO | General Staff Officer |
| HOW | Home Office Warrant |
| IGC | Inspector-General Communications |
| IO | Intelligence Officer |
| OSA | Official Secrets Act |
| MCO | Military Control Officer |
| MI-1(c) | Secret Intelligence Service |
| MI5 | Security Service |
| MI6 | Cable and War Trade |
| MI6(d) | Munitions Intelligence Branch |
| MI7 | Press Censorship |
| MI8 | Cable Censorship |
| MI9 | Postal Censorship |
| MO5G | Security Service |
| PoW | Prisoner of war |

| PSL | Possible Suspects List |
| R | British double agent in Holland |
| SWL | Special War List |
| T | Tobert Tornow |
| W/T | Wireless Telegraphy |
| WTID | War Trade Intelligence Department |

# ORGANISATION OF MI5'S G (INVESTIGATION) BRANCH

MI5 underwent three significant wartime reorganisations. In August 1915 MO5A became MO5G and consisted of five sub-sections: G, G1, G2, G3 and G4. In October 1915 G was further sub-divided into five sections and two new sub-sections, with G2 acquiring G2(a) and G2(b).

In April 1916 G2 absorbed G2(a); and G2(b) and became G6. In September 1916 G3 became D Branch. In January 1917 G2 was sub-divided into four sub-sections. G5, previously Oriental Affairs, was redesignated E Branch. Simultaneously, G2(a) became G4. Later the same year G3 became H Branch.

- G1: Sedition and peace propaganda
- G2: Counter-Espionage
- G2(a): Intercepted communications
- G2(b): Port Control
- G2(c): References from F Branch
- G2(d): All other sources
- G3: Photography, chemistry and technical research [later H Branch]
- G4: Intercepted correspondence [previously G2(a)]
- G5: Oriental Affairs, later Translations
- G6: Special enquiries [previously G2(b)]

# INTRODUCTION

IN 1921 MI5's Director-General, Colonel Vernon Kell, authorised the preparation of a comprehensive account of his organisation's operations during the Great War. His motives for doing so were partly to do with protecting his budget, primarily concerned with a struggle then raging within Whitehall to take control of the rival Secret Intelligence Service, and everything to do with the creation of a detailed record of what had been accomplished just before, and during the conflict, in relation to the then untold story of a massive German espionage offensive. It stands, therefore, as a unique record of a hitherto unknown dimension of Great Britain's intelligence history, and is all the more remarkable because the original author also had the benefit of post-war interrogation reports, for example of the German spy-master Hans Eils and, most helpfully, access to the roster of 136 agents compiled by the Zweigstelle staff at Antwerp, a copy of which was seized by the Belgian Sureté. Because this study would not be declassified for some ninety years, only those with a legitimate access to MI5's famous Registry could apply to read this extraordinary history. Even a century later, the declassified version still contains a few redacted passages, usually intended to conceal the true identity of a particular agent.

In pursuit of his various objectives, Kell commissioned an academic, Dr Lucy E. Farrer, to undertake the massive task of sifting through the records of hundreds of individual investigations, and then to create, in some ten volumes, each of more than two hundred pages of typescript, a veritable treasure trove of historical data which recorded MI5's extraordinary role in detecting and countering the Kaiser's efforts to construct a large spy network in Great Britain from 1905 onwards, and then to infiltrate significant numbers of agents through neutral countries, principally the Netherlands, Belgium, Norway, Denmark and the United States.

A graduate of the Sorbonne, Farrer took her PhD in literary history and in 1908 published an account of the life and times of Claude de Sainliens, a Hugenot refugee who arrived in England in about 1554, taught French in London for more than thirty years, compiled one of the first English-French dictionaries, and worked in Lewisham under the alias Claudius Hollyband, an Anglicised version of his surname.

As a scholar, Farrer had plenty of intelligence experience, having served in MI5 during the war; she summarised MI5's files, and the manuscript of her volumes was typed in April 1921 under the supervision of a Colonel Jervis, and then in January 1922, passed by a Major Phillips to a civilian clerk, H. M. Cubb. The entire work was then archived.

In the early days Kell's entry into the counter-espionage field was supported by a tiny staff, and undertook various duties, including liaising with the Home Office and military authorities, and acting as an interrogator of especially recalcitrant suspects. His outside investigations were conducted by two retired detectives, Superintendent William Melville and Inspector Regan, both formerly of Scotland Yard's Special Branch. For enquires further afield, Kell relied upon local constabularies, with very mixed results as all too often the German spies spotted the somewhat inept, supposedly clandestine, surveillance. As will be seen, Kell was also dependent on cooperation from the GPO, and the interception of the mail and telegrams, on warrants issued by the Home Office, was a crucial instrument in countering foreign espionage.

As for the German spies, they were undoubtedly well-briefed, professionally managed and often quite colourful. Take, for example, Mrs Emily Riley of Sheerness and her four beautiful daughters, Nellie, Patricia, Edith and Emily, all of whom became romantically involved with German agents. Patricia married Karl Hentschel who embezzled a huge sum of money from the Germans and decamped with his wife to Australia, taking her sister Edith too. Emily, a shop assistant, would marry George Pelling, an artificer in the Royal Navy. Edith would be courted by Captain Friedel Fels, the German intelligence officer sent to find the absconding Hentschel. Connected to them were Edith's fiancé Philip Penrose, who taught at the Royal Navy's Mechanical Training Establishment at Chatham and later worked at the Woolwich Arsenal, and another Royal Navy non-commissioned officer, George C. Parrott, who was Patricia's lover. Parrott's son-in-law, Gunner Francis Deacon, and his son Charles, were also serving in the Royal Navy and were implicated. This network, encompassing the strategically important naval bases at Chatham and Sheerness, was but one of several spy-rings never previously documented which monitored the movements of British warships, reported on naval exercises and researched the performance of new weapons and tactics adopted by the Royal Navy.

Although in recent years some historians have disparaged both a supposedly amateurish German effort to collect intelligence in England, and Whitehall's bungling response, it would seem that the Kaiser's spy-masters, led by the very energetic Gustav Steinhauer, took a highly professional approach to building networks and even attempted in 1915 and 1916, through the use of Josef Marks and the double agents John de Heer, Marius Hoogendyk and Charles van Ekeren, to learn more about his adversary. Operating from Wesel, and later from various bases in neutral Holland, Steinhauer and his Naval Intelligence counterparts recruited a series of agents to travel to Great Britain under various covers to collect and transmit valuable intelligence. After the war MI5 received from the Belgian Sureté a list of German agents enrolled in Antwerp, and the list is impressive, proving not only the guilt of suspects against whom there was insufficient evidence to bring a prosecution, but also demonstrated how the Germans adopted the ingenious method of selecting pairs of American journalists to travel to London and Amsterdam, having them exchange ostensibly innocuous telegrams as a means of conveying information about the movements of warships. MI5 probably would never have uncovered this particular scheme if it had not been for a British correspondent in New York who was approached and pretended, having taken advice from MI-1(c), to play along and participate.

Such stratagems were thought to have originated in World War II, but it is clear from the pages that follow that, by 1915, MI5's security apparatus covered the globe and enjoyed access to all letters entrusted to the Royal Mail, all overseas telegrams, and to a group of experienced detectives who could conduct discreet enquiries about suspects in Spain, Holland, Norway and Sweden.

Although censorship provided plenty of leads to enemy espionage, MI5 also took full advantage of two other useful sources in Rotterdam, a port which would become something akin to a front-line in the intelligence war. There the enterprising British consul-general, Ernest Maxse, incurred the disapproval of the Foreign Office by indulging in some very undiplomatic conduct, of the kind that enabled him to give advance notice of the impending departure on missions to England of some German spies, such as Haicke Janssen, the Dutch cigar salesman arrested in London in June 1915 and executed on 30 July. Another profitable source was Richard Tinsley, an extremely energetic and effective British Secret Intelligence Service officer who genuinely ran his own shipping business in Rotterdam while simultaneously managing a network of agents who kept suspects under surveillance and occasionally succeeded in penetrating some of the local German spy-rings. By using the very considerable leverage of the commercial Black List maintained by the Ministry of Blockade, which could ruin a foreign trader, Tinsley proved highly successful in recruiting valuable informants, among them Frederick Graff who compromised numerous putative German spies. The redoubtable Tinsley is credited with tipping off MI5 to the departure of Leopoldo Vieyra in 1916 and directing the investigation in Amsterdam of all those associated with George Bacon, the American journalist MI5 considered its best, most impressive adversary of the war.

The German strategy of recruiting agents who could operate under plausible journalistic cover proved effective, and a ring involving Rutledge Rutherford and Charles Hastings was uncovered. The investigation eventually identified the organisers in New York responsible for their recruitment, and they were imprisoned.

Tinsley also acquired the evidence that ensured the conviction in

1917 of August Patrocinio, and undertook the dogged detective work that led to Albertine Stanaway's internment in December 1916. A French dress-maker living in London, she turned out to be a key figure in a very extensive network involving numerous other German agents.

Accordingly, the Farrer Historical Report, even in this edited version, represents the British counter-espionage experience during the Great War, and is unique in being the only account of its kind of the Kaiser's pre-war and wartime intelligence offensive.

*Nigel West*

## PREFACE BY DR LUCY FARRER

THE experience of MI5 between 1909 and 1914 allowed that there was only really one active enemy, the Germans, and that their conception of espionage embraced the whole life of the state: naval, military, economic, political and social information, and often details of the conduct and fortune of private citizens were of interest to them. There are signs that their agents stirred up discontent and strikes, but the commercial penetration of this country was partly due to our own legislation (the Patents Act).

During the later years of the war, owing partly to the disruptive and deterrent impact of MI5 acting in England, and Ml-I(a) acting abroad, partly to the progress of hostilities ashore and afloat, the Germans seem to have laid even greater stress upon sabotage and the fomenting of discontent and revolutions. Fewer agents were sent into the country for espionage proper since our armies were, for the most part, abroad, and naval espionage was carried on chiefly by seamen and travellers on board neutral merchant vessels.

Throughout the war, the Germans attached considerable importance to the voyages of their agents who were cross-examined by competent persons as to the ships, mines, etc. which they had seen at sea. The results achieved by air-raids, the effects upon the popular morale of such terrorist acts and of the stress of submarine warfare, the question as to whether hospital ships carried munitions of war, the anti-recruiting and peace propaganda campaign, were questions and methods peculiar to the state of war.

But speaking generally, the difference between the methods and aims of German espionage in peace and war is one of degree and emphasis rather than of quality. Its elements are so various and inclusive that in legislation the wider term, 'German agent' is now substituted for that of spy, and similarly the expression 'Defence Security Intelligence', of larger connotation than 'counter-espionage', has been adopted to express more adequately the work done by MI5.

The unity of the attack is demonstrated in the long line of spy cases from 1911 to 1917; these cases are related to one another by one or more common factors, such as a spy address, or a knowledge of new developments and often the relation is so close that one case will throw a flood of light upon another. This is so true that even though the Special Intelligence Bureau broke up the German organisation at the outbreak of war, it is possible to discern at least one of the links between the pre-war and wartime organisations. That link is Miss Brandes, once secretary to Baron Bruno von Schroeder and his agent in charitable work. As such she must have been, almost inevitably, in constant touch with Adolf Evers, a prominent member of several outstanding German charitable institutions and associations including Libury Hall, and with various German pastors of suspect attitude. The case of Charles Wunnenburg, who combined the organisation of sabotage with that of espionage proper, illustrates this unity from another point of view. Each spy case is indeed an entity, the details of which require mastering for itself; but each spy case is also only one link in a long chain and its details must be mastered and called to mind in dealing with all other cases.

From these considerations one law emerges: success in investigation depends upon mastery of detail and the corollary of this is that no one can foretell what detail will not prove to be of primary importance either in the case itself or in some later one. Of chief importance are contacts: the best instance of this is the contact between Charles Wagener, William Klare and Abraham Eisner at Portsmouth; the police failed to establish contact between Klare and Wagener – the man who betrayed Klare had been ready to act as a postbox to Wagener. Again the tedious enquiry about Eisner would have been shortened if his contact with Klare had been realised sooner. Hence, tedious though it may become, all contacts should invariably be noted.

From the considerations set forth in the preceding paragraphs, it follows that both in peace and war, espionage proper should be dealt with by one counter-organisation, the repository of continuous records, traditions and methods. Further it would seem to be of advantage to the State that there should be at all times free interchange of information between the department dealing with counter-espionage (the Defence Security Service) and that dealing with the preservation of peace and order (the Public Security Service).

## Investigations

The qualities required of the investigator are mental alertness, elasticity, knowledge of men, intuitions, an accurate and powerful memory combined with imagination, judgement to choose the right method of handling a case and the moment to strike, besides the special knowledge of counter-espionage legislation and preventive measures, some knowledge of law, legal procedure and the laws of evidence. He should also know one or two languages thoroughly.

Whether in peace or war, the investigator works under cover and uses both methods, ordinary and special machinery. The ordinary machinery consists of other government departments working in their ordinary routine but set in motion at the request of the investigator. The special machinery consists of methods peculiar to counter-espionage but carried out by ordinary government departments specially conceived and constituted in time of war.

The aim of the investigator is:

1. To discover enemy agents.
2. To collect evidence against such persons.
3. To bring them to justice or to nullify their efforts.

Two main classes of spy exist: the foreigner, whether resident or on a mission, and the traitor, whether of British or alien origin. Detection comes either through the action of the bureau or it may follow on information received from some outside source. The sources vary in peace and in war.

## Sources of detection in peace

*Inside:*
1. The Precautionary Index.
2. Home Office Warrant.
3. Spy contacts established in pursuing an investigation.

*Outside:*
1. Private informer.
2. Military or Naval.
3. Government Offices.
4. Police.
5. Chance: a returned letter or a letter picked up and submitted, a conversation overheard and reported.

## Sources of detection in time of war

*Inside:*
1. General check on the transmission of money orders, telegraphic orders, cheques, drafts.
2. General check on telegrams.
3. General check on passenger traffic at ports and certain areas, Home Office Warrants and special checks.
4. British Intelligence services at home and abroad.
5. Foreign Office.

NOTE: The first of the Inside Sources does not seem to have led to the detection of any proved spy but it supplied information which was of great value during the war. The second and third sources frequently overlap and the second is the most important source of detection in time of peace.

*Outside:*
1. Special Departments.
2. Censorship.
3. Passport Office.
4. Military Permit Office.
5. Allied Services.
6. Police.
7. Private informers, both British and foreign.

Of all these sources by far the most important are the agents employed by British officials in touch with MI-1(c). The action taken depends upon the class of spy and the source and nature of the information received.

If it be a case of information lodged against an alien or civilian by a private person the first step will be probably verification of the details through police enquiry; if the accused be a serviceman or a government official the enquiry will begin in the department to which he belongs.

If the existence of a spy be known, but his personality in doubt, the first step will be identification. The means of identification most successfully used was the comparison of handwritings. The best way of procuring a specimen of handwriting was by securing it from the local post office's receipt signed by the suspect, but this of course presupposed that the enquiry had reached a point at which suspicion is directed against a definite person. For especially interesting identifications, the case of Armgaard Graves, Fred Ireland and Frederick Gould before the war, and the case of Carl Muller and John Hahn and that of Kenneth de Rysbach during the war, are worth special study.

Sometimes the bureau employed its own special agents in this difficult work, as happened in the cases of Alfred Hagn and Eva de Bournonville.

The second stage of investigation, i.e. the collection of evidence, shows important differences in peace and war. In peace it might be a long and tedious process involving the repeated shadowing of an agent and the postponement of arrest until, by a series of measures elaborated between the bureau, the police and the post office, it became known that certain incriminating documents would be found on the criminal or in his house. In war, the spy's movements might be known beforehand and he would be invited or taken to Scotland Yard on arrival, duly cautioned and interrogated, and if he failed to extricate himself, would be arrested. His interrogation might be put in evidence against him. The difference of procedure is due to the difference in the authority sanctioning proceedings; in time of peace it is in the hands of the law officers of the Crown. In time of war it is in the hands of the Competent Military Authority.

There are thus two stages in the collection of evidence: (1) before and evidence to justify arrest (2) after arrest and to prepare the case. Both stages consist of a series of verifications: the man's civil status, movements, business, money affairs and receipts, communications, friends and associations both in England and abroad form the object of enquiry. In addition, in every spy case in which information was sent to the enemy, verification of its truth and value was given in open court.

The preparation of the case took place under legal direction. One principle governs in both peace and war, and that is secrecy. In peace the trial takes place in open court and is fully reported, therefore it is essential to conceal counter-espionage methods. Both for this reason and for reasons of evidence, much damning information against the criminal cannot be produced in court in time of war; with control of the press and trial by court martial, there is less risk of exposing the methods of counter-espionage, moreover the special preventive measures are necessarily known to the enemy. Secrecy therefore bears upon another aspect of the case; the enemy must be kept in the dark as long as possible as to the actual arrest of his agent and the nature of the charge.

There is, however, one difficulty in wartime, the spies may be neutrals and as a matter of courtesy and prudence, an official, whether of the embassy or consulate of that neutral country is present at the trial. He is of course held to secrecy – but presumably he furnishes a report to his government. By whatever means, whether by a process of inference or by leakage, the record of the spy cases shows that the Germans arrived at pretty accurate results as to the fate of their spies and the weak points in the tactics which led to their arrest, and in searching for fresh methods they laid bare the weak points of our defence.

It is the business of the investigator to note these results and to offer suggestions for strengthening prevention to those persons who deal with that side of counter-espionage i.e. originally F Branch, now renamed A Branch.

In conclusion: the pre-war possible suspect list was the means of educating the police in certain aspects of a work that to all was novel and the police were inclined to consider that if a man was outwardly respectable and clear of any criminal suspicion, he could not be a spy. The county constabulary worked on the whole very well with the Metropolitan Police, who had not had the same opportunities in peace, worked well on the outbreak of war but not so well later. The German view was that the police could be moulded to suit their ideas by treating and bribes, and this suspicion does not appear to be entirely unfounded. The war itself may partly have educated the public but the lessons would soon be forgotten. It is impossible for the general public to have any idea of the extent of an enemy's espionage attack, and the majority are still found to discredit the allegations against the Bolshevists. The best security of all might be a contented and well-informed general public.

It is as well to emphasise strongly here the limitation of this report, and the large area of the uninvestigated field. Much has been done in the time available, but much has been omitted, and the report though apparently voluminous, necessarily omits much that should be included. Most historical reports are more or less misleading for it is very difficult to write down the truth very satisfactorily. It is so often not only difficult but impossible to know what is the truth.

# CHAPTER I
# MI5 Pre–War

THE Special Intelligence Bureau was started in October 1909 by the Committee of Imperial Defence, at the insistance of the Imperial General Staff, with the object of counteracting the efforts of the German government to establish a spy organisation in the United Kingdom. The work, and consequently the organisation of such a bureau, is naturally divided into two main branches:

1. The investigation of particular cases involving a definite suspicion of espionage.
2. The construction of legal and administrative machinery calculated to embarrass, penalise and, if possible, to frustrate attempts in general and for the future.

On 1 October 1909, Captain Vernon G. W. Kell took up the duties as above and from the inception of MO5 (later MI5) as a bureau and with only the one officer to carry on the work, the duties tended to fall under the two heads mentioned above and then a third dealing with the administrative work as a whole. By 1913, the bureau consisted of three branches eventually known as F, G and H, each with its own special functions.

As far back as 1908, the DMO had drafted a memorandum to the Chief of the General Staff regarding the unsatisfactory position the country was in as regards the matter of German espionage and point out that there was no staff to watch suspicious cases even when reported and at best they could only be superficially investigated and then dropped. Co-operation by other government departments was almost impossible to obtain.

During the early days of the bureau's existence the 'G' or Investigation work had to be done by the one or only officer who was in charge of Captain (now Colonel) Kell, which necessitated his constant absence from the headquarters in London to make personal enquiries into cases and to get in touch with local naval, military and police authorities to assist him. In March 1910 he was given a secretary and later, on 1 January 1911, Captain Kell obtained the services of another officer Captain P. L. Stanley Clarke of the Suffolk Regiment, and the division of the work of the bureau began to divide itself more definitely into the Passive (Preventive) and Active (Detective) Branches, though as a matter of fact both officers functioned on the two duties.

At the commencement of the bureau's existence, Captain Kell in his G Branch capacity had to investigate some interesting and curious cases of which those known as the Frant and Rusper cases are typical. In the first case a German who gave the name of De Corina took a farm in the neighbourhood of Frant in Sussex, Here he went in ostensibly for poultry farming but it was noticeable that the farm at Bartley Mill was a great rendezvous for Germans, most of whom seemed to spend the greater part of the time cycling and motoring all over the country. De Corina himself was a typical German and it was quite obvious that he could not be making his living from the proceeds of the farm. Although nothing was ever discovered which could definitely connect this man with espionage the whole circumstances of the case were very peculiar and suspicious and the extremely secluded position chosen for the scene of their operations as well as the difficulty of watching it lends colour to the belief that it was used as a centre for espionage.

The Rusper case was similar. Two Germans appeared at considerable intervals of time, each furnished with a recommendation to a gentleman living in the village of Rusper, from a certain baroness whom this gentleman declared he had never heard of before. Those German pretended to know nothing of one another but rapidly struck up an acquaintance, and it is evident that whether they knew one another or not each had a very intimate knowledge of the other's concerns.

William Melville MVO OBE who, since his retirement from Scotland Yard in 1903 had been employed by the War Office, was sent down to investigate the case, put up in the same house and caused these gentlemen some perturbation. They cross-questioned the landlord closely about him, being especially anxious to know if he understood or spoke any foreign language, and were visibly relieved when the landlord assured them he did not. Shortly after Mr Melville's arrival the two gentlemen quarrelled (it was evidently a put-up job) and refused to speak to each other during the remainder of Mr Melville's foray. They were constantly moving about the village of Rusper. In this case too there was no definite proof of espionage but the circumstances were very suspicious.

In November 1909 MO5 sent Melville to investigate one Karl Hentschel who advertised a school at Sheerness and who stated he would also visit Sittingbourne and other places. Melville, after enquiries, concluded he was in the German Navy and a spy. This investigation, which also brought into the case George Parrott and the Rileys, was continued during 1910.

So far the bureau in its G capacity had only two detectives, Melville and Herbert Dale Long. The former, however, was too old for such work as constant observation and the talents of the latter lay in rather a specialised direction which rendered him in some ways unsuitable for this class of work. It was, therefore, felt necessary to add to the staff of detectives and Captain Kell applied to be allowed to engage two suitable men. Captain Kell got in touch with the head of the Military Police at Aldershot as a very possible aid in certain cases that might occur in any army centre.

It was becoming daily more evident that it was necessary to have a staff of special detectives as those belonging to the ordinary police force of the country, however excellent they might be as regards crime, had not got the necessary degree of tact to carry out the delicate enquiries involved in espionage cases.

In July 1910 Melville had been sent over to Ireland to investigate the O'Brien case. It appeared that a certain Kate O'Brien, who had a brother in the Royal Artillery at Portsmouth, had written to say that she had plans of the Portsmouth defences and considered them of value. There was some doubt as to whether this could be the case and Melville was sent to find out further information about the plans in the sister's possession, it was however, found that it was an ordinary map of no military value so no further steps were taken.

On 5 September 1910, a telegram arrived from the GOC Portsmouth defences to say that some of the officers had arrested a Lieutenant Siegfried Helm of the 21st Pioneers (German Army) in the act of sketching Fort Widley. The next day Captain Bonham Carter came up with all the necessary evidence about Helm's espionage. Then the unsatisfactory state of the law under the Official Secrets Act of 1889, came prominently to notice.

On calling on the Public Prosecutor in regard to the case he gave it as his opinion that the necessary evidence was at hand to apply for a fiat from the Attorney-General to prosecute Lieutenant Helm. As, however, that official was away on the Continent it was necessary to wire for his authority to carry out the arrest. In consequence it was necessary to detain Lieutenant Helm in military custody until 4 p.m. on 7 September at which time he was handed over to the civil power. The German officer was eventually tried and was bound over in his own recognisances of £250, to come up for trial if called upon to do so. As a matter of fact the fort he was sketching had been long out of date and could be of no possible interest to Germany, but the case is illustrative of the difficulty of taking proceedings against a suspected spy. This was one of the many cases that helped towards the framing and production of the Official Secrets Act 1911.

In August Franz Heinrich Lozel became a subject of the attention of MO5G also Walter E. Wilson at Portsmouth, about whom Melville was sent to make enquiries.

Early in 1911 Heinrich Christian Wilhelm Schutte became an object of suspicion and the attention of MO5 was called to the case of Dr Max

Schultz at Plymouth whose actions and movements appeared suspicious, and Captain Kell took up the direction of the cases on 6 August 1911.

In April the Chief Constable of Kent forwarded a report about Lozel and he was placed on the Special War List (SWL) for Kent under the heading 'Search'. A hairdresser, George Wittstruck, at Sheerness was also a subject for enquiries.

In order to obtain information at the ports from ships' captains who were in a position to act in a certain measure as scouts on the high seas and in the enemy's harbours, Captain Kell obtained the services of Lieutenant B. J. Ohlson of the Royal Naval Reserve as Mercantile Marine assistant on 10 May 1911. By the end of June 1911, Lieutenant Ohlson was doing regular work for G Branch and through him the names of those merchant shippers plying between London and the Continent who were discreet and willing to keep their eyes open and report useful information were received.

In August, the consent of the Home Secretary to grant warrants in suspected cases of espionage for the opening of letters in the post provided MO5 with a much needed form of assistance in their duties. About this time, one Charles Wagener at Plymouth became an object of suspicion to MO5 who placed him on the SWL under the heading 'Arrest'.

On 18 August a warrant for the arrest of Max Schultz was issued under Section 1, sub-section 2 of Official Secrets Act 1889 and he eventually went for trial to the Exeter Assizes on 3 November, found guilty and sentenced to twenty-one months' imprisonment. This case also introduced a German agent named Gustav Neumann, of whom we knew, and also Edmund Ahlers and Francis L. Holstein.

On 22 August 1911, the new Official Secrets Act was passed into law and the work of counter-espionage was thereby greatly facilitated.

The Home Office Warrant (HOW) on Otto Kruger brought proof that one Johann Engel of Falmouth was in receipt of a subsidy of £40 a year from the German Secret Service fund. He was placed under observation in September but nothing suspicious was noted. He was placed on the SWL heading 'Arrest' and arrested on 4 August 1914.

By the end of September much work had been done by the bureau
to assist and simplify G Branch's future activities. The registration of
aliens in the areas under the jurisdiction of Chief Constables of counties
had made considerable progress, returns having been received from
twenty-eight. Eight counties were already furnishing regular reports on
the arrivals, departures and change of address of aliens, mostly along
the coast, and other counties were preparing to furnish similar returns.
Returns of aliens, in all government establishments, under the Admiralty,
were received and registered. Lists of possible suspects to be reported on
every three months had been started by some twenty Chief Constables
and the first installments of reports had been received from four counties.

The case of one Heinrich Grosse who had established himself at
Portsmouth during the crisis of 1911 (the Agadir incident), in the name
of Captain Hugh Grant had been engaging the attention of the bureau
during the year and the man was finally arrested on 4 December. He was
indicted on five counts under the OSA 1911 and eventually brought to
trial on 9 February 1913, found guilty and condemned to three years'
imprisonment. Mixed up with the case we find Heddy Glauer who
though probably not a spy was possibly a political agent and a friend of
Joseph King MP who played an active anti-British part both before and
during the war.

Towards the end of the year suspicion fell on a Second Class Stoker,
Frederick Ireland, and his uncle Otto Kruger, and a warrant was taken
out for all correspondence to the latter's address.

The check on Steinhauer brought the name of Walter Reimann
of Hull to notice as a German agent engaged particularly in obtaining
information about the Humber defences.

Early in January 1912, steps had been taken to extend the work of the
bureau by getting in touch with the police of the boroughs and cities,
and in April the Home Secretary's letter of introduction had been sent
to Alfred Arnold, the Chief Constable of Rochester. He had replied
stating his willingness to help and asking for an interview and in May,
Captain Drake went to Rochester and laid before the Chief Constable,
the bureau's suspicions concerning one Frederick Gould.

At the end of January, letters were intercepted showing that undoubtedly one Charles Wagener was a German agent and during the year investigation and enquiry into this case took place, and also that of William Klare at Portsmouth.

In February the Second Class Stoker in the navy, Fred Ireland, mentioned before, came under more positive suspicion because it was known that his uncle (Otto Kruger) was an agent residing in the United Kingdom and in the pay of the German Secret Service. It was found he was endeavouring to acquire information as to certain secret experiments that were being conducted, with the objective of communicating it to a member of the German Secret Service. He was arrested on 21 February and dismissed from the Royal Navy as it was not considered advisable to place him on trial owing to the nature of the correspondence which would have to be produced in court. Kruger, who played an important part in this affair, at first fled the country, but returned, and observation kept upon him, his correspondence intercepted and examined. He was one of the German agents arrested on the outbreak of war.

Another case which became suspect at about this time and which was of importance was that of Gunner Parrott, a warrant officer RN employed on shore duties at Chatham. With him were implicated Karl Hentschel and Mrs Emily Riley. This was a long and interesting case and is set forth in full detail. After being dismissed from the navy in August 1912, Parrott was eventually tried in January 1913 and condemned to four years' imprisonment and on release, interned under Defence of the Realm Regulation 14B. An intercepted letter from John James Hattrick of Plymouth to the 'Head Intelligence Department, War Office, Germany', offering information and giving the wording of an advertisement to be placed in the *Daily Mirror* if the offer was accepted induced MO5G to take action, Melville impersonating a German agent. In March also a German Secret Service agent was discovered at Southampton but he left for Germany before any steps could be taken to arrest him.

In April the division of the bureau became more definite and Captain Drake late the North Staffordshire Regiment, who joined on the 1st was placed in charge of the investigation of cases (i.e. G Branch) of espionage.

In May MO5 took steps to find out which agents Heddy Glauer and Armgaard Graves had been in touch with. Graves was quietly released to act as an agent for MO5.

A very large number of suspected cases of espionage had been investigated though the only ones that had been brought to trial by the end of 1912 were Heinrich Grosse, Frederick Ireland, Otto Kruger and Armgaard Graves.

Notes of the methods employed by foreign secret service agents in the work of counter-espionage had been printed and were being issued to all Chief Constables so that they might have every opportunity of co-operating with Captain Kell. Contact had been made by Lieutenant Ohlson with six steamship lines trading between British and Continental ports, including those in Norway, Russia, Germany, the Black Sea and the Mediterranean.

In December 1912, Captain Eric Holt-Wilson DSO was transferred to the bureau from the Royal Engineers in succession to Captain Stanley Clarke, taking over the organisation of the Preventive Work, the correspondence relating to the routine supervision of the 'possible suspects' and German Institutions, the interior administration of the bureau's record and indexing system, and the financial accounts.

In this year, 1913, the bureau developed into three branches identical with the F, G and H of February 1918, the G being that of the detective branch.

Owing to a remittance of £10 sent via August Klunder at the end of February, MO5G got on to the track of Heinrich Schmidt (or Henry Smith) of Devonport. During his absence his room and property were examined and though there was clear proof of his intention to spy there was not sufficient evidence to secure conviction.

During the year a new form of attack by the German Secret Service came to the notice of MO5, in the shape of incitement to treason. It was chiefly directed against the navy and action was taken by the Admiralty to counteract it. The method was attempts by foreign agents (living for the most part in Denmark) at the wholesale perversion of naval personnel and others by pretended, literary work. It was brought to notice that communications were being received by naval officers and others requesting them to contribute technical articles to publications which it was alleged were being started abroad in the interest of professional naval and military circles. The attempt was on the whole one which might well have succeeded as the writers disclaimed any wish to obtain confidential information and merely posed as being desirous of producing a review which should be interesting to sea-going or engineering circles as the case might be.

On 26 June William Klare was sentenced to five years' imprisonment for attempting to obtain a secret naval work and Karl Hentschel was remanded on 24 October, on his own confession, for inciting the commission of offences for which George Parrott was undergoing four years' imprisonment.

During this month Karl Hentschel, who had returned from Australia gave himself up to the police, signing a statement embodying accusation against George Parrott. The exposure was very inconvenient and forced the hands of the police with whom MO5 were keeping in close touch over the case. Investigations followed as to Robert Tormow, Captain Friedel Fels, Captain Steinhauer and Max Dressler.

During July, arrangements were made to test the scheme for the arrest, search or observation of the known agents whose names were in possession of the Chief Constables. Before this could be carried out the precautionary period was proclaimed and the messages, instead of being sent out as a mobilisation test, were despatched in earnest. Of the twenty-two German agents in England, all were arrested with the exception of one, Walter Riemann, who escaped a few days before the declaration of war. Of the others, as it was not considered advisable at this stage to try them, they were all held in detention under an order from the Home Secretary. The effect of this order was that they were imprisoned as securely as if they had actually been sentenced. The following is the list of those agents arrested, together with the centres of their activities:

1.  Rummenie, Antonius J. London
2.  Stubenwoll, Karl. Newcastle
3.  Meyer, Carl. Warwick

4. Kuhr, Johann. Newcastle
5. Buchwaldt, Oscar. Brighton
6. Hemlar, Carl. Winchester
7. Apel, Fred. Barrow
8. Laurons, Max. London
9. Lozel, Franz. Sittingbourne
10. Hegnauer, Thomas. Southampton
11. Schneider, Adolf. London
12. Von Wilier, Karl. Padstow
13. Kronauer, Marie. London
14. Rodriguez, Celso. Portsmouth
15. Diederich, Fred. London
16. Klunder, August. London
17. Heine, Lina. Portsmouth
18. Schutte, Heinrich. Weymouth
19. Sukowski, Fred. Newcastle
20. Kruger, Otto. Abercynon
21. Engel, Johann. Falmouth

*

In January 1912 the check on Gustav Steinhauer brought evidence that he was in treaty with a man writing from Grimsby and Hull.

Walter Rimann (alias Gustave Friese, alias Germanikus), of Roslyn House, 24 Spring Street, Hull, sent in two reports answering test questions. One of these questions had involved some enquiry concerning Mildred Burkinshaw of 3 Cleethorpe Road, Grimsby. She was, Rimann said, the owner of a cheap sweet-shop which catered for seafarers. She had been there seven months, lived a most retired life and consorted only with foreign sailors and the crews of British torpedo-boats. Among other articles she sold 'piquant if not exactly indecent postcards'. This circumstance recalls the cases of Charles Wagener and of Solomon and Abraham Eisner.

In February, Rimann was summoned to Hamburg and engaged at a

salary of £3 a month, if his reports were worth it. His ostensible work
was to write articles for a well-known German periodical dealing with
literature and art on behalf of 'Professor Kluge', a well-known Germanic
philologist. This cover he was most precise in keeping up, even when it
involved patent absurdities. His own reports he signed 'Gustav Friese'.

Rimann was instructed to report on the Humber defences; the
Germans were especially keen to locate the minefields, and the base of
the mine-sweepers, and to obtain any information about new methods
and equipment connected with mine-laying and sweeping.

Rimann's reports cover much ground; he deals with the
coal situation, the strike and hampering dearth of coal-wagons, the coal
tonnage imported into and exported from Hull, and the amount carried
in coast-wise traffic. He reports about the East Yorkshire Territorial
Association, the batteries at the mouth of the Humber, the Admiralty
works at Killingholme, Immingham Docks, negotiations connected with
alterations and additions to the works, and any new project mooted.

Steinhauer insisted upon getting the results of personal observation
and objected to accounts of the visits of important people since these were
reported in the press. He instructed Rimann to get into conversation
with naval men and to ascertain from them details relating to the special
exercise of the Naval Reserve.

In October 1913, Steinhauer is particularly pleased with Rimann's
three last reports. One of these had given particulars of the Fleet
manoeuvres: the names of the ships forming the invading Squadron
and of the troops on board them, details of an attack on
Immingham and of the disguise of repair ships and transports. Attempts
to ascertain the disposition of the trawlers or anything material about the
verdict of the umpire had, however, failed.

The two other reports dealt with fleet manoeuvres near Spurn Point,
and their intimate connection with the fleet manoeuvres; the details
comprised an account of two floating-docks, of hydroplanes coming
from Yarmouth, of wireless attached to hydroplanes, of the altitude of the
flight, etc. Afterwards Rimann sent a picture postcard of the Hydroplane
Station at Bridlington.

The correspondence lasted from January 1912 until the outbreak of war during this time Rimann went once to Germany for Christmas 1915, and had at his own request, an interview with Steinhauer at the railway station at Berlin. It is worth remarking that Steinhauer never once seems to have visited Rimann in Hull, although he and other German agents seem to have entered England frequently by that port. The passage runs: 'I too have been there several times and had always intended to visit you, but then there came unforeseen delays, and the visit did not come off.'

Rimann seems to have been the only German agent resident in or near Hull, but others may have come and gone to his house. There is evidence that Steinhauer would have letters of instruction to Rimann posted locally by an agent passing through, and that one at least of Rimann's visitors travelled back to Germany on some merchant ship.

'John Moreenstern' wrote to warn Rimann of the date at which the Helen Heidmann would reach Immingham and of the time of her probable departure so that 'Mr Bode' could go on board. Mr Bode was a young man of about twenty-five, a student of philology and theology in the University of Kiel and he had been spending some weeks with Rimann. The next letter showed that Rimann had still not been able to locate the mines at the mouth of the Humber, a task with which Bode's journey may have been connected.

Rimann's nervousness is apparent: in August 1912, he begs Steinhauer to avoid using 'direct expressions' if possible; and Steinhauer replies complaining of the too obvious care with which Rimann's letters are sealed. However, a few months later, Steinhauer veiled questions as to the position and movements of the 7th Flotilla under the guise of discovering the whereabouts of a nephew, whose prolonged silence caused anxiety. The excuse however may have been genuine as the incitement to treason attack had by then begun.

The correspondence about the 7th Flotilla continued during March and April and ended with Rimann sending a plan of Immingham's deep water dock on which the moorings of the torpedo-boats were marked in pencil.

The anxiety caused by the arrest of Gould in February 1914 led to fresh precautions. Rimann had explained a long interval in his reports by the fact that the names 'St.' and 'P...m' had figured too prominently in London and begged Steinhauer to give him a fresh address and to avoid posting letters of instructions in Potsdam.

Steinhauer conceded the fresh address: Rimann was to post to any name at Brauerstraase, Potsdam, an hotel and receiving centre for Steinhauer's correspondence; it was also agreed that instructions should be sent in envelopes printed 'Zeitschrift fur Literatur & Kimatgeschichte'.

Steinhauer, meanwhile, had enquired in various quarters for dangerous press-cuttings where his own name may have been printed in full, and as none were produced, he was reassured and concluded Rimann had been mistaken. He then told Rimann to write to either Braueratrasse or to Allee Sanssoucci. The correspondence also shows that, from the very beginning, arrangements had been made for communication at the outbreak of war and it would seem that, in that event, Steinhauer contemplated Rimann remaining at his post.

In the letter of March 1912 accepting the engagement, Rimann says he will start on his article dealing with Friesian roots and asks for the name of the 'K. correspondent'. The answer came that he was to write to: Miss Henny Deininger, c/o Mrs T, Steinhauer, etc. But in May 'Kluge' was at last able to send the name of Herr Paul Eisner, Dr Priemeseg 10, Copenhagen, who was engaged on philological research, and to whom Rimann was to apply in case of urgency. No use was made of this address and it was not again referred to until just before the outbreak of war.

Professor H. Julius warned Rimann that 'next month' would be a favourable time for writing his article on Friesian roots: E was helping and it would be sufficient to send letters to E in K. Fjordsallee 23, or to the writer's own address. If the telegram was sent, Rimann was to begin wiring in conformity with the agreement.

On 1 August a wire came from 'Ewald' Guhrau, near Breslau, Rimann's home, informing him that he had not been called up and that money was on the way. Rimann replied by wire to Eisner, Copenhagen, asking for an explanation of the telegram. This, however, he did not await this, but he borrowed money and left for Zeebrugge on 1 August.

£4.17s.6d which had been telegraphed from Guhrau, was received in Hull on 3 August and sent after him.

On 19 and 22 February wires were despatched to Steinhauer, Allee Sanssouoi 4, Potsdam, from the Beverley Road Post Office, Hull. The address of the sender, which was not to be telegraphed, was 34 Spring Street. The sender was making an appointment for Sunday morning. As Germanicus had written a few days before from Hull saying; he could travel on 22 February the telegrams were attributed to him and so his name and address were discovered.

The first paper relating to the enquiry, is, however, dated 23 April 1913, and this shows that MO5 had, in the interval, ascertained many particulars about the sender. He was a teacher of languages, who pretended to be an ardent promoter of the Anglo-German entente. MO5 wrote informing the Chief Constable of Hull of these facts, and of their suspicions and asked for cautious enquiries with, if necessary, observation of the man.

In reply, the Chief Constable sent a careful description of Rimann, whom he described as a foxy looking person. Late in September 1913, Lieutenant Ohlson went down to investigate. He took lessons of Rimann, whom he found willing to discuss naval and some military matters but not to be drawn into confidence.

Through Lieutenant Ohlson the following details also came to hand: Rimann had served in a German pioneer regiment and visited Germany every year; he had been in Hull eighteen years and owned property there but in spite of his long residence he was an obvious German and spoke with a German accent. He was one of the best teachers in the town and had plenty of pupils there. He had formed an association for the purpose of studying German literature and had induced some of the local notabilities, including the postmaster, to serve on the committee.

Some of these statements, about Rimann's annual visits to Germany and his owning property in Hull, seem not altogether borne out by other papers in the file. It is probable that Rimann was about forty-five years of age and had reached the stage of biennial military training. Also, as regards his means, on the outbreak of war he was badly off. He was renting a house at £25 a year and had to borrow money for his journey.

Lieutenant Ohlson reported that he had asked only two questions relating to the Service: one had references to the discussion then raging about the shortage of men; the other was about the strategic importance of Hull.

Enquiry was renewed in April 1914 when Rimann wrote regretting that he could not supply certain information as his informant had been ordered south. The word used was, 'Gewahrsmann', which means informant. The translator seems to have confused it with 'Gewehr', or gun, for enquiry was limited to ascertaining the name of any man, 'supposed to be a gunner', Royal Garrison Artillery, who had recently been transferred to the south of England from Stallisborough Battery or other defences round Hull. Only one such name was returned and no action seems to have been taken.

Walter Rimann had been placed on the Possible Suspect List in 1911 and in 1912, on the SWL, heading 'Arrest'. But when action was to be taken he had already escaped. As he had gone to Zeebrugge he was put on the Special War List for Belgium with the note: 'Wanted if in Great Britain' and, as his wife remained on at Hull, the Chief Constable was informed that it was desirable she should be removed under the Aliens Act. She went to London.

In September, her daughter wrote from Germany, where she had found refuge in the family of Countess Bernstorff and was staying at Hintenburg-bei-Lassaim, Lauerriburg. Rimann had found his way back to Silesia but had not been then called up. The daughter had tried every conceivable means of getting letters through but the obstacles seemed to have been as great in Germany as here.

As Rimann was trying to get in touch with his wife, Mrs Rimann's name was put on check. Some correspondence between herself and Mr J. Enerson of Twyer's Wood, Hedon, Hull, allowed that the latter was taking care of her interests. The two families were evidently very intimate.

The Chief Constable of Hull knew that Mrs Rimann was trying to get back to Germany and suggested that she should be subjected to special search, but she managed to get away while MO5 were concluding arrangements for the same.

Enquiry about Rimann was renewed in November 1914, when Sepp Hoftbauer of Messrs. Riccardo Hirschfeld & Co. of Milan, wrote asking him to have his baggage forwarded abroad through the American consulate. Sepp Hoftbauer had been staying at Hull with Rimann, and had left hurriedly on the outbreak of war. His baggage had been examined carefully and nothing suspicious found in it. He was said to have been a student and this seemed likely as he had a quantity of books such as a student would possess.

More interesting was a report which came to hand in August 1918, that Captain Strasser, the commander of a Zeppelin which was destroyed off the north-east coast, had been seen at Walter Rimann's house in Hull before the war. His portrait was identified by a resident of Hull, whose statement received support from a local policeman. The policeman did not remember the face, but he had been told that Strasser either lived in Spring Street or 'had a pal in Spring Street'.

Three questions referring to information imparted by him at a meeting with Steinhauer in Germany. The verbal explanations had not been understood. The answer to this letter shows that the subjects of these questions were mines, minelayers and sweepers.

★

Charles Frederick Wagener stated that he was born in Germany on 8 May 1879. He came to this country from Antwerp, and from 1899 followed the calling of ship's steward. Existing official papers, however, bear varying statements as to the city of his birth and his identification papers are said to confirm his claim to German nationality, and also to prove that he was employed for some years as interpreter to Messrs. Thomas Cook & Son.

He was at Plymouth in 1909. In 1910 he occupied a room at 9 Shirley Road, Southampton and occasionally made a trip on an American boat. During that year Wagener was receiving letters and money in £10 and £5 cheques (? notes) from Germany; he himself despatched a good many registered packets and corresponded with a man in Berlin named Tobler, who had precise and correct information of his journey from New York

on board the SS *Philadelphia* in April 1911 and hoped to meet him in
Brussels in May 1911. Wagener had then left Southampton saying he was
returning to Germany but instead he had opened a shop in Portsmouth.

MO5's attention was called to Wagener at the end of January
1912 when letters were intercepted that Wagener was trying to renew
intercourse with Tobler. Several of his letters seem to have slipped
through the post unnoticed, but the replies of 'T', which came via Karl
Ernst, showed that the employers did not trust the man and insisted upon
obtaining the exact titles of confidential books about wireless, torpedoes
and submarines before making further arrangements. A meeting at
Ostend was proposed for 16 March; it fell through owing to Wagener's
dilatoriness in posting. A ticket and journey money were then sent for a
meeting on the 31st, but Wagener did not go. In reply to an indignant
letter from 'T', Wagener wrote to Mr Henri Adam, Petit rue des Longs
Chariots 10, Brussels, a lying excuse that his home and all his papers
had been burned and he himself injured in a disastrous fire and this he
supported with a newspaper cutting. He gave a new address: c/o Mr
Rosenthal, 71 Queen Street, Portsea, Portsmouth. A third meeting was
proposed for May and Wagener hoped to bring confidential books as
well as the list but by May he had not even obtained the list.

In July 'T' wrote again to ask Wagener what 'his friend' had provided.
The reply came that nothing could be done for the moment as 'the
friend' was away but he would return the following week; Wagener also
acknowledged receipt of £5. There the correspondence seems to have
ended. Other letters now in the Reimer file of Wagener's correspondence
should be ascribed to Heinrich Schutte and, possibly, to Carl Ernst.

The address Henri Adam, 10 Petite rue des Longs Chariots, Brussels,
had been used by Patricia Hentschel in her correspondence with 'T' in
March 1912. Enquiry was instituted at Portsmouth on naval lines. As the
first two letters came in, Mr Ohlson called at the dockyard police station
and showed the police copies of them. In return, very excellent and full
reports were received from Inspector Savage. Wagener it appeared had
come to Portsmouth in 1911 and had opened a business as a silhouette
cutter in Queen Street, Portsea.

This was not a success so he took to canvassing for and executing orders in public houses. His customers were chiefly lower-deck naval men. At night he would call on a stationer named Abraham Eisner whom the police viewed with suspicion. He would stay talking with this man till 11.55 p.m. On one occasion Eisner noticed observation was being kept and tried to find out the reason.

Having seen the letters from Germany, the police knew exactly what was aimed at and accordingly supplied MO5 with a list of the titles of confidential naval books on the required subjects, including the Manual of Wireless Telegraphy and a document entitled 'Instructions for Fitting W/T in Destroyers. M.I.C. 2. W/T'.

As no evidence against Wagener was obtained, and as these titles could easily be sent by post, Inspector Savage thought Wagener would be trying to obtain the books themselves. He therefore suggested stopping the man and searching his effects if he were seen about to leave Portsmouth for Ostend on the day proposed. But Captain Kell advised taking no action. Wagener was to be discreetly and quietly watched, to he followed to town, and pointed out to Melville.

The police reported also that on 28 March Wagener had proclaimed that he had received a ticket and journey money from his mother, who wished him to go to Germany and from that date till 4 April he had spent money lavishly on drink and entertaining his friends. He had also stated that instead of going to Germany he would sell his ticket in London.

Meanwhile, on 29 March, he had visited the shop of Levi Rosenthal, a barber of 71 Queen Street, in Portsea. A month later Wagener gave this to 'T' as his postal address and he was still using it in July when the correspondence closed. Now Levi Rosenthal was the informer and chief witness in the William Klare case. To anticipate events, in May 1913, MO5 made enquiry about Wagener's correct address stating that the police had given two addresses, 8 Bishop Street and 13 North Street, Portsea, and that a third address: 35 Paradise Street, Landport, had been received from a source not stated. It will be noticed that no mention of Levi Rosenthal's address was made.

The police kept observation for about a month without obtaining any direct evidence of espionage; Wagener frequented low haunts and conversed much with naval men but it was not possible for the police to overhear the gist of these conversations. Therefore they suggested discontinuing the risky business of continuous observation and employing a naval man as a kind of agent. MO5 would not allow this; they required only occasional reports as to Wagener's whereabouts and observation was discontinued.

When MO5 enquired about Wagener's address in 1913, the police stated he was living in Southampton in a common lodging house and was said to be employed on a mail boat. Mrs Wright, his fanner landlady, was referred to; she supplied the information given above, allowed copies to be made of Tobler's letters to herself enquiring about Wagener's movements, and gave the police a photograph of Wagener.

Renewed enquiry in September 1913 elicited the fact that he had left Southampton and, on 17 July, had applied at the General Register and Record Office of Shipping and Seamen for information about his discharge book which had been stolen the week before. In his application he stated that he was born at Magdeburg and had last served as saloon steward on board the *Oceanic*. The Agreement Paper of the *Oceanic* showed that he claimed to be a native of Hamburg, that he had served as carver steward on the *Oceanic* from 16 April to 3 May 1913, and that he had served previously on the *Philadelphia*. On leaving Southampton he expressed the intention of obtaining a post as interpreter with the Orient Steamship Company and returning to Southampton in December.

Since 1911 Charles Wagener had been an object of suspicion to MO5 who had in that year placed him on the SWL under the heading 'Arrest' but after July 1913 he never returned to Southampton and no action could be taken under the general preventive order of 4 August 1914. It was afterwards found that he had transferred his operations to the north-east coast.

In March and April 1914 he had been in trouble for various offences committed at South Shields. In July he went to North Shields and the Tyneside police placed his name on their register on 23 August 1914. On

3 September he was charged under the third schedule of the ARO and was sentenced at Newcastle to two months' hard labour. When released he was taken to the infirmary and the Board of Guardians then tried to recover his identification papers which had been deposited some years before as security for a loan with Alfred George Mills, a stationer in Portsmouth. There is no record of whether the papers were recovered but Mills made a signed statement as to their contents. After leaving the infirmary Wagener was taken to the internment camp at Lancaster in April 1915 and in 1917 he was at Alexandra Palace.

★

The nationality of William Klare, of 33 Osborne Street, Southsea, was not identified. He was in London working as a kitchen porter in 1902. He married in June 1905, at a registry office in Camberwell and made no declaration of German nationality. Even before marriage he had lived on his companion's earnings as a prostitute. The pair went to Portsmouth in September 1905, and in October 1907 took a house in the name of May, the name used by Ellen Klare. About August 1910, Klare took a separate lodging at 33 Osborne Road, a house rented by W. E. Roast, Stoker Petty Officer, of HM Yacht *Victoria and Albert*. He stayed with the Roast's more than two years and moved with them to 44 Oliver Road, Eastney, in April 1912. It was his habit to visit his wife daily and to have meals at her house. In 1911 he served on the *Olympic* as steward or cook's mate. He also worked during eighteen months for a German dentist in Victoria Road. When this man left, Klare set up some apparatus at his own lodgings and put a dentist's plate on the gate. He did very little work however and went out at irregular hours. In 1910-11 he received only about one postcard, but in 1911-12 he had more letters and he frequently received letters from Southampton.

In April 1912 Klare took a house for his wife at Southampton. She was there three months, he spending the weekends with her. In July she went to 17 Sydney Street, Plymouth for a month. Klare spent the last fortnight of the month, with her, and wrote to the Roasts giving them that address for forwarding letters. After leaving the Roasts on 19 July he called there five or six times for letters and in September 1912, two letters did come and were given to him.

In September the Klares had returned to Portsmouth and were together in 7 St Paul's Road until mid-November, when Klare moved to 57 Hudson Road, and Mrs Klare to 1, Unity Place. While at Hudson Road he received a few letters. One was from Germany.

In November 1911 a letter from Portsmouth signed 'W. H.' was intercepted on its way to Herr. G. F. Steinhauer, Potsdam. 'W. H.' offered the services of a dentist, who had been 'here' ten years, knew many naval officers and artificers, had opportunities and leisure for obtaining useful information, and was a trustworthy man. A good deal of correspondence passed before the name and address of the dentist was discovered. Then a letter from 'Richard', posted in the Hanover train from Berlin, was stopped, presumably owing to the handwriting having been identified as that of Mrs Seymour's, Parrott's correspondent. It was addressed to William Klare, Dentist, 33 Osborne Street, Southsea, and it gave directions for the 'transport of a patient to Ostend' and for a meeting, day and hour to be previously wired by addressee, at the Hotel d'Allemagne. The patient would need a rest of twelve to eighteen hours after the journey. For seven months nothing more was intercepted.

In July 1913 'C' wrote to Richard Hugo Dinge Esq., Furbringerstrasse 21, Berlin, that he had not yet attained his object but the doctor's expenses had continued up to the 25th and a promise had been given to carry out the poor chap at the first opportunity. Everything else was 'good'. In December a substantial Christmas present was promised to Klare if the operation was carried out by then. A new address, J. Sturtz, Bornemann's Hotel, Hanover, was to be used for letters, the telegraphic address remained as before.

Six weeks after, 'Allen' replied that the operation could be carried out, but only between Wednesday and Saturday, and £20 must be sent to arrive on Tuesday evening or Wednesday morning. But if addressee had lost confidence, which would not be surprising, he was to send one of his friends to look into things. The right doctor had now been found.

As there was no reply, 'Willi' wrote again suggesting that a friend should be sent to investigate; all was prepared but the doctor would not operate without sanction from the principal. Willi's assertion was supported by a postscript in another handwriting and by a letter from W. H. certifying that the business was genuine this time.

Willi wrote again on the 5th to suggest carrying out the operation on his own initiative, and on the 12th he wrote his address at the head of the letter and begged for an answer: 'Yes' or 'No'.

Then he wired – but the message passed unperceived by the authorities. In reply there came a wire accepting this proposal and this was followed by a letter which explained the delay. Owing to an accident to the intermediary, Klare's letters had never been forwarded until enquiry had been instituted on receipt of his telegram. A new address for letters was given: H. Peters, Potsdam, Brauerstraase 1/2. If Klare agreed to a meeting at the Hotel Cosmopolitan, Bristol, he was to wire merely the date; if he was also bringing the patient he was to add 'Yes' after the date.

In the correspondence itself there is no evidence that Klare received money from abroad, but, as a fact, he did receive money at Christmas 1911, in February and March 1912 – in all £55 according to his own statement. Little of his correspondence was intercepted; it may have been directed to his wife, a name and address or to some agent.

In reading the correspondence two slight errors of interpretation were made. W. H.'s statement that the dentist had been 'here' ten years was taken to refer to Portsmouth whereas it probably referred to England. Secondly, the 'patient' was taken to mean a naval man who would be going abroad with Klare; in fact a confidential book was meant.

On receipt of W. H.'s letter MO5 begged the dockyard police to identify the dentist recommended as suitable for employment by the German Secret Service. This they could not do and, when his name and address became known from the intercepted letter, they were puzzled because the facts they could glean about him did not quite tally with W. H.'s recommendation. Moreover, observation was extremely difficult owing to the position of the house where Klare was lodging. Besides, it seemed an unlikely place for a dentist to live in. A supplementary report, which is not to hand, seems to have been made on 8 January. Then Captain Kell stimulated the zeal of the police by showing them copies of the intercepted letters and asking them to obtain evidence on which to base a prosecution. The police kept such observation on Klare as they were able – they supplied details of his appearance and of his life at Portsmouth, and a tracing of his handwriting which showed that he spelt his name 'Willy Klare'. (In his correspondence the name was written in English form with a 'C'.)

He was undoubtedly an undesirable alien but there was no evidence of his being a spy and he had not left Portsmouth by the train which would connect with the afternoon boat to Ostend. Altogether the police thought that W. H. might have been referring to another man. Further reports were sent in on 20 February and 8 March but these are not in the file. In March, it will be recollected, the case of Wagener was taken in hand and the police were fully engaged upon watching him. Only limited observation was kept upon Klare, and that showed that he frequented the same public houses as Wagener but the two men had not been seen together and there was nothing to connect them. On 4 April, Klare and his wife had taken return tickets to Southampton; on the 6th he had been seen at Portsmouth station talking to two well-dressed Germans for three-quarters of an hour.

The case subsided until October, when Levi Rosenthal, a hairdresser of 71 Queen Street, Portsmouth made a statement to the police: on 18 October a man whose name he did not know had offered him £200, with prospects of obtaining nearly twice that sum, if he would get from the dockyard a confidential book on submarines.

To draw the man on, Rosenthal had pretended to accept the offer saying that he had done that kind of thing before and he had made an appointment with the man to call at his shop on the 21st. Then he had told the story to a town councilor named Privett, and Privett had sent the police to take down his statement.

Levi Rosenthal, it will be recollected, was known to Charles Wagener and had supplied him with a postal address for his spy correspondence.

But there is no evidence in the file that either the police or MO5 remembered this circumstance. If known, it certainly would have been convenient to ignore it, if on the other hand it was unknown then it may have been due to some defect in registration or in tracing. The system of keeping Carl Reimers' correspondence in files apart might be responsible for a slip of this kind.

The police kept in touch with Rosenthal and casual observation upon Klare but nothing further happened during November. Then in mid-December MO5 warned the police that Klare was expected to be sending information of importance abroad during the next fortnight, and the police accordingly kept him under observation as close as was compatible with safety. He was followed to many different public houses, to a hairdresser named Hammel and finally to Rosenthal's shop, where he remained twenty minutes. He was carrying a despatch case. Soon after he had left the shop Rosenthal came to the police to tell them that the spy had called. He had said he had been unable to keep the appointment on 21 October. Rosenthal had then pretended that everything had been ready and he had been looking for Klare but could not find him. Klare said he should have asked Hammel and Rosenthal replied, 'I didn't know that you knew Hammel.' Rosenthal had then offered to introduce Klare to a man who would get the book and promised to call upon Klare to arrange this matter. £30 or £40 would be given to the man.

The police considered that Rosenthal's action in reporting the call proved his genuineness as he could not know that they were watching. They also suggested that some trustworthy naval man should be introduced to Klare as the person who could obtain the book. But this was not thought desirable. Observation was to be continued, corroborative evidence collected if possible and note taken of Klare's associating with naval men for the purpose of obtaining information.

Klare anticipated Rosenthal and called again at the shop on 10 January 1913, to ask whether Rosenthal had seen the man and when the book could be procured. There would be £25 to £30 for the man and £100 for Rosenthal and Klare. The book wanted was not about submarines but about the working of torpedoes. Klare would write to

Germany for the money, and his letter must go via London which would involve a delay of a few days.

Rosenthal reported to Inspector Savage who, in spite of instructions received, did not think it advisable to bid Rosenthal break with Klare, as it was obvious that the only way to catch Klare was to trap him.

Captain Kell saw the DPP and, with his consent, went to Portsmouth to confer with the Admiral Commanding-in-Chief about taking measures which would lead to the arrest of Klare. Charles John Bishop, a pensioned naval writer, then employed as office-keeper of the C-in-C's office, was introduced to Rosenthal as a go-between and the police carefully rehearsed with each the part he was to play. The same evening Klare called on Rosenthal to say he had received £30 but more would not be sent until the book had been procured. The following day Rosenthal definitely promised Klare that a naval man would obtain the book and, after careful enquiry by Klare as to the qualifications of the go-between Rosenthal arranged for a meeting, which took place the same night, between Bishop and Klare. Klare then told Bishop that the book wanted was the very latest edition of the Annual Report of Torpedoes and he described the look of the book exactly. Afterwards he warned Rosenthal that Bishop must be careful not to show the notes received in payment. He asked that the book should be delivered in time for him to cross to Rotterdam by the Great Eastern Railway boat. Although confirmation had thus been obtained of Rosenthal's accusation, the police urged that the business should be completed and Klare arrested as he left 71 Queen Street with the book in his possession.

But, as will have been seen from Klare's letters to Germany there was a hitch on the question of money. Klare had to put off the final meetings until 5 February and then, as the money had not come, he wished Bishop to act without previous payment. Bishop declined and Klare said he would write to his employer's wife and arranged to see Bishop on the 12th. On the 11th, as he was still without money, he wrote out a telegram, addressed to Nakpatus, Berlin. He asked

Rosenthal to send it and allow the reply to be sent to his shop, for he himself was afraid to be seen at the post office. Eventually however he was too nervous to allow Rosenthal to send the wire.

Then on the 17th Klare called on Rosenthal with a telegram he had received in answer to one he had himself sent. The next day he put this telegram and the form he had written out for Rosenthal in the fire; on the 19th at 10 a.m. he called with the letter from Berlin, which confirmed the telegram, and as Bishop came in, the letter was shown to him by Klare and translated by Rosenthal, and then burned.

On the 17th Inspector Savage had telephoned to MO5 that Klare had received a wire agreeing to his proposal to take the book over at his own expense. Sir O. Matthews, being referred to, agreed that the money transaction between Klare and Bishop might be foregone. Accordingly at the meeting between Klare, Rosenthal and Bishop on the morning of the 19th, it was arranged that Bishop should hand over the book at 4 p.m. Klare said it would be easy enough to convey it out of the country, the difficulty lay in getting it back past the Customs, but he would wrap it in underclothing and put tobacco on the top, then declare the tobacco and the book would pass unnoticed.

The delivery of the book was carried out as arranged and Klare was arrested soon after leaving Rosenthal's shop. Klare was brought up on 20 February, and evidence of arrest having been given he was remanded for a week. The charge was that to the prejudice of the State he had in his possession a book containing valuable information contrary to Section 8 of the Official Secrets Act. He was told that other charges would be made of inciting Rosenthal and Bishop. On hearing the charge he accused Rosenthal of having incited him. Klare appeared before the magistrates on 20 February and was remanded till 27 Feburary. On behalf of some German calling himself Schwartz, Mr Gordon Cummings wired Klare offering to send his solicitor to defend him and Klare accepted. The solicitor was a Mr Adrian de Fleury, of French descent, who had married the niece of a German hotel proprietor settled at Marie Kerke in Belgium.

On 27 February Klare was further charged with inciting Charles

John Bishop to obtain the book and with unlawfully receiving it. Some cross-examination took place about the telegraphic code address 'Nakpatus' and the police afterwards applied to MO5 for information on the subject; but they had none to supply.

The defence also tried to elicit from Inspector Savage the name of the first informant in the case throwing out a hint that it was someone in the Secret Service; but counsel for the Crown pointed out that the case was limited to the period between 18 October 1912 and 19 February 1913, and the magistrates upheld him. The hearing was resumed on 6, 15 and 20 March. The defence was concentrated on the cross-examination of Rosenthal.

Rosenthal was born in Prussian Poland and his parents brought him to England and settled at Hull when he was two or three years old. Then they moved to Newcastle. Rosenthal learned his business as a hairdresser, went to New York for some years, returned to Newcastle in 1876 and then worked in several hairdressing shops in London. He then took up business on his own account in Portsmouth, where he had been for about twenty-one years. He had occupied the premises in Queen Street for eighteen or nineteen years. He could not read and he could only just sign his own name.

The defence wished to prove that Rosenthal had frequently met Klare before October 1912, had begged Klare to get him work for the German Secret Service, had said he could get anything from the dockyard, and had admitted procuring a signal book for a German officer two years before. Rosenthal denied these charges, he held his own with counsel, but made no attempt to explain why a man whom he had seen only once before should have asked him to obtain a confidential book. Oddly enough, counsel did not press the point.

Bishop's evidence was definite: it was Klare, and not Rosenthal, who had asked for and described the book, and Klare who had received a letter in German accepting a meeting at Bristol (for Brussels). Inspector Savage gave evidence that a book of paying-in slips of the Capital & Counties Bank in Southsea, had been found in Klare's room and contained the following entries:

- 1 March 1912 £10 in notes
- 2 March 1912 £9 in gold
- 16 March 1912 £20-10 in notes
- 18 May 1912 £25 in notes

The defence persisted that the prime mover in the plot was not before the Bench and put Klare into the box to make a statement about his relations with Rosenthal. Klare said that Rosenthal first mentioned spying at the end of February or beginning of March 1912. He had known him for five or six years and he asserted that Rosenthal had incited him to procure the book. It was a case of allegations and counter allegations and Klare broke down badly in cross-examination about his intended journey, the letter from Germany and the telegram to 'Nakpatus'. Besides points that had a direct bearing on the procuring of the book, counsel for the Crown laid stress on Klare's private life and his wife's movements. Inspector Savage was recalled and again cross-examined on the evidence of immoral living, but not necessarily of spying, which had been collected against Klare in the nine months preceeding October 1912.

Klare was committed for trial on all four counts and the case came up on 26 June at the Winchester Assize. The question of incitement was brushed aside and Klare was found guilty of having, for a purpose prejudicial to England, obtained a book which would be useful to an enemy. Before sentence was passed, Savage was called to make a statement. The facts that Klare did little work, spent the greater part of the day in public-houses with servicemen, that his wife's clientele consisted of the same class of person, and that he was much in her company, were interpreted in one way - that he used her as a source of information.

Klare was sentenced to five years' imprisonment. He was amazed at the sentence and attributed it to the judge being a German-hater. He had been condemned on the word of a Jew who would have been only half believed in Germany. He expressed the intention of petitioning for a reduction of sentence and suggested to his sister (Mrs Clara Schneider) that she should approach Baron Speyer, if opportunity served.

To a fellow prisoner Klare made statements about German methods of spying and their policy on the outbreak of war. The Germans relied on their spies who swarmed in every rank of life; through them they would get the upper hand. They counted besides on the treachery of Englishmen, whom they had in their pay. They made a point of knowing the private circumstances of officers, officials, secretaries and ministers, and bribed gamblers or those in difficulties. For two or three years running Klare had got from two officers stationed on one of HM ships the loan of the Annual Report of Torpedoes and the Manual of Torpedoes and had gone with them to Ostend and Brussels. Besides, the secretary of an English minister kept the Germans informed of the intentions of the British government.

On the outbreak of war every move would be wired to America while the British authorities should be watching only the cables to Germany. A policy of terrorism would be adopted; reservoirs would be poisoned, churches, railways, viaducts blown up, important officials would be shot or kidnapped. Moreover landings would be made on the west coast of Ireland and on the Isle of Wight. The submarines would play a most important part in the war.

The statement was written down by Newton and handed to the prison governor after the outbreak of war. An attempt to procure from Klare the name of the secretary failed as he did not know it, and he refused to give the names by which he had known the two officers whom he had accused of treachery.

Klare was kept in prison till practically the end of his sentence. He was then served with a deportation order and repatriated. He was blacklisted on 1 November 1918. In connection with this successful prosecution £10 was given to Bishop, £20 were distributed among the dockyard police and £20 went to Rosenthal.

In February 1914 Rosenthal appealed for help on the grounds that his action as informant had materially injured his business and he was then in straits and receiving threatening letters. Enquiry was made by the police, who believed his story. He was granted a further sum of £10 on condition that he signed a document to the effect that he had been liberally rewarded already for his services to the police, that the present payment was an act of grace, and that he understood that no further application for assistance would be entertained. Levi Rosenthal accepted the conditions and signed the document.

The case of Klare showed that the Germans had scored a considerable success, whether by their agents at Portsmouth or elsewhere, and comparison of the files of Charles Wagener, William Klare and Abraham Eisner throws a little light on the existence of a gang of spies at Portsmouth.

As regards Klare, he was introduced obviously by a man of some authority. 'W. H.' may be identical with W. Herpers who afterwards posed as an editor. He may have been a travelling agent: at any rate he wrote twice from Southsea spontaneously and at an interval of fourteen months. On the second occasion he guaranteed that Klare's hopes were well-founded and that the money must be sent, it was no doubt he who added a postscript to Klare's second urgent letter. In order to give this guarantee 'W. H.' must have known and approved of Rosenthal's share in the business.

As regards any possible connection with Wagener: during the first seven months of 1918, Wagener was trying to obtain the exact titles of confidential books on wireless, submarines and torpedoes and possibly also some of the books themselves; Klare on the other hand was from the beginning trying to obtain a book ('the patient was to rest twelve to eighteen hours after the journey' to Ostend) but it was not till October, after Wagener had dropped out, that he mentioned a book on submarines, and this he corrected in January 1913 to the Annual Report of Torpedoes.

The exact title of this book was the Annual Report of Torpedo School. In asking for it Klare showed such accurate knowledge of its appearance as could only have been obtained in an authorised manner. While Wagener corresponded with Henri Adams in Brussels, Klare wrote to Richard or 'Richard Hugo Dinge' in Berlin and later on to an address in Hanover and one in Potsdam. The two men therefore aimed at a similar objective, simultaneously, but they sent reports to different centres.

But after Wagener dropped out, Klare seems to have had at his disposal the special information which Wagener was instructed to collect. Technical evidence at the trial showed how difficult this was to obtain as the books were printed under secret bond and none but officers might even see them. How then was this information procured?

Was it through the indiscretion of printers, for German agents cultivated the acquaintance of printers, and had Klare got in touch with such men through his intercourse with the stationer? The question of Klare's connection with Abraham Eisner has been dealt with in that case. Suffice to say here that in 1919, when the recession of the order against Eisner was under discussion, it was dismissed on the grounds that there was no mention of it in Klare's file and that the police had kept the man under constant observation before his arrest. This sounds plausible, but the Klare file is imperfect as there are at least three police reports missing. The case dragged on for fifteen months, and continuous observation was impossible. Moreover neighbours and business connections sometimes know even more than the police.

Levi Rosenthal plays a doubtful part. His story was that he had met Klare once five or six years before: Klare said that Rosenthal, whom he already knew, had come to him in the end of February or beginning of March, and begged to be enrolled as a German agent. Does this explain why at the end of March Wagener called upon Rosenthal and finally used his address as a postbox? It must be remembered Klare took no risks: nothing incriminating was found on him or at his house; he was clever, he sent his wires unnoticed; is it likely he would have approached a man of whose past and sentiments he knew nothing on so dangerous a business as stealing a confidential book? Klare, no doubt, did incite Rosenthal; at the same time it seems at least probable that Rosenthal had, as he himself said, 'done the thing before'.

Lastly, there is the man Hammel, who knew both Rosenthal and Klare, and knew where Klare was to be found. The defence called him as evidence that Rosenthal had lied about his movements.

The determination of the Germans to get the confidential book was evinced by their pursuing this object at Portsmouth and Chatham simultaneously. In October 1912, Frederick Gould was offered £200 for the Gunnery and Torpedo Manual of 1909, with Addenda and £200 for the Annual Report of Torpedo School for 1912; and in January

1913, a bait of £400 was offered him for the 1911 edition of the Annual Report of Torpedo School.

The German agents were supposed not to know each other and to act independently but it is impossible to believe that the vultures gathered round a carcass do not recognise each other, there must have been a scramble to get there first.

As a last comment, the dangerous use to which the Germans put their exact knowledge of the aspect of Secret Books was illustrated in the case of HMS *Queen* when a signals book was stolen and replaced by a dummy exactly like the original.

★

Karl Paul Gustav Hentschel (alias Atlantis, alias 'Ch. G. Hills') of 96 Invicta Road, Sheerness, was probably of German descent. In 1913 when concealment was no longer possible, he claimed German nationality, stating he had served one year in the German Navy and had then gone into the German Merchant Marine and knew every port on the German seaboards. He gave William Melville the following account of his engagement as a spy.

While in Berlin in 1908 he had advertised for a situation as a correspondent, and was engaged by letter by Robert Tornow, member of a foreign correspondence bureau, to go to London, mix with people, and hear what was going on. This was at a time of crisis – no doubt the Moroccan crisis which lasted from about September 1908 to February 1909. A few weeks later he was sent to Devonport as a clerk to assess the situation and report what was going on.

He received £10 a month for reports on the movements of warships which were posted to Max Dressler, a confectioner, who also let rooms at 22 rue de l'Ouest, Ostend. Hentschel found himself hampered as a foreigner at Devonport and the salary was too low. He left and went to Essen and reported this through Dressler to Tornow. Tornow then offered him £15 a month and £15 bonus to go to Sheerness. He was to watch the movements of ships, mine-laying etc. Then a secret code was sent him and he was told to obtain the naval signal code. He went to Sheerness in April 1909. In June he distributed circulars as a teacher of languages. He taught French, German and Italian and also navigation. At first he had as pupils a good many naval officers, lieutenants and commanders, and through technical conversations with them he would find out anything he wanted to know. From a petty officer of HMS *Diamond* whom he met accidentally at Sittingbourne, he learned about mine-fuses and the newest mine-sweepers, and a fitter gave him some drawings. But his own pupils explained to him the working of range-finding and fire control instruments. He also learned about the lights inside and outside the harbour and other information required by his employers. In October 1909 Hentschel again advertised at the school at Sheerness and stated he would also visit Sittingbourne and other places. Within five months of his setting up as a teacher, MO5 sent Melville to investigate. Hentschel told Melville he was born in Holland and brought up in Germany. He objected to giving any references but could produce good ones from the Freiderich Wilhelm Gymnasium, Berlin, and he referred Melville to the Reverend Mr Tozer, minister of the Congregational Church at Sheerness.

Further enquiry showed that Hentschel's statements as to dates, motives and personal circumstances varied. He had about twenty pupils. He had spoken of having been much at sea; he had come to Sheerness for his health or else because he thought it a nice place. He had independent means and was teaching for something to do. He had much correspondence, and was doing well with teaching in spite of frequently changing his address. Two of his landladies suspected him of being a spy. Melville concluded that he was in the German Navy and a spy. Some years later Mr Tozer produced a letter from Dr Meinarius, minister of the Lutheran Church at Munster, Westphalia (which Mr Tozer believed to be in Holland) agreeing to Hentschel's joining the Congregational Church at Sheerness. This provided cover for Hentschel's work and nationality. Cover for his journeys abroad and correspondence was provided by Hentschel's engagement to Amelie Wetzel, of whom he would sometimes speak as his wife. She lived at Maastricht. When it became inconvenient he broke off the engagement, and after a hurried journey abroad announced that his 'wife' had died.

On receipt of Melville's report NID and the GOC East Coast defences were informed and officers were warned not to patronise Hentschel. On 15 December 1909 Hentschel married a shop assistant, Patricia Riley, and within a few weeks moved to Chatham and set up a school at 7 Waghorn Terrace. He intended to visit Sheerness three days a week. This move portended the breaking of fresh ground. It is possible that, owing to the action of MO5, Hentschel's clientele in Sheerness had diminished; it is certain that through his wife and her family he was adding largely to his sources of information. The Rileys lived at Chatham. They had seen better days. John Riley the father, a broken-down deputy bank manager, had become traveller to a tailoring firm, had embezzled money, and disappeared. The mother, Emily Riley, was a heavy drinker and in the habit of raising money in any way she could. There were at least four attractive daughters, Patricia Hentschel, Emily (afterwards Mrs Pelling), Nellie and Edith. These girls had many admirers and friends among naval men in Chatham.

It was in February 1910 that his wife Patricia found out her husband's real work and offered to help him. He meanwhile was procuring from abroad better cover of his supposed Dutch nationality. There are in his file three, to all appearances, official Dutch papers emanating from Rotterdam: his parents' marriage certificate; a curious passport for inland use only; and a kind of identity book, valid for one year, extracted from the National Register on 5 April 1910.

Concerning these papers, Karl Hentschel subsequently told William Melville that they were given him by Robert Tornow; his father's name was correctly given, his mother's name was spurious. The father's name, Ferdinand Wilhelm Johann Hentschel, is pure German, the mother's, Elise Wilhelraine Elisabeth van Dyke seem a mixture of German and Dutch. The copies of the marriage and birth certificate were made on 20 June 1899.

These false papers recall those carried by Dr Max Bolton in 1910 and a statement made by Theisen to the effect that Steinhauer had his offices in Rotterdam. It is to be supposed that the official Dutch seal for a foreign passport could not easily be fabricated. Patricia worked hard for her husband and she enlisted in his service her mother and sisters, and also George Charles Parrott, Chief Gunner on HMS *Agamemnon*. She had known this man since 1908 and had several times borrowed small sums from him for her family. After her marriage she continued to correspond with him with her husband's knowledge, and eventually she lured him to betray his country. This result seems to have been achieved in three stages, corresponding with Parrott's movements and promotions.

Parrott served on HMS *Agamemnon* from 28 January 1907 to 27 August 1910 when he was transferred to the *Pembroke*; at the end of September 1910, he was put in charge of the range at Sheerness. From August 1909 the *Agamemnon* had been repeatedly engaged in exercises off Sheerness, Portland and Portsmouth; she had also visited Cromarty and Queensferry. In February 1910 she was exercising off Portland; she was in Chatham Dockyard from 7 May to 15 June, took part in the grand manoeuvres off Portland from 26 June to 19 July, and was paid off at Sheerness on 26 September 1910.

At the end of September, Parrott, according to Hentschel, offered in Mrs Hentschel's presence to supply any information that was wanted. Parrott answered questions and was engaged at a monthly salary of £8 rising to £10. Parrott however, asserts that Patricia Hentschel persuaded him to answer questions and overcame his scruples by offering him a £5 note. Fresh lists came in about every ten days and he received from £5 to £7 for answers. The questions dealt with guns, armour and steering qualities of ships, oil capacity and radius of submarines, interference with wireless telegraphy. In the fifth or sixth list, he was asked to obtain a complete list of the confidential books and documents supplied to ships. He refused and tried to back out, and was threatened with exposure. He then consented on condition that all writing should be destroyed in the presence of both parties, and a code of the names of flowers was arranged for use in the work.

In February 1911, Parrott got very nervous and tried to break off, but Patricia induced him to continue the work. Parrott had then received £85 which he kept in his locker at Sheerness. Then the two men quarrelled and Parrott threatened to expose Hentschel, but was calmed down by Patricia and the affair ended for the time being with the departure of the Hentschels for Australia. He lent Patricia £65, of which she paid back about £45. Parrott never seems to have resumed relations with Hentschel.

Hentschel states that a few days after Parrott's engagement he produced four volumes of the Half-Yearly Gunnery Progress. The last issue of the half-yearly summary dates from January 1910; it was replaced at the end of that year by the annual summary. The four volumes presumably of 1908 and 1909 were taken to Ostend and thence to Berlin and Tornow gave Parrott £40 for them. They were not of much value.

In the next four months (October 1910 to January 1911) Hentschel says that Parrott supplied S3 confidential books. From the imperfect indications of the titles given by Hentschel some of these are believed to have been the following:

1. The Flotilla Signal Book (issued 1908, addenda 1911) (Secret List 11), Parrott said the Germans offered him a £1,000 for this. Gould was asked for this book in the autumn of 1912; the signal book was stolen eventually from the *Queen* in February 1914.

2. Addenda to Torpedo Manual Volume III. The Manual on the Heater Torpedo (issued 1909). These books had been copied on sheets by some educated man, not Parrott. The sheets were taken abroad and photographed. On Hentschel's own evidence it seems improbable that Parrott supplied these two books.

3. Torpedo Manual (three or four volumes, issued with addenda 1908, 1910, 1909, 1911). Gould was asked for the 1909 edition in October 1912 or else Annual Report of Torpedo School (issued annually since 1905). This was obtained from HMS *Actaeon*. Parrott's evidence goes to show that these two books were not supplied to the Germans and Frederick Gould was being asked in October 1912 for the Annual Report of 1911. The request was repeated to Gould and to William Klare in January 1913.

4. Manual of Gunnery (three volumes, issued in 1907, 1902, 1922) and addenda to Volumes I and II 1909. Gould was being asked for this in October 1912.

5. The Employment of Cruisers and Destroyers 1906.

6. Instructions in Defence Matters 1907. Very Secret. List I. Steel Safe or else. Memorandum on the Regulation of Traffic at Defended Ports in Time of War 1909 (issued for the CO's personal use, List II.)

7. Manoeuvres Report for 1909 (issued January 1910). Parrott is said to have received £500 for this; Parrott told fellow prisoner Rayner he was offered £500 for this by 'Richard'.

8. A Book on Fire-Controls, presumably one of the three following:
   (i) Handbook of Fire Control Instruments, 1909.
   (ii) Information relative to Fire Control Range-Finding and Plotting, 1909.
   (iii) Fleet Fire-Control and Concentration of Fire Experiments, 1909.

9. A book on minesweepers.

10. Other books.

These books were photographed at Ostend by Robert Tornow who brought two assistants and special appliances. Four were photographed in one night. Parrott was paid £600, £500, £250, £150 and other sums.

Patricia Hentschel told the Chief Constable of Kent that she had carried abroad two books for Parrott; she thought one of them was about torpedoes, the other about the distribution of the Fleet in wartime. She may have been referring to books on the list given by Karl Hentschel but it is possible that these books were conveyed abroad by her in July 1912.

Parrott, on the other hand, denied having supplied confidential books to Hentschel. He declared the only book he had delivered was the handbook of the 6-inch gun. But there is support for Hentschel's contention as regards books on gunnery and fire control.

In talk with Rayner, Parrott stated that while on board the *Cambridge* (between 1903-1906) he had had the three volumes of the Gunnery Manual and had burned them in order to get rid of them. He must have been referring to old editions of no value. These he may have offered to Hentschel and they may have been rejected.

A minute dealing with the preparation of the case shows that, at the written request of Parrott, confidential books were issued to him from a library at Chatham; that confidential books were returned by him on 20 February 1911 and on the 11 March 1911, and that one of the books 'contained information regarding fire control and was the latest book issued by the Admiralty on that subject'. This curiously worded statement might refer to the signal book, for when a confidential signal book was stolen from the *Queen* it was stated in the press that among other secrets, the book contained details of the Percy Scott Fire Control System.

The break with Hentschel took place in March 1911. On 3 April 1911 Parrott deposited with the Conservative Club Building Fund the sum of £100, which would seem to be a larger sum than his professional income would warrant. But even allowing for the fact that Parrott kept money received from the Germans in his locker, the sums he banked, invested, and disbursed are too small to make it credible that he gained much from the sale of confidential books. It was thought probable that Parrott did not receive as much for his services as he had expected and that that was the cause of the quarrel between the two men. It is also probable that Parrott did not supply all the books mentioned by Hentschel, but that he did at least give Hentschel the titles of a number of confidential books. This was a service of some value and it is worth noting that in January 1912 Wagener too was asked to send in a list of confidential books which would go to prove either that Parrott had not supplied the complete list asked for or that a check on his data was required. One of the difficulties of estimating the truth of a spy's statements lies in this – that there was undoubtedly a good deal of gossip in the Service and that accuracy as to dates was not observed; hence a spy would attribute to himself the achievements of others or else to one date what was accomplished by himself at some other time. The truth seems to be Hentschel claimed to have received from Parrott and delivered to the Germans all those books (1. Mentioned in conversation with Parrott at any time; 2. Specially asked for by 'Richard' of Parrott; 3. Actually supplied by Parrott in 1911 and 1912).

In October 1910, the police at Sheerness sent in a report about Hentschel which touched upon his copious correspondence with Maastricht in 1911, and his receipt of money from abroad and stated that he said he had been a captain in the Merchant Service. He sometimes received letters addressed to Captain Karl Hentschel.

Hentschel's name was noted on the Black List No. 18. He had been on the possible suspect list since October 1909.

In March 1911 the question of officers taking lessons with him was again raised but no action was taken lest his suspicions should be roused. Orders were given to instruct military officers not to discuss naval or military matters with foreigners.

On 29 March 1911 Hentschel was reported to have left England. No doubt he had gone to the Continent to wind up his affairs before going to Australia. Hentschel and his wife sailed for Australia on 24 June 1911 and MO5 heard of his departure in October.

This closes the first part of Karl Hentschel's case. MO5 at that time knew nothing beyond what had been reported by Melville, Major Bright, and the police in 1909 and 1910; there was no proof against Hentschel and no suspicion against his wife, her family or Parrott. The one danger anticipated was the indiscretion of officers during their lessons with Hentschel and against that only very limited precautions could be taken. It was not until August 1911 that a new weapon was placed in the hands of MO5 by granting warrants in special cases for the opening of letters in the post.

When he left for Australia Hentschel had quarreled not only with Parrott but also with his German employers. The reasons for these quarrels are not clear, but there is evidence to show that one motive at least was jealousy, personal and professional. Hentschel was a suspicious man; his wife had been actively employed carrying books, etc. to Ostend on at least three occasions and he was jealous of her relations with both Parrott and with Tornow. Her attitude may have given him cause for jealousy. Letters from Tornow and from another married man both reveal a peculiar tenderness for Patricia. Moreover, Hentschel accused Parrott of making love to her.

From an employer's point of view, Hentschel may have become an unsatisfactory agent; he had probably taken to drink and he may have kept for his own use money given to him for other purposes. 'T' afterwards mentioned two sums, £300 and £250 for which some reparation had to be made. One of these was a sum of £500 which according to Hertschel had been given to him to start farming in Australia. Patricia too declared her husband had embezzled £1,700 but 'T''s letter disposes of this statement. Parrott declared that Hentschel had sold his 'connection' to the Germans for £1,000; that would bring Hentschel's profits of a more or less illegitimate kind up to £1,550. It was Charles Wagener who told [XXXX] that it was he who found Parrott through a commercial traveller and Wagener, alias Steel, alias Brown, was running a spy bureau at 394 Edgware Road and 15 New Oxford Street. Combining all these statements the following may be the facts: Hentschel could do no more with Parrott, the two men quarrelled over Patricia and probably over the £300 which Hentschel received from the Germans and did not share with Parrott. Hentschel then sold his connection to Wagener and decamped to Australia with the proceeds. After a time the Germans heard of this and sent Fels over and Fels, through Wagener, picked up the Rileys and Parrott. Between the Rileys and Wagener, Parrott was coerced into acting for them. He had been able to ignore letters from Germany but yielded to personal pressure under the influence of fear and cupidity.

Hentschel, out in Australia, heard of this and immediately wrote to Parrott demanding a sum of £250. 'Richard' in Berlin was informed, let Parrott know that he was not to worry, for the matter would be arranged from Berlin, and promptly cabled £50 to Hentschel. This supplied funds for the return of the pair and accordingly they landed in England in March 1912. Meanwhile MO5 had been empowered to take out a HOW for suspect correspondence and had thereby discovered the activities of Parrott, Mrs Riley, and others. With intercepted correspondence we get on absolutely firm ground.

On arrival Patricia wrote to Robert Tornow who was already expecting her return, begging him to re-engage her husband. She sent two copies of her letter one via Schulzer, 28 Misinesmier, Rotterdam, the other via Otto Kruger. This latter was intercepted; eventually it was delivered to Kruger's house after his flight to Germany and was burned by Mrs Kruger.

Various spy trials had taken place during the Hentschels's absence and the reply to Patricia showed that the name Tornow had been exchanged for Thibaut and the Ostend address for that of Henri Adams, 10 Petite rue des Longs in Brussels. Thibaut was prepared to re-engage the Hentschels provided a promise were given never again to blackmail 'gardener who was the cause' of Karl's success. Patricia then wrote that she hoped to resume partnership with Gardener and was most anxious to meet Captain Fels and that her sisters were looking forward to seeing him again. Hentschel went abroad, saw Thibaut, and promised to deliver up any correspondence at all in his hands, and was re-engaged at a lower salary than before.

Next came a wire from Rotterdam bidding him continue negotiations as money was being sent. This it would seem, referred to a plan for buying a public-house, which fell through. The wire was followed by a registered packet despatched from Rotterdam by Ch. Beaumont. But nothing further seems to have passed and in June Hentschel set out for Australia and was followed by his wife and her sister Edith in July. A HOW had been taken out for Hentschel's correspondence; it was cancelled on 15 October 1913.

Parrott had no doubt refused to have anything to do with Hentschel and Hentschel's services as a German agent were not needed for Gould was at work at Rochester, Parrott at Sheerness, and the Riley girls at Chatham, and Mrs Riley may have been carrying documents to the Continent.

Very soon after Patricia reached Australia, she was planning her return, and Thibaut was undoubtedly anxious for it. Parrott had been dismissed from the navy in August and 'T' was communicating with him through Mrs Riley. At the end of August, Parrott was to be informed through this channel that a very satisfactory arrangement had been made with Charles and that the old friendly relations were being kept up. This means that Hentschel was receiving a salary of £30 a month for keeping silent.

In September 'T' was still feeling hopeful about Charles and quieting Parrott's fears. At the same time he complained of the large sums received by Charles and Patricia in the last year and made it clear that Mrs Riley's pension depended on Charles's good behavior. In this letter Hentschel gave Mrs Riley Charles's address: 31 Woolcott Street, Darlinghurst, Sydney, and a check was immediately placed on it, apparently without result. Supplies were forwarded to Charles from Berlin via the Bank of Australia, and the Deutsche Bank, and the Diskonto Gesellschaft.

It seems evident that Charles and Patricia had separated for the time being, for, late in October, 'T' had heard of her impending return and was preparing to see Mrs Riley after that had taken place. He also wanted to see Charles's letters and was most anxious that the man should stay in Australia as it would be best for them all.

Patricia and Edith returned to England in February 1910 and for a time Patricia settled at Gravesend. Then 'T' made a mistake: he stopped Hentschel's allowance by a clumsy trick which would deceive no one. He must have argued that exposures would not matter much since Parrott was by then in prison.

In March 1913, a mourning card announcing the death of Robert Tornow on a journey to America was sent to Hentschel via Klunder. Possibly this had something to do with Graves's journey to America in company with Stammer in February 1913. Then, in July, the remittances stopped and Hentschel returned home, arriving on 23 September.

The news must have been posted abroad at once for, on the 30th, 'Ch. Fischer' wrote from Berlin acquainting Mrs Riley with the reported death of Fels, and saying that anything that would have been of interest to Fels was to be sent to Miss Mary Kennedy, Brauerstrasse 1/2, Potsdam. 'Flapper' immediately wrote to inform Hentschel, who meanwhile sent Henri Adams a threatening letter to 'Mr R. P. or Successor'. Hentschel was using the alias 'Ch. J. Hills'.

On 15 October Schulz wrote to Nellie promising further particulars of the death of Fels but Hentschel was not to be convinced. Fels, it appears, had been in England and at the Rileys as late as September 1913.

On his return from Australia Hentschel went to Mrs Riley's house at

82 Pagitt Street in Chatham and found that Patricia was earning her living as manageress at Bennett's Hotel in Weybridge, a place much frequented by airmen. On 29 September Hentschel left Mrs Riley's and went to London. He wrote begging his wife to return to him and she refused; on 15 October he went to Weybridge to see her again and she still refused to return. Meanwhile he had been communicating with Scotland Yard under the assumed name of Atlantis. He wrote three letters offering to give information about the German Secret Service and traffic in confidential naval books, on condition that the safety of everyone he mentioned should be guaranteed, that he should receive a sum of money, and employment in the British Secret Service. The expenditure of £100 was sanctioned and an advertisement in the terms required by Atlantis was put in the *Daily Telegraph* asking him to call. On the 10th Atlantis called at Scotland Yard and Mr Melville identified him as Hentschel.

A further meeting was arranged which took place on the 15th, Hentschel received none of the guarantees he had asked for and was preparing to leave without making any revelations when Melville broke down further resistance by addressing him by name. Hentschel then told the story of his life and dealings with Parrott and the German Secret Service.

Meanwhile, Hentschel had spared his wife and her family and continued his efforts to induce her to return to him. It was her final refusal that drove him to desperation. Late at night on 21 October he took his two little children to the police station at Chatham and there made a scene. The police persuaded him to go home with the children. He had been drinking heavily and was confused. In his rage he told the family that he had given himself up as a spy and had betrayed them.

This was anticipating events but, as will be seen, it frightened the Rileys into concerted action to protect themselves and their connections. Emily Pelling clung to him to prevent the final rupture. On 22 October Hentschel came to town with the children and Mrs Felling and, after sending threatening telegrams to his wife, he gave himself up as a spy to the city police. He made a signed statement embodying the accusations he had made against Parrott and the German Secret Service in his interview with Melville.

The exposure was highly inconvenient for once in the hands of the police the matter had to go forward. The Foreign Office would not, the Admiralty could not intervene. Hentschel was detained in custody for a fortnight in order that his statements might be investigated. He was brought up at Westminster on 8 November and charged with having on his own confession incited, 'George Charles Parrott ... to disclose official secrets ... during the years 1910, 1911 and 1912'. At this hearing the written statement he had made to the police was referred to in general terms only, as it was inadvisable to make public the extent of the disclosures made to a foreign power.

The solicitor for the defence suggested that this was a confidential communication in return for which Hentschel had received £30 from the police, and an engagement in the British Secret Service at £5 a week. It is probable that Hentschel was too bemused to have realised the difference between his communication to Melville and his voluntary statements to the police, for after his arrest he had written to reassure the Rileys and to beg for the intervention of 'Uncle' or 'Cousin' in whose death he did not believe. But his mistake was eagerly seized upon by the prosecution, who withdrew the charge with a fine show of clemency. Sir Archibald Bodkin admitted in court that a confidential communication had been made to and a payment of £30 received from an authority specially constituted to deal with similar cases.

Hentschel was discharged and *John Bull* contrasted the case of the self-confessed spy who could not secure a conviction, try how he might, with that of the convicted spy who was released and promoted to a post in the British Secret Service. Hentschel left prison on 18 November. He saw his wife on the 19th and fetched away his little boy. Then he took out a gun license, bought a pistol, and threatened his wife with it. At her instance he was rearrested on the 22nd and charged with threatening to kill Patricia Hentschel. The threat was useful to Patricia whose file became that of the innocent wife coerced into acting against her country's interests.

At the first hearing of the charge against Hentschel, the threatening telegrams he had sent to his wife on 22 October were produced. Further evidence was required as to the despatch of these telegrams and the case was adjourned. Between the first and the second hearing the GPO contrived to mislay the originals of five of these telegrams, with the result that, although Hentschel was committed for trial, the more serious charge was withdrawn, for lack of sufficient evidence. He was bound over for twelve months and discharged. The file does not contain any detailed press notice of the trial, for the DPP was not concerned, but Patricia Hentschel had complained of the result to the Chief Constable of Kent, who communicated with MO5 and they supplied the solution given above. Hentschel went abroad. He wrote to Nellie Riley once or twice from Antwerp and stated his intention of going to China.

Hentschel had stated that the Annual Report of Torpedo School had been received from the *Actaeon*. It was discovered that First Writer W. R. H. Greene had been serving on the *Actaeon* from either 7 March or 8 April 1910, and had been relieved on 2 December 1911, at the request of his commanding officer who did not trust him. At the beginning of 1912, Greene was on HMS *Diamond* and he was discharged for unsatisfactory conduct on 24 April 1912. His shore address was 20 Imperial Road, Gillingham. He had spoken of his intention of emigrating.

Enquiry concerning Parrott was also revived. Hentschel's statement was shown to him and his reply to it has been already discussed. His comments on other points were interesting: he threw doubts on the integrity of George Pelling, Engine-Room Artificer on board a torpedo-boat of the Chatham Division and of Mrs Riley, who he said, had tried to blackmail him and had forced upon him in 1911, an introduction to Captain Fels; and he stated, that 'Tom' and 'Richard' were, he believed, identical and that his own trip abroad had been taken with a view to extricating himself from the position in which Hentschel had left him.

Thus the Rileys and Pollings were definitely incriminated by Parrott and their relations with Fels, a German agent, exposed. On 22 October, the day after they thought Hentschel had betrayed them, anonymous information was given to the Secretary of the Commander-in-Chief at the Nore that Hentschel had returned from Australia, was living with the Rileys, his relations, that he had a brother-in-law, George Palling, in the navy, and that he had given himself up as a spy. The informant was Philip Owen Penrose, civilian schoolmaster of the Mechanical Establishment Training at Chatham. His reason for anonymity was no doubt the fact that he had known the Rileys intimately for about a year and was engaged to be married to Edith Riley. His somewhat tardy information was inaccurate but represented what the Rileys believed at the time.

Penrose next volunteered the information that Captain Friedel Fels had, during Hentschel's absence, visited the Rileys for the purpose of paying his addresses to one of the daughters. Having been submitted to a severe interrogatory concerning his acquaintance with the Rileys, and his connection with Fels, Mrs Riley and Parrott, his replies were too guarded and showed too correct a knowledge of the Rileys' doings to be satisfactory. Moreover he declared he had seen Fels only once and that in September 1913, whereas Mrs Riley had admitted that Fels had been frequently to see them in August of that year. Penrose repeated the story of the Rileys that Fels had originally come over to trace Hentschel who had embezzled money; he also repeated Mrs Riley's explanation of her motives in going repeatedly to Rotterdam, and asserted her innocence. He was censured by his commanding officer for want of frankness, for not having kept his position or acted in accordance with his duty. There was an obstacle in the way of removing him from Chatham but, after war had broken out, when he went to live with the Rileys, he was told to choose between his connection with that family and his post. He preferred to resign. A search of his old rooms and of the premises at the Rileys was made without result. Subsequently in 1916 he obtained a post as draughtsman in the Royal Arsenal. This being reported to MI5 they eventually procured his discharge. He then obtained work with the Napier motor-manufacturing firm.

Parrott had not hesitated to denounce Patricia and the part she had played as beguiler. She herself acknowledged this part: she was to find out, she said, those officers and non-commissioned officers who were in need of money and open to bribery.

Eventually in May 1914, through a friend of Hentschel's, certain definite charges were made against the Rileys. These charges had been made to the friend by Hentschel himself. Thanks to their efforts Hentschel had received information which he could not otherwise have attempted to get; his own pay was increased and Patricia had received a gratuity of £150; she had obtained from Parrott in lieu of Talbot, who was moved, specimens of the English high explosives and information about the manoeuvres; she had been repeatedly to Ostend and was sometimes accompanied by her sister, Emily (later Mrs Pelling, who was then unmarried); Emily had typed out confidential reports about secret signals, torpedoes, minesweepers etc. Nellie and Edith had often gone with Patricia and Emily on their excursions in search of information. Mrs Riley had gone to Ostend twice, to Rotterdam once and had received money and instructions. She had known she was being shadowed. The same informant stated that Pelling had known Hentschel since 1910, when he took lessons in German.

He and Hentschel had always been enemies but he became extremely friendly with Fels and was photographed with him. Pelling had spoken of having had a Manual of Torpedo School given to him 'by an officer who had forgotten to ask for it back'. As regards Penrose, the only cause for suspicion was that he had known Fels.

Patricia assumed the name of Howarth and continued her work at Weybridge. She worried the Chief Constable of Kent with her fears about Hentschel and even hinted that a fresh case of espionage was developing in her neighbourhood. In May, after receipt of the specific statements made by Hentschel to a friend, enquiries were made as to the date of her marriage, the £150 received from German sources, and her addresses when she returned to England in 1913. On the whole Hentschel's statements were substantiated. In August 1910, Hentschel and his wife had bought furniture from a local firm on the agreement that the total cost of £154 should be paid off in monthly installments of £10 but on 19 October 1910, £136 was paid by, it was believed, Mrs Hentschel: the sum was made, of two £50 notes, two £5 notes and gold.

Talbot, an employee of Chatham Dockyard who was to have given Patricia specimens of high explosive in 1910, was also identified from data given by Hentschel and was connected with the Pellings. When he promised the specimens Talbot was expecting to be transferred to Upnor Magazine, the transfer did not come off so Patricia obtained the specimens later on from Parrott.

On the outbreak of war Bennett's Hotel was searched but nothing incriminating was found. In February 1916, enquiry was made as to Patricia's residence and she was still managing Bennett's Hotel. A check was placed upon her correspondence, but it was cancelled in March 1917 having produced nothing of interest.

Following Hentschel's confession to Melville, MO5 undertook further investigations concerned with German agents abroad and the connections of the Rileys at home. Hentschel had mentioned four agents:

- Robert Tornow, whom he identified with Theisen, aged sixty-four and Chief of the German Secret Service;
- Captain Fels, Theisen's assistant, aged about thirty-five and a captain in the German Army;
- Captain Steinhauer, a police officer, aged forty-five, resembling a Maltese, who had journeyed through England in 1911 as a traveller in optical instruments;
- Max Dressler, a confectioner and keeper of a private hotel in which German agents met their employees and photographed documents brought from England.

The statements regarding Dressler were verified. Dressler had opened a confectioner's shop at rue d'Ouest 22, Ostend in 1909, and had run it in conjunction with the Hotel Pension Gretry, 70 rue Longue. The rooms over the shop at 23 rue d'Ouest were used as an annexe. Dressler had had electric light installed in them. The business had not paid and had been given up at the end of October 1910. Two Germans had stayed there on and off.

Mademoiselle Fotsch, the manageress, who was staying at Sunderland at the time of the enquiry, denied having ever heard the name of Hentschel, or having seen Tornow but she had heard Dressler speak of him. So far as she knew the rooms had not been used for photographic purposes. Enquiry about Fels was more complicated and led to preventative action.

When the Hentschels went to Australia on 24 June 1911, they took with them Nellie and Edith Riley, who returned at some date unknown, but before February 1912. Mrs Riley remained at Chatham with her daughter, Emily Pelling, and in July 1911 Captain Fels appeared at Chatham, posing as a schoolfriend of Hentschel, and an author. Ostensibly at work on a guide book, he struck up a great friendship with the Pellings through whom Hentschel later said, that he had been able to find out anything he chose about naval matters. Hentschel heard of Captain Fels's visit and threatened Parrott with exposure. According to Parrott, Mrs Riley also tried to blackmail him. In January 1912, the Germans were dealing with these attempts from Berlin, while Mrs Riley was backing them up by wiring to Hentschel: 'No business doing here.'

These details are necessary to assess the correspondence between Mrs Riley and 'T'. Concerning these letters and several visits which she paid to Rotterdam, Mrs Riley afterwards declared in an interview with William Melville that they dealt solely with the affairs of Karl Hentschel and her daughter, Patricia. She had doubts of the validity of her daughter's marriage, and Fels had told her to write and enquire of Hubert Carr, known also as 'T' or Thompson, about the matter.

She did so, went abroad repeatedly, once even in July, while George Parrott was under arrest, and saw Thompson. Her description of the man left no doubt she had seen Theisen, who had told her that Hentschel had got into trouble with a woman abroad and had embezzled money. Melville thought she was lying and certainly her pretended ignorance of the fact that she was dealing with German agents was a lie. But there is some truth in the statement about the woman abroad (particularly the story of Hentschel being already married, and of his engagement to Amelie Wetzel); he had certainly wrung money from his employers, although it is not certain that he embezzled money entrusted to him. Analysis of Mrs Riley's relations with 'T' bears out her statement that she was wholly concerned about Hentschel and her daughter's affairs.

On the other hand, 'T' sent messages by her to Parrott, when direct communication was unadvisable and Mrs Riley's efforts on behalf of her daughter seem to have been designed to secure provision for Patricia and the buying of Hentschel's silence. Here her interests and those of the German Secret Service were identical.

In December 1911 MO5 became aware of Mrs Riley's existence through a letter sent via Carl Gustav Ernst, acknowledging Mrs Riley's communication of mid-November, and arranging a meeting with her at the Maas Hotel in Rotterdam on 25 December. The meeting was then postponed and ultimately put off for weeks. But when 'T' heard that Patricia was on the way home, he sent Mrs Riley £6 and arranged to meet her on 25 February 1912.

Mrs Riley evidently accepted the meeting, but did not go. Her house was being watched: detectives even went to Rotterdam, and saw there Theisen, travelling under the name of Thibaut, and another man who seems to have been somewhat younger than Fels. The detective stated that Theisen was also known as Charles 'T' of Cologne.

On 17 March Mrs Riley went to Rotterdam, and, almost immediately afterwards, Patricia and Hentschel resumed communication with the German Secret Service.

While Hentschel was still in England and negotiations were being continued, Mrs Riley was refused an interview, but when his departure for Australia either was immediately at hand or had taken place, she was summoned once more to Rotterdam for an interview to take place on 25 June. At this time, according to Hentschel, she was blackmailing Parrott for £500, an unlikely story but she may have asked for a small sum. At that meeting some small fixed pension or payment was arranged for her on condition that Charles gave no further trouble. The sum sent for July and August was £5. It was some time after this meeting that 'Richard' wrote to Parrott acknowledging the receipt of 'three nice novels'; these might have been conveyed abroad by Mrs Riley.

Negotiations with Charles were satisfactorily terminated, Patricia's living was thereby assured, and Mrs Riley was bidden to inform Parrott of these facts. Then she was asked to tell Parrott to write to the Germans about his affairs, and accordingly she sent somewhat urgently for Parrott, who had been dismissed by the Royal Navy. The news of Parrott's dismissal was wired out to Hentschel from Berlin and £30 monthly promised for Hentschel's silence.

The next series of letters shows that Charles and Patricia must have separated and that 'T' was keeping in touch with Charles, while Mrs Riley had lost sight of him. In October Mrs Riley was expecting trouble with Charles, because Patricia and Edith were coming home. 'T' then wishes to see Charles' letters, and thinks that Charles will certainly stay in Australia: if a meeting with Mrs Riley seems advisable he will arrange for it to take place after Patricia's return. A month later 'T' asked anxiously whether Patricia was coming home, and in January her letters showed that she would start on her journey the following month.

After Patricia's return in February 1913 there was an interval in the correspondence of many months and then, as already stated, came the news of the sudden death of Fels. With this letter Mrs Riley's direct connection with German agents ceased altogether.

The correspondence with Germany which had died out during 1913, revived after the return of Karl Hentschel from Australia. Mrs Riley was informed that matters which would have been of interest to Fels must now be sent to Fischer and addressed to Mrs Mary Kennedy at Brauerstrasse 1/2 in Potsdam.

But for a moment Hentschel's outbreak acted as a check. The girls had noticed that the house was being watched, and postponed a journey to Flushing to meet Fels, who had now assumed the alias A. Schulz. But in the first part of December they contrived to slip abroad, apparently unnoticed, and agreed with Schulz that he should obtain employment for them with Charles Fischer. Fischer then offered them a salary of £1 a month, with a capitation fee of £10 for every Commissioned or Warrant Officer, needing money, whom the Germans should succeed in inveigling into the service through the agency of the girls. Special fees were also to be given for special orders, and Pelling was asked to renew with Fischer the work she had begun with Fels.

It seems that the girls prepared to accept these terms, but as some of their communications passed unseen, it is not certain that they supplied any names. They wrote to many young men in the services and in the Merchant Marine, but there is no evidence of these men giving them information. That, however, was not in the bond. What seems more conclusive is that no money was intercepted on its way to them, and that in June 1914 Schulz asked Nellie for a definite answer as to what they proposed to do about 'Ch. F's' affairs. There is evidence too that the girls were seeking other and honest employment.

Nellie, meanwhile, had written to Fels about the Hentschel case, attributing his release to the prudence of certain authorities. But for a time and until Hentschel had left England, she begged Fels not to write to her. As soon as she thought Fels had left Europe however, she raised the embargo on letters, and suggested that Fels should come to England. Instead, however, of his coining over, Nellie went abroad to see Fels, meeting him at Brussels on 9 and 10 May. Later he refused to come to England claiming he was too busy, but he held out hopes of another meeting abroad. This letter contained the question about work for 'Ch. F', and Nellie may not have answered it. The war came to break off the correspondence. These are the facts as far as can be ascertained from correspondence. They do not seem very incriminating but it is to be noted that no letters from England were intercepted.

Action in the Rileys' case began in February 1912, when the detectives went to Ostend, and saw Theisen, but not Mrs Riley. Later on the attestation papers of Drummond Hay, a son of Mrs Riley's, who had been farming in Australia then returned to England and enlisted, were forwarded to MO5. He seems to have been turned out of the army.

In November 1912, after the arrest of Parrott, anonymous information began to come in against the Rileys and their connection. Patricia is said to have gone with Parrott, to Sittingbourne, on his journey of 13 July 1912. Karl Hentschel was said to have met Parrott at Ostend (this was false but Parrott said that William Klare was there) and the address of his relations-in-law in Chatham was supplied. In April 1913 the Admiralty was told of possible treachery among their personnel. MO5 informed them that the letter obviously applied to Mrs Riley and Hentschel. But it was supposed that the publicity of the Parrott case, and an interview which Melville had with Mrs Riley in February in connection with that case, and also the fact that Hentschel had gone to Australia, would act as deterrents, and safeguard British secrets.

In June 1913 Mrs Riley was living with Emily Pelling and Patricia Hentschel at 88 Pagitt Street in Chatham, a house evidently rented by George and Emily Pelling. MO5 was interested at that time in preventing her from taking a situation as cook in the household of an officer or dockyard official. They were also making enquiries about her artificer son-in-law. The police stated that he had not visited Pagitt Street since December 1912, but could not supply his name, which was eventually discovered in Melville's report of February 1914.

The Admiralty trace showed that George Pelling had served in the *Actaeon* from 1 March to 8 August 1911. The police identified Pelling as Mrs Riley's son-in-law, an artificer serving in a torpedo boat, HMS *Cheerful*, stationed off Harwich with the 8th Flotilla. In December 1913, Mrs Pelling was placed on the PSL.

When Nellie took up correspondence with Fels and Schulz, and a definite offer of work was made to herself, her sister and George Pelling, an enquiry was asked for about the whole family. The reply came that Edith was engaged to Penrose, and Nellie was visited by Captain Fels. Then came information about, Mr Riley. The photograph of Fels was obtained, and the members of the group with whom he was photographed were identified as George Pelling, Emily Pelling, Nellie and Edith Riley. At the same time information was obtained about John George Riley, a clerk in the ASG and employed in the headquarters office at Cairo.

The letters contain repeated references to Edith's ill-health. She does not seem to have been able to work for her living, but she maintained an affectionate correspondence with various young men belonging to the services, and to the Merchant Marine. Enquiries were made as to the identity of some of these, but without result.

MO5 endeavoured to obtain the removal of Pelling and Penrose from their posts, on account of their connection with the Rileys,

Hentschel and Fels. Pelling was put on the SWL under the heading 'Search'. Patricia meanwhile had changed her name to Howarth.

While the case about Hentschel was still pending she made an effort to suppress any evidence of her own connection with espionage. There was one letter which caused anxiety and that was the duplicate sent via Otto Kruger in March 1912, in which she had applied for her husband's re-engagement in the German Secret Service.

In February 'Gerald' wrote from Brighton, that Mrs F (or Mrs R, probably) had just assured him by letter that a certain communication had been destroyed, no one had ever called to make enquiries about it, and no incriminating evidence would ever be forthcoming from that quarter. 'Gerald' added that it would be too risky to forward that letter, and he took the precaution of posting his own under cover to Edith Riley. Enquiry failed to elicit any information about 'Gerald' who had written from Brighton.

It seems that Penrose's suggestion that Mrs Riley should be interviewed in order to enable her to prove her own innocence was to have been acted upon, but eventually the interview was indefinitely postponed, as the party was being broken up by Karl's departure, Patricia's leaving for Weybridge, and Pelling's prospective removal. As for Nellie, Edith and Penrose, it was impossible to deal with them without revealing too much inside knowledge. Penrose was, however, as we have seen, submitted to a severe interrogation concerning his relations with the Rileys, and failure to report the visits of Fels.

In April the police reported that Mrs Riley had moved to 10 Elm Avenue in Chatham, and a HOW was taken out for this address. She was also placed on the SWL heading 'Search'. An entry on the SWL states that she had been on the Arrest List since 1911 and was transferred to Search on 29 July 1914. During April Mrs Riley had been in great trouble as she had to appear in court because she was being sued for non-payment of a debt.

The following month Nellie Riley was shadowed on her journey to Brussels, and the man she met was identified as Captain Fels. In order to assist the police, the photograph of Fels with the Rileys was circulated, and it was suggested that for the actual shadowing none of the local police should be employed, but Sergeant Andrews was to watch for her coming and going at Dover. She was followed from Chatham and pointed out to the police at Charing Cross: she was then followed to Dover, and pointed out to Sergeant Andrews there. Sergeant Andrews pointed her out to Fitzgerald, who followed her to Brussels. At the same time enquiries were being conducted as to the truth of various statements made by Karl Hentschel about the family. He had accused Mrs Riley of going to see George Parrott when the latter was under arrest at Chatham, and of reporting afterwards to the German Secret Service abroad. The allegation was false as regards Chatham, but it was ascertained that Mrs Riley had visited Parrott in prison, at Brixton on 6 September 1912. There is no record of Mrs Riley's journey abroad in connection with that visit.

After Nellie's visit abroad, action was taken against George Pelling. An interrogatory was drawn up on lines similar to that of Penrose, but it does not seem to have been used. As he was nearing his pension, he was merely transferred from Harwich to the Mediterranean. Hentschel had also stated that the Rileys were in the habit of going to the Royal Naval Barracks on visiting days, but the Chatham police denied this.

Further information was procured about John Riley, Patricia's father, from the Detection Branch of the Constabulary at Maidstone, the city John Riley had left about twenty-five years before. As the result of finding that the dockyard police had no photograph of the Riley girls, Major Kell suggested that, as a matter of routine, copies of photographs of known suspects circulated to officers at the Ports should also be circulated to officers at the dockyards, with a view to preventing such persons from obtaining information in those areas. Nellie and Edith Riley were placed on the SWL, heading 'Search'.

In March 1915 information was received that Karl Hentschel, who had gone abroad in 1914, was returning. This revived interest in the Rileys. It was ascertained that Mr and Mrs Riley had moved to Mortlake in about October 1914, and that Nellie and Mrs Pelling and a much younger sister were living at 44 Ewart Road, Chatham.

Quiet observation was to be kept from time to time. A year later action under DRR 14B was being contemplated against Mrs Riley, Mrs Pelling and Mrs Hentschel, but as there was no case against them since the outbreak of war, the authorities were content with taking out Home Office Warrants for the whole family, and casual observation was asked for, especially with regard to visitors.

The police reported that Mrs Riley and her daughters, Mrs Pelling, Nellie, Edith and two younger ones together with Patricia's two children, were living at 53 Rosslyn Avenue in Barnes. The HOW taken out on 27 February was cancelled on 17 November 1917.

Nothing auspicious was discovered until Philip Penrose was found to be working at the Woolwich Arsenal, and Edith to be frequently visiting Chatham and bringing back strange stories from there. The ensuing enquiry showed that Penrose was living in the same house as the son of a German who was fighting against the British. He was eventually discharged from the Arsenal, and Major Kell thought that a Prohibition Order should be made out against the Rileys, but this does not seem to have been done.

As a result of the HOW on the Riley family, a warrant was taken out for the letters of Sergeant-Major George Barnes of 34 Boundary Road, Chatham, who wrote about some enquiry into the loss of papers. This warrant was cancelled in March 1917.

In that month Nellie Riley was supposed to be corresponding with Grandjean at Lausanne, and a warrant was taken out for the correspondence of Mrs or Miss Riley, but without results so it was cancelled in September 1918.

★

A great part of the evidence concerning George Parrott has been dealt with necessarily in the study of Karl Hentschel's case; there remain for discussion his work as an independent agent, and the investigation connected with it. For the events between March and December 1911, our sources of knowledge are several statements made to the authorities and to private persons by both Hentschel and Parrott. In so far as they relate to the Hentschels and Rileys, these statements have been examined already.

As regards Parrott's entry into direct relations with the German Secret Service, he declared in a signed statement that it took place under pressure from Mrs Riley towards the end of 1911. She compelled him to be introduced to Fels to whom he spoke once only and for a moment at the railway station at Chatham.

Talking to Rayner, a fellow prisoner, Parrott's tale varied somewhat. He told Rayner the early history of his connection with Hentschel and declared that up till February 1911 he had received £85 from that agent. On leaving the German Service, Hentschel sold his connection to Charles Wagener for £1,000, and this exposed Parrott to blackmail. Mrs Riley proceeded to blackmail him for small sums and the Germans wrote to him twice, but he ignored their letters. In July 1911, Fels wrote to him from the Ship Hotel at Queensborough and Parrott went to see him, but refused to work for him. On mentioning that the Hentschels owed him £45, however, Fels immediately refunded the money. Then Parrott asked what they wanted; Fels said: the Signal Code, and offered £1,000 for it, but Parrott does not seem to have taken the bait.

Parrott met Fels again at Mrs Riley's, when George Pelling was there courting Emily Riley, and he still refused to work for Fels. But he met him also at the Shakespeare Hotel in Dover, where Fels was posing as a commercial traveller; moreover Parrott knew Fels' postbox in England. Eventually, a £20 note seems to have decided Parrott to move. He says this was given to him by a woman named Roma, possibly a pseudonym for 'Richard'.

Parrott thought 'Richard' and 'Tornow' were the same person but the description he gave of 'Richard' does not tally with Melville's description of Tornow or Theisen. The truth seems to be that Fels and Mrs Riley paved the way and brought pressure to bear; Parrott was not very difficult to persuade and the rewards were put at a high enough figure to tempt him. The direct connection seems to have begun on 30 September 1911, on which day Parrott went to Sittingbourne and proceeded with a stranger to Dover, saying that he was going to Paris or Ostend.

Early in December 1911 'Richard' was arranging a meeting with Parrott at some regular place of call which needed no specifying, and expressing pleasure at meeting 'so soon'. In this letter he already made use of the cover under which all further communication was carried out, namely, that of an intrigue with a married woman. He sent his letter via Otto Kruger to 87 Alexandra Road, Sheerness, and addressed it to 'Mrs Seymour'. The letter was so worded as to make it appear that 'Richard' would call at that address at 3 p.m. on the 16th and spend the night there. It will be remembered that in December 1911, Steinhauer was on a tour of inspection in England but it is probable that the meeting-place intended by 'Richard' was Ostend. Next, 'Richard' promised to extract Parrott from certain difficulties, Hentschel's attempts at blackmail. This letter proves that Parrott was then writing to 'Richard' but through some channel which was never identified, for not one of Parrott's letters has been preserved.

In March 'Richard' made arrangements for meeting 'where we met last time,' and the times and routes given showed this to be almost certainly Ostend. 'Richard' was then, he said, expecting news of 'PH' (Patricia Hentschel). The rendezvous was fixed for 6 April, and Parrott was to indicate in his acceptance whether a camera would be required. The meeting was accepted, but it is not certain that Parrott went to it. On 25 April, 'Richard' offered £60 for documents No. 1 and 2, and promised to bring the 'little balance on the 4th'.

Parrott certainly went to this meeting, for 'Richard' mentioned his return journey and suggested another meeting at Whitsun to which Parrott was asked to bring a nice novel, and asked to be allowed to keep the coloured photograph which he had received from Parrott at the last meeting.

Then a meeting was proposed for 22 June at Brussels but Parrott could not go, so the 29th was proposed instead; but this also fell through, owing to special measures taken by the Admiralty. Then he was told that up to 14 August, he must go to Ostend but, after that date, to Rotterdam and he must first send a wire to show whether he was bringing anything.

Parrott went to Ostend and met a gentleman who called himself the

Chief of the Staff. At this meeting scouts were posted to warn 'Richard' of possible intruders and at a sign from one of them he shifted his place. One of these scouts was William Klare. At parting, 'Richard' gave Parrott a note for £25.

On 6 July 'Richard' acknowledged receipt of 'three nice novels' received that day and appointed a meeting for the 14th. He gave the address: Richard Dinger, Furbringerstrasse, Berlin.

The wording of 'Richard's' first letter misled the authorities who expected him at Sheerness, whereas it is almost certain the rendezvous was at Ostend. At the request of MO5, observation was to be kept at Sheerness on Mrs Seymour and 'Richard'. 'Mrs Seymour' did not exist, and 'Richard' did not appear. It was ascertained however, that the occupant of 87 Alexandra Road was a Mr Parrott.

The misunderstanding and consequent failure of the observation led to explanations with the Chief Constable of Kent, who requested that in future all available information should be given to the police at the time of asking for observation. MO5 replied with the suggestion that the letter, of which they had already in the first place given the gist, was purposely worded so as to mislead and begged for enquiry about Mr Parrott. The police reported that he was a Chief Warrant Officer in the navy, and in charge of the range at Sheerness; that he had a wife and daughter, aged twenty-one, and owned a two-seater car in which he toured the country when on leave.

'Richard's' next letter pointed to a rendezvous at Ostend on 5 April. William Melville, Superintendent Grey of Chatham Dockyard and Sergeant Hibbard of Sheerness were in observation from early morning on the 5th. But Parrott got away with his wife in his car on the afternoon and was lost sight of. Melville crossed to Ostend and continued observation on the 6th and 7th but without result. He concluded that the appointment had been cancelled by wire.

It has been said that Mrs Riley had noticed she had been shadowed abroad about three weeks previously: she would have warned Parrott, and it is extremely probable that he was aware of the observation of his house on the 6th and motored to Sittingbourne to put off his journey by wire.

Superintendent Grey reported that Parrott had gone motoring again on Saturday the 6th, his movements on Sunday the 7th could not be traced, and on Monday he was seen in Sheerness Dockyard. A description of Parrott's car was obtained and forwarded to the Chief Constable of Kent with a request for any information as to his movements in the car or suspicious circumstances. When it became certain that Parrott was selling secrets, the naval authorities at Chatham and Sheerness were informed of the facts and the Civil Engineer in charge of the dockyard promised to take special precautions.

Parrott went abroad early in May and he evidently took some plan with him. He does not seem to have been shadowed on this occasion but subsequently, when meetings were proposed for Whitsun, 22 June and 29 June, special measures were taken. He was kept under observation from 24 to 30 May and 2 June. He was seen to visit the Britannia Hotel and the Conservative Club at Sittingbourne. From 3 to 14 June he was kept too busy at Sheerness to be able to leave, and observation began again on 14 June.

Regan reported that he had motored out of sight to Rochester; that his appointment would end in August; and that his daughter was to be married in the first week of August. Parrott was consulting timetables, and expressing great annoyance at not being able to get away. Neither he nor his family were seen to send any wire.

Observation was also kept at Dover on 22 June but Parrott was not seen. Regarding the proposed meeting with 'Richard', on 29 June, much discussion arose as to the means of preventing it. The Law Officers of the Crown refused permission to arrest on the facts and letters laid before them, but suggested that the Admiralty should act ultra vires and arrest and search on their own warrant. The Admiralty declined such high-handed action under the Official Secrets Act. A way out was found by assigning to Parrott duties that would prevent him leaving Sheerness during the weekend. Regan and the local police were also detached to keep observation but had nothing special to report, beyond the fact that Parrott appeared to be under some form of arrest in his own home and was entertaining a party of naval men on Sunday. Some enquiry was made about the motorcar in which the party arrived but nothing useful was ascertained.

Copies of correspondence connected with Parrott were given to the DPP immediately after, as it became known that Parrott had communicated documents and was preparing to meet 'Richard' again, a fresh consultation took place between MO5, the Admiralty and the DPP. The Admiralty agreed to allow Parrott to be treated as a civilian; the DPP agreed to allow search of his premises on suspicion, provided he sent the telegram accepting the meeting; for this together with evidence already available, would constitute the grounds for the 'reasonable suspicion,' required by the Official Secrets Act.

Notice was received that Parrott had applied for, and been granted, fourteen days' leave as from 13 July, and had given as his address during that period as 6 Edinburgh Road, Plymouth, which was the address of his father-in-law, G. Crouch. But the GPO reported that at 6.50 p.m. on 11 July, a wire signed 'Seymour' and addressed to Richard Dinger, Furbringaratrasse, Berlin, accepting a meeting for Saturday, had been handed in at Sittingbourne.

Superintendent Tett was instructed to keep observation and on the afternoon of 13 July, two boys called at Chatham Dockyard with a message for Gunner Beaton [sic] of HMS Fervent to the effect that Parrott expected to see him that night at ten o'clock. This was thought to be a blind, as there was no one of that name or standing on HMS Fervent. On the other hand, Gunner Deacon, of HMS Fervent but attached to the Actaeon, was Parrott's prospective son-in-law.

On the evening of 13 July Parrott went by rail to Sittingbourne accompanied by a young woman who was afterwards anonymously reported to be Patricia Hentschel. At Dover, he was stopped as he was going on board. He stated that he was a civilian: he was searched and documents in his bag showed his identity, address and profession. Moreover, the piece of the letter bearing Dinger's address was found on him and he then admitted his identity and status: he was, he said, going to see a lady and begged that his wife should not be informed. He was allowed to continue to Ostend but William Melville followed him and saw a suspicious meeting take place between him and a foreigner who obviously feared detection. The meeting lasted about one and a half hours and Parrott returned to England by the next boat. Melville gave a somewhat vague description of the agent, that he was a man of about thirty-five to forty, with dark hair and moustache, height about 5 feet 9 inches, which did not tally with Parrott's description.

On receipt of Grey's report Parrott was recalled from leave, and asked for an explanation. He admitted the fact of his journey, which was taken in order to meet a young lady. He declared his ignorance of the King's Regulations forbidding an officer to go abroad without leave. Pending the Admiralty's decision, he was confined to barracks. It was decided not to prosecute under the Official Secrets Act but to interrogate him concerning the motive of his trip, the personality of Dinger and his connection with the man, the telegram and arrangements for the meeting. He was, if he adhered to his lies, to be confronted with the reports of the two detectives. Parrott maintained he had gone abroad to see a lady whom he had once met accidentally here and from whom he had concealed his real name; she had given him the address of Dinger, and suggested he should write there to propose a meeting at Ostend in July; he had wired to her under his assumed name, Seymour, but no one came to meet him at Ostend. He had lied about his status to Inspector Grey, whose position of authority he had not at first known. He strenuously denied that he had met and talked with a foreigner at Ostend, but he admitted some part of Melville's statement about his visit to that town.

As Chief Gunner, Parrott would take seniority among warrant officers and seniority over midshipmen; he was in receipt of the full pay and allowances of warrant officers which amounted to £255 12s. 6d. per annum, he was entitled to a pension of £98 11s. 3d. a year and had been selected for promotion to commissioned warrant officer.

On receipt of Parrott's answers, another meeting of government departments was held and the Attorney-General again refused to take action under the Official Secrets Act. The Admiralty therefore decided that Parrott should be dismissed the navy. He was perturbed, but showed no surprise and on being asked he asserted he had no confidential Books in his possession. He left the Royal Naval Barracks on 15 August and MO5 asked for supervision of his movements and copies of the local papers.

Turning now to the question of what he achieved during this period: a very important point of the investigation was concerned with ascertaining what confidential books had been issued to Parrott. This list is not now accessible, but certain books had been issued to him from Chatham at his request on 16 January and returned on 17 February 1911 and a second batch of books was issued on 27 February and returned on 11 March 1911. Since then none had been asked for, or issued from, Chatham and none had ever been issued from Sheerness. If then the registers of the issue of confidential books could be trusted, the most dangerous period of Parrott's activities was limited to the time of his intercourse with Karl Hentschel. On the other hand, 'three nice novels' were mentioned on 6 July, and Parrott himself insisted on the carelessness with which books were kept and mentioned many different ways of gaining access to them. Then we know that Patricia Hentschel conveyed two (or else one), books abroad for him and there is a possibility that this occurred between Hentschel's departure for Australia in June 1912, and Patricia's departure in July of the same year. But Parrott's vivid description of the photographing of books abroad is that of an eye-witness. Hence we may conclude that he sent books via Hentschel and via Patricia and that he carried over something himself, but that he did not procure the greatest prizes obtainable.

It is possible that when first he began to obtain confidential books for wrong purposes, Parrott used legitimate means of borrowing them but that when he acted independently, this was too dangerous. As his education in villainy progressed he adopted some of the methods he revealed to Rayner. Negative evidence, however, goes to prove that the signal code, the Annual Report of Torpedo School and the Report of Manoeuvres, for which 'Richard' offered £500, were probably not among the books sent abroad. As remarked previously, such money payments as we know of do not represent a quarter of the value of these books and the Germans were asking for them elsewhere.

Parrott, during this period, seems to have received a monthly salary and £50 special payment for two documents. We do not know what the price of the 'three nice novels' was to be. But, whether the documents were of much value or not, as an expert and trusted Gunnery Officer, Parrott could give very valuable information by word of mouth. This no doubt accounts for 'Richard's' insistence on personal interviews abroad, as 'Richard' himself dared not set foot in England. Parrott described him as a man of about fifty and of forceful personality. He had a large head and a square-cut beard. He had been in the army and was a teetotaller.

Observation was continued on Parrott after his dismissal from the navy and Chatham Dockyard reported that on 23 August that he had moved to 32 Juer Street, Park Road, Battersea, where he was renting four rooms. Reports were also received about Parrott's son, a Shipwright Artificer in Sheerness Dockyard, and his son-in-law. His daughter had been quietly married to Warrant Officer Francis Joseph Deacon on 24 August.

Early in September, the case had become public and there was great agitation in Chatham. It was officially stated that Parrott had fallen under suspicion of communicating information to a foreign power, and his services had therefore been dispensed with. This agitation was referred to by Frederick Gould in his letters to Heinrich Schmidt.

The address in Battersea was placed on check and a letter was intercepted from G. Couch, from 6 Edinburgh Road, Devonport, referring to the long delay in settling Parrott's case. It was discovered that Couch was Parrott's father-in-law, and a pensioned petty officer who had served as coxswain to many admirals-in-charge of the dockyard, and was considered a very respectable man.

Then Parrott received orders to review a public-house at Witham and Uxbridge and about the same time Mrs Riley wrote begging Parrott to call as she had a message for him. ('Richard', it will be remembered, had written to her that Parrott was to communicate with him.) After this invitation, intercourse began again between Parrott and the Germans. As the letters from abroad were sent via August Klunder they were intercepted, although the precaution had been taken of addressing them to G. Couch, c/o P. Williams, tobacconist, 136 King's Road, Chelsea.

A meeting, to be arranged by coded telegram, was proposed to take place at Brussels, but eventually 'Richard' agreed that it would be wiser to await the decision in Parrott's case. Parrott, however, was not to be afraid of Karl, with whom arrangements had been made. From 'Richard's' letter it would appear that at first Parrott had hoped for a revision of his case. That hope died out and he went to Rotterdam to fetch certain documents and to come to terms with the Germans. There was some discussion about the documents returned; Parrott received back three, and 'Richard' declared he had never had more. A sum (£5 for £500) had been granted in order that Parrott might set up in a bar. He was to go to Hamburg, via Grimsby, and to take with him any documents he still had that might be useful. Parrott obeyed the summons and was at Hamburg on 18 October and there received part of the money promised. As it was too dangerous to send the balance by post, he was bidden to go to Rotterdam on the last week of October to receive the balance, of which £100 would be brought by hand. He was to post the receipt abroad. Again 'Richard' referred to Patricia who, as he had heard from Mrs Riley, was on her way home. In close connection with this statement, 'Richard' added that he was expecting soon to receive from Parrott 'good news for our business'.

Several letters followed in November and Parrott was sent to Portsmouth and Devonport to verify rumours about mobilisation of the Second and Third Fleet. Then he was thanked for his prompt answer and was ordered north to the Firth of Forth to supply answers to a list of other questions, with £10 enclosed for travelling expenses. He was to act on his own responsibility and report abroad at once on hearing rumours of mobilisation. Between the end of September and early November 1912, Parrott had gone abroad at least three times and had received a sum of £500 probably, and one of £10.

Observation was at first kept upon his house but it failed, for Parrott had been warned through the wife of Police Sergeant McKinley who lived in the same street. Parrott manoeuvred and arrangements were made, most likely by Fels, for his disguise. Hence he got abroad repeatedly, unnoticed by Regan. However, Regan saw him return from the journey to Grimsby and watched his movements. He was calling for letters at the tobacconist's shop. Later on Regan ascertained that a journey had taken place via Folkestone and Flushing on the *Cronje-Nassau*; this knowledge came to hand at least a fortnight after the event.

Meanwhile the Admiralty was kept informed and, with their consent, a HOW was taken out for Deacon's correspondence as it was known that Parrott was writing to him and that Parrott's son Charles was living at Deacon's house. Nothing to incriminate Deacon transpired but, after Hentschel's revelations, his case was examined in October 1913. He had not always been a satisfactory officer, but between December 1911 and December 1912, he had improved remarkably and had earned a recommendation for promotion. In 1913 the Deacons kept aloof from the Parrotts and did not write to them, but in 1914, when Karl Hentschel's case was still fresh and enquiries connected with it were in progress, MO5 placed Francis Deacon on the SWL, heading 'Watch' and recommended that in view of his relationship with Parrott he be removed from his station. It will be remembered that Hentschel detailed he had received certain books in manuscript from the *Actaeon*, the Torpedo School to which Deacon was attached. Parrott subsequently told Rayner he could ruin his son-in-law by holding up his finger, and the mysterious message to Gunner 'Beaton' (probably a mishearing for 'Deacon') on the eve of Parrott's journey in July 1912 might have some bearing on this accusation. It is quite likely, however, that Parrott was revenging himself for Deacon's studied neglect after his fall. In 1917 it was stated officially that there was nothing to connect Deacon with Parrott's treachery.

Meanwhile, enquiry was being made into George Parrott's financial position. In April, May, and June 1911 he had deposited sums of £100, £10, and £20 in the Conservative Club Building Fund. In July 1911 he had bought a car for £30 and in July of the following year, he had exchanged this car for another and had bought a motorcycle, the whole transaction amounting to about £63. His deposits had been made in gold, and a considerable sum had been withdrawn, apparently to purchase the motorcar and cycle. In February 1912 he opened both a current and a deposit account with the London Westminster & County Bank. On 10

February he had deposited £50 paid in ten £5 notes, and all his deposits were made in cash or notes. A note for £20, which he deposited in May 1912, was traced to T. F. Melik Dadaeff, who went abroad via Victoria Station on 26 April 1912.

Other notes were traced to Johann Frederic Wilhelm Woolff, Post Langen, Berlin, and to Paul Wilscheck & Co., Berlin. Since 1895, Paul Wilscheck had been director of an institution making investments on behalf of officers and officials.

Immediately 'Richard's' letter of special instructions was intercepted, arrangements were made for the arrest and search of Parrott. He was arrested as he left Williams' shop with the unopened letter in his hand so it could, therefore, be produced in court. Parrott was charged on 18 November with having communicated to another, information calculated to 'be useful to an enemy'.

The facts of his journey to Ostand and East Kant on 13 July, and its bearing on his subsequent connection with a German agent were examined. The interesting news came from a firm of private detectives, S. Street & Co., of the Edgware Road, which was acting for Parrott. The steward of the Grimsby Line proved his journey to Hamburg; the stewardess of the *Cronje-Nassau* swore to at least three journeys made to Rotterdam, she believed, at the end of the summer; and evidence was given concerning the notes paid into his bank by Parrott. He was committed for trial and no notice was taken of an attempt to upset the finding on a technical point. Counsel for the defence had called attention to the fact that the Attorney-General's fiat had not been given until a witness had been called.

Meanwhile, MO5 pursued their enquiries. Parrott had not made use of his return ticket from Grimsby, which was found at the search of his house. It was thought he might have been travelling in Scotland in search of information. His photo was circulated to various important centres, but no one had seen him in those parts recently.

Then anonymous informants connected him with a somewhat undesirable woman staying with the Hentschels named Marie or Maria, who was at Weymouth in 1908–9. Nothing came of that enquiry but much more important was information connecting him with Patricia both before and after her marriage, and with Karl Hentschel. It seems probable that then, for the first time, the meaning of the various references to 'PH' in 'Richard's' correspondence with Parrott became known. It was also noticed that a German hairdresser, George Wittstruck, had taken over Parrott's house at Sheerness, and had been missing ever since Parrott's arrest. Enquiry was also made as to the address in Edinburgh Road, Devonport, with results already recorded. On 4 December 1912 Mrs Parrott was reported to have left Juer Street, and she moved to 73 Lower Richmond Road, Putney.

The trial of Parrott took place in January 1913 and he adhered to the story that he had gone to Ostend to meet a lady, but he now admitted having met there a man, who explained that the lady could not come. The notes from Germany had been sent by Mrs Hentschel, wife of a German teacher at Sheerness, in repayment of a debt of £45, and with this sum Parrott had opened his deposit account. He explained 'Richard's' questions of 1 November by saying they referred to a specimen newspaper article, which he was to write with the prospect of being engaged as a correspondent in compensation for the loss of his employment here.

For the defence, counsel raised the points of Parrott's excellent service on the *Agammemnon* and his integrity with regard to the plans of that ship; of his ignorance of anything worth communicating concerning ship construction; of the facts that the confidential books borrowed had been returned in 1911; and that Parrott declared he had not communicated them to anyone. The most damning admission Parrott had to make was that he had destroyed every scrap of paper he could that had come from the foreigner who was to employ him. He was found guilty, but as the judge took the view that he had been entrapped by a woman so the full penalty was not inflicted. He was condemned to four years' imprisonment with a hope of reduction or remission of part of the sentence provided he made a full confession.

Parrott appealed against the sentence but the appeal was dismissed. His family broke off relations with the Rileys, or the Rileys broke with them, in December 1918. Mrs Riley was a relative of Mrs Parrott.

Concerning events during the period July 1912 to November of the same year, Parrott afterwards volunteered to Rayner some information: at the interview at Hamburg, Parrott arranged with 'Richard' for a lump sum in compensation for his dismissal from the navy. Half the sum was paid that day, the rest was handed over at Rotterdam by a stranger. Parrott was shadowed at Rotterdam to make sure that no British agents were following him.

At Hamburg, he said he saw a gunnery expert who questioned him for an hour; and an engineer, a torpedo technician, and an executive expert who, with 'Richard', examined him for two hours. They considered the English were far ahead of the Germans in the details of ship instruments and they proposed to give Parrott a billet at Wilhelmshaven to do there the same class of work that he had been doing on the *Agamemnon*. Parrott agreed to this, provided he could arrange matters comfortably for his wife in England. Then he began negotiations for a public-house at Greenwich, and for the time being undertook a roving commission for the Germans.

He had contrived to hide from the police diagrammatic sketches of torpedo directors, scott fire-directors, and a new mercury sight for rolling and pitching, and these he hoped to sell later on. His counsel was paid by the German embassy and he meant to work for the Germans on his release. He also told Rayner that the Germans were paying his salary to his wife, that they had set her up in lodgings and had launched his son Charles in life, and that they were nursing the connection, not so much on account of what they had received, as of what they hoped to get. Parrott, in preparation for future activity, was studying colloquial German.

After Parrott's imprisonment, a check had been kept upon the letters and movements of his family. His statement was both corroborated and modified by the correspondence of Mrs Parrott and Dorothea with 'Richard' to whom they had appealed for help; but the Germans did their best to evade interviews and reduce the help given to a minimum. But 'Richard' was compelled to give way: Fels at first sent £5, then 'Richard' sent £50 and finally, under veiled pressure from Parrott, he saw Mrs Parrott at Rotterdam, and arranged probably to pay her rent afterwards procuring for her son, Charles, access to the detective agency of Charles Brown at 13 New Oxford Street, a man already known to be in touch with the German Secret Service.

In August 'Richard' refused to do more for her than he already promised, and about the same time, C. Brown was writing a dissatisfied letter to Charles Parrott, complaining of the boy's leaving him without a word. But Mrs Parrott went on giving trouble: she began claiming repayment of old debts from the Rileys and 'Richard' intervened to protect them. He sent her £10 and promised the balance of £80 for their next meeting, which was to take place at Wesel on 7 November. For the journey he sent her £5 in connection with this meeting and it is worth noting that the date was fixed shortly after Karl Hentschel gave himself up as a spy. Mrs Parrott sent newspaper cuttings about the case for 'Richard' and acknowledged receipt of press-cuttings and of a photo. Charles Parrott, too, was summoned to see Charles Brown in connection with a case that was coining on in November.

The Germans continued to send remittances to Mrs Parrott at the rate of £10 a month, and even after the outbreak of war 'Doris' wrote to ask for money.

In February 1914 C. Brown supplied lodgers for Mrs Parrott. These, Parrott said, were a mere blind, and in reality German agents, for Mrs Parrott had contrived to keep her husband informed as to her connection with the Germans. By a transparent code she let him know that 'Uncle Will' was sending money, that Fred (Freidel Fels) had not been seen for three months, that Hentschel and Patricia were home for good and the Rileys had had no dealings with her since early December 1912 (the date of proceedings against Parrott). Only 'Nellie' had written asking her to sell 'records', which of course she had not got.

In February, Parrott asked anxiously whether the 'records' had been recovered from 'Cousin Nell' and whether 'Uncle Will' had been heard of. And again in June, he repeated his enquiries about 'Cousin Nell' and 'Uncle Will'. He also asked for news from Tabard Street. It has been shown that Nellie Riley continued intercourse with Fels after the rest of the family had apparently withdrawn from the game. Parrott's reference to 'records' may mean that certain compromising documents belonging to him had been entrusted to her keeping. On the other hand there is another possible explanation. It was at this time he was assuring his wife that he would regain a position as good as that he had lost, and that he was studying German hard. He was bidding Charles write down all messages and questions for him and bring to their meeting a notebook and pencil so as to take down any messages sent in reply. The correspondence seems about as damning as anything could well be and it led to the Home Office Warrants being taken out on:

- Frithjof Sørensen, Centrofte, Copenhagen. 16 April 1913 to 8 May 1913.
- A. Hocke, 25T Carstensgade, Copenhagen, about September 1913.
- Charles Brown, 13 New Oxford Street (for the second time).
- Mrs Parrott, 73 Lower Richmond Road, Putney.
- Any lodgers at her address, 22 April 1914.
- Hermann Hillebrandt, 12 Queensthorpe Road, Sydenham, 30 April 1914.

This last warrant was taken out because some of the notes sent to Mrs Parrott were traced to Hillebrandt who was said to travel much on the Continent. It was kept till 31 May, but confined to foreign letters. On 11 May, William Becker of 15 Barbarossastrasse, Berlin, wrote from 37 rue d'Hautevllle, Paris, to say he was returning to Berlin almost at once.

MO5 were kept informed of Mrs Parrott's removal and in June, when Parrott's correspondence would by prison rules be beginning, MO5 asked for copies of all letters sent out or received by him.

In October he made the statement already discussed concerning his dealings with Karl Hentschel.

When Mrs Parrott went abroad in November she was shadowed to Victoria Station. In consequence of the letters passing between husband and wife, it was suspected that traffic was again going on; Parrott's cell was searched, without results, and he was transferred from Maidstone to Parkhurst Prison to get him beyond easy reach of his family. At an interview with her husband in prison, Mrs Parrott, who had not known in the early days of his connection with the Hentschels, pressed him to give all the information in his power in order to obtain remission of his sentence but he refused to admit having sold confidential books. Obviously, disclosure would have prejudiced his chances with the Germans.

On about 19 December the authorities became aware that Mrs Parrott was getting correspondence through to 'Richard' unnoticed. Special observation was arranged with a view to detecting the channel and the daughter was seen to post a latter. Action was taken at the local post office and, as a result, enquiry was made about the occupier of Ulleswater, Watling Street, Devonport who, it was thought, might be Nellie Riley; but nothing that seemed pertinent came of the enquiry. It was ascertained that the house was occupied by John Mustchin of unknown nationality, his wife, and his daughter aged eight. 'Cousin Nellie' had written from that address to Mrs Parrott in September 1913 suggesting that George Parrott had betrayed himself in talk with George Wittstruck at Sheerness. Eventually, too, Parrott went to live at Ulleswater in Devonport.

This raises the question as to whether by 'Cousin Nell', Nellie Riley was meant, whether it was not a pseudonym for Mustchin, or else the name of Mustchin's wife, and finally whether this was not the safe place of hiding for Parrott's documents and money.

Observation was kept on Mrs Parrott and the children and her lodgers during February, and the posting of letters duly noted. Also the place of employment of Charles Parrott was ascertained. Mrs Parrott was in difficulties at that time and trying to obtain employment for her daughter in *John Bull*'s offices, no doubt in return for information of value to that paper.

Then came Rayner's revelations with Parrott's half confessions – for he never did admit having given to Karl Hentschel more than the handbook of the 6-inch gun, declaring that Hentschel might have obtained the books he said he had obtained but, in that case, not from Parrott himself. Parrott, however, stuck to his statement that the person who at last persuaded him to enter into direct relations with Germans abroad was a highly-placed lady, aged about twenty-two, and that when 'Richard' met him at Ostend, and he had to confess to having been searched and deprived of 'Richard's' address on 13 July, 'Richard', after some hesitation, made him memorise the name and address of a Graf or Grafin, who lived at Dusseldorf. That such a person existed and played a high and romantic part in German espionage, became known during the war.

In March 1916, a certain Miss Alice Joyce applied for the address of the prison in which her favourite uncle, George Parrott, was confined. Her name was placed on check, and she was refused employment in Devonport Dockyard. The check was cancelled in August.

As Parrott's sentence was due to expire on 9 February 1917 it was decided that, in view of his record and known sentiments, he must be interned under the DRR and the order was confirmed on 22 January 1917. On 5 February 1919 Parrott was conditionally released and he was to report his address and his employment and any future change of address or employment to the Metropolitan Police. He went to his wife's house in the Lower Richmond Road for a few days and then, on 10 February, he took up his abode at Ulleswater, Watling Street, Devonport. It was supposed that he had quarreled with his wife, and possibly Karl Hentschel's revelations about Patricia Hentschel was the cause.

A record was kept of the letters he received and tracings taken of envelopes. This was considered all that could be done safely, since any opening of letters would be carried out at Dartmouth by persons not expert, and Parrott was considered too clever not to notice tampering with his letters or observation directed against him.

★

The three cases treated above may be considered practically as one, at least at regards the requirements of the German Secret Service; the evidence thus collated and related with evidence from the case of Frederick Gould and William Klare goes to prove that Karl Hentschel

exaggerated his achievements whether brought about through George
Parrott or through other agents; that the most valuable books or other
documents supplied by Parrott were conveyed abroad by Patricia Riley
and by Parrott himself; that although Parrott underrated what he had
supplied, it is nevertheless true that he was a valuable agent and that
the Germans meant to retain his services if possible; that, probably his
greatest services were rendered by word of mouth. The importance of
his visits abroad may be gauged by the fact that they were undertaken at
great and known risks; they were made reluctantly and under pressure
from 'Richard', who dared not come to England.

Concerning 'Richard', no definite knowledge was obtained of his
personality, but he was evidently either a man of mark or a marked
man. Probably, he was a high official of the German Naval Staff. Had
he been identical with Theisen or Theisen's underling, or Steinhauer, or
Fels, Melville surely would at some time have noted it, for he had seen
Theisen and his subordinate in June 1912, Steinhauer in 1903, and Fels,
he saw in 1914.

There is evidence in the case of Parrott of extreme vigilance on
the part of the Germans from April 1912 onwards. Other spy cases
had been a warning to agents, and Parrott knew when he was being
watched. He used his motorcar more than once to get out of range. His
telephoning from Sittingbourne while Sheerness Post Office was being
watched is another instance of alertness. Finally, the Germans tried to
evade observation by appointing Brussels as the place of meeting and,
when this did not work, they adopted counter-shadowing at Ostend
and elsewhere.

MO5 doubted there being a woman in the case: the woman is there
the whole time. The case centres round Patricia Hentschel's love and
despair, Parrott's loyal and most efficient helper, 'Richard's' hope. From
the repeated references to Patricia in 'Richard's' correspondence with
Parrott, we see what a role she played in Parrott's activities. Between
September 1911 and February 1912 we do not know at all what Parrott
contrived to do for the Germans, but he took documents abroad in May
1912, and he sent others in July 1912, and Patricia was said to have been

connected with his own journey in July 1912. On the other hand after Parrott's imprisonment, Patricia seems to have definitely broken with Hentschel, which would probably not have taken place had she still been acting for the Germans, which brought about the exposure of the whole system. From that exposure, the Rileys and Pellings never recovered.

Karl Hentschel's great achievement was his bringing such a person into the business, his fault that he fell too much in love with a fascinating woman, who knew how to retain her hold on men. Passionate jealousy wrecked him and he took to drink. He lost his wife's affection owing to his own conduct and Mrs Riley's report of his behaviour before marriage probably was not without weight. He certainly attributed some of the disaster to her and spoke of her as a wicked woman.

As regards the minor characters in the case, George Pelling always disliked Hentschel and it would seem that if he supplied information he did it through Fels. Hentschel's claim to have learned much through Emily is most probably false for the Pellings were still in the courting stage when Hentschel was in Australia, in the autumn of 1911 and after Hentschel's return in 1912 he could not have obtained much information. Mrs Riley probably told the truth when she said she confined her intercourse with Tornow to efforts on behalf of her daughter, but she suppressed the truth about Fels and Theisen's activities.

There is no proof that Nellie and Edith Riley ever achieved anything for the Germans. Nellie was probably genuinely in love with Fels and the will was not lacking, but fear prevented her from acting. Edith did act as cover for Patricia on one occasion. She was a flirt, undoubtedly, but she did not keep up correspondence with Fels, Schulz or with Fischer and it is probable that Philip Penrose, her fiancé, was until October 1913, honest in his belief in the trustworthiness of the Rileys, whom he had known intimately for a comparatively short time, and that when the exposure came, he acted hastily in self-defence.

It is interesting to see how Karl Hentschel could not get on without Patricia, nor Patricia Hentschel without George Parrott, nor Parrott without her help as a carrier. Had the Germans been content with documents only, the necessary proofs against Parrott might never have been obtained.

With regard to obtaining these proofs, the long drawn-out case of Hentschel demonstrates admirably the true value of the Home Office Warrant. Without it MO5 were absolutely in the dark as to what was going on; with it, they were able to watch proceedings, take preventive action, and at last to bring Parrott to book. One thing is noticeable; the omission to detect the letters passing out of England. Parrott, Mrs Riley, and the Riley girls, got their letters through unnoticed. It seems evident that the ingenious system of getting specimens of handwriting and then observing the posting of letters and taking action at the local post office, a system successful in the case of Heinrich Grosse and of Mrs Parrott, was not carried out at Chatham and Sheerness.

Another noticeable feature is the betrayal to Mrs Parrott by the wife of a police sergeant of the fact that Parrott was being watched; Parrott's counter of disguise and sending his bag away by a boy are worth recording. It seems clear that agents got to know the detectives and the measures they took. On the whole, observation fails as often as it succeeds.

Karl Hentschel himself corroborated the Rileys' statement concerning the object of Fels' first visit to England: Fels, he said, had come over in the first instance to find him, had then introduced himself to the Rileys and had been introduced by them to George Parrott and it was in consequence of this visit that Hentschel had begun his blackmailing from Australia. The Rileys stated that Fels had come to trace Hentschel who had embezzled some £1,700 belonging to the German Secret Service.

Parrott stated that Fels spoke very fluent English with a German-American accent. Mrs Parrott told the solicitor defending Karl Hentschel that Fels had spent July and August 1911 at the Prince of Wales Hotel in Chatham; that in August 1913 he was daily at Mrs Riley's house in company with Nellie Riley and Mrs Pelling; that he was engaged to Nellie Riley, and that Pelling and Fels had been photographed together. His last reported visit to the Rileys took place in September 1913. When Hentschel returned to England, Fels spread rumours of his own death but shortly after resumed relations with the Rileys under the alias 'A. Schulz'.

According to the interview of Atlantis (the alias adopted by Karl

Hentschel) with William Melville on 15 October 1913, Hentschel came to England in 1908 – when there was some crisis on. He went to Devonport and was told to report anything he heard. He was there four months and sent in reports only on the movements of warships. He was sent to Sheerness in April 1909 to watch movements of ships, and mine-laying, etc. and he was asked:

I.   To obtain a Naval Signal Code.
II.  Questions about range-finding, the instruments used for this and for fire control.
III. The newest invention with regard to minesweeping.
IV.  Exact position of lights inside and outside Sheerness Harbour. Whether any change during manoeuvres. To specify fixed and moving lights. The rules regulating the use of lights during night attacks.
V.   The stations and duties of patrol-ships during manoeuvres.
VI.  Where the submarine factory was. Whether cruisers or battle-ships carried submarines.

It should be noted that Frederick Gould afterwards declared that the Admiralty telegraphic code and the signal code had been delivered to the Germans in October and November 1911. In this he was not referring to his own achievements, but he must have been thinking of George Parrott's. Gould had dropped communication with Steinhauer after receipt of a letter in September 1911 and he did not resume communication until the arrest of Heinrich Grosse in December 1911, which enabled him to bring pressure to bear on the Germans. Karl Hentschel was out of England from March 1911 until March 1912, and according to Parrott, the first thing that Fels asked of him was to procure the Naval Signal Book.

After Nellie and Edith Riley had been definitely offered employment by the Germans, the photograph of Captain Fels was circulated to the police at the dockyards, and at Queensborough, Folkestone, Dover and Harwich, in order that if he should come to this country, his movements should be reported to MO5. Some time later a group photograph was obtained of Captain Fels, the Pellings, Nellie and Edith Riley. From Parrott's conversations with his fellow-prisoner Rayner it was ascertained that Fels had a postbox at the Aldgate Hotel, 76 Aldgate High Street in East London, and that he was an unscrupulous character who would stick at nothing; he had even drugged the Rileys in order to search their house. A HOW was taken out for Fels at the Aldgate Hotel, but had to be suspended owing to complaints of delay from the hotel. Enquiry showed that Fels was known at that hotel and at one time used to stay there frequently, but he had not been there for some time. He was supposed to be in the cigar trade.

In May Nellie Riley went to Brussels to meet Fels and she was shadowed by Fitzgerald who saw her meet a man resembling the description of Fels given by Karl Hentschel. Later the same person met Lina Heine in Ostend and in June it was arranged that £25 should be spent on finding out all that was possible concerning his movements and acquaintances. At this point, his story breaks off.

★

John James Hattrick (alias Walter J. Devlin) of 41 Crymell Street, Stone House, Plymouth was born in the Wirrall, Cheshire in April 1888, and after seven and a half years' service in the Royal Navy, he deserted from HMS *Queen* in June 1909; he was recovered but was not claimed for further service. He then obtained work as naval canteen assistant on board ships, but tired of the work. In March 1912 he wrote, using an illegible signature, to 'The Head, Intelligence Department, War Office, Germany' offering information and giving the wording of an advertisement to be placed in the *Daily Mirror* if his offer were accepted. The letter was stopped and William Melville, impersonating a German agent named 'A. Pfeiffer', inserted the advertisement giving the address 54 Shaftesbury Avenue.

Walter J. Devlin answered the advertisement from the Sailor's Rest, Devonport and the correspondence continued for some weeks while Melville, cleverly imitating the style of a German agent, induced Devlin to show his hand and finally to drop all disguise and give his true name and address. At a meeting which took place at Devonport on 16 May 1912, Hattrick wrote out an engagement promising to find out and to forward any naval or military intelligence required by the Germans in return for a salary of £30 a year. The following day Hattrick, having taken Melville, whom he believed to be a German agent, into the dockyard, was there detained on a charge of attempting to communicate information to a foreign power. In reply he said his object had been to obtain money from the Germans and then go abroad. He was then photographed and released after being cautioned that the case was held in abeyance and that its revival depended on his good behaviour, that his photograph and description would be circulated to all dockyards, naval barracks, ships, and prohibited places and that, if found near them, he would be arrested as a suspect.

The fright cured him and when MO5 enquired about his conduct in August of the same year, and after the police had called at Cremyll Street, Hattrick wrote somewhat pathetically to implore them not to let his 'only friend' know of 'that affair'. MO5 suggested telling him that provided his conduct remained sound nothing would be done to injure his prospects. Hattrick went into the Merchant Service and in September 1912 his discharge papers were marked: 'Conduct very good'.

This is an interesting case of prevention at its very best and the affair never passed beyond these shores. The interests of the country were protected and in all probability a citizen was saved. The drawbacks, however, of the agent provocateur method were such as to restrict its application to the smallest possible number of cases. The handling of the case of Ernest Evans shows an ingenious variant of the method.

★

Abraham Eisner, a tobacconist and stationer of 3 Edinburgh Road, Portsmouth was first brought to the notice of MO5 in connection with Charles Wagener. Observation revealed that Wagener had visited Eisner on 16, 21, 22, 23, 28 and 29 March 1912, always, with one exception between 11 and 12 p.m., an hour which suggests either great intimacy or unwarrantable business. The first visit took place on the day on which Wagener would have gone to Ostend, had the ticket and money been forthcoming; the last visit took place after Wagener had announced he would sell the ticket sent him for the meeting at Ostend on 31 March, after he had called at the shop of Levi Rosenthal. The abrupt cessation of intercourse with Eisner (Wagener was under observation till 10 April but no other visit was recorded) seems to betoken a quarrel. A quarrel actually did take place, though we do not know the date, and Wagener complained that Eisner had treated him, a fellow countryman, very badly. It is further to be remarked that no letters from Wagener to Germany were intercepted until after intercourse had ceased between the two men.

The Portsmouth police believed Eisner to be a German Jew and they viewed him with suspicion – on what grounds they did not state, but no doubt the dockyard police were in touch with the borough police and knew the talk of the town. Eisner's character was not good. In business, he was a rogue and he had been twice prosecuted for selling indecent postcards in 1906. The charge was proved and he was fined; in 1911 it was dismissed. He told a neighbour that the postcards had been sent him from Germany by his father, Solomon Eisner, and in this connection it may be worth noting that a charge of having committed a similar offence was proved against Charles Wagener at North Shields in March 1914 and against Solomon Eisner in London in May 1914. During the war the existence of an obscurity code became known; whether picture-cards were ever used the writer is unable to say.

In May 1914 MO5 were made aware that Eisner was photographing warships. He afterwards stated he had obtained leave from Lord Charles Beresford.

Attention had been called in October 1913, to the undesirability of allowing the publication of picture cards of any portion of the naval and military defences and it was decided that the publication of that class of card must be stopped. The police at the ports were requested to watch for such cards and to warn the vendors that they might be prosecuted under the Official Secrets Act. It must have been in consequence of this action that the police at Portsmouth reported Eisner. As the papers have disappeared it is impossible to say how far MO5 prosecuted their investigation. The only reference to the episode is contained in a minute of 1915.

The facts as regards Eisner were suspicious. He had been running a very small tobacconist's business, had been recently through the bankruptcy court, and yet was running a motor car worth £700. He told the police that he bought it out of the profits of his sales of photographs to naval men, but in June 1914 he told a neighbour that the money came from a legacy in Germany. He could not have pretended to make a profit of £700 in under a year or two, and the question arises whether he was engaged in that kind of business at the time of Wagener's visits. If so then it is worth noting that Wagener was a silhouette-cutter by trade and that, according to Armgaard Graves, spies had to memorise the outlines of British warships from large charts of silhouettes.

Another source of profit came to light some years later owing to the indefatigable efforts of the intelligence officer at Portsmouth. It appears that in 1912 Abraham Eisner began touring the southern provinces as a traveller in watches and cheap jewellery of German make, and in that capacity visited various places in the Aldershot Command. Why, if his purpose was innocent, did he not mention this source of income (he did a good trade) to the police in 1914? This is only the first of many evasions, not to say lies, which do not seem ever to have been realised by those dealing with the case here.

In May 1914, Eisner sought to put himself right with the police by handing to them one of the spy letters disseminated in Portsmouth by Celso Rodriguez. There were so many of these letters that the action had no special merit.

At the outbreak of war, MO5 had in their files evidence of Wagener's unseasonable visits to Eisner and of Eisner's trade in photographs of warships; they knew that he was viewed with suspicion by the Portsmouth police, and that he had received a letter from Rodriguez. He had not, however, been placed on the SWL.

Early in August 1914, Eisner registered as a Russian subject born at Kalisz on 30 September 1884. He had come to England from Russia in 1896 and had married an Englishwoman in 1907. As he had no documentary evidence in support of his claim to Russian nationality, the military authorities decided that he and his wife must leave the district. This order was given verbally by the police on 28 August 1914 – two days before the promulgation of DRR 24A, which gave power to make the order. Eisner and his wife at once obeyed and as a consequence of Eisner's efforts to get permission to return, the matter was brought to the notice of MO5 The lawyers employed by Eisner forwarded a certificate of Russian nationality obtained from the Russian consul-general, and an affidavit in which Solomon Eisner of 122 High Street, Whitechapel, supported all his son's statements with the exception of the date of arrival in England. He stated that he brought the family to England in 1891 and that Abraham had gone to Portsmouth in the following year.

Enquiries instituted by MO5 showed that in his affidavit Solomon had suppressed a vital fact: the family had spent five years at Leipzig and one year at Antwerp on their way to England. Moreover he had antedated his arrival by ten years. Abraham Eisner, too, while admitting the facts about his photography at Portsmouth, and that he had visited Leipzig every year on business, lied about his visit in 1912, which he attributed to having spent his honeymoon there. He had married in 1907. These discrepancies and evasions passed unnoticed.

Enquiry of the Portsmouth police as to the facts of Eisner's eviction produced a vague letter. Abraham's statement that he had come from Russia, and the date and circumstances of his marriage were set forth, as also was the fact that his private home and business had been searched without result, and that he had been ordered to leave Portsmouth. MO5 assumed that their question had been tacitly answered and that Eisner had been expelled under DRR 24A. Accordingly, they referred the lawyers back to the Competent Military Authority and forwarded to them what seems to have been an undated copy of DRR 24A, but again no notice was taken of Abraham Eisner's suppression and misstatement concerning his arrival here, which resulted clearly from a comparison of the reports of the Metropolitan and Portsmouth police.

The Officer Commanding the South Coast defences having refused permission for Eisner to return, the question of his naturalisation, which had been applied for in September 1914, was revived, but MO5 refused to recommend him. Next their attention was called to other members of the family. In August 1915 David, a brother of Abraham, was expelled from Plymouth, and in October of the same year Charles, another brother, travelling for the Beehive Watch Company of 125 High Street, Whitechapel, was seen at Southampton with an undesirable alien who had been expelled from that district.

Then Philip Halpern, travelling on behalf of David's firm, the City Postcard Company of 40 Mansell Street, London, tried to get into important munitions districts in Lanarkshire; a month or two later the City Postcard Company was supplying cards with the forged stamp 'Passed by Censor' to a stationer at Folkestone. The method invariably followed by all the family was to submit gracefully to any protest or suggestion of the police and to begin again elsewhere. Then, acting on information received from the intelligence officer, Portsmouth, the intelligence officer at Aldershot wrote informing MI5 (G2) of Abraham Eisner's transactions with jewellers in his district: the business seemed genuine and a good deal of money had passed hands, but the intelligence officer wanted to know more about Eisner.

MI5 left the decision as to whether Eisner should continue his travels in the Aldershot district to Major Gunn and sent a précis in which no mention was made of Eisner's former connection with Charles Wagener.

Then Eisner applied as a Russian to be allowed to join the Labour Battalion and the intelligence officer at Portsmouth sent a précis of information he had collected tending to show that Eisner was not of Russian, but of German, nationality and that he had been connected with German agents. The neighbouring tradesmen had repeated scraps of Eisner and his wife's talk from which it appeared that he was liable to military service in Germany, and he himself had said more than once that he was a German. On this point some of the evidence was eventually traced back to Wagener. The intelligence officer called attention to the discrepancy between the date of arrival in England as given by Abraham and Solomon, respectively, in official documents. The date on Abraham's shop was 1902. The evidence as to Eisner's connection with German agents had been taken mostly from MO5's letters to the dockyard police, and thus, at length, MO5 became aware of this evidence contained against Eisner in their own files. To this the intelligence officer added other vague evidence: on leaving Portsmouth Eisner had entrusted the conduct of his business to his brother-in-law, M. Myers, and I. Zeffertt. Zeffertt had taken a hat to Mr Taylor to be ironed, and out of the lining there had dropped two letters from Berlin. These Taylor had handed to the police who had destroyed them before informing the military authorities and without making a copy or translation. Taylor also declared that he knew Eisner had employed a short hunchback during the period before his arrest and trial, and John Henry Pedler signed a statement to the effect that he had often seen William Klare with Eisner. Taylor was the manager of Dunn's shop which was situated opposite Eisner's business premises. He could, if asked, sign a statement, but he did not wish for publicity. Moreover, John Henry Pedler signed a statement to the effect that he had frequently seen Eisner with the hunchback during the period before the war.

In addition the intelligence officer stated that the order evicting Eisner had been made verbally and that in April 1917 Mrs Eisner had been allowed to return to Southsea, and her husband had been given leave to visit her once a month.

The question arose whether this man should be interned. It was decided to verify Wagener's evidence against Eisner's, but no steps were taken at Portsmouth, and no notice was taken of the strange action of the police. It was considered too late to intern Eisner and the intelligence officer was told that there was nothing in the information supplied upon which action could be taken at that time. Wagener's evidence, when it came, was rejected as unsatisfactory. But Wagener's declaration that Eisner had told him he was a native of Leipzig and Mills' signed statement to the effect that Eisner had told him he was a German subject was passed over. Captain Coltart was accordingly informed that nothing had been proved by Wagener's statement, but he insisted that further information might be obtained from Aldershot, so enquiry was pursued there and in London, where Eisner had registered on 30 March 1916. The police, in reporting, called attention to the suppression of material facts in this entry. He had registered as a traveller in watches and had given as his business address as 122 High Street in Whitechapel. Both the London police and the intelligence officer at Aldershot considered that Eisner's business was genuine, and stated that he had been definitely rejected for military service.

MI5 now enquired to know the address at which Eisner actually resided. The reply came that he was seldom at has registered address and as much in Portsmouth as anywhere. Enclosed with this information was a notice from the Chief Constable that the military authority had cancelled the concession under which Eisner might visit that area once in three weeks. The list of the stamps recently inspected by the police in Eisner's identity book recorded five visits during nine weeks, and the Metropolitan Police wished to prosecute for this irregularity and for incorrect registration. The intelligence officer at Portsmouth was informed and was asked for a copy of the original order against Eisner. He replied that none had ever been made; thirty-four people had been removed in 1914 and 1915 without any order except a verbal one, and they were kept out by the threat of applying for an order should they attempt to return. The appointment of an intelligence officer at Portsmouth dated from 1916 and Captain Coltart complained bitterly of the negligence of the police; he had compared the entries in Eisner's identity book with those in the Register kept by the Portsmouth police and the results show that Eisner's journeys were entered either in his identity book or in the Register, but never in both. Needless to say, the Register at Portsmouth showed no irregularity. Eisner told the police in London that he had received verbal permission to go to Portsmouth once a fortnight, but this was denied by Inspector Ford. The Chief Constable of Portsmouth wrote that on this question Inspector Ford had referred Eisner to the military authorities and sent documents to prove that from the outset the police had objected to making any concession at all.

With all these irregularities on the part of the authorities there could be no case for prosecution; but MI5G applied for a restriction order under DRR 14. The grounds adduced were Eisner's frequent visits to Germany before the war and his known connections with other suspects and alien enemies on the grounds which might have been adduced in 1914. The order was served on 4 May 1918 and it was rescinded after many petitions and much debate on 9 May 1919. In this connection Inspector Ford distinguished himself by telling Mr Myers, Eisner's father-in-law, that he must apply to Colonel Kell, head of the Secret Service. The next month Lieutenant-Colonel de Watteville, reporting on the Portsmouth Intelligence Service, records that the garrison intelligence officer complains of the apathy of the Chief Constable of Portsmouth in questions affecting the relations of the naval, military and civil population, does not trust him, and does not credit him with sufficient authority to enforce the application of intelligence precautions by his men. The case of Abraham Eisner illustrates the difficulty of dealing with a suspect ally, but it cannot be said to reflect credit on the investigators. The complete facts of the case seem never to have been grasped. Let it be said at once that there was no proof against Abraham Eisner: there was also no serious attempt to get to the bottom of the facts. That MI5 were unconscious of the evidence contained in their own files until 1917 may be due to initial defective registration or training in May 1914 when Eisner first came under suspicion; that the lies and evasions of himself and his family passed unnoticed in October 1914 may be due to pressure of business and to there being apparently no Special Branch to deal with a suspect ally; and that when the intelligence officer at Portsmouth had collected a good deal of evidence from the neighbours, no attempt was made to sift it and obtain something definite from them, from the family, and from the police is less to easy to explain. It may be that as all these cases depend upon mastery of detail and that detail lies buried in a confused mass of documents when fresh evidence comes in, the officer in charge adjusts it to his last minutes rather than refresh his memory by referring to facts previously set forth.

The case also shows vagueness and laxity if nothing worse, on the part of the borough police. There seems to have been friction with the intelligence officer but even in June 1914, MO5 had to represent to the Chief Constable that he was supplying as regards the possible suspects merely those details which were required for the General Register of Aliens.

★

Heinrich Schmidt (or Henry Smith), of 43 St Aubyn Street, Devonport, arrived in that town on 24 February 1913, and it was not his first mission to England as a spy. He may have been engaged at Kiel by Herr Paul, alias Passarge, and had been sent to Rotterdam on 20 February, there to receive further instructions from Hanaan and his salary which came from Hamburg and amounted to £10 a month.

Schmidt has dealings with Hanaan and Passarge. From the circumstances that he wrote to the governor of the prison at Gluksstadt and that no references could be given to Schmidt for his 'work at G', it may be imagined that Schmidt had been an inmate of the prison. His correspondence with his mother at Hamburg and with a friend named Mosbach at Kiel shows that both these persons 'knew the nature of work here'. In writing to Schmidt, Hanaan used paper stamped (in German); International Journal for European Marine published by Dr J. Morrow and a staff of permanent collaborators at all the more important harbours at home and abroad, but based at White Brothers, a printers in Berlin.

Hanaan wrote from Rotterdam, and Passarge's letters were posted there. Schmidt, who was supposed to report twice a week, wrote once a week only, and sent his reports at first by channels unknown to us but he kept a record of his letters, and it was one of failure. He failed to get into the dockyard or to get the right employment, or the right friends. He arrived in England just after the arrest of William Klare and from his subsequent reference to this case, it seems probable that he was too scared to make any determined effort. He declined to become a commercial traveller and applied instead for a clerkship on the Western Morning Herald. Hanaan then prepared faked references with dates and particulars to suit Schmidt's fancy.

Schmidt was summoned to Brussels on 20 April, he there saw Passarge and was given the character prepared by Hanaan. No use was ever made of this. Schmidt found work for himself as a scullery-man in a hotel and returned the false character in July 1913. On 14 April Schmidt had been instructed to write via Hugo Marscheid at 206 Boomgardstraat in Antwerp, instructions which he obeyed with some reluctance. Then his reports were intercepted, but there was nothing in them. The last remittance noted in the files was sent on 26 May 1913 and the last report to Rotterdam, one showing great prudence and hesitation, was dated 9 July 1913, it is possible the correspondence continued until October.

Schmidt's actions aroused the suspicions of his landlady's son, Mr Wakeham, who informed the borough police, and they reported to the Chief Constable of Devonport. He, however, delayed communicating with MO5 who meanwhile had got on to Schmidt's track owing to a remittance of £10 sent via August Klunder at the end of February. MO5 got the dockyard police to make enquiries and they then discovered that the borough police had the case in hand. However, the dockyard police took up the work and carried it through. They reported Schmidt's friendship with a waiter at 29 Marlborough Street, a restaurant frequented by naval ratings. They telegraphed Schmidt's departure to London and his intended absence of three weeks, and while he was away they procured a copy of his photograph which Captain Drake saw and identified as that of a spy whom he had previously noted.

When Schmidt was making arrangements for his journey, he was said to have packed a portmanteau and to have left it at the station, but the police failed to discover it. During Schmidt's absence (he was away three weeks and spent nearly all that time in London), the police got in touch with Mr Edwards, owner of the restaurant in Marlborough Street, and found Schmidt's effects there. Meanwhile MO5, having learned through Schmidt's correspondence that he had left behind incriminating documents, caused his luggage to be searched. The records of his letters were found as well as his letters from Hanaan and Passarge. Captain Drake went to examine them and decided that although there was clear proof of Schmidt's intention, there was not sufficient evidence to secure conviction. Schmidt was therefore merely kept under observation.

In July the police reported that Schmidt was in touch with a Leading Signalman, and a private in the Marines named Palmer, and that he had obtained a situation as storekeeper at the Duke of Cornwall Hotel, Plymouth. Schmidt's friends were warned by their commanding officers to be careful in having dealings with a foreigner and a special enquiry was made about Palmer, who was believed to communicate information to the *Western Morning News*, but his commanding officer had no reason to suspect leakage.

In December MO5's enquiry brought the report that Schmidt had not been seen lately at Plymouth; but he was there, still acting as waiter on 20 February 1914. No entry of registered letters could be traced since October 1913, hence it seemed certain that the German Secret Service had cast him off. He left Plymouth on 2 May and went to Deyshart, Sark. The police noticed his absence but made no enquiries until requested to trace him just before the war. A wire was sent to the GOC Channel Islands to arrest and hand Schmidt over to the military authorities for detention pending deportation. He was arrested at Guernsey on 12 August and held as a PoW.

All through this investigation MO5 and the dockyard police exercised the greatest caution, preferring to forego certainty about the spy's movements rather than risk giving him the alarm. The overlapping of sources of information, being the private informant and the Home Office Warrant on Klunder, involved two police departments, local and Metropolitan. It is to be noted that in such special investigations the action of the Metropolitan Police was greatly to be preferred to that of the local police, because of Special Branch's greater speed and precision. No report concerning Schmidt seems ever to have been received from the local police, who were no doubt sufficiently engaged.

\*

In April 1913, through the correspondence of Heinrich Schmidt of Devonport, the address of Hugo Murscheid at 206 Boomgardstraat in Antwerp, became suspect. The check placed on it brought to light in May the existence at Barrow of a German agent, who had been recruited at Copenhagen. By means of details contained in his letters abroad, he was soon identified as Fredrik Wilhelm Henrik Apel.

Apel had come to England apparently destitute at the beginning of May and had called on the German consul who sent him to the Sailors' Institute. Subsequently, he received money from Germany addressed to him c/o the German consul at Barrow. His ostensible reason for coming was to look for a married sister who had eloped with a British ship's engineer. He explained the remittances from abroad as coming from an uncle who was interested in his quest. He stuck to these stories consistently, with the exception that having first given the uncle's name as Hugo Munscheid, he afterwards degraded Hugo Munscheid to the position of confidential clerk, and substituted as to his uncle a man named Carl Cornelson.

Apel drifted from house to house and lived to a considerable extent upon the charity of Mr Conway Milne, a port missionary and head of the Sailors' Institute. After several vicissitudes, Milne found him work with a German pork butcher named Osterlein, whom the police believed to have become naturalised as a Briton. In March 1914, he left this employment for work as a labourer at the Barrow Hematite Steel Company's Wire Works, and in July he was at the Kellner Partington Paper Pulp Company.

As an agent Apel was untrustworthy and a failure. He had been sent to get work at Vickers and to report on the constructions in progress for the British Navy. Having tried but failed to get employment at Vickers, owing to his German nationality, he complained of English patriotism and of the absurd precautions taken. To save face with his employers he invented the story that he had found work as a casual labourer at the dock, that he had made friends with the Chief Pilot of Vickers, and had at his invitation gone for a trip on the *Congo* when she was on her trials and that a night-watchman of the 'Technical Bureau' had admitted him to that office and shown him plans.

In his first report, Apel announced the forthcoming laying-down of a British cruiser, and afterwards sent what purported to be her dimensions. He declared he had discovered a secret for hardening steel applied in work on foreign orders, and that he would discover other secrets later. Also he had been on board a Japanese warship. He used code in his letters, referring to information generally as 'health' or a 'lawsuit', to ironclads as 'Horse Hector', to plans as 'Hypothsken' (mortgages).

In June 1913 he went to Manchester and thence to Hamburg to meet his employers. He took with him plans which were photographed. On 1 July 'C' wrote from Rotterdam absolutely refusing to send any more money until value had been received, and in August 'W. Klein', Poste Restante, Berlin, informed him of the failure of the photographs and asked for news. It may be worth noting that this was one of the methods of obtaining information recommended by George Parrott.

In September, 'Leon' wrote from Brussels to confirm receipt of Apel's letter to 'Herr. C' who was away. In December, 'A.S.' wrote from Petersburg that he had given up expecting any good result and bidding him to be careful in the use of addresses, but if he could get the things wanted they would fetch a high price 'here'. This was followed by another letter to the effect that the gentlemen in Petersburg had become impatient and had obtained the information through another man who was in direct communication with them, but that if Apel had the goods they could he brought to the next meeting. The writer enclosed four questions about the *Emperor of India* and said the answer was to be sent to A. Sampler at the Brussels Poste Restante, Bureau Central, as he had ceased connection with the other gentleman (Hugo Munscheid). Apel replied to this letter and sent his communication as directed, but it was returned from Brussels as undeliverable. This letter of Apel's reflects the nervousness caused by the arrest of Frederick Gould: 'One must go slow', he says, and he begs that no more letters should be sent from Brussels.

In April 1914, Apel wrote again urgently demanding an answer and money. He gave some account of shipbuilding on the Clyde by Vickers and directed this letter to Hugo Munscheid and left it with the Port Missionary who was to enclose a note confirming Apel's statements. Mr Milne, the port missionary, wrote a note and despatched it with Apel's to Antwerp, after having had a translation made of Apel's letter. Mr Milne had appealed to Hugo Munscheid to pay his nephew's debt of £2. A resume of Apel's letter was supplied apparently by Mr Mine himself to Vickers who forwarded it to MO5. The reply to Mr Milne came on the 15th casting off nephew 'Fred' forever, and enclosing the £2 due to Mr Milne. The illegible signature began with 'M'.

Apel disappeared in May 1914 but in July a letter showed that he was in Barrow, and still in communication with his employers. He proposed to take two plans to Hamburg that week, and wanted money for 'his man' whom he would bring with him. There is no record of any reply to this letter. Enquiry regarding the unknown German agent began on 26 May and on 8 June the Chief Constable of Barrow supplied details which left no doubt that the agent wanted was Apel and that he was a liar. Police observation was asked for, and at the same time Vickers were informed of the facts. The police acted intelligently and recorded the following payments: soon after arrival a post office order for £7.10s; on 27 May 1914 a £5 banknote (number and date of issue) from Rotterdam; on 30 May 1914 another £5 banknote from Copenhagen sent by an aunt named 'Thora'; on 11 June 1914 two £5 banknotes (number and date of issue of one of them), from Berlin, previous to Apel's going to Hamburg.

In the whole course of the investigation no further remittances are recorded, but it is possible some money was sent. Simultaneously with reporting about Apel, the police had sent information about Bernard Schenk, a German who had been engaged as one of the crew on the *Ying Swei*. This was a cruiser built by Vickers for the Chinese government. Schenk had sailed with the ship to Falmouth and returned with her to Barrow as some alteration was required. He had then obtained work in the Riggers Yard. As he was reported to be a Naval Reservist of the Submarine Department, the police kept him under observation but before reporting to MO5 they had been in communication with Vickers and had learned that Schenk had entered Vickers' employ on 17 December 1913, and had left them of his own accord. He had gone to work on the dredgers on 12 February, supposedly to earn more money. The police from time to time supplied information as to Apel's movements and correspondence. Regarding letters, it had been found impossible to put a check on at Barrow, as Apel was at first receiving communications through the German consul and the opening of such letters could only be done by a skilled official, but a check was of course placed on the addresses of Apel's correspondents. This, however, was concealed from the police at Barrow. They worked with great zeal and in July reported the arrival of a telegram addressed to Apel which was then traced and found to contain the word: 'Gratuliere' (I congratulate). This Apel explained as code, meaning 'the goods were coming'. Apel was being kept under special observation at this time, for he was talking of plans for a fresh start in life – but these did not materialise.

In September 1913 Conway Milne had written to Hugo Munscheid about Apel asking that Munscheid should communicate with his nephew on the subject of paying a debt of £2. Unknown to the police, the letter was intercepted and enquiry made as to the identity of Mr Milne and it was then learned that Milne had been helpful in giving information about Apel to the police, but Major Kell was afraid the enquiry might have let the Chief Constable of Barrow into the secret of the Home Office Warrant on Munscheid.

In November 1913 a British agent in Brussels wired to England to stop a letter from Sampler to Apel, but the letter being unimportant was allowed to proceed. It is almost certain that this was a communication inciting Apel to fresh exertions. In February 1914 special warnings were issued to Vickers and to the police at Barrow that Apel would be trying to obtain information about the *Emperor of India*, but the Chief Constable reported that Apel was quietly at work and gave no sign of seeking such information. In March however, the Chief Constable at Barrow reported his change of employment from driving a cart for a pork butcher, to working as a labourer in the steel company's wire works, at the same time forwarding Munscheid's reply to Milne discarding Fred. MO5 concluded that Apel could be disregarded.

In June the police forwarded to MO5 the returned letter from Brussels with the information that Apel had left Barrow, and his whereabouts were unknown. In July enquiry revived since it was obvious that Apel was still in touch with the Germans.

Since 9 June 1913 he had been on the SWL under the heading 'Arrest' and he was detained on 4 August and searched. He possessed nothing but what he stood up in, and nothing incriminating was found at the search. He was charged with contravening the Official Secrets Act, but the charge was not proceeded with. He was interned under the Aliens Restriction Order and taken to Preston Prison.

The case is interesting as an illustration of the first form of attack upon the private shipyards, an attack which was anticipated in May 1911. It was then proposed to draw up a list of all foreigners employed in private yards doing work for the government. Whether the list was so drawn up and whether, in consequence, the clause which prohibits foreigners from being employed upon works of defence was inserted in government contracts does not appear. But it is clear that the harmonious action of MO5, Vickers and the Barrow police completely blocked Fredrik Apel so far as direct access to information was concerned. The whole of his case, however, cannot be understood unless it is related to a wholesale attack upon the personnel of the British Navy, an attack which reached its climax in 1913.

'Carl Cornelson' and 'A. Sampler' were two of the pseudonyms of a person or persons directing this movement, which had for its object the making of traitors in the Royal Navy; they were also in touch with Apel who, it will be remembered, had complained of the insurmountable difficulty of his German nationality. Owing to this difficulty, the attack upon the navy had been extended to the personnel of the dockyards and private yards and it was no doubt part of Apel's business to supply the names of Britons who could and would give information. They would then be approached directly by letters from Brussels, Copenhagen, Petersburg, etc. All through 1913 such letters were coming into the country in quantities. In October, Sampler had sent three of them and this led to an enquiry at Brussels undertaken by a British agent.

This seems to be the explanation of the 'unimportant letter' to Apel of 19 November which the agent had seen and wished stopped. He had seen three documents in Sampler's portfolio and had evidently related their contents with each other, but his detailed report did not come in until 12 December, too late for action in the case of Apel.

The documents here referred to are the following:

1. An empty envelope, stamped with an unused Belgian stamp and addressed to F. Apel, c/o W. Ossterlein, etc.
2. A postcard (address and addressee not given but the context seems to show it is for Apel), in which Sampler begs for news and threatens the recipient with the displeasure of someone in Petersburg: he tries to arrange for a meeting and has sent money.
3. A postcard in Russian addressed to Mons. Boyle, p.a. Mme Sievers, St Petersburg, running: 'Prospects in Barrow are good: hope to be able soon to place at your disposal English collaborators'.

In February the gentlemen in Petersburg had obtained some part at least of what they wanted; they were in direct communication with someone at Barrow. It is very tempting to connect the contents of this letter of Sampler to Apel with one from Josephine Steer, giving the address 1 Newington Crescent, London, but bearing the postmark Barrow-in-Furness, and addressed to Mr J. Steer, Pannierstrasse 2/3, Neuholin, Berlin, in which the writer says, 'So Leon got to Berlin alright, he is not to be trusted five minutes alone, 'Leon', it will be remembered had written to Apel from Brussels in terms showing that he was a subordinate of 'Herr C'.

Apel's reply to Sampler was returned evidently as a result of the exposure of Frederick Gould. Brussels was suspect and no doubt for a time Sampler dared not collect his letters. Apel communicated next with Antwerp, although he had been told that that address was no longer in use. In dealing with the case at this point, MO5 took Hugo Murscheid's letter to the missionary seriously, although it seems rather to have been a blind. In any case Apel's change of work which followed soon after receipt of Sampler's letter of February 1914 may quite well have been connected with a change of intention. Early in his career he had promised to discover secret processes of hardening steel, a task which would have been more easily carried out by an employee in the steel works than from the box of a butcher's cart.

If idle, Apel was also cautious; he veiled his visits to Hamburg by spending a few days at Manchester on the way. By July, he may really have obtained a recruit and information from the steel wire works and have veiled his intention by leaving that employment for the apparently harmless paper pulp works. The fact that nothing was found at the search does not preclude his being in possession of valuable knowledge. This however, is mere conjecture; he may have remained incurably feckless and certainly he was destitute.

★

Izzel bin Aladdin was one of a group of Turkish naval officers who went through a gunnery course at Whale Island (HMS *Excellent*) from November 1910 to March 1911. Thence he went to HMS *Lord Nelson* from March 1911 to September 1911. He returned to Turkey in October of that year.

Aladdin came to London in about August 1913 and went first to the Imperial Hotel for a week and afterwards to 17 Grenville Street for a month. On 3 October he purposed to go to Portsmouth. Owing to a check on Carl Ernst's address, MO5 became aware that Aladdin, alias Maurice, was in touch with the German Secret Service. An intercepted letter endorsed W. C. Brown of the Imperial Hotel at Russell Square and signed Foti Vassilyadi, was addressed to Mr A. Alaadin [*sic*] at 17 Grenville Street. The writer described a method of sending monthly remittances through the Constantinople and London branches of the Deutsche Bank. This would cause no remark as the Deutsche Bank was much used by Turkish firms and by the government. A credit would be opened in Aladdin's name at the London branch and payment would be made to the order of a supposed relation in Constantinople.

Aladdin's sign-manual would prove his identity and on drawing his money for the first time he was to use a password. Aladdin communicated with the Germans via Mr Henry Adams and was also given the addresses of Bicker & Worth and M. Muller of 81 Pacheco in Brussels. Of the four letters of this correspondence Aladdin wrote one only and that was to acknowledge the instructions sent about his pay. At the same time he announced his intention of going to Portsmouth on 3 October.

After December 1913 no further letters were intercepted. The Home Office Warrant for Aladdin's address was taken out on 23 September and on 3 October the dockyard police at Portsmouth were asked to look out for Aladdin, but on no account to begin making enquiries. William Melville then called at the London address and obtained a description of the man, and heard that he had left saying he was going to Torquay and that letters were to be kept for him – but none had come.

From the Admiralty, a list of Turkish officers who had been attached to the Royal Navy was obtained, and it was headed by Aladdin's name. Inspector Savage was then seen by appointment and asked to make every effort to get in touch with the man, but he was unable to find Aladdin in Portsmouth. However, he discovered for himself the previous connection of a Lieutenant Biayuk A. Aladdin with the navy, and comparing a hearsay description of this person with that given by Melville of Aladdin, he concluded that the one might be identical with the other. The identification was established by means of a photograph supplied by Savage and shown casually to Aladdin's landlady in London.

The case is interesting because of the personality and nationality of the spy and of the arrangements made for remitting salary without arousing suspicion. Aladdin, so far as one can tell, wanted a little extra money for a pleasant excursion and to send to his wife back in the east. On our side the extreme caution observed by MO5 in initiating enquiries in London and Portsmouth is to be noted, as also Inspector Savage's cleverness. Further, the case led to a fresh protective measure; Major Kell arranged with the Admiralty to furnish from time to time a list of all foreigners attached temporarily to our navy.

★

In 1913 a new form of attack came to MO5's notice, under the guise of pushing the sale of a work on the navies of the world or cover for the work, and completing the work, which was to be published by a Danish, Russian or French firm. Evidently the Germans sought to gain direct contact with and information from officers and men of the Royal Dockyards. Names of naval personnel were obtained by German agents here who were directed to send in the names of officers or men who were poor, or had a grievance: with the same object in view, the daily press was scrutinised for the reports of court martial and of Admiralty enquiries, and advertisements were inserted in the daily and weekly papers announcing that manufactory agents were wanted to introduce an absolutely new article of general interest to naval circles; knowledge of special branches not necessary; only those who have a good connection with seamen need apply – offers to Soedermann, Hotel Bristol, Copenhagen.

This advertisement appeared in *Lloyd's Weekly* in December 1912 and others were published in the *Weekly Dispatch*, the *Daily Telegraph*, and the *Daily Mail*, in February 1913. These advertisements were answered in December and in February, respectively by five men, who were: W. Collier, Armourer's Crew, HMS *Minerva*; Corporal Buckley, Royal Marines, Gosport; W. G. Benson (no occupation given), 6 Johnson Terrace, Devonport; A. Semper, Retired Ship's Master, 12 Allison Road, Harringay; and James Kiernan, a pensioner and steward of the Beatty Club, a favourite resort of the naval officers.

In all these cases the applicants were answered from Copenhagen by Sonderland, or Lindstrom, manager for Soedermann, under the date of 17 February. The replies therefore were dealt with in batches, and considerable delay in answering might indicate that investigation was being made on Gustav Steinhauer's behalf into the suitability of the applicant.

Each of the applicants, according to his status, handed in the replies received either to the police or to a commanding officer. Corporal Buckley was instructed to continue the correspondence and did so under the guidance of MO5. His case can be quoted as typical. The three Soedermann replies received by him reveal some common denominators. An agent was required to push the sale of a book which a Danish-Russian firm is about to publish on the navies of the world and purchasers were likely to be found among naval men. Precise details of the applicant's connection with officers, petty officers and functionaries of the dockyards were required; applicants were to collaborate by writing articles demanding expert knowledge of matters relating to the British Navy, or to find some naval man who was competent to do so.

The replies often mentioned that several novelties and modern inventions were missing, so publication had been postponed; reports on specified points were required: these had to be more explicit than newspaper articles; handsome reward was offered for introduction to competent and willing collaborators. Invariably, six questions were enclosed. The commissioning correspondent also complained that some answers sent by the applicant were too short and simple; only special information was needed; other questions were enclosed; £5 was sent for the answers already received; promise of better pay was offered for detailed answers to a second list. At this point MO5 got Buckley to close the correspondence, and they obtained for him a reward of £5 and a recommendation for promotion.

The method followed by the Germans in setting their questions was to ask the same general questions of two different people with one or two questions of special application to the man's circumstances. The attack begun by advertisement was quickly followed by the method of direct approach. In this case there were slight variations in the letter sent: if the Germans knew nothing beyond the man's name and rank, he would be asked vaguely to collaborate by writing articles for the publication in question; if he were wanting money, there was a mere offer of an easy way of earning money; if he were known to be poor and efficient, he might be asked directly to write articles which would be treated as 'Private and Confidential' and, failing his reply, he might be written to again explaining that there was an easy way of earning money (signed Dostoyevsky and Ch. Beaumont).

A commodore based at the Royal Naval Barracks in Devonport, who recently had been court martialed, was offered money which he need not repay, provided he would do business for a Russian house. On his reply that he would be glad to earn something, he was told that naval information would be required, and he was asked to spend the weekend at any place in Belgium he chose, and travelling expenses would be paid in advance.

The case of Gunner J. E. Robertson, HMS *Bulwark*, illustrates the attack upon a man with a grievance. Robertson had been tried by court martial for drunkenness and acquitted. On 8 May 1913 a letter purporting to have been written from the Grosvenor Hotel in London was sent suggesting that he would be well-qualified to contribute articles on the artillery of the British Navy. By order of the Secretary to the Commander-in-Chief, Portsmouth, and under the guidance of the dockyard police, Robertson answered this letter and received in reply a list of questions, with the promise of £15 for satisfactory reports, secrecy as to his name, destruction of reports sent, discretion in the posting of questions, and a postal order of 20/- was enclosed. Chernakoff was the pseudonym used by the German agent.

By far the largest number of letters was composed of the vague circulars addressed to men about whom the Germans knew no details. The recipients in most cases seem to have handed up the letters voluntarily, but the gigantic nature of the undertaking and other considerations led to the adoption of action by the Admiralty.

On 31 December 1912 the address of Mr J. Soedermann at the Hotel Bristol, Copenhagen, and on 11 January 1913 the address of Nik Chernyakoff at the Palace Hotel in Lucerne, were sent to August Klunder on picture postcards and were thus brought to MO5's notice.

In that month, the name Chernyakoff became known to MO5 as being definitely connected with incitement to treason and then in February the advertisement ruse was reported, and Soedermann's connection with it. Also, more names of apparently would-be traitors emerged, including those of Green at Flexborough, Yarmouth, and of Ernest Evans. Green became known through a letter returned from abroad as undeliverable, and Evans through Steinhauer's instructions that Carl Ernst was to enquire about him. Through Evans' correspondence the name of Carl Cornelsen became known, and on 15 March, the *Daily Mail* published the two letters which had been received by A. Semper and, as a result, MO5 were able to read in various intercepted letters that Soedermann had handed over his business to Chernyakoff.

MO5 were also able to learn much from Steinhauer's letters to his intermediaries here. He would ask, for instance, for a copy of a paper in which a particular advertisement was about to appear and addresses of various persons connected with the scheme.

The large scale on which the Germans were going to work was indicated by their request for quantities of envelopes of different sizes and sorts: Klunder was to send sixty well-gummed envelopes; Ernst at request, send from 250 to 300 envelopes by sample post and as these were returned, he despatched 305 by parcel post. On 26 May, two letters inciting treason, signed Popoff, came through the post to Ernst and in June two letters were posted to Klunder. For special reasons the two addressed to Gunner Robertson and to George Sheppard were allowed to go through. Others that followed were stopped in the post.

Meanwhile, MO5 had received the correspondence of Gunner Robertson, and had pointed out to the Secretary of the Commander-in-Chief, Portsmouth, the danger of encouraging answers to the inciting letters, since the rewards offered were large and might corrupt the morally weak. They suggested that if any answer at all were sent, the opportunity of drafting it should be left to themselves. MO5 also wished that favourable notes should be taken of the action of those who handed in these letters.

In July, the Secretary wrote to MO5 that the publishing firm was particularly active, and MO5 then requested that all letters handed in to the naval authorities should be forwarded to the bureau. Finally, with the help of MO5, a Weekly Order was drafted enjoining upon the recipient of any such letters that he should not make any answer but hand it up together with the envelope to his commanding officer. This Order was issued about the end of July. The Admiralty had also in some cases adopted MO5's policy of thanking the men who brought the letters to their notice.

The letters were sent to MO5 and were collected in a file known as the Treason Box. The index bears entries of about 150 such letters, which were despatched by agents whose pseudonym changed continually. At least eighty such pseudonyms are recorded.

Enquiry made at Brussels in October 1913 showed that the letters were sent in batches from Germany to foreign centres whence they were either posted or brought by hand to distribution centres in England. There is some reason to think that, with the exception of Soedermann and Chernyakoff, each pseudonym covered one batch only of not more than three letters. The index never records more than three letters to one name, sometimes there are two and sometimes but one. In such cases the missing letters may stand for cases of neglect, treason, or failure in the post.

★

According to his record, Ernest Evans deserted the Royal Navy in 1904, but was returned and was discharged in 1906 for having been in civil custody. He was re-engaged on September 1915 and then invalided out at Chatham, and pensioned. He then obtained employment at an explosives factory at Gretna, but was discharged following MO5G's intervention. A check was placed on his correspondence and he was traced to Woolwich Arsenal where he was working as a gun-examiner. He left at own request and was traced to Brighton. The check on his correspondence continued from 3 August 1917 until 15 May 1918. Evans changed his name to Reginald Northcote and obtained employment as examiner at the Brighton Motor Coach Company to which he was sent by the Aeronautical Inspection Department. However, he was found to have altered his discharge certificate having erased the words 'Civil Custody'. When challenged, Evans said that no action had been taken by the navy, no action by the Aeronautical Department, and that he had been employed at Vickers Air Works in Crayford where his conduct had been found to be satisfactory. This case arose out of the Soedermann answers. Evans had answered an advertisement but the Germans did not reply until Ernst had verified his existence.

Then a meeting was arranged to take place at the Hotel Cosmopolite in Brussels on the morning of 23 February. MO5 had of course followed the correspondence and the case was dealt with on novel lines that would effectually prevent the Germans from engaging Evans. Melville first saw Evans to assure himself of his identity. Then, posing as Soedermann, he interviewed the man at Brussels, in the Grand Marine Hotel, on the evening of the 22nd and again on the morning of the 23rd, and saw him off to England by the 1.16 train to Ostend.

Soedermann induced Evans to sign an application for employment in the German Secret Service, but warned him that should nothing come of the application it would be owing to the fact that Evans had left the Royal Navy seven years earlier. Meanwhile 'F', who was an MO5G agent, was impersonating Evans at the Cosmopolite and when the representative of Chernyakoff arrived, F professed absolute ignorance of anything to do with the affair. The German waited at Brussels till the evening of the 24th on the chance of the real Evans appearing.

Evans waited for about six weeks, then he wrote again to Soedermann on 13 May and at the same time made arrangements to sell his knowledge to the British Secret Service. When accused he gave a true account of his interview with William Melville, he was dealt with gently and warned of the danger of getting in touch with German agents. Evans had been on the SWL heading 'Watch', but the entry was cancelled on 29 July 1914. But he was a marked man and although the case was dropped, when he was again brought to the notice of MO5 they followed his movements with perhaps undeserved suspicion.

One more case of incitement to treason deserves mention. W. E. Robson, an electrician on HMS *Cochrane*, answered the advertisement. MO5 received the stock letter of 17 February and wrote accepting its suggestions. His letter was intercepted and the Home Office Warrant on his name produced a letter from Portsmouth dated 14 March with a passage referring guardedly, but in a tone of alarm, to the episode, and in a way that threw doubt on the loyalty both of Robson and the writer. The letter purported to be written by a woman and was signed 'Rose'. A copy of the letter was sent to Sir Graham Greene but on the same day, Robson reported the matter to his Admiral Commanding. In February 1914 MO5 recalled the incident and asked for enquiry to be made by the police at Portsmouth, on the grounds that they were not satisfied that Robson had made a complete avowal or discontinued his correspondence.

The report furnished by the police showed that Robson's wife and child occupied part of 59 Wadham Road, North End, Portsmouth with a pensioned naval engine-room artificer named Rose. It would seem that in this case the intervention of a navy man brought Robson to his senses.

★

Gosta Olai came to live with Reuben Salter at Vansittart Street in Harwich on about 9 September 1912. He gave out that he was a Swede studying the English language, and he received remittances in Swedish money which he changed at the consulate. About the first week in November he was planning to go to a London college.

Inspector Sandercock, who had been stationed at Harwich with a view to detecting cases of espionage, drew the attention of MO5 to Olai's suspicious intercourse with Robert Burn Nichol, a torpedo coxswain of Torpedo-Boat 26. Nichol was known to have spoken disloyally and to have boasted of having documents stolen from HMS *Vernon* concealed in his bunk. Two days later, Sandercock reported that on 5 November,

Nichol had awaited Olai's return from London in a tavern, and at a late hour of the evening had produced documents from the lining of his cap and from his person. Olai had then noted down the contents.

A search warrant for Olai and his rooms was taken out at once and executed, but nothing was found. Olai, however, left Harwich suddenly either on the 12th or 13th and went to St Anthony's at Torrington Square in London. Torpedo-Boat 26 had also left Harwich for Sheerness, and it was supposed that Olai intended to work with Nichol from London.

Meanwhile, Leading Torpedoman Alexander of Torpedo-Boat 26 had also become implicated with Nichol and Olai. Circumstances aiding, the commanding officer of Torpedo-Boat 26 obtained the information that Nichol and Alexander were engaged in business which they dare not discuss openly, involving the receipt of money and communication with a particular address. A search of Alexander's effects produced one of Olai's cards bearing an incitement to discontent and treason saying he was a fool to stay in the navy when there was money to be earned outside. Moreover, Nichol was spending his time stirring up strife on the mess-deck. By an ingenious combination of the commanding officer of Torpedo-Boat 26, Nichol and Alexander were separated and Nichol was discharged to the depot at Chatham.

MO5 kept Olai under observation and he left the boarding house in Torrington Square penniless on 25 November, but in the course of the following weeks he received two remittances and departed for Sweden on 16 December. He had been very silent at the boarding-house and had had no visible occupation. Moreover, a letter received by him from his landlady at Harwich had shown that he was acting in collusion with someone else. In November, he had written to Nichol asking for news of the Italian accident and showing that he given money both to Nichol and Alexander. In January 1913 Alexander wrote congratulating Nichol on having obtained the other book, and asking for Olai's address.

The prompt action of the commanding officer of TB-26 merely postponed further treachery: the men remained scoundrels. On the other hand, the value of the power to search on suspicion is here apparent. It seems to have frightened Olai and interfered with his efficiency. Probably his worst achievement was the legacy of discontent which he left behind him. Robert Burn Nichol (who had been on the Watch List) and Gosta Olai were put on the SWL under heading 'Wanted if in Great Britain'. There is no record of what happened. Nichol was transferred from the Watch to the Arrest List on 2 July 1914.

★

In October 1913 22-year-old Dorothy Chalmers despatched letters from her home at 69 Leyland Road in Southport, couched in almost precisely similar terms to an officer of HMS *Suffolk* and of HMS *Lancaster* whose names she had seen in the Naval and Military Record of which she was an assiduous reader. She expressed great interest in naval matters and asked each officer to become her naval correspondent. The letters were supposed to emanate from an agent of a foreign power and were forwarded to the Admiralty in accordance with the order of July 1913. On 16 December Major Kell wrote to the Chief Constable of Southport explaining the circumstances and asking for enquiry about the lady. The Chief Constable forwarded particulars stating that he saw no cause to suspect her.

In March the case was revived by the action of the officer commanding the Royal Naval Barracks Devonport. He wrote direct to the Chief Constable asking for enquiry and the Chief Constable reported the matter to Major Kell. Investigation showed that Miss Chalmers had written in much the same terms as stated above to a young officer who had brought the letter to Commander Pilcher and by the letter's instructions answered it in suitable terms. The correspondence continued and in all about six letters were exchanged between 19 and 28 February.

The terms of the girl's letters were foolish, but it was not quite clear whether her intentions were innocent from the point of view of the Service. Her correspondence was watched from the 17 March to 30 April and eventually it was decided that she was merely foolish. Her mother was warned of her daughter's behaviour and of the suspicions attaching to it and she undertook to put a stop to it. Commander Pilcher was rebuked for taking action before reporting the matter to the authorities and so running risk of impeding the action of the department properly constituted to deal with such matters.

# CHAPTER II

# 1914

EARLY in February 1914 letters were intercepted which showed that the German Secret Service was transferring its very determined attack upon the loyalty of the navy from the personnel afloat to the personnel of the dockyards. The first group of agents to come under investigation consisted of Peter Gregory, Lina Heine, Celso Rodriguez, Sam Maddick, Francis Bubenheim and his employee, E. J. Knight.

Under the guise of collecting articles and materials for a Russian paper which was to keep track of all the navies of all the world, A. Kutusow, giving the address: c/o Mme Muller, Pachecostrasse 81, Brussels, was carrying on the work begun by Soedermann and continued under the names of Chernyakoff and Lindstrom. How he gained touch with Gregory, a ship-fitter of Portsmouth Dockyard, was never ascertained, but most likely it was by the distribution of a typed circular through the Inland Post.

On 7 February Edwin J. Gregory wrote from 23 Copnor Road, Portsmouth, to A. Kutusow, chez Mme Muller, Pachecostrasse 81, Brussels, enclosing an article on the recruiting and training of naval men, and suggesting for his next subject the training and differences of the engineering branch of the British Navy. He asked to be paid at a flat rate of £2 for every article, long or short, and once more protested that he would supply no information prohibited by the law of 'this England'.

Kutusow replied that the information received was neither accurate nor according to promise and he enclosed a list of questions about the manpower in certain ships and in the barracks, about the fitting of wireless on submarines, and the storage and supplies of fuel oil. He also enclosed £2 for the next report.

To this Gregory answered indignantly that he was not a spy and would not give the required information, not even for £30, much less for so paltry a sum as £2; but if Kutusow really were an editor, he would be glad to discuss matters in a personal interview. And Gregory returned the questions but kept the £2.

Kutusow expressed great surprise; he alone as editor could write the articles for his paper; the information asked for was not for publication but for his own use, he was writing about all the navies of the world and must be able to judge of the whole. And he was only asking for such details as anyone living in Portsmouth could easily get to know. Besides, the more detailed the answers the better the pay.

With this explanation Gregory was satisfied; he wrote that he would answer the questions but he required an advance. He even became very anxious when the answer to his letter was delayed and wrote a second and a third time. This third letter was not seen by MO5. Eventually Kutusow returned the list of questions, and after an interval sent £2, and finally explained the various delays by his having been obliged to send to England for more postal orders. At each stage of this correspondence, action was taken with the objects of identifying the writer, collecting proofs which could be produced against him in open court, and rendering his action harmless.

Major Kell wrote to Sir Frederick Wodehouse, Assistant Commissioner, New Scotland Yard, asking that the officers at the dockyard should ascertain who and what Edwin J. Gregory was. Through Mr Fetherston of the Investigation Branch of the GPO application was made for the production of the postal orders sent from Berlin. These were forwarded to MO5 on 5 March. On 28 February the dockyard police reported that it was Peter, not Edwin J. Gregory, who lived at Copnor Road. Edwin was a bricklayer employed in the dockyard, 'but Peter Gregory, who was supposed to be the father of Edwin, was a pensioner artificer engineer of the Royal Navy and at that time employed as a ship-fitter in the manager-construction department of the dockyard.

Edwin J. Gregory had been kept under observation for some days but without result.

When Gregory proposed a meeting with the foreign agent Scotland Yard was informed in order that it might watch proceedings. On 20 March, Major Kell wrote to the police suggesting that Peter Gregory was using his son's name, or the son was using his father's address, as cover for dealings with foreign agents and he asked for specimens of the handwriting of each, but the police now discovered there was probably no connection between Edwin and Peter, for the only son of Peter Gregory was said to be Frederick Charles William, a draughtsman employed in the Mould Loft, and had recently left his father's house after quarrelling with him. They enclosed specimens of the handwriting of each of the three Gregorys. None of these being recognised as that of Kutusow's correspondent, recourse was had to a ruse. Mr Melville wrote under the name of Morgan to enquire about an Edward Gregory who died intestate, and, in the required handwriting, there came a reply, signed either E. Gregory or Gregory, for the signature might be read either way, acknowledging the relationship and asking for the enquirer's credentials. Morgan then pointed out the strange circumstance that whereas he had addressed his letter to P. Gregory, he had received a reply signed E. Gregory. Gregory bluffed, declared he had signed with his surname only and threatened to place the matter in the hands of a solicitor. And there the affair ended.

Having thus made sure of his man, Major Kell wrote begging the central authorities to inform the dockyard police that Peter Gregory was in touch with a foreign power and using the name Edwin J. Gregory as cover. He also brought the case before the Admiral Commander-in-Chief, suggesting that if Gregory were able to obtain confidential information at his post he should be quietly transferred to other work. The Secretary replied stating that Peter Gregory was not in a position to learn much and that when his job was finished he should be transferred to the tool-shop but Frederick Charles, the son, was employed in a place so secret that even the writer himself was not admitted to it and he might be giving valuable information to his father. Captain Drake's answer exonerated the son.

Early in April it had been noted that although the address Stiller, Pachecostrasse 81, Brussels came out during the Gould trial, the incident seemed to have passed unnoticed by the German authorities and no fresh address had been given to Gregory. Still, one at least of his letters had slipped through the mesh, so the precaution was taken of sending specimens of his handwriting to the GPO with the request that they would watch for any fresh address to which he might be writing.

In spite of this however, on 4 May, Kutusow acknowledged receipt of a letter of which there is no trace in the file. It contained Gregory's answers to some of the questions. Kutusow enclosed £2 but he was dissatisfied with the replies; he enclosed a fresh list and if satisfactory answers were received a regular weekly salary would be offered. The new questions required exact information about the fitting and number of tubes on ships of the Iron Duke class; the number, range and speed of torpedoes carried by them; the reliability of the gyro when the torpedo was used at its highest range; about the torpedo tubes, heavy guns and armour of the *Queen Elizabeth* and *Royal Sovereign*, then under construction; and the date on which the battleship of the year's programme was to be laid down.

Moreover the omission noted above was silently made good, the envelope was endorsed: 10 rue des Longs Chariots, Brussels, but Gregory did not take the hint; he replied to the old address saying that he was anxious to answer these questions but it would be much more difficult and he would have to pay more for the answers.

A. Kutusow then forwarded £2 to cover the next set of questions and endorsed the envelope: Jaecker, 10 rue des Longs Chariots. About a month later Gregory wrote, still to the old address, that after making every effort and running great risks he could not get the information about the new ships, it was altogether too dangerous a job, but he could write articles. The correspondence ceased at this point.

When the second list of questions passed through the post, the police were informed that P. Gregory had already cashed postal orders at Southampton in the name of Edwin J. Gregory, that it was likely that he would soon be receiving others from abroad, and it was particularly desirable to connect him with these. General observation was asked for, for the next few days, but such that he should not suspect he was being watched.

Two receipts for registered packets from Brussels, dated 16 April 1914 and 5 May 1914 and signed E. Gregory, were submitted on 8 May but the police had to report that they had never seen him enter a post-office, though several letters had been delivered at his house.

Two other receipts seem to have been extracted for Mr Fetherston. Gregory was placed on the list of men to be kept under observation on the outbreak of war and in October the dockyard police pressed for some action to be taken. On 3 October, Gregory applied for leave so that he might volunteer as an artificer engineer and his application was forwarded to MO5 for consideration, but while they were consulting as to whether the authorities would be justified in dismissing the man without reason given, the police wrote again pressing for some definite information upon which to act: Gregory, then in the tool-shop, was constantly applying to be moved to some place of greater interest in the dockyard where he could see what was being carried out in the way of fresh construction and fittings.

MO5 replied that, although there was no doubt that Gregory had been for some six months engaged in correspondence with a foreign agent, there was no reason to believe that he had been able to give any important information, and, in view of certain difficulties about bringing a charge under the Official Secrets Act, they would submit the case for disciplinary action to the decision of the Admiralty. This would relieve the police of further responsibility.

A précis of the facts was forwarded to the Admiralty and the question was definitely raised as to whether Gregory should continue to be employed, and if so, whether he ought not to be removed from Portsmouth. His case was compared with that of Mott and an offer was made to draw up the necessary questionnaire should the Admiralty decide to mete out the same treatment to Gregory. There is no record of their Lordships' decision.

The case offers a good instance of the graduated attack of the German chief spy. At first the information is to be supplied in articles of a general and innocent nature. Then definite questions, such as anyone living on the spot could easily answer by reference, apparently, to a navy list, follow. These questions have some relation to the subject on which the victim was willing to supply information and the fiction of writing for a newspaper is kept up. Money is sent and the cupidity of the informant aroused. Then, when he has accepted the money and is in the tills, the thrust goes home and the real question, which from his specialised knowledge he might be expected to answer, is put, together with the barely veiled offer to engage him as a paid spy.

Another, more topical feature of the case, is the Gould trial looming in the background; 23 and 25 February, 4 and 11 March 1914, mark the first stage of that case, and the trial and judgement took place on 3 April. The committal for trial on 11 March doubtless took the Germans by surprise and Gregory's recantation of 12 March remained unanswered for more than a fortnight. This gave time for at least two letters to reach the suspect address in Brussels safely. The change of address was probably deliberately delayed in order to test the action of the British Post Office.

Lastly the psychology of the victim is of interest. Alert and suspicious, unscrupulous and a coward making a brave show, it is probable that his protests of patriotism were not altogether a pose. He was out to make money but on his own terms. That he was on a dangerous tack he knew from the start, his words and his mean sheltering of himself under a fellow worker's name prove it. But he had neither the intention nor courage enough to carry out the worst treacheries and Gould's heavy sentence acted as a deterrent.

★

Lina Mary Heine, born at Holzweiseg, Prussia in 1893, arrived at Portsmouth on 13 March 1914 and ten days later began work as a teacher of German. At the end of March, Max Power Heinert or Heinricht, formerly agent for a firm of coal and briquette merchants, also arrived at Portsmouth ostensibly for the purpose of studying English. He was Lina's husband but the connection was kept secret; he used, however, to visit her under pretence of taking lessons from her, but such visits are recorded by Heine's landlady as having begun about early June. Entries in her diary show that between 1 April and 29 July she went fourteen times to Emsworth, six or eight miles from Portsmouth, between Havant and Chichester, journeys which may conceal meetings with Heinert. After his arrival Heine moved to 6 Pelham Road, where she occupied two rooms. Heine afterwards stated that she had been recruited for the German Secret Service at about Christmas 1913, by a bogus advertisement in the *Berliner Tageblatt*; a lady knowing English was required to fill the post of teacher of German in a Russian language school in England. She answered the advertisement and was persuaded to take up Secret Service work.

Heine's reports were sent to a man with a Russian name and addressed to hotels in different towns in Germany. Letters to her from Germany were dealt with as follows:

Lists of questions were posted to Miss Claire Fouquet, poste restante, Southampton; remittances were sent, on one occasion at least, in an envelope endorsed Henry Court, Imperial Hotel, London; friendly communications signed in turn, Uncle, Aunt, Ruth, Ellen, would come acknowledging her letters and asking her to fetch from Southampton and forward to Basle letters for Miss Claire Fouquet, or warning her that a remittance was coming from Henry Court. All such communications came via Schneider or August Klunder.

The check on Schneider's correspondence brought Heine's activities to the notice of MO5 at the beginning of April, but in spite of all their efforts no proof of her spying was obtained for several months. Special agents were sent to shadow her from 17 to 23 April, but nothing suspicious was observed, and she was never seen to post a letter. Her pay of £15 was sent regularly every month and the postmaster of Portsmouth was able to forward her signature for the first of these remittances, dated 16 April 1914. After that she allowed the servant to sign the slips, possibly out of precaution. The postmaster also noticed and forwarded to MO5 an advertisement of Heine's offering her services as a teacher. Ohlson was sent to take lessons and he succeeded in obtaining a specimen of her handwriting. In the course of five lessons he could make nothing of her, only he managed to learn that a certain officer at the Royal Naval College was an intending pupil of Heine.

In May Heine was followed to Ostend and was seen to meet Captain Fels. Early in July the check on A. Hocke, Carstensgarde, Copenhagen, which had been running since 27 August 1913, produced a letter from Heine. She sent a sketch of the searchlights at Portsmouth as they had appeared on certain dates in June, and she answered a few questions of a list posted to her in April. She was put on the SWL and arrested on 4 August 1914.

Heinert was with her and as he could give no satisfactory account of himself he also was arrested. The police then discovered they were man and wife and that Heinert had, since 1 July, been living in the house of Leigh Kendall, a private tutor, who had given him lessons in English. Kendall had seen nothing suspicious in Heinert's actions and conversations. Next it was discovered that Heinert had a brother, Walter Heinricht, a musical instrument maker living and owning four shops in Glasgow. Heinricht also was arrested but as there was no evidence against him he was released.

Heine and Heinert were interned in Portsmouth Prison pending deportation. At some date between 1 August and December, Heine confessed to her guilt but declared that her husband was innocent. He died in prison suddenly on 1 December 1914 and Heine was subsequently moved to Aylesbury Gaol.

The Home Office wished to release Heine, but MO5 declined to entertain the idea that any term short of three years' detention was an adequate punishment for her crime. As Heinricht, her brother-in-law, corresponded with her, some fresh enquiry was made about him. He had been interned as a prisoner of war in September, and his shops had been searched, but as nothing incriminating was found and there was no suspicion against him he had been released in December 1914. Six months later his wife, Molly Heinricht, was the subject of a presumably satisfactory enquiry.

Heine appealed to be repatriated in 1916 and was again refused on the grounds that if she returned to Germany she would be sent to spy in Allied territory.

A repatriated German tailor's assistant named Hermann Otto Nather, published in the *Premdenblatt*, a lying account of the cruelty of the British authorities towards interned civilians and prisoners of war, stating as an instance the case of an Austrian officer who had been interned with his wife in Portsmouth Prison and had died there. The case was raised by the Austrian Government through the American ambassador. The draft of the Foreign Office reply identifying the supposed victim as Heinert or Heinricht and giving the true facts concerning him was submitted to MO5. Twice during 1917 the question of Heine's repatriation was raised. Colonel Kell kept to his view that release was impolitic and eventually she was recommended for internment under DRR 14A, on the grounds of her hostile origin and association with German Secret Service agents here and on the Continent and of her being a professional spy. The Order was made on 28 February 1918.

On 11 December 1918, the DMI had placed Lina Heine on the list of women who were to be held during demobilisation, but as it was evident that these women, eleven in number, were suffering much from the prolonged captivity. MI5F asked that their cases should be reconsidered on the grounds that the principle of prevention and not punishment, which had governed in interning them, should also be applied in the question of release. The Home Office consented and Colonel Kell raised no objection to the release, subject to the immediate repatriation of all these women. On 21 March 1919, a Deportation Order was made against Heine, who sailed for Rotterdam on 1 April.

The case is of interest for the greater subtlety of the German methods employed. If Heine gave the correct date for her enlistment in the German Secret Service, the interval between Christmas 1913 and March 1914 must have been spent in training as a spy. She may, in fact, have been the 'Limma' whom Steinhauer mentioned to Gould in January 1914, as having just 'been put in the way'. Heine's success in baffling our agents shows that she was an accomplished spy. It is possible that Heine got her husband to post her letters, or else that she posted them in the Isle of Wight where she went frequently.

Another interesting point is the false report made by the repatriated German. It shows the danger of letting such people go. But his report and Heine's repeated efforts to obtain release serve to emphasise a weak point in the policy of interning spies without previous trial and conviction. It gave rise to endless petitions and to the claim that the trial had been quashed because there was no proof against the accused – consequently he or she was unjustly imprisoned.

★

The real name and nationality of the spy, who passed as a Spaniard named Albert Celso Rodriguez, is in doubt. He arrived at Cecil House, Western Parade, Portsmouth, on 26 March 1914 and at once got employment at the Berlitz School, 14 Hampshire Terrace. On 30 March he sent an urgent message, which was to be wired on to 'Holloway', announcing his change of address through the well-known spy agency: Mr Adams, 10 Petite rue des Longs Chariots, Brussels. Then came obviously the first communication from Berlin in Schmidt's handwriting but signed 'Harry'.

Rodriguez's first commission in England was to ascertain the facts about Sam Maddick. While reporting about the man, he volunteered the information that several officers had come to Portsmouth to be examined for the rank of lieutenant and he specified one officer of the line who had just concluded a loan for £200.

Regarding the correspondence that followed, certain points show that additional precautions were adopted by the Germans after the trial of Gould. Several of Rodriguez's letters passed through safely unnoticed by us, but one letter, dated 8 May, which Rodriguez claimed to have sent, and of which there is no record in Reimers' file, was lost in transit, so a new address, e.g. Mevrouw E.C.A. Groot-Verwer, Koningennenweg 91, Haarlem, was sent for Rodriguez's use.

In the interests of safety, 'Harry' or 'Holloway' limited his communications with Rodriguez to what was strictly necessary and sometimes wrote in French and posted in Amsterdam letters were sent gummed into their envelopes, and the pay was remitted in French

banknotes, two precautions which were also observed in the case of
Lina Heine. Sheets of question were forwarded to Rodriguez and many
of them repeated questions sent to Heine but the two spies, although
they arrived almost at the same time and were engaged in collecting the
same information, were never seen to meet and probably were quite
unaware of each other's existence. It is known also that both of them
made excursions to London and the Isle of Wight. Rodriguez revived the
'Incitement to Treason' circular under a new form; he launched typed
circulars of questions which were to be answered for a new English or
English–American Naval Review, offering five shillings for each answer
and £70 for the Annual Report of Torpedo School. The replies were to
be sent to Harry Ford, Poste Restante, Brussels, and an allusion in one
of Steinhauer's letters shows that after collection there, they were to be
posted back to Rodriguez at Portsmouth.

The first type of circular was sent to various civilians in Portsmouth
and the neighbourhood on 16 April. It was followed by a more elaborate
one offering £5 for a set of correct answers with the chance of earning
£5 a week by such easy methods. A pencilled postscript threatened
reprisals in case of betrayal. This circular was signed Robert Wilson,
Post Office, Southsea, and was launched on 2 May. Eisner and Company
received one of these and handed it to the police.

An out of work labourer named Graham then brought in to the
police one of these circulars signed Harry Marbas or Markas, Post Office,
Southsea. Graham connected it with a chance meeting he had had in
Victoria Park with a man resembling Rodriguez.

Lastly, a letter addressed to Miss Caddy Morrison, 2 Herbergstrasse,
Berlin, with an enclosure addressed to the 'Ghrieg toinietermium' and
signed by H. Ellison, Post Office, Southsea, was returned from Berlin as
undeliverable. The letter purported to come from a gunner who offered
to give information regularly at a salary of £6 a month. On receipt of the
letter to Mr Adams, Brussels, MO5 took out the necessary Home Office
Warrants, informed the Admiralty that there was a spy at the Berlitz School,
and requested the dockyard police to keep observation on Rodriguez and
the borough police to verify the address for the Register of Aliens.

The dockyard police sent in a special report giving the description of Rodriguez and Maddick, whom Rodriguez had visited on 23 April. Rodriguez had moved to 30 Ashburton Road, Southsea.

On 25 April Rodriguez came up to town. Portsmouth informed the Metropolitan Police by wire and the man was shadowed to 194 Green Lanes, the house of a Jew named Louis A. Sions, and thence back to Oxford Circus, where he managed to shake off his pursuer. He was not seen again at Ashburton Road till the morning of the 28th, when he took steps to protect himself: he applied at the consulate offices for a passport to be made out in the name of Alberto Rosso, Professor of Languages, Berlitz School, native of Carteolona, Pavia, Italy. His application was sent to the Italian consulate.

Through the post office, MO5 obtained a registration slip signed by Rodriguez. Meanwhile the circulars had been coming into the dockyard and borough police who forwarded them to MO5. At first these circulars were thought to be a hoax, but the Graham incident aroused MO5's suspicion that they might represent a genuine spy effort. Home Office Warrants were taken out and arrangements made for the identification of the person calling for letters addressed to Wilson, Marbas and Ellison at Southsea Post Office. A careful comparison was made of all the handwriting with that of Rodriguez with the result that he was declared to be the author of all the circulars as well as of the Ellison letter. This letter was interpreted as a draw to test the safe working of the post between England and Germany. A few days later corroboration of the result of the handwriting test was received in a letter from Holloway, who asked how long he was to go on calling for letters addressed to Ford.

Rodriguez sent a stupid boy to collect letters for Marsab at Southsea Post Office; he was told there were none and that in any case Marsab himself must call for them or supply his messenger with a written authorisation. Rodriguez therefore called in person for the letter to Ellison.

About this time he moved to 60 Clarendon Road and boasted in his reports of the interesting people he met in the boarding house. Melville, who was sent down to enquire, ascertained that there were no other foreigners in the boarding-house and no one there had naval or military connections.

By the end of July the borough police sent in a report that Rodriguez had left Cecil House on 6 April but they had not discovered his present address. This was acknowledged with the request that, if possible, the address should be picked up.

On 12 July Rodriguez sent answers to several questions and propounded a scheme for opening an art school, which scheme his employer was inclined to accept. But he quarrelled with Rodriguez's answers and said the only things of any interest to Berlin were the official and confidential books and plans. On 2 August Home Office Warrants were taken out for Rodriguez at the post offices at Chichester and Ryde on the Isle of Wight.

Rodriguez had been on the SWL since early April and he had been the subject of enquiry by both the dockyard and borough police; accordingly, when the warning letter of 30 July was received, these two departments concerted measures for dealing with all persons on the SWL. Rodriguez, Heine and Henri or Louie Schneider were to be kept under observation and arrested by the dockyard police. Between 30 July and 4 August careful watch was kept upon these suspects. It was known that Rodriguez and Heine were both preparing to leave. Rodriguez took his luggage to a grocer's shop with instructions that it was to be forwarded to A. C. Rosso, Regent House, Seaview, Isle of Wight. Then on 3 August, the wife of the manager of the Berlitz School informed the borough police that Rodriguez was a spy and produced letters on 3 August: proof. He was arrested at 11.15 p.m. and charged under Section 6 of the Official Secrets Act. Proceedings thus passed into the hands of the borough police. Rodriguez was dealt with under the ARO and interned in Portsmouth Prison on 12 August 1914.

From the German point of view it would seem that their policy of direct incitement to treason in naval and dockyard circles was a failure, thanks to the general loyalty of the men and to MO5's methods. Hence the attack was broadened to include the purely civilian element in the ports and, as the Continental post was known to be unsafe, methods of posting in England were introduced. This involved a corresponding change in the wording of the circular; the news was now wanted for an English or English-American review. However the amazing clumsiness of the circular and of Rodriguez's notes was bound to mar the plot.

With the special precautions taken in the cases of Heine cum Heinert and Rodriguez we have clear evidence of the employment of two unconnected agencies working in the same port. Both were sent into the country for the purpose and not resident here. This policy may be an outcome of the bitter experience gained in the Hentschel case.

The chief feature in the investigation is the immense use made of the Home Office Warrant for this one case no fewer than six names and eight addresses were registered. Lastly, owing to the action of a private individual Rodriguez would have been captured and possibly convicted even had he escaped the notice of MO5.

★

Sam Maddick was born at Westminster in October 1874. From 1 March to 12 October 1912 he was at work in Devonport on all kinds of electric installations on ships of a new type: he left Portsmouth at his own request and went immediately to Chatham, where he worked mostly afloat running electric leads on ships. He left Chatham on 21 December 1913. Where he spent the next few months is unknown. Rodriguez said that he had been a chauffeur in London, but on 11 June 1913, he took up work in Portsmouth Dockyard and was employed on ships and on yard machinery. At Chatham and at Portsmouth he had been somewhat irregular in attendance at work and in March 1914, he was away for several days and stated on his return that he had been to Paris to look for a job and did not depend upon his weekly wages.

Late in April, A. Ransom, Hotel Stadt, Konigsberg, Potsdam, wrote to Maddick in terms that showed Maddick had offered his services to Germany but in the wrong quarter; Ransom, however, was willing to accept them. A good deal of correspondence followed in the attempt to arrange a meeting. Maddick wished it to take place in London, but Ransom would not hear of this. He proposed Brussels, on 9 or 12 May but Maddick was afraid to go. Finally, Maddick proposed to take 'samples' abroad at the end of May or beginning of June and the matter was clinched in a letter posted at Ostend and endorsed M. Dressler, 71 rue Longue, Ostend, enclosing £4 and arranging for a meeting at Ostend on 7 June.

On 1 June, however, Maddick confessed his intention to the dockyard authorities and was arrested. His statement showed that he knew what he was about; he had deliberately offered information to the German Admiralty and this not for the first time he had received communications from an Information Agency which he said was undoubtedly German, although this, the agency denied; he intended to raise money for going abroad by selling worthless information.

The search of Maddick's house brought to light Ransom's letters and also the fact that the man had visited Paris in March 1914 and Brussels probably at a later date. Also a letter was found written from Paris under the date 11 September 1915.

Maddick was charged with attempting to communicate information to a person other than a person to whom he was authorised to communicate it. He was brought up on 2 June and remanded till the 9th. His confession was reported to MO5 who had been watching the case since 20 April, when instructions had come through to Rodriguez to make enquiry about Maddick on behalf of the Germans. MO5 too had caused discreet enquiries to be made and the dockyard had supplied information which showed that Maddick was seeking for better opportunities of spying and had been visited by Rodriguez.

In May it had been decided to arrest Maddick on his journey abroad and then two technical difficulties arose. The magistrate refused to grant a warrant for arrest because MO5 would not include Maddick's intercepted correspondence in the evidence and the police at Portsmouth objected to searching Maddick's premises without a warrant as that would preclude their right of forcible entry. Luckily, the Official Secrets Act covered both these difficulties as it allowed for arrest on suspicion and search, in a case of extreme urgency, on a written authorisation of the Police Superintendent. MO5 decided upon these measures and to make the search dependent upon the finding of incriminating documents upon the person of Maddick.

In the event, neither of these measures was required, but watch was maintained all through May, and measures for the arrest were again taken towards the end of the month. In mid-May, on account of injuries to his head, Maddick had been removed for a month to Forton Oil Works, where he could work out off doors without being a danger. This time he was taking a certain amount of leave and was seen to go frequently to Victoria Park and the railway station. Then came his fear and defection.

MO5 took charge of the conduct of the case against him and a good deal of evidence was collected to show his intention and opportunities of treachery. After the remand however, it became known that he was not of sound mind. He was discharged and ended up in an asylum. During the war he escaped but was re-captured and, as the doctor thought that although not insane, he yet required watching, he was interned under DRR 14B. He offered his services to the government, but was refused, and eventually MI5 recommended his immediate release under the conditions imposed upon alien enemies. On these terms he was released on 27 January 1919, and went to work on a farm at Bromley, Kent.

★

Born at Bischheim, near Strasburg in Alsace in 1886, Karl Franz Joseph trained as a high-class mechanical engineer and was employed by the Allgemeine Elektricitatsgeaellrachaft in Berlin from 13 April 1909 to 30 September 1910. Then, from October 1911 to October 1912, he was manager of the Birmingham branch of the AEG in the Welding Department. He left Birmingham to go to the Madrid branch and was employed chiefly at Barcelona before he returned to Germany. He had been discharged from the German Army as medically unfit and remitted to non-combatant service with the 1st Landwehr in February 1912. In October 1913, he obtained employment with Messrs. Marks & Clarke, patent agents, at 57 Lincoln's Inn Fields and in March 1914, he went to the Electrical Company, 122 Charing Cross Road, and while there he had the opportunity to see good plans of aeroplanes.

He wrote to an officer in Strasburg asking to be admitted to the German Secret Service, and in the last week of March met a Colonel Kolbe at Brussels, and arranged to organise an espionage service for the whole of the south coast of England, with special reference to dockyards and aeroplane stations. He was to receive no salary but his expenses were to be paid.

In mid-May, relying on the warrant for Schneider, MO5 intercepted a letter to Francis Bubenheim acknowledging letters of 12 and 14 May and, in answer to his request, offered him an appointment for a year at 420 marks per month; a code was also encolsed, together with strict instructions that it was not to be issues to any subordinates. The code covered the information required in time of strained relations or war, and stated that in peacetime only occasional reports on the sailing of warships, and merchantmen intended to be used as armoured cruisers, would suffice. With this code came a set of questions on aeroplanes. In connection with the requiring of information on the sailing of merchantmen it is to be noted that on 28 February 1914, the *Army and Navy Gazette* had reported an abatement made by Winston Churchill to the effect that twelve vessels of the White Star Line had been armed at the expense of the company with material drawn from Admiralty stores; the process of arming merchantmen had been confined to food-carrying ships with the intention of providing for their self-defence in time of war.

Further correspondence showed that Bubenheim was on the point of obtaining a situation with the firm of Victor Tischler, patents agent, in Vienna, and that he was expected to go there early in June. Moreover, Jean Delpiano, who wrote illiterate French, was undertaking enquiries for Bubenheim in Brussels, the object being apparently a certain lady.

Concerning Victor Tischler's firm, MO5 made enquiries through the Foreign Office which ascertained through the British embassy in Vienna, that the firm was genuine and enjoyed a good reputation. In June Bubenheim received £5 from Kolbe, and his requests for more pay for himself and his subordinates was refused.

As Bubenheim's letters were passing through unseen, William Melville was instructed to keep the man under observation with a view to obtaining a clue to the correspondence. Observation was impossible owing to the nature of the building and to the fact that Bubenheim was not the only lodger and his appearance was unknown to Melville who ascertained that Bubenheim had been absent since the 29th and that he was frequently away on business for a week or more at a time. Bubenheim had in fact gone to Germany via Brussels. On his way back he stopped at Rotterdam on 2 July and on the 4th offered to give information about the German spy organisation to the British consul there. He was referred to Inspector Frost, the representative of the Metropolitan Police stationed at Rotterdam, who, on his reporting the matter, was instructed to have nothing to do with Bubenheim. At the hotel, Bubenheim used the alias Charles Wilson. Meanwhile MO5 despatched Melville to Rotterdam to interview Bubenheim and caused the man's rooms at 67 Adelaide Road, Shepherd's Bush, to he searched. Nothing incriminating was found but certain documents seized corroborated Bubenheim's statements to Melville and to Frost. Bubenheim gave to the police the name and address which he used in London – his real name, Karl Franz Joseph which was found on his papers, he suppressed. He lied about the source of a remittance which he was hoping for from Berlin.

Of his work for the Germans, Bubenheim gave the following account which has been summarised from his interviews with Sergeant Frost and Melville. He was deputed to organise an espionage service for the whole of the south coast of England, and he was to pay special attention to dockyards and aeroplane stations. In support of this statement he showed Frost a plan of the Military Flying Station at Farnborough. This had white sectional drawings on a bright blue background. In May he had obtained a salaried post in the Service. He had taken several sketches of aeroplanes to Brussels and sometimes Kolbe Junior had to come to London for them. There were three Kolbes in the business: Colonel Kolbe (Senior) aged about forty-five, Captain Kolbe (Junior) aged thirty-seven to forty, Kolbe III aged thirty-five.

Bubenheim was disgusted with their treatment of him; they paid badly, depreciated his work and Kolbe III had bullied him on the subject of supplying the names of impecunious English officers. Bubenheim had in his employ E. J. Knight, 4 Marathon Paddock, Napier Road, Gillingham, a labourer in Chatham Dockyard, who was expected to give merely information about the pressure of work in the yard. With much difficulty Bubenheim was induced to give the name of James Gray, 119 Queens Road, Farnborough, a clerk in the Inspection Department of the Royal Aircraft Factory, Farnborough, who had supplied several important sketches of aeroplanes.

The Germans were anxious to obtain plans of Short's hydroplane, of White's biplane and Wright's stabiliser, and Bubenheim proposed to decoy the Kolbes over to London by proffering sketches and false information. He asserted that Kolbe held an agent, a naval man, at Sheerness and this man had gone to Ostend on 29 June. (It is possible that this agent was E. J. Knight.)

Letters to Germany were to be sent to Mrs Anne Mayland, 158 Gustav Adolfstrasse, Berlin, and letters to Amsterdam to Mynheer A. B. J. Hemker, 46 Jan van der Heydenstraat.

Melville gave Bubenheim £6 for his information, but discouraged him from hoping for employment by the British Secret Service. Bubenheim however, came to London and engaged in correspondence with W. S. Morgan, 54 Shaftesbury Avenue, an address to which persons seeking to enter into communication with MO5 were referred.

Bubenheim tried to procure through Melville a drawing of Short's hydroplane saying that an old one would do, provided it were marked '1914, Confidential' and he asked for money. He also asked for the name of a smart young officer who could play the part of being willing to receive a bribe. Kolbe, whom Bubenheim had invited to come over to receive the drawing, however wrote that the journey was impossible, and the drawing must be sent by post. A few days later Kolbe remitted 450 francs to Bubenheim. Melville answered Bubenheim to the effect that no drawings could be supplied, but a suitable reward would be given for the name of the British traitor at Sheerness. On this point Bubenheim had nothing to say. On 16 July he once more asked for money and then the correspondence with Morgan stopped, but on the 14th Bubenheim had also written to Kolbe and in reply was bidden to go to Cologne. MO5 decided not to watch him off, as it was undesirable he should be made aware that his intentions were known. Bubenheim, however, did not go to the meeting. Home Office Warrants had been taken out for the two foreign addresses mentioned by Bubenheim but they yielded nothing.

Bubenheim was placed on the SWL heading 'Arrest', and the telegram concerning him was sent but he seems to have disappeared. When MI5 enquired of Scotland Yard in November 1915 they had no papers dealing with Bubenheim. An effort was made to trace him at 67a, Adelaide Road, but Mrs Grandjean, his landlady, had left in July 1915 and nothing was known about the man. The enquiry was not altogether fruitless, for the case of James Gray was then gone into, as it would seem, for the first time.

Immediately after hearing of this man's connection with Bubenheim a Home Office Warrant had been taken out for Gray's correspondence without apparent result.

On 28 December 1915, Captain Carter gave instructions to obtain all particulars about Gray through MI-1(a). Owing to sickness there was some delay. Then Major O'German wrote that Gray had been employed at the Factory since December 1913, that he bore a good character and occupied a position of some trust. MI5 then ascertained that James Gray was occupying one of the Royal Aircraft Factory cottages, 28 Finehurst Cottages, Farnborough.

A HOW was taken out and a check put on for foreign correspondence. The Censor submitted a letter from E.L.S.G., Park Hotel Mooser, Vevey, to J. E. B. Gray Esq., 42 Cambridge Road, Aldershot, Hampshire, dated 16 June 1916, with the remark that the addressee might be identical with the person on check. The letter seemed harmless and was forwarded to its destination and no attempt was made to verify the identity of the addressee. In July 1916, the Home Office Warrant and check were cancelled as unproductive. On the other hand Hemker's address in

Amsterdam was blacklisted for six months, but without any results. Meanwhile direct enquiry came from the Royal Aircraft Factory as to James Gray's character as he was then acting as Secretary to the War Distress Relief Fund.

MI5 took action through Major Gunn, the intelligence officer at Aldershot, and for the first time Gray was interrogated as to his knowledge of and dealings with Bubenheim. Gray stated that he and Bubenheim had served at the Napier Motor Works from about July to September 1913. Bubenheim's pay of 25 shillings a week was supplemented by remittances from Germany which he said came from his mother. He used to say that in Birmingham he had been in receipt of £300 a year. In September 1913, he took up a situation with Messrs. Marks & Clarke and moved his lodgings to 58 Birkbeck Road, Acton, the residence of Mr Burman, another clerk employed by the Napier Works. Gray went to Farnborough in December 1913. At the first interrogation Gray denied having written to Bubenheim after taking up the post at Farnborough and accounted by a lie for the fact that Bubenheim had given him a private address. When this was proved, Gray admitted having corresponded with Bubenheim up till June 1914, and stated that his letters were sent to 58 Birkbeck Road, Acton, where Bubenheim lived.

Major Gunn stated that Gray was thought at the factory to be unreliable and expressed the opinion that, although Gray might not go the length of acting treacherously in time of war, he was shifty and might very probably have given Bubenheim sketches of aeroplanes and, if so, with full knowledge that he was giving them to an aggressive pro-German. The enquiry was taken up at Acton.

Mr Burman of 57 Shakespeare Road, stated that Bubenheim had lodged with him at that address from about September 1913 to March 1914 and had not 'since been seen or heard of' Enquiries in the neighbourhood brought evidence that Bubenheim and Gray had been intimate friends. Thereupon MI5G wrote to AOIC giving an account of the facts about Gray and Bubenheim and suggesting that Gray should be quietly transferred from a position where he could obtain information of value, but must not be allowed to suspect that the transfer was due to his connection with Bubenheim. There is no record of what was done at the factory.

A circumstance seems to have escaped notice here or stronger measures might have been taken. Gray gave a wrong address for Bubenheim's letters. It is of course possible that 58 Birkbeck Road, and 57 Shakespeare Road cover the same house. But from March 1914 onwards, Bubenheim was not living there, and that letters were not forwarded to him from there is obvious by the terms of Mr Burman's statement. Another point, that of the letter from Switzerland, will be dealt with in the summing up of the case of Bubenheim and Knight.

In 1914 MO5's action probably stopped further mischief and, after his confession, Bubenheim no longer dared to employ Gray. But it is exceedingly likely that he gave Gray some hint of danger and that to some extent Gray was forearmed against the interrogatory. Why nothing was done about Gray earlier does not appear. Probably other considerations interfered; there had been already a good deal of correspondence with the factory about W. F. Brown and George Beatty. Also, MO5 was obviously over-weighted. Some arrangement seems to have been lacking to ensure the police sending in reports of action taken by the direction of MO5 on the outbreak of war.

Knight had been in the Royal Navy as a writer. He bore the character of being good at his work, intelligent, industrious and willing. For reasons unknown he had been discharged to shore. When he came to the notice of MO5 he was employed on ordinary labouring duties, e.g. non-confidential work on HMS *Leviathan* in Chatham Dockyard. Enquiry showed that he had come down in the world through drink. Early in May, 1914, E. J. Knight was found to be in direct communication with Herpers, an editor in Berlin.

He had, he afterwards stated, answered an advertisement requiring the services of a naval correspondent for an important Continental paper. In reply he received questions referring to the construction, armament, searchlights and wireless of HMS *Lowestoft* and also to submarines of the E class then under construction at Chatham.

Correspondence showed that Knight was to go to Brussels on 11 May. Regan was sent to get in touch with the Chatham Dockyard police, to verify Knight's activities, and to follow him to Dover, where he was to be pointed out to Sergeant Andrews for future identification. Knight evaded the observers and he was absent from work without leave from 11 to 18 May and then returned saying he had been to Manchester. On 21 May he offered to give to the Admiralty information about German espionage. The Director of Naval Intelligence suggested that Knight should be told to give his information to the dockyard authorities. But Knight came up to the Admiralty on 22 May, and appeared there drunk. On 29 May he sent in a claim for expenses and on the 30th wrote that he had a letter from Wallkenraedt asking for naval information.

On the suggestion of MO5 Knight was discharged from the dockyard without reason given; his claim against the Admiralty was disallowed whereupon he complained of being victimised.

Meanwhile, he continued his correspondence with Herpers asking for and receiving £3 for travelling expenses; this was followed by a remittance of £5, and appointments for a meeting in Brussels were first made for 14 June and then for 21 June.

An exchange of wires between himself and Herpers, c/o Hubert Cam, Neutralstrasse, Welkenraedt, took place with reference to the remittance of the £5, and for this address a HOW was taken out.

Through the police at Chatham MO5 had tried to procure from Knight the letters he had received from abroad, but Knight declined to say much and garbled the facts. He stated that at his own request the German was coming to an interview at Dover. MO5 proposed to arrest Knight if he attempted to go abroad. Shadowing being difficult, he was to be identified at the port of departure and arrested as he went on board. For this purpose Regan was sent to Chatham to become acquainted with the man's appearance, and he watched him for an hour. Thence Regan proceeded at once to Dover in order to point Knight out to Sergeant Andrews there. The police at Chatham kept watch till about the time that Knight would be leaving for Dover. Knight, however, did not move. On 12 June he had a confidential talk with Inspector

Gray; he proclaimed his loyalty, stating that if he were taken on again at the dockyard he would show the letters from the foreigner. He asked Gray's advice with regard to levying £3 from the German for travelling expenses to Brussels. (This money he had already received.) Gray declined to advise him.

Captain Drake then wrote cancelling the orders for 14 June. He suggested that Knight should be warned of the dangers he was running and pressed to make a frank statement; he was to be told that he had been discharged for absence from work without leave and the facts regarding his trip to the Admiralty were to be put before him. The police were warned of Knight's lie about the £5 and Gray was told to have no further confidential talks with the man.

The DPP decided that arrest was possible only if Knight should try to go abroad: he could not be prosecuted for communications with a foreign agent in view of his having made a partial confession of the transaction. But if he attempted the journey and incriminating documents were found on him, his defence would fall to the ground; if there were no such documents he could be warned and discharged.

On 16 June, Knight was seen by the Superintendent of the dockyard and the gist of Captain Drake's letter was explained to him but he declined to make a statement.

The precautions which had been taken on 14 June were renewed for 21 June, but Knight did not move. He was drinking heavily. The £5 note received by Knight was eventually traced back to a Mr Emile Bunge, a traveller largely connected to the Argentine who had received it from the Banco Espanol on some date subsequent to 3 April 1914. At the time of tracing, Bunge was in Germany and receiving his correspondence forwarded daily through the Banco Espanol. Then came news of Knight's connection with Bubenheim. Knight was placed with Bubenheim on the Search List but there is no record of what happened.

For a moment interest in him revived in November 1914, as a letter, which was eventually traced to Edward Frank Knight of Hayling Island, was at first attributed to E. J. Knight. In July 1917, there was another false scare connecting E. J. Knight with a visit to Ostend in conjunction with

Victor Tewel. It was then ascertained that E. J. Knight had left Gillingham about two and a half years previously, and a former neighbour stated that he joined the army at the beginning of the war. Knight seems to have been in communication with the German Secret Service abroad, both directly through Herpers, and indirectly through Bubenheim and the question arises how he got in touch with Bubenheim. There are various possibilities connected with Herpers, Kolbe and the Rileys.

(a)  W. Herpers first appeared as an organising agent at Portsmouth; it was on his recommendation that William Klare was taken on. Assuming that the name covers one definite personality when Knight got in touch with Herpers, the latter might have handed on the name to his successor, Francis Bubenheim.

(b)  More probable is the second possibility, that the three Kolbes cover the identities of Theisen, Steinhauer and Fels, the chief agents dealt with in these reports. The description of the Kolbes given by Bubenheim do not exactly tally with the appearance of Theisen, Steinhauer and Fels, but descriptions of the same individual vary according to their origin and moreover it is not necessary absolutely to trust Bubenheim.

It seems possible that Kolbe Junior stands for Fels, who was said to be an aviator, who frequently came over to England before the Karl Hentschel fracas, but avoided coming after that affair. It will be remembered that in April and May 1914, he refused to come to England to meet Nellie Riley, so too in June Kolbe Junior found it impossible to come to England to see Bubenheim's drawings of the Short hydroplane.

If Kolbe Junior and Fels were identical, Knight might have been brought to his notice by the Rileys who knew Chatham Dockyard intimately. On the other hand it is possible that the Rileys were directly acquainted with Bubenheim. The following trace is slender but worth mentioning; while at 67a Adelaide Road, Shepherds Bush, Bubenheim was lodging with a Mrs Grandjean, a widow, who had been in occupation since 1913. She had another male lodger whose name was not known.

She left the house in about July 1915. In March 1917, Nellie Riley was stated to be corresponding with a Sergeant Grandjean at Lausanne but nothing was obtained from the check on this correspondence. It is however, interesting that a James E. B. Gray of Aldershot, who may be identical with James Gray of Farnborough received from Vevey a letter signed E.L.S.G. Had this letter been traced and the identity of the recipient verified interesting results might have followed.

Bubenheim and Knight therefore both seem to have somewhat more importance than would appear at first sight. It is singular that both these men simultaneously should appear to be playing a double game. It is impossible to say whether they really meant to betray the Germans or not, both had come down in the world, both were rascals, and both were in need of money and receiving money secretly from Germany after embarking upon and indeed persevering in face of discouragement in negotiations with the British Secret Service. The consequence is that both fell under strong suspicion of having been put up to the job by the Germans, who had suffered severely in the course of the winter of 1913–14.

To sum up from the point of view of German espionage: in the case of Bubenheim, Knight and Gray, we seem to have the nucleus of a fresh organisation with its base in London and built, it is possible, partly out of the shattered organisation that had Chatham and Rochester for its centre. The arrangements made for the arrest of Knight are to be compared with those for shadowing Nellie Riley. They show an advance in method due no doubt to the enhanced appreciation of the difficulties of recognising and shadowing suspects. The tricks of George Parrott and Frederick Gould had not been wasted.

★

The second group of German agents to come under investigation upon the outbreak of war consisted of Adolf Schroeder (alias Frederick Adolphus Gould-Schroeder or Gould, alias Gouldstein, alias Gould-Schivner) and Stephen Horvath.

The duration and intricacy of the investigation of the Adolf
Schroeder/Frederick Gould case, the peculiar interest attaching to the
man himself, and the heavy penalty inflicted upon him render it one of
the most important of the pre-war cases.

There is a mystery about Gould. He impressed those in authority
as one better born and educated than his circumstances would seem
to warrant; he had been accustomed to command and he could hold
his own in the society of gentlemen. But he was a liar, a falsifier, a
blackmailer, a spy. He called himself a good and faithful Prussian and his
correspondence shows that he could bully and sneer but did not cringe.
He had a suspicious temper with men of the humbler class. While in
London he associated with reputable adventurers, but at Rochester, for
the purpose of spying, he sought out and made friends with naval men
of excellent character. He seems always to have been fond of drink but
the police never had occasion to complain of the management of his
business. In his family life, too, there are the same contrasts. To his wife
and eldest son he was callous, but he remained faithful to the artistic,
clever Jewess who took her place, and he was an affectionate father to
the nine children she bore him.

As regards his antecedents everything about him is uncertain, even
his parentage and the date of his birth. A kind of legend grew up about
him. It was stated, for instance, that he was the son of the German
attaché and that his mother was an English woman, but on Schroeder's
marriage certificate, the name and occupation of the father are given
as Carl Ludwig Schroeder, upholsterer, and Schroeder's injured wife
declared that her mother-in-law was a typical German. Jessie Schroeder
of 62 Thornhill Road was one of the witnesses of the marriage.

Search for Schroeder's birth certificate was ineffectual but that does
not prove his foreign origin, for it was not until 1874 that the deposit
of such documents at Somerset House was made compulsory. Gould
stated repeatedly that he was born in Germany in 1854, and that he
came to England in 1858, but in 1884 he gave his age as twenty-six.
The independent testimony of a school-fellow, Carl Bernhard Reimers,
corroborates Gould's next statement: that he went to the German

school in the Savoy. After that, investigation founders in the quicksand of conflicting accounts. He is said to have returned to Germany, or alternatively to France, in 1868 to complete his education. When the Franco-Prussian war broke out, he joined the German Army and served in it three years, as he told his wife, or else twelve years, retiring with the Iron Cross and a captaincy, as he stated when he was applying for a post in 1903.

In this application, he said that he returned to England in 1882 and was employed with a firm of engineers until 1886. He then travelled in Canada for two years, came back to England in 1900, and, after an unsuccessful venture in business, became an agent in the Secret Service. As such he travelled over the greater part of Europe, but the risks proving too great, he retired from the service and returned to commercial life. Most of this statement is false and it leaves the years between 1888 and 1900 unaccounted for. On the other hand, the wife's story passes over in silence the years between 1873 and 1884.

On 11 October 1884 Adolf Frederick Schroeder married Elizabeth Fenton at Holy Trinity Church, Islington. He described himself as a clerk and, according to his wife, he was employed as a furrier's traveller. On 23 September 1887, Mrs Schroeder had a deed of separation drawn up on account of her husband's conduct with Mrs Maud Sloman, whose real name was Rebecca Sloman. She was the daughter of Professor Sloman, a well-known entertainer, and herself performed in public as a whistler. After the separation Schroeder stole and falsified his wife's marriage certificate, substituting the name, Rebecca Solomans, and the date, 11 July 1887, for the original entries. The police furnished a paper drawn up from birth certificates bearing the name and date of birth of six children born of this union between March 1891 and September 1901.

There were besides three elder children: a married daughter, Clara Abbott, Henry and Maud. In the entry of September 1901 the surname appears as Gould Schroeder. If the birth certificates were of British origin this would tend to show that the family was established here from 1891 onwards.

After his conviction Schroeder stated that he was first employed by

Steinhauer in 1890 for espionage against Russia and France; he was to get in touch with necessitous officers and obtain information about hasty mobilisation, armaments, etc. From 1895 to 1908 he said that he directed his activities against Great Britain, naval information being his objective. Letters found in the house in Merton Road, bearing the date 1897, showed that he had than assumed the rank of captain, and that he was engaged in some vague dealings with a brewery not unconnected with friends in Paris. He was also corresponding with the notorious Captain Stephens, who was employed first by the French Secret Service, and then from May 1898 till March 1899 by our own, after which he returned to the French Service.

Schroeder was brought to the notice of our Intelligence Department by the 'O' and 'A' letters written from Paris in 1898. A German named Schroeder, alias Gould, is said to have signed the deed for the sale of the Ryde Hotel which the French staff were to acquire for the purpose of spying in England, but the scheme fell through. He is also said to be trying to levy blackmail on 'A' (Captain Stephens) and to have reported to Berlin that 'A' was a French agent in London. Then Schroeder quarrelled with Stephens, but when Gould-Schroeder transferred his quarters to London they became great friends. In 1902, or early in 1903, he told C. B. Reimers that he was an agent for the Germans and that he had taken the name of Gould.

The next record of him comes from a letter-book which was found at Rochester and handed over to the police in 1914. From this it appears that in May and September 1903 he was at Manchester working as agent for a firm of index-card makers, and was at the same time engaged in the exportation of rifles to Hamburg. His correspondent in that city was a man named Herr Moritz Magnus. At the end of September he quarrelled with Stockalls and came to London where he found employment with the Baby Arc Lamp Company. He took up his residence at Earlsfield and was known to his friends as Captain or Major Schroeder or Captain Gould.

Between 1900 and 1908 he was frequenting Mooney's in the Strand and a public-house in St Martin's Lane where music-hall artists went to gather. More interesting is the evidence of his work for Steinhauer. On 7

October Gould wrote to Steinhauer giving the names and addresses of two necessitous British officers, both of whom had retired long before 1904, who had promised to give information about naval and military matters. Following this up, a week later he acknowledged receipt of Steinhauer's letter, but complained of bad remuneration and declined to act unless £8 were sent him by return.

If we may believe Pierre Theisen, it was in 1904 that the German Secret Service for the navy was created. Its office was at Potsdam and its activities were mainly directed against Great Britain. Jacobs was head of this service and Steinhauer's subordinate, who afterwards worked his way up, and had an office at Rotterdam. Theisen had met him at Brussels. Melville, who was afterwards MO5's agent, had met Steinhauer, then a police official, in 1901 and had been struck with his foreknowledge, possibly obtained through Gould, of Captain Stephen's career.

In 1907 or 1908 Gould spent a month at Leith where he passed as a cigar merchant of the name of Gould-Schivner. He spent money freely on entertaining naval men and he was even photographed with a group of artificers from a torpedo-boat then in port for repairs. He received money by registered post and many telegrams purporting to come from his wife. He was very talkative and an ardent Freemason. In 1908 the Germans seem to have initiated a more vigorous campaign of spying in this country and Gould was probably not very useful in London. For this reason, perhaps, he was encouraged to move to Rochester where, on 24 July, he acquired the license of the Queen Charlotte Hotel, taking possession in the following October. The venture was not a success financially or from the point of view of espionage. Though Mrs Gould appeared at concerts given in the men's quarters of the naval barracks and once performed at a reception given by the Commander-in-Chief to officers of the Japanese Mission, the Goulds obviously could not gain access to the society of officers nor was their hotel of a class to attract them. On the other hand, it was nearer to naval and military quarters than any other public-house and was much frequented by the rank and file. A Lodge of the order of Buffaloes was formed and called the 'Sir Frederick Gould Lodge', and the meetings were held in the Queen Charlotte.

The police noticed that Gould was superior to his work and viewed him with suspicion, meanwhile the Germans gradually dropped him. In March 1911 Gould was borrowing £10 to pay Knight and it was doubtless owing to the desperate state of his finance that Gould wrote the letter which first brought him to the notice of MO5. This letter is dated 13 December 1911 and it is addressed to Steinhauer, Allee zur Sanasouoi 4, Potsdam. The Home Office Warrant placing a check on Steinhauer's correspondence had been taken out in October 1911, consequently Gould's letter was intercepted. From this point onward direct touch with Gould was maintained through his correspondence.

The embarrassment caused to the German Secret Service by the arrest and indiscretion of Grosse was Gould's opportunity for forcing their hand. He wrote complaining of Steinhauer's insulting letter of September, and of the way in which he himself had been shelved, and he threatened to reveal both to the Kaiser and the authorities here, the bungling of Steinhauer and of the Marine-Amt. He hinted that although he had always been a good Prussian, if he were not re-employed he would change sides. He could give information here identifying Petersen with Steinhauer and he could show that he had been given the same address at Ostend as had been given to Schulz. Steinhauer replied, but there is no record of the letter, and on 9 February 1912, Mrs Gould intervened. She reminded Steinhauer of Gould's excellent and discreet services, urged him to arrange for an interview, and pointed out the wonderful opportunities she and her husband enjoyed at Rochester.

Steinhauer must have yielded, for Gould wrote proposing a meeting at Crefeld-am-Rhein and wired on the same day to say he was coming. He wrote for money and sent two other wires urging a reply. All three wires he endorsed with a false name and address. Steinhauer answered the first telegram on 5 May and appointed Cuxhaven as the rendezvous, and subsequently sent a £10 note. Having obtained Gould's address (the HOW for Gould's letters was taken out on 3 May), and direct evidence of his intended treachery, MO5 called upon the Rochester police for help. Early in January steps had been taken to extend the work of the bureau by getting in touch with the police of the boroughs and cities, and on 29 April, the Home Secretary's letter of introduction had been sent to Mr Arnold, Chief Constable of Rochester. He had replied stating his willingness to help and asking for an interview. On 6 May Captain Drake went to Rochester and laid before the Chief Constable his suspicions concerning Gould. Mr Arnold supplied a description of Mr and Mrs Gould which was afterwards verified by Regan. He sent by post a specimen of the handwriting of Gould's son, Joseph, then in the Royal Engineers, as well as confirmation of Gould's intended journey abroad. This had been obtained by a ruse: a policeman had served him with a jury summons, whereupon Gould had declared he was expecting to be called away on business at any moment. Gould was then placed on the SWL under the heading 'Arrest'.

MO5 wrote asking for photographs of Gould, specimens of his handwriting, which were supplied in due course, and any other details that might occur to the police. They asked Mr Arnold to inform them as soon as Gould left Rochester, and to inquire into the identity of Captain Bront or Pront of the SS *Westria*. On 5 May the police forwarded a photograph of Mrs Gould, with the statement that Gould had come to Rochester on 3 October 1908 from some address in Putney, and that his real name was said to be Gouldenstein. Captain Bront or Pront and the SS *Westria* were unknown in the port of Chatham. In reply Captain Drake explained that MO5 believed these names and addresses to be merely a cover used by Gould in communication with a foreign agent. This is a typical instance of the care taken throughout the investigation to keep the police interested in the case and informed of all those circumstances which could be communicated to them, without always revealing the very precise nature of the knowledge in the possession of MO5, of the source from which it has derived.

The interview at Cuxhaven took place between 13 and 17 May, and by Steinhauer's influence Gould was taken on trial for four to six months at the rate of £15 a month. He was to obtain confidential books in use from 1908 up to date and to receive special rates for these. But he was no longer under Steinhauer's orders and henceforward Steinhauer's role was to be that of the friend and adviser who accepts presents from, and might possibly enter upon profitable private business with Gould, but who has nothing to do with espionage.

Gould was put under the orders of F. Schmidt, a so-called banker's agent, whose agent in Berlin directed him to send fortnightly reports under cover to Mme Duller, rue du Theatre 33, Brussels. Schmidt informed Gould that they would both of them be working on their own responsibility and at their own risks. Schmidt would supply funds out of his own pocket, but as he would be paid only by results, he depended upon Gould to furnish material that would bring in good return. He asked whether the letters were to be sent to Gould from Germany, Belgium or England. Concerning the personality of Schmidt, Gould stated afterwards that the name stood for Steinhauer, but he made this statement only after circumstances of his trial had made it obvious that the name was known to our police. It may have been a true statement, but Gould's tone in addressing Schmidt, and Steinhauer's tone in referring to Schmidt, is one of respect. But Schmidt too is a subordinate, who experiences some difficulty in dealing with the Generalstab. It is possible that Steinhauer was playing a double game with Gould, which Gould afterwards discovered.

The correspondence was punctuated by visits abroad and on these occasions Gould seems to have met 'Herr P' or 'Petersen', and not his employer, Schmidt. Only once, in January 1914, did Gould push on to see Schmidt at Cologne after interviewing 'Herr P' at Brussels, and then Schmidt objected. 'Herr P' was identified by the French Sureté Generale as Pierre Theisen, a Belgian in German pay who had done much work in France in the early 1890s, and who may have been connected with Gould then.

He was afterwards made head of the German Secret Service in Brussels and, in 1908, he was said to be directing operations in England and to be coming to England to look for a good agent. He is the Robert Tornow or 'T' of other spy cases, notably the Karl Hentschel case. It is possible that 'Mme Mueller', through whom Gould's reports were to be transmitted to Schmidt, was one of P's numerous aliases. The point is one of importance for Gould objected strongly to cover addresses as delaying matters when immediate action was necessary, and when his very first letter to Schmidt via the Brussels address miscarried (there is no evidence to show that we stopped this letter), he insisted that the agent was untrustworthy, and that the name and address must be altered, and he carried his point by writing direct to Berlin. But whether Mme Mueller stands for Theisen or not, Gould used to meet 'Herr P' at Rotterdam or Brussels, when 'Herr P' would inspect the documents brought, have them photographed, and transmit the photographs to Berlin together with a report of Gould's plans. C. F. Schmidt would then submit them to the authorities, and send to Gould the resulting criticisms and orders.

Other methods of eluding observation were the use of vague general terms and of a cipher code. For specific comments or questions Schmidt would write the significant word in cipher. Gould had accepted the code but was never at pains to use it. Yet he showed considerable nervousness; for his first telegrams he used a false name and address; he refused to notify the despatch of his reports by sending a picture postcard to Brussels, on the ground that this would arouse the suspicion of the postal authorities; when going abroad he repeatedly took steps to conceal his destination from the police. Thus, on his very first journey, he told a policeman he was going to town to sell some whinny, but he was seen directly after on the down platform with luggage labelled for Dover. Acting on the request of MO5, the Rochester police immediately sent warning of Gould's departure and described his appearance; on 17 May they reported his return home.

Meanwhile preventive action went hand in hand with investigation. By reference to the Admiralty, to whom a list of Gould's sons was sent, a report that he had a son serving in the navy was proved to be unfounded. The Rochester police supplied the information that he was with an engineering firm in London.

Concerning Joseph Gould, of the Royal Engineers, MO5 made inquiry of his commanding officer at Chatham, and learned that the man could do no harm where he was but that an early opportunity would be taken to get rid of him. In September 1912 Joseph was moved to Bulford Camp and after his father's arrest he was placed in the reserve.

His origin was known in the regiment and, although he had never given any real cause for suspicion, when war broke out he was left at home and eventually sent out of harm's way to the Gold Coast, and MI5 was informed of his return in July 1918.

Special observation was kept upon Gould, and one of MO5's agents, J. Regan, succeeded in establishing friendly relations with Gould and reported from time to time items of interest; for instance, that Gould was employing one of his sons, aged fifteen, to reproduce drawings obtained from Rotterdam, or that Gould was talking freely about the sums of money spent by Germany in fomenting revolution here.

Gould's first letter to Schmidt was lost in the post, and he wished to write direct to Berlin instead of Brussels. He was ordered to send letters to Paris, but this he declined to do as the delay would be too great. His reports began at the end of June. They were posted to the new cover address: C. Roland, Hotel Stadt Konigsberg, Potsdam, and at CR's request he used for alternate letters 1/2 Brauerstrasse, Potsdam, which was merely another version of the same address. His reports were of a general nature describing the existing discontent and the shortage of men in the navy, as well as incidents in the manoeuvres, and in August CR complained of receiving only newspaper information and threatened to break off relations unless Gould adopted better methods; he must go to Portsmouth as he had suggested (letter of 20 August). Gould replied that he was going to Portsmouth about 7 September. He hoped to obtain full particulars of the new fire director, and the latest gunnery book and he was also in touch with a wireless operator at the Admiralty.

Some letters of Gould's then passed through unnoticed giving particulars of a signals book that he was trying to obtain. Schmidt refused the 1908 Boat and Vocabulary Signals Book and anything not marked 'secret and confidential', he asked for the other part of the book and even wired definitely refusing the part of which Gould had sent details. But Gould carried the day by pointing out that when once he had paid his agent £50 for this book he could 'make him deliver others'.

MO5 noted, incidentally, that the required signal books would all have been kept in the captain's steel safe on a ship, but as they were in constant use on the bridge, access to them was fairly easy. The other part of the book required by Schmidt was no doubt the addenda issued in 1911.

Schmidt at last accepted the book provided it were marked 'secret and confidential' and appointed a meeting in Rotterdam. Accordingly on 10 October Gould wired from Dover Pier arranging for this to take place on Saturday 12 October. The wire was despatched, but a notification of non-delivery was received from Berlin by the office at Dover, and Gould, anxiously waiting in the Hotel Leygraaff at Rotterdam, on the one hand telegraphed to his wife to repeat all messages, on the other hand got into communication with Steinhauer by telephone.

Steinhauer, with difficulty, found C. Roland, who sent £80. Gould apparently submitted the 'sample' for photography and returned home on 17 October. Police Sergeant Andrews identified him as he stepped from the packet at Dover. On the same day CR wrote bitterly disappointed at his purchase: a few pages torn from a book had been foisted on him and the whole thing was worthless. In future Gould must state definitely whether he was offering a whole book or merely a fragment. Rotterdam must remain the place of meeting, as there was no photographic apparatus at Ostend; telegrams must be confirmed and the name Roland must be changed, as it was easily mis-spelt, Gould must write to Paul Beck, Brauerstrasse 1/2, Potsdam.

On 25 October Gould retorted that owing to the delay at Rotterdam immense difficulty had been experienced in returning the sample – but soothingly he added that he hoped to secure from Portsmouth the Torpedo and Gunnery Manual. Schmidt then offered £200 for the Gunnery and Torpedo Manual of 1909 with addenda and £200 for the Annual Report of Torpedo School for the current year. This was afterwards corrected by Steinhauer to 'Theodor Beck'.

Meanwhile, MO5 kept the Admiralty informed of each important point of Gould's progress in September. A list of the staff employed at the Admiralty Wireless Station was obtained and in October the Commander-in-Chief at the Nore was warned that Gould was trying to obtain a confidential book of naval signals. He replied that the necessary precautions would be taken.

On receipt of Schmidt's letter of 26 August, Captain Drake wrote warning the Rochester police that Gould would be going to Portsmouth for ten days and, in order that he might be shadowed while there, they were sending Inspector Savage of Portsmouth Dockyard to Rochester to 'become acquainted with the spy's features'. Inspector Savage went to Rochester, but did not find the police there very helpful, ostensibly because inquiry and observation were impeded by their being so small a body that Gould knew them all by sight. However, Mr Arnold promised to let MO5 know when Gould left the town. Then the Chatham police were asked to help by watching the railway station and the Rochester police were specially warned that Gould might be leaving on 6 September. In spite of these precautions Gould contrived to slip away unobserved; he was missed on the 6th and many anxious messages as to his whereabouts passed between MO5 and Rochester and Portsmouth Dockyard. He was lost – but late in the evening of the 6th he returned and, it was thought, not from Portsmouth, but from Sheerness. Next day he inquired about the Sunday passage via Folkestone and Arnold begged that the Folkestone boat should be watched, but on 10 September Gould was still at home. The police at Folkestone and Dover were directed to give Captain Drake any assistance in their power, and any message they sent to the Central Office was to be telephoned on at once to MO5. Still Gould did not move. On the 30th observation was discontinued by the Rochester police. It was resumed by an agent of MO5 in the first week of October. Arnold, being anxious about Gould's intimacy with the mayor of Chatham on account of the persons whom he might meet at official receptions, consulted MO5 as to the advisability of warning the mayor. MO5 left the Chief Constable to act on his own discretion, but suggested taking no action unless it were absolutely necessary.

Investigation was also started at Chatham since Gould seemed to draw his information from that quarter. The Metropolitan Police were informed that Gould was trying to procure a book of naval signals and the help of superintendent Tett of Chatham Dockyard was asked for particularly with a view to discovering his naval friends there and to watching their movements. Mr Quinn therefore directed Superintendent Tett to give MO5's agent all possible assistance. The Admiralty also were warned of Gould's intentions.

The events of 10, 11 and 12 October are not recorded in Gould's file, and the narrative that follows has been compiled from the papers of the Metropolitan Police. On 10 October, Captain Drake with the Chief Constable of Folkestone called upon Sergeant Everest at the port of Folkestone, and gave him a description of Gould, who might be leaving for Germany and was supposed to be intending to convey abroad a confidential torpedo signals book. The same day, at 4 p.m., Gould's wire to Potsdam appointing a meeting for 12 October, was signalled to the GPO from Dover Pier and next day, Captain Drake with Detective Sergeant Andrews 'from the Secret Service Department' saw the telegraphist to whom Gould had handed the telegram and begged him to take particular note of the sender's appearance with a view to subsequent identification if necessary. (Owing to special circumstances this wire was not included in the evidence against Gould, but at first Captain Drake had intended to call the telegraphist as witness, and had found it advisable to warn the man to avoid any reference to himself and the Secret Service). On 12 October, Captain Drake called at Scotland Yard at 10.30 a.m. to say his agent at Rochester had reported Gould's departure for Folkestone or Dover and he was going to those ports at once to speak to the officers there. At 2 p.m. Captain Stanley Clarke called to ask for the assistance of the police at those ports, as Gould had left Rochester with important documents which he was conveying to a foreign state. Superintendent Patrick Quinn of Special Branch directed the police at Dover and Folkestone to stop and search the man as he was about to embark. But Gould escaped. Regarding this the police records merely say: 'The man was not picked up'. It appears that MO5's agent had seen Gould leave Rochester by rail for Dover on the 11th, and Mrs Gould circulated the story that he had taken one of the children to Dover and had then gone to Leith via Chatham, a story which Captain Drake was able to contradict. It seems probable that Gould suspected he was being watched and contrived to get away in the morning before the police arrangements for his arrest could he completed. Arrangements were made with the Customs to search Gould's baggage (and possibly person) thoroughly on his return but in the interval something must have become known to MO5 about the nature of the book he was conveying abroad, for, on 14 October, Captain Drake wrote to the police that, from information received, Gould would probably have parted with the book he was conveying abroad; he was expecting to return not before Thursday, and it would be better for the Customs not to examine his luggage too closely lest they should arouse his suspicions; but the police were to look at him well so as to recognise him, should he attempt to go abroad again. Sergeant Andrews, however, reported that he had seen Gould disembark at Dover on 17 October, and that Customs examined his baggage closely.

This episode led to a reconsideration of the procedure to be followed in arresting on suspicion. Such arrests would have to be effected by the police, on whom would lie the responsibility of justifying their action, Under Section 6 of the Official Secrets Act, any person reasonably suspected of having committed, or having attempted to commit, or being about to commit, an offence under the Act might be apprehended and detained. It had become apparent by Captain Drake's letter of 14 October that Gould was not carrying valuable information and a doubt arose in Superintendent Quinn's mind as to the validity of police action in such a case. His view was that, by the requirements of the Act, reasonable suspicion must be based on evidence which could be produced in court, and that, failing such evidence, if nothing incriminating were found on the person arrested, a successful action for damages or assault might be brought against the police. Captain Drake's view was that in such a case when the evidence, although not producible in the court, showed that action was imperative in the interests of the state, the police might plead privilege of information supplied by the War Office which it was not to the public interest to disclose. On 24 October the Chief Commissioner decided that he could not give directions to the Commission or police to arrest and search without warrant, persons who were supposed to be carrying some paper or thing which might not be regarded as important by the military authorities, since, in that case, no defence could be put forward in a court of law. But he would, after consultation, take the risks, provided he were satisfied that a particular person were conveying to the agent of some foreign power an instrument or drawing of a highly secret and important nature. In consultation with the Secretary of the Admiralty, the Secretary of the War Office, and the Secretary of the Home Office, MO5 drew up a letter, which should be sent to the DPP whenever circumstances demanded the arrest of some person suspected of conveying information abroad. This letter signed by Sir Graham Greene was first used on 31 October, and in the case of Gould.

The policy of shadowing and arresting Gould could be more easily carried out because on 10 October the Rochester police had at length secured six photographs of him. These MO5 asked Superintendent Quinn to have circulated to the naval ports in case Gould should go there in search of information and the Rochester police were informed that there was no longer any doubt as to the business upon which Gould was engaged.

Following up Sir Graham Greene's letter demanding Gould's arrest, the photograph was also sent to the ports of Queenborough, Dover, Folkestone and Harwich with the information that Gould might shortly attempt to convey abroad secret documents about torpedoes, and in that case, the port to which he was travelling would be notified by a wire signed 'R'; he was to be minutely searched on suspicion of contravening the Official Secrets Act, and if any incriminating documents were found on him, he was to be taken to the local police station; the officer in charge was to be acquainted with the circumstances; the facts were to be telegraphed to headquarters and instructions as to the charge would be sent; special precautions were to be taken that Gould did not destroy any document or piece of paper however small. If nothing incriminating were found, he was to be discharged with an apology, and if he asked any questions, he was to be told that the charge originated with the police.

This was followed by a memorandum to the effect that Gould might succeed in slipping away from his house unobserved and the police must therefore keep a sharp look-out for him and act on their own initiative in carrying out the instructions already received. Evidence against the man might also be found at his house. Mr Melville was therefore sent to Rochester to arrange with the Chief Constable for a search of Gould's premises, which was to be carried out as soon as intimation had been received of his arrest. The search could be made either under a warrant signed by a Justice of the Peace or, in extreme urgency, under an order signed by the police authority report. Three days later Mr Melville reported that these arrangements had been made, that police officers from Queensborough, Folkestone and Harwich had been to Rochester to look at Gould and P. S. Andrews of Dover had also seen him. The importance of the matter had been impressed upon all these officers. In reply Captain Kell sent to the Chief Constable at Rochester a copy of the telegram upon which he would have to take action. Meanwhile, following up clues supplied by the Rochester police, efforts to establish Gould's identity had been made in London, but no trace of the name of Gould or Guldenstein was found on the special register of the Criminal Investigation Department or on the General Register of the Home Office, nor could either name be found in the Naturalisation Lists.

The next period of the correspondence is from October 1912 to September 1913 when Schmidt broke off relations with Gould. During the autumn and winter of 1915 the letters reflect the turmoil caused by the Balkan War and the nervousness which resulted from the arrest of Parrott on 15 November 1912, and his trial on 11 January 1913. A new factor appears in the correspondence; Gould obtains an aide who supplies him with reports. This involves additional work in the conduct of the investigation as these reports have to be traced to their source.

On 28 October, Gould who had scoffed at the cover address used by the German Secret Service, now asked to be written to via London. After his journey abroad in December, Schmidt wrote to him through August Klunder, and, as an additional precaution, the letters were addressed to Gould under an alias which was frequently changed. Besides this, the opening sentence of the letter would imply that the recipient was only temporarily at Rochester. The aliases used were: John Steffenson, George Allen, Stuart Moore, George Parker, Charles Graham and Charles Schattock.

C. F. Schmidt also changed his own cover address and directed Gould to write via the bankers, Broker & Wirth, 46 rue du Congres,

Brussels. But Gould had a rooted objection to any address in Brussels; he took no notice, at first, then he was told to go on writing to the old address; then he adopted the new address, under protest presumably, for Schmidt wrote in some annoyance to say that the address given was quite unremarkable and the only other at his disposal in Brussels was the one (Muller, rue du Theatre) which Gould had refused.

Moreover, in December Schmidt prepared an improved code and invented a scheme to enable Gould to draw money if war broke out. Both of these were to be communicated at a meeting at Rotterdam, but eventually the code was sent by post. From 28 October onwards, the report are full of rumours connected with hasty mobilisation and, on 15 December Schmidt asked definitely whether there were no signs in the dockyard of special preparation for war. But throughout the eleven months of the period in question Schmidt's chief objective was the Torpedo Manual and his insistence upon getting it shows the importance the German Staff attached to it.

On 15 November Gould enclosed with his own letter a report, signed 'T', written in a strange handwriting and giving information about certain nucleus crew ships, the equipment of certain vessels with rapid mine-sweeping gear, and the arrival at Sheerness of two 9.2 guns for land defence. Schmidt had been on the point of terminating the contract, but the effect of this letter was immediate; mine-sweeping gear was about as interesting to the Germans as torpedoes. He wrote thanking Gould for the most interesting reports just received, and suggested he should spend more time and trouble on procuring information; a permanent appointment depended upon this. A few days later he begged his 'Dear Brother-in-law' to meet him at Rotterdam but Gould, hoping to get samples from Portsmouth, put off the meeting till Friday 6 December. Schmidt accepted that date and asked Gould to wire if he were bringing samples so that arrangements could be made for photographing them.

Though unrecorded in the file, it is clear from Schmidt's next letter that Gould did wire to put off the photographer and consequently went abroad unhindered. After his return from Rotterdam, Schmidt wrote that it was to be regretted that Gould had had to put off 'Herr P' on account of his friends having been unable to come but 'Herr P' had given 'good hopes for this month', and three times in succession did Schmidt write urgently demanding completion of this business, but in vain. Gould ascribed his failure to the paralysing nervousness caused by the 'Gunner's' (George Parrott's) trial. Then Schmidt offered £400 for the 1911 edition of the Report of Torpedo School. This was double the price he had offered in October 1912 (to Klare whose letters about obtaining this report were at that moment being delayed in Germany). Meanwhile, though unsuccessful in obtaining information about torpedoes, Gould had pursued minor objects. His informant had supplied him with details and diagrams of mine-sweeping gear and methods in use in the navy, details and diagrams of the defences of the Medway and particulars of the structure and place of storage of the Sheerness boom defence. And on 25 January came details and diagrams of the Dover defences with especial reference to the boom defence. All this information was allowed to go through as it was not of sufficient importance to require confiscation and MO5 wished to keep their hands free to deal with Gould.

Besides this he held out hopes of getting details of the Percy Scott Fire-Director. The importance attached to obtaining this information is shown by reports received at Scotland Yard and at the Admiralty. A journalist told the police that on some date previous to 10 January 1913, a German journalist, Fred Manasse, had asked him to procure details of the fire-director, and had read a list of points concerning which he required highly confidential information which had not appeared in the press. On the 15 January 1913 the Admiralty was informed that a lady had been approached by a German of her acquaintance, who asked her to help him procure one of the sights connected with the Percy Scott Range-Finder; three other men were working for him with the same object in view and success might bring in a sum of £800. Finally in the same letter in which Schmidt offered £400 for the Torpedo School Report, he asked for a sketch and precise details of the new fire director and for details of the fire control fitted on the *Thunderer*.

The record of the investigation during November and early December shows that MO5, being satisfied that Frederick Gould was not obtaining valuable information, now tried to put in practice a policy which had been successful in the case of George Parrott, but, owing to the cleverness of the professional spy, they failed.

During November Gould was reported to have changed his habits and to be attending closely to his business; he seldom left the house which was less resorted to by naval men than formerly. When Regan was sent to relieve Melville he found that Gould was inventing another pretext for a trip abroad; moreover conversation at the public-house showed that the Goulds knew George Parrott, their friend Jack Shepherd had said he knew Parrott had been shadowed abroad three times, and Gould was silent and anxious.

Then the correspondence showed that Gould might be going abroad, hence on 28 November, four ports were warned and two officers were sent from Scotland Yard to shadow him on his trip but they were recalled the following day. On 3 December Regan reported that a dinner and smoking concert which was to have taken place on Friday 6 December, had been postponed till 20 December, and he thought Gould would cross on 5 December; subsequently he noted that the daughter had just posted a letter.

On 4 December as the journey seemed imminent, the police at the ports were informed that Gould might be going abroad in a few days, but, as he would not be carrying incriminating documents, he must not be stopped, nor must the two police officers who would probably be shadowing him, be recognised. These two officers were again sent to Rochester and together with MO5's two agents, Regan and Fitzgerald, they kept close watch on Gould until 11.30 p.m. on Wednesday 4 December. On 6 December Regan missed him at the bar, and ascertained from the wife that Gould was 'upstairs sleeping off the effects of a rough night'. This being reported to MO5, the two officers were recalled to Scotland Yard. Then, on the 7th, a report was received from Sergeant Sandercock of Harwich that Gould had crossed to Rotterdam on the 8th and had returned that day. When Regan called at the Queen Charlotte on the 7th and 8th, there were signs that the family suspected the house was being watched. He had cleverly eluded the police for the third time.

The leakage continued. Schmidt had sent a fresh cipher code on 24 January, this was followed up by a long questionnaire, covering a immense field of naval armaments which was completed, at Gould's special request, by questions on tactics, to which Schmidt added one question, supplementary to the long list, on the Percy Scott Fire-Control. Besides this, as a connection to Gould's nervousness perhaps, Schmidt asked him to submit the name of some person who would procure books of fleet signals and fighting instructions. Schmidt would approach him cautiously and Gould would incur no risk. Subsequently Schmidt offered £25 for the name of any deck officer who would be willing to work for him.

On 25 February Gould sent answers to questions 1, 4, 6, 11, 11a, 12b, 26, 28, 34a of the questionnaire; on 7 March answers to questions 34 (n) 34 (o) and 35 with some information about mine-sweeping on 18 March he stated that the fire director was not quite satisfactory, but was to be submitted to severe tests after Easter. On 28 March he sent answers to Nos. 3, 4, 5, 6; on 7 April he sent answers supplied by his informant to questions Nos. 3, 7, 8, 9, 10 of the questionnaire. In this letter too reference is made to a particular book dealing with torpedoes which has 'a couple of items about fire control'.

In spite of all this work Schmidt was dissatisfied and again threatened to break off relations with Gould, who had spoken of a special secret surveillance exercised by the authorities in England. But Gould mollified him somewhat by offering for sale a torpedo drill book, edition of 1913. This was not a confidential book but it was issued to officers and instructors only. Gould offered to convey it abroad together with the Admiralty chart of the Medway. Schmidt wished to see the book at Rotterdam or Ostend, which seems to imply that facilities for photographing documents had been set up there. Then he wrote that the book and the chart were of little use but he would like them to be sent by post. But Gould's man had to account for the things – or the loss of them – on Monday, and the only way was for him to obtain week-end leave from Devonport, and bring them to Rochester. Gould pressed the purchase saying 'the Thing is full of useful information', and Schmidt at length agreed to a meeting at Rotterdam, Hotel de France, on 3 May. Gould went and returned via Folkestone on the 5th. At that meeting a quarrel must have taken place, for on 16 May Gould writes that he is leaving for London on 24 May; he is being blackmailed at Rochester; he has a good offer of work in London but he could act as postbox for the German Secret Service. At the same time he has hopes of getting a sample. After consultation with 'Herr P', Schmidt agreed to prolong the contract for three months, but he insisted that Gould must go to Devonport. Whereupon Gould postponed the transfer of his business, promised to go to Devonport and on 5 June offered a sample for the following week. Schmidt hoped it would prove of more value than the last and told Gould to travel direct via Harwich. But Gould never went, he had not even seen the book although he declared he had been twice to Devonport, and he sent misleading information about torpedoes. On 6 September Schmidt wrote finally to break the contract, but he told Gould that should he ever obtain anything of value, he was to write to the address in Potsdam as the Brussels address was no longer available. Gould replied that he was leaving Rochester as soon as possible.

During this period the chief objects of MO5 were to identify Gould's informants and to protect Admiralty secrets from being tampered with. This involved correspondence with the Admiralty and naval officers, which must now be dealt with, together with certain facts in the correspondence, which it was more convenient to reserve for this special chapter than to mention in their chronological order.

Since early October of 1912, efforts had been made to find out the names and occupations of Gould's naval friends and one of the first names submitted was that of 'Billy' Knight, a carpenter's mate. He was a Chief Petty Officer attached to HMS *Actaeon*, at Sheerness Dockyard. At first suspicion fell on this man and an effort was made to identify him as the writer of the letters. Specimens of the handwriting were sent through the Commander-in-Chief at the Nore to the captain of the *Actaeon*, who returned them saying he had been unable to connect them with anyone on the ship. Regan however had previously reported 'Billy' Knight's recent retirement from the service, and that it was said he intended to settle at Devonport, his birthplace. The inquiry was therefore not pursued.

A better clue was afforded by the letter which contained a sketch of Dover defences. Inquiry elicited the fact that, on 19 December 1912, a party of six riggers had been sent from Sheerness to help in fitting the nets of the Dover boom defence and Captain Kell guessed that the culprit would be one of those employed on this work. But specimens of handwriting obtained from this group of men were insufficient to prove identity and further specimens could not be procured without causing remark. For a long time suspicion rested on George William Shepherd (the Admiralty form), Gunner, known as 'Jock or Jack Sheppard', an intimate friend of Gould, and a First Class Petty Officer attached to HMS *Pembroke*, the stores department of Chatham Dockyard. However, there was some doubt as to the man's name. The police at Chatham identified the photo as that of George William Shepherd, Gunner, and the 'trace' from the Royal Navy Barracks, at Chatham, gives the name, George William Shepherd, adding the private address used by Jock or Jack Sheppard. Regan also identified the photo as that of Jack Sheppard but Commander Booth Allen of HMS *Pembroke* wrote of him as Petty Officer Sheppard. There was also a petty officer named George Howard Sheppars who may have been identical with George W. Shepherd, as the trace of the two men were strikingly alike.

In answer to Schmidt's request, Gould had submitted this man's name and photograph stating that he would do anything for money if he were cautiously approached. When employed in the Stores Department he had embezzled to the extent of £2 a week and now he was moved to other work he was very poor. Schmidt at once wrote to George Sheppard (the form of the name used by Gould) but he concealed his connection with Gould, signing under the name Alexandropf, and giving the address as the Palace Hotel in Lucerne. He said he could offer him a means of earning money easily and suggested that Sheppard should send an address to which particulars could be forwarded without risk. Sheppard, fearing a trap (his remarks about Parrott have been quoted already), did not answer but showed the letter to Gould, who wrote rebuking Schmidt for his bad English and want of caution. Then Schmidt wrote again and enclosed £1 as earnest of his intentions. Sheppard showed this letter to Commander Booth Allen of HMS *Pembroke*, and so somewhat tardily cleared his character.

Up to the end of April, however, Captain Drake thought that Sheppard was the purveyor of news and documents to Gould, and made the usual inquiries at the office of the Commander-in-Chief, the Nore.

Schmidt's acceptance of the torpedo drill book led to the identification of the writer of Gould's reports, for when Schmidt's telegram had come through, Gould immediately wired to Thomas James Mott to meet him that night. Now Mott's name was on the list of men who had been sent to Sheerness to rig the boom at Dover.

On 30 April Captain Kell informed Mr Pullen of the discovery made and asked whether Mott was a position to disclose anything of importance. Mott, a former Torpedo Coxswain had been employed for about a year in the dockyard. The question of how to handle the case was discussed with the Superintendent of the dockyard. It was agreed to keep him on without any remark but to take steps that he should not be employed on any confidential work. Later on he seems to have been kept so busily at work that he had no time to meet Gould – if we may believe Gould's statement – and in any case the precautions taken were successful for Mott wrote on 25 August confessing to Gould that he had failed miserably. It has been shown already that the information he supplied to Gould was not valuable, nor could certain definite references made to the contents of the book offered for sale in April be traced to any torpedo book known to Captain Villiers, HMS *Actaeon*.

Mott's name was put on the SWL for Kent, the police kept some watch upon his movements, and the naval authorities were specially warned when Gould was proposing to put special pressure on Mott in order to save his own reputation. In February 1914, Sir Graham Greene was warned that in view of Mott's connection with Gould it would be wise to move him from his station and after Gould's conviction the question of the man's discharge from the dockyard was again mooted, and the further question arose as to whether in that case he should be told the grounds of his discharge. But because intercepted correspondence could not be produced as evidence and Mott might deny the charge and get his case taken up publicly, it was agreed not to interrogate him but to frighten him thoroughly. A semi-official letter drafted by MO5 and initialed by the Secretary of the Admiralty was sent to the Commander-in-Chief at the Nore, requesting him to instruct the Superintendent of Sheerness Dockyard to send for Mott and tell him that in the course of investigations it had been discovered that he had been in touch with a foreign agent under gravely suspicious circumstances, and that to communicate information to a foreign power was a felony punishable with seven years' imprisonment. He was to be invited to make a signed statement after being duly cautioned that the authorities might use it against him. This policy was successfully carried out and on 30 April Mott signed a statement denying everything.

Another man in touch with Gould was J. M. Pinkard of HMS *Cyclops*, a repair ship. From the 'trace' of his services by the Admiralty it appeared that his conduct was very good; he was intelligent and might be very useful to the enemy if he were not trustworthy. MO5 wrote asking that he should be kept under observation by the police of Chatham Dockyard and he was placed on the SWL for the army and navy. On 19 February 1914 his name was submitted to Sir Graham Greene with the suggestion that he should be removed from his station on account of his connection with Gould. As regards preventive action concerning the care of official documents, it will suffice to note once and for all the principle followed by MO5: as soon as they had particulars of the photos or maps offered to Schmidt, inquiry was made of the naval authorities as to the value of these objects and a warning was given as to Gould's intentions. During this period the police reported Gould's various items of interest connected with Gould's children; Maud, for a short time, was a barmaid in a small public-house at Folkestone; Adolphus was at work in the Haymarket and living with an elder brother Henry, at Clapham. Gould, changing his habits, was going out at night, in the direction of Chatham and coming home the worse for drink.

Since Gould had grown suspicious of Regan, another special

agent was sent down to report and he, as well as the Rochester police, discovered that Gould was intimate with a German-Swiss of the name of Klocken-Busch who had lived in Chatham for twenty years.

In May the Rochester police reported the removal to London of the whole family, with the exception of Gould and his daughter Violet, and, through an intercepted wire, MO5 obtained their town address, 340 Merton Road in Wandsworth. Gould stayed on at the Queen Charlotte, occasionally going to London for a few days while Mrs Gould took his place at Rochester. Then towards the end of October the police noted signs of Gould's approaching departure. He was having a hundred cards printed with a notice to the effect that he was sole agent in Kent for John Brown's Whiskies – and the police knew of no such brand in Kent.

Gould moved to London on 30 December 1913 and MO5 were acquainted with the fact by the postmaster and the Chief Constable of Rochester. Shortly after, the Chief Constable forwarded to MO5 two books which had been found in the Charlotte after Gould's departure. One of these was a press copy containing a number of letters written by Gould during the years 1903 and 1904. The reference already made to this book in the reconstruction of Gould's part are sufficient proof of the value of this find.

In January 1914 Gould resumed relations with Schmidt at the Hotel Stadt Konigsberg, Potsdam. Writing from Wandsworth that he had found a good chance for a 'sample' he begged for an interview in order that he might unfold his plans. Schmidt answered from Cologne, where his office had been established for some months, suggesting that Gould should go to Brussels on the 23rd, provided he had discovered a better source of supply than the last. Gould went to Brussels, but apparently also pushed on to Cologne, whence he wrote to Steinhauer urging, presumably, that a questionnaire should again be sent to him. For Steinhauer replied: 'For the present I must get Mr P's opinion, before that it would be no use to send you a request, that does not all go quite so quickly as you think'. And Schmidt wrote on 29 January, enclosing a duplicate of the questionnaire of February 1913, in accordance with Gould's request to Herr P; he added emphatically that Gould was to start on his journey only after hearing from Germany and to go only to the place indicated.

The cover address given by Herr P. was Madame Mueller, Pachecostrasse 81, Brussels. Gould's first letter dated 29 January to this address slipped through the post unnoticed for there is no trace of it in the file and C's men were directed to inquire. It was an important letter offering certain drawings for, on 5 February, Schmidt replied that he would give only £10 for the 'pictures' as they were too old. Gould was to go to Brussels on Friday 13 February. Meanwhile, Gould seems to have intended to enter upon some strange business conducted in collusion with Steinhauer and a man named Austin Fryers, director of the British Cinema Productions. While still at Rochester Gould acting with Austin Myers had been engaged in a very questionable attempt to wrest money from Mr Forde Ridley, formerly the MP for Rochester. Gould offered to procure for him a knighthood or baronetcy, and demanded the payment of certain fees to the officials who would exert influence in his favour. Mr Forde Ridley did not covet this honour and in some alarm broke off the interview. Then Gould and Austin Fryers turned their attention in another direction.

On 29 January 1914, two letters addressed to Steinhauer and apparently bearing on business connected with the British Cinema Productions were intercepted in the post. In the first Austin Fryers mentioned Gould as his introducer and approached Steinhauer with the suggestion that he should secure for the British firm exclusive rights over German films and in exchange the firm would send good English films to Germany. In the second F. A. Gould-Schroeder, writing on note-paper of the British Cinema Productions Ltd., announced that a letter addressed to Major Schroeder was lying at the post office. Steinhauer was to fetch it and 'read it carefully and perhaps some good business might come of it'.

After Gould's arrest the DPP was asked to examine the question of Gould's connection with Austin Fryers, but the inquiry elicited little of importance; Austin Fryers was said to be connected with speculative concerns and to have a small office in Shaftesbury Avenue; he associated with theatrical people and had no influence in Court circles. And the question remained unsolved as to whether the business proposals to Steinhauer were genuine and for his private advantage, or whether it was connected with some new scheme for conveying information out of the country.

The rest of the correspondence was taken up with haggling for better terms with Schmidt who wired on 9 February offering £30. Gould could supply charts of Bergen and Spithead and a 'pilot' chart, as well as a cruiser drawing and gunnery drill book of 1909 and he asked first £80, then £60 for the collection. Schmidt wired again curtly: 'For thirty' which Gould accepted. His wife would convey them abroad passing under the name of Mrs Jackson – but they were to ask no questions of her.

On 9 January, as already stated, the Rochester police forwarded to MO5 the letter-book containing damning evidence that could be produced in court, and the authorities began preparations for the arrest of Gould. Statements of his movements were prepared and he was specially kept under observation. He was allowed to go to Cologne unimpeded, the police at the ports being merely instructed to watch for him and report his passage.

On 6 February a letter from Sir Graham Greene demanding Gould's arrest was sent to the Chief Commissioner of Police; on 9 February the police at the ports of Folkestone, Dover, Queensborough and Harwich were referred to the memorandum of 1 November and warned to keep watch for Gould and a description of him was also sent to Gravesend; on 13 February sworn information was laid before the magistrate at Bow Street and a search warrant was taken out against Frederick Gould otherwise known as Major Schroeder; on 18 February the police were requested to watch all trains arriving at Sheerness during the next few days as Gould was expected to be going there to fetch confidential documents.

On 19 February Mr Hetherston of the GPO's Investigation Branch gave special orders that a particular letter addressed to Gould was not to be intercepted in the post but the time of delivery was to be reported when returning the order. This letter was delivered to Wandsworth in the 8.55 p.m. delivery on 19 February. MO5 must then have known that Gould was in possession of a particular incriminating document. On 21 February the police at Chatham Dockyard and at the Admiralty

Pier, Dover were instructed that if Gould or his wife attempted to leave England the following day they were to be stopped and special care was to be taken to prevent destruction of any documents, or communications passing from the one to the other.

Mrs Maud Gould was arrested in the Continental train for Dover at Charing Cross on the afternoon of 22 February 1914 after the police had ascertained that she had taken her ticket to Ostend and Melville had surprised her into admitting her identity. Lying on the seat of the carriage and concealed by her rug were three envelopes containing the gunnery drill book, the charts of Bergen and Spithead and the cruiser drawings. On her way to the police station at Bow she tore up a scrap of paper unnoticed by the police, but the pieces were seen and picked up when she dropped them on leaving the cab. The fragments were pieced together but as some of them were missing the message so recovered was incomplete. It ran 'Petersen', 'Pacheo', 'arrival in ssels'.

Mrs Gould was searched and detained at the station. A return ticket to Ostend was found on her. When the charge of having committed an offence under the Official Secrets Act was read over to her, she denied all knowledge of the nature of the documents she was carrying; she said she was taking them to Ostend and then to Brussels, and that she tore up the address to which she was going.

The same afternoon F. A. Gould was arrested and searched at his house. The photograph of Steinhauer, posted at Potsdam on 13 February, and also the two telegrams of the 9th from Schmidt were found on him. The premises were searched and there were found a quantity of letters with the date 14 February written on them in ink; also the falsified marriage certificate. There were besides some letters and postcards in German signed 'St.' and the list of thirty-eight questions.

A search was instituted at the Queen Charlotte and a portfolio full of ordnance charts of the coasts – especially of County Galway and Wales – and river estuaries and five plans of railway stations in London was discovered by the Rochester police. The Goulds were brought up at Bow Street on 23 February, they were remanded till 25 February and again till 11 March. Mrs Gould was let out on bail.

Meanwhile, Captain Drake in consultation with the DPP, Sir Charles Matthews, set about the preparation of the case sifting the evidence so as to ensure conviction while concealing the existence of a counter-espionage organisation, the methods employed and the amount of information regarding the German Secret Service acquired by that organisation. The work involved many consultations with Sir Edward Troup of the Home Office. The point to be settled was the extent to which use should be made of the mass of evidence procured under Home Office Warrant for opening Gould's correspondence. It was decided to limit the evidence produced in court to that which would have been retained under the ordinary usage of the GPO, to telegrams dating back not more than two months, and to receipts for registered packets dating back not more than two years. The mass of correspondence and the letter-book found at Merton Road and the Queen Charlotte could also be produced. Of these documents the two letters to Steinhauer from the letter-book, showing that Gould was procuring agents for the Germans and accepting commissions from them in 1904, the letter to Mr MacMaster of 1903 giving details of Gould's past history were put in evidence, and also Schmidt's telegrams of 9 and 19 February.

An official from the accountant's department of the GPO was to be subpoenaed to produce the receipts for registered postal packets despatched from Berlin and also the telegram of 19 February. The arrest naturally caused great excitement and many persons came forward voluntarily and made statements to the police. Most of this testimony has been mentioned in the course of this narrative, for instance that of Carl Reimers in which Gould condemned himself out of his own mouth. Reimers was to be called at the trial.

An effort was made to trace the purveyor of the incriminating documents. Suspicion fell on Harry Schroeder, who had been employed from 2 to 6 February on heating apparatus in the basement of Block 4 of the Admiralty. He had been discharged on 6 February but had been seen by a man, who had known and suspected Frederick Gould as far back as 1910 or 1911, coming out of the Admiralty on 20 February. No proof however of Harry's complicity was obtained but the inquiry elicited a severe comment from the Secretary of the Admiralty who pointed out how little care was taken by the Office of Works to select suitable men to carry out repairs in government offices.

Evidence was also collected on the value of the documents found in Gould's possession. The maps and charts found at the Queen Charlotte were submitted to an expert, who stated they were non-confidential and could be bought by the public, but taken as a whole the collection indicated that the owner was particularly interested in ports, harbours and railways of vital strategic importance.

William Llewellyn, a staff clerk in the Admiralty's hydrographic department, was to identify and appraise the charts found on Mrs Gould: the chart of Spithead labelled: 'This chart is to supersede No. 394 which latter is to be destroyed in the presence of the captain. 594. Spithead Skeleton. No. 17, Folio No. 1'; and a chart of the approaches to Bergen marked Skeleton Index No. 10. Folio No. 12. These he identified as Admiralty property by their peculiar linen backing and by the labels attached to them. Once Admiralty property they would remain Admiralty property for all time. They had been issued to one of HM ships or to a chart depot in one of the dockyards. The chart of Spithead was in official custody in December 1912 and almost certainly as late as October 1915. The Bergen chart had been in the Admiralty at Whitehall, through a chart depot, and on a ship. It was in official custody in July 1910 and possibly as late as October 1913. Copies of both charts could be bought from a map-seller for the use of the Mercantile Marine or of yacht-owners.

Louis Rivers Croisdale, engineer in the Commander-in-Chief's department at the Admiralty was to identify the print copy of an Admiralty tracing of an unarmoured cruiser. This was a confidential document and the property of the Admiralty. The original tracing was in use from March 1909 till the end of 1911 and the print was used in connection with the building of two ships in 1909, and of two others in 1910. The last two were completed in 1913 and the print showed the general arrangement of the main and auxiliary machinery in the ship with certain essential features of the design of the ship. Three sections of the vessel were shown illustrating important points of the design. Twenty copies of the print had been prepared, a number sufficient to issue to firms together with the invitation to tender for the contracts, while retaining enough for official use. Fifteen copies had been issued to ship-building on the express understanding that they were to be kept secret and these were all returned.

Evidence concerning the questionnaire was to show that the answers would be of the most confidential nature dealing with the latest developments of guns, armaments, torpedoes, mines, and kindred matters. Only one who had technical knowledge and was in close touch with recent developments in our navy could have framed them. Besides this, police evidence was to be called dealing with Gould's journeys abroad in May, October and December 1912; with the search for documents establishing Gould's identity; and to establish the finding of documents at both houses. Also evidence of private persons connected with the transfer of the Queen Charlotte and, the agreement for the occupation of the house in Merton Road. Besides the preparation of the case, MO5 set on foot various subsidiary inquiries. The banknotes received by Gould were traced but no fresh discoveries resulted; a list of the names of Gould's sons was sent to the Admiralty and the names of his naval friends were supplied to the Director of Public Prosecutions; an enquiry was instituted into the nature of Gould's relations with Lieutenant Herbert Stokes, Royal Navy of HMS *Natal*; a photograph of Gould was sent to the French Sureté Generale who identified 'Petersen' as Pierre Theisen; communications were also received from the Belgian Sureté Generale with regard to this man.

Finally, Frederick and Maud Gould were charged on 5 March, with Sir Archibald Bodkin prosecuting, the hearing was resumed on 11 March. Counsel for the defence urged that there was no evidence to prove that the accused had obtained the documents but only that they were in possession of them. The charge should therefore be one of misdemeanour and not of felony. Both the accused were committed for trial, the woman being allowed bail as before.

The trial took place at the Old Bailey on 3 April before Mr Justice Atkin. Frederick Gould pleaded guilty to the charge of having feloniously obtained and attempted to communicate certain plans and information calculated and intended to be useful to an enemy. The Attorney-General summarised the evidence already given in the magistrate's court and submitted for the judge's perusal the questionnaire, which it was not considered advisable to read or discuss in public. The defence was that Gould had never admitted being a spy; that the maps found at the Queen Charlotte were harmless and had been bought at a sale for half a crown; that only two of the documents found at Gould's house were of a dangerous nature and they had been deposited there for some person who was to call for them.

Gould was sentenced to six years' imprisonment with a recommendation for deportation at the end of his sentence. In passing sentence the judge laid stress upon the abuse of the hospitality of this country committed by Gould and the iniquity of his methods in luring necessitious officers to betray their country.

Maud Gould pleaded not guilty to a charge of receiving information and the charge was withdrawn as there was insufficient evidence to prove that she knew what she was doing, Gould was imprisoned at Brixton and while there made various statements to obtain mitigation of his sentence. But Captain Drake doubted his information on any point. In Maidstone Prison, Gould was able to identify only the vocabulary signals book, small size, and the old economic code, then obsolete, as having been sold to Germany in 1911. He also stated that Klockenbusch of Southend and an engineer named Percy King should be watched, and some observation was kept on the family. Harry Schroeder went first to Newport, Monmouthshire, then abroad and Mrs Gould returned to the stage. In February 1915 she spent some days with a troupe at Dover, but there was no reason for interfering with her. She corresponded with her husband in the most affectionate terms and appears to have hoped that he might be released in October 1918. This however, was not allowed and directions were given that her correspondence should be carefully watched. Some enquiry was also made about Frederick Charles Schroeder, the son of Gould's wife, Elizabeth Fenton, but there was no ground for suspicion.

In summing up the Gould case we may distinguish points that concern the case alone and points that arise in relating it with other cases. The investigation was of enormous length and involved an extraordinary number of officials, inclucing the police at Rochester, Chatham, Portsmouth, Harwich, Dover and London, and post office officials at Rochester, Dover and presumably London. Such an investigation gave opportunities for disagreement on the part of the several authorities involved and for leakage.

MO5 were scrupulously courteous and conciliatory; they made every effort to ensure harmonious co-operation with every department, and also between the several branches of the constabulary engaged in the enquiry. Yet there are traces of a difference of opinion between MO5 and the central police authorities on the question of arrest on suspicion, such a difference perhaps, as arises naturally from the different training and outlook of the military and the police. The military background of MO5 may constitute a difficulty in dealing with the spy cases: such a possibility should at least be kept in view. On the other hand, there seems to have been some friction between the police of Rochester and of Portsmouth Dockyard, the latter being under the Metropolitan Police.

There may have been no leakage, and probably was none, but the case illustrates the extraordinary difficulty of police observation. In a big town the prey escapes, in a small town the hunt is seen and guarded against. Moreover, with such a network of spying as the Germans had organised, any special measures taken at any danger-spot, such as a dockyard or port, would be noted and reported. Consequently a long investigation is to be avoided both on the score of expense and difficulty. MO5 tried to close on Gould many times; he evaded them easily showing an expert knowledge of his trade. In conclusion, several points arose from grouping the cases. It seemed the spies knew each other and each other's work, in their own centre and in different centres.

The case is the last in a long series. The evidence collected in the study of the series seems to prove that, contrary to what was supposed, the spy was not isolated; he did not act in ignorance of what others of his own grade were doing; he knew not only spies working in his own neighbourhood but those in distant fields. How else should Parrott have recognised Klare at Ostend and what was the meaning of Gould, who was a failure at Rochester, being repeatedly told to go to Portsmouth and Devonport? Besides, we have, in various assertions of the spies, evidence that seems to prove they pooled their experiences. This, of course, might not take place directly but indirectly through the German spy-master.

As evidence of direct communication between spies we have a link connecting Lozel with Karl Hentschel and Hentschel with the Rileys and Parrott with Wittstruck and with Gould in the Chatham district and with Klare in the Portsmouth district; Gould with Klockenbusch at Chatham and with Kronauer in London (and possibly also Kent); Wittstruck with Kronauer and Ernst; Grosse seems to have had some connection with Kronauer and a question that needs answering is why did Patricia Hentschel assume the name of Howarth? That was the name of a firm at Singapore which had employed Grosse on his discharge from prison; this form of the name sometimes also is used by mistake for Horvarth and Howard.

The evidence seems to prove that the business of spying like any other business becomes a family affair; the action of the Germans in supporting the families of their victims who came to grief tends to make it hereditary, while normal pressure tends to make it spread collaterally.

MO5 laid great stress on obtaining information as to a suspect's friends and associates. The police were not always able to supply this and it may be asked whether it might not have paid to act on the assumption that a suspect in a district was a friend of and working with, a known spy in that district and to give the police a hint to work on the lines of such an assumption. Possibly, too, the Home Office Warrants might have been extended in that direction. Mrs Riley, for instance, had been definitely asked to send her letters through the intermediary of some friend and while the Gould correspondence is on the whole admirably complete, that of Parrott and the Rileys is not. Wittstruck's correspondence might possibly have supplied some valuable information with regard to the Chatham and Sheerness group.

After Frederick Gould's arrest his true name was established by a London County Council Inspector who had discovered it on one of the Gould children's birth certificates. He brought the fact to the notice of the police and called their attention to another case of the same kind that had occurred in his district. The children of a foreigner named Horvath attended school under the name Howard. In years gone by the Horvaths had lived in the district and had frequently visited the Continent. They had then left Southfields and gone to Golder's Green. They were supposed to be friendly with the Goulds and had returned to the district and gone to live at 297 Wimbledon Park Road, at about the time the Goulds went to Merton Road. Horvath was reserved and resentful of official interference; at the time of Gould's arrest he was harassed by business worries. No enquiry seems to have been made but Horvath's name was put on check. He was found to be corresponding with Berlin, to be receiving by parcel post, very small quantities of a special sort of wire, and to be expecting the visit of a certain Herr Sannig, head of the firm and at that time engaged on a business tour.

He was also expecting the arrival of Fritz Kramm from Berlin. Taut seemed to avoid answering Kramm's letters. Herr Sannig fell ill suddenly at Amsterdam and returned to Berlin. The writer of most of the letters subsequently announced that Sannig's visit to England was given up but he himself might come later.

The suspicious circumstances were Horvath's apparent unwillingness to write to Fritz Kramm in Berlin; the fact that his breakdown in health and postponed journey of Herr Sannig coincided with the apparent breakdown of Walter Reimann's journey in March 1914; but the correspondence might be genuine. The Home Office Warrants which had been taken out for Horvath and Fritz Kramm were cancelled on 30 April, having produced nothing after 25 March. War broke out and on 15 October 1914 MO5G reported Stephen Horvath, a mantle manufacturer at Kentish Town and Highgate, to the CID as a suspicious character who should be watched. The police replied that Horvath had registered as a Hungarian subject, that he had five children all born in England; he was an electrical engineer, and had lived in this country fifteen years. He was then the principal of the Corona Lamp Works Company of Asham Street, Kentish Town. Casual observation had been kept upon him, and there was nothing suspicious to report.

In July 1915, the Home Office referred to MO5 Horvath's application for exemption from internment which was favourably considered. Two years later, however, Horvath's neighbours were insistent for his internment, and 45,000 residents of Wandsworth signed a petition in that sense. Enquiry made by the local police failed to produce anything substantial but the police reported that Horvath had never expressed good sentiments towards this country. Enquiry was made at Horvath's place of business, where he was found to be doing work of national importance in producing tungsten under the supervision of the Ministry of Munitions. There was nothing on which MO5 could act and Horvath was known to have an enemy, Mrs Clutterbuck-Barnett. Then William Jones, a neighbour of Horvath's, wrote explaining Horvath's position; he was loyal, was a denationalised Hungarian, all his children were British except the eldest son, who for special reasons had been born in Hungary. The case was brought up again in September 1918, as that of an unnaturalised Austrian, with a son of military age not serving, and a daughter engaged to an officer of the British Army. Horvath behaved insolently to the Special Constable who was sent to inquire but his papers were in order and no further action was taken. The ambiguity of the position of Stephen Horvath and still more of his son was obviously the cause of great offence to the public. The police were to blame in that they had given incorrect information to MO5 as to the nationality of all the children. The point seems to be that a more prolonged enquiry in 1914 might have given more certain results.

The LCC Inspector considered the man's actions suspicious and there was sufficient in the correspondence to raise some doubt. The connection with the Gould family seems never to have been verified and it is obvious that if there had ever been any guilty association, Horvath would have been particularly careful while Gould's case hung in the balance and for some time after Gould was sentenced on 3 April. The records of this early part of the case are almost certainly incomplete;

if there was any police enquiry at all, the probability is that Horvath would have known of it and have been extra cautious. With the expiry of the Home Office Warrant all chance of clearing up doubts vanished.

★

The third group of enemy agents to be investigated after August 1914 proved to be of rather less significance and consisted of a dozen men. They were Friedrich von Diederichs, a 65-year-old pensioned German naval commander; George Beatty; Private Harry Sampson; Carl Meyer; Robert Blackburn; Frederic Sukowski; Carl Hemlar; Karl Stubenwoll; Edward Durkin; Antonius Rummenie; Thomas Hegnauer and August Reichwald.

Von Diederichs was the son of a German admiral. He came to England shortly before the outbreak of war and wrote letters to Captain von Prieger, head of the German Secret Service, at 38 Konigin Augustastrasse, Berlin. This was already known to be the headquarters of the German Admiralty's intelligence branch and had been the subject of a HOW that had been taken out for the name 'Streckel' at this address on about 22 July 1914.

In these letters he gave details connected with British naval mobilisation, asked for certain addresses at A (Amsterdam) and R (Rotterdam) to be sent him, suggested that a simple code for urgent telegraphic communication be supplied, and that arrangements should be made to remit money in case of war.

He wrote to his brother Hermann von Diederichs KK at the same address and Hermann replied that his wishes would be carried out. The day before a letter had come through from Berlin rebuking von Diederichs for his long screed, the contents of which could be read in the newspapers, and warning him to be careful not to show himself so much in public. The HOW for von Diederichs was taken out on the 27 July and he was placed on the SWL on 29 July.

Enquiries showed that he had been some days in London before taking up quarters at the Kenilworth Hotel on 24 July, and that he had left the Kenilworth on 29 July, as it was supposed en route for the Continent.

When arrested in town on the 4 August there were found in his possession a pass issued by Korvettenkapitan von Muller, of the German embassy, stating that von Diederichs was going to his unit and requesting facilities, and also the return half of a ticket to Flushing issued 1 August 1914. The other half had been used, said von Diederichs, to visit his brother. He was detained under ARC and all requests for release or mitigation of his sentence were refused on the grounds that it was fairly clearly established that von Diederichs was a naval officer sent on a special mission of espionage just before war broke out.

He was repatriated in March 1919. In Brixton Prison he came in contact with Grosse who befriended him as von Diederichs could speak very little English. Afterwards both men were transferred to Reading and there eventually von Diederichs learned what Grosse's past had been. In consequence, when Grosse was being repatriated, von Diederichs, with the consent of the governor of the prison, cut out of a bible which he had given to Grosse an inscription of warm friendship. Grosse was furious and reported the matter to von Muller at The Hague. The only thing that calls for comment in this case is the really shocking translation of von Diederichs's letters.

★

An American aviator named George Beatty came to England in June 1913 and had introductions to officials at the Royal Aircraft Factory, Farnborough, to Graham White and others; obtained possession of eleven sheets of drawings of the British experimental aeroplane; he tried to sell them first to the US War Department and then to private firms. The drawings were signed Crouch. The military attaché at Washington had been told these facts by a Canadian, unknown to him. The report reached MO5 in due course, after MI-1 had communicated with the Superintendent of the Royal Aircraft Factory.

The Superintendent had already been told by Rogers, one of his inspectors, that certain BE drawings had been sold to a private firm in America and the inspector had been offered £10 a week to go and make BE aeroplanes in America. The Inspector had accepted the offer and asked for it to be put in writing. The Inspector was of the opinion that the drawings had originated in Handley Page's office as Beatty shared lodgings with Handley Page; was frequently in his office and had been surprised with Handley Page under circumstances which embarrassed both these men. A further report embodied the following details and inferences. In August 1913, two BE drawings were at Handley Page's. Beatty was having his aeroplanes repaired there. Early in December he went to America, and returned thence on 15 January 1914, and on 20 January he told Inspector Rogers that a company in Connecticut had a complete set of copies of drawings and that a company had been formed for the purpose of building BEs. The company had a promise that all future improvements of BE aeroplanes would be sent them. On 9 February Rogers had found Beatty sitting familiarly with Handley Page although previous to that Beatty had given no sign of knowing Handley Page.

The enquiry was narrowed down to four possible firms who were in possession of the latest BE drawings, e.g. British & Colonial Aeroplane Co. Bristol; Hewlett & Blondeau, Clapham; Graham White, Hendon; Handley Page, Cricklewood and Hendon.

MO5 had recourse to two Metropolitan Police detectives and GPO warrants were taken out for the addresses of Beatty at London Aerodrome, Hendon and 1 Park Drive, Golder's Green. A check had been put on for the address of the Handley Page factory at Cricklewood for letters from the United States to Beatty and Handley Page. The name of the draughtsman at Hewlett & Blondeau's was obtained: it was Halberg. An attempt was made to buy back one of the original drawings – through Colonel M.

Letters to Mr William H. Workman, of 1 Park Drive, Golder's Green, which may have been an alias used by Beatty, were intercepted. Beatty started a flying school at Hendon on Monday 16 February. Melville, in conversation with Beatty, found that Beatty knew that the confidential drawings given out to contractors were called 'blueprints'.

Mr O'German was to prepare an identifiable drawing of a tail-plane but whether this was done does not appear. Beatty was to be proposed as member of the Aeronautical Society and Mr O'German warned the chairman who had already received a warning letter from the Canadian or American society. Mr O'German suggested that Major Kell should tell the chairman about the case and get to see this letter.

Some action was taken but the result is unknown. In this file is a copy of *Flight* for 18 October 1913 which contains some drawings and an account of certain details of a BE aeroplane. These had been supplied it was said by the Superintendent of the Factory and it may be that these drawings were the source of the whole trouble.

Beatty's financial position seems to have been unsound; he had interests in various commercial undertakings of which Scotland Yard took note in August 1914. Up until 2 July 1914 Beatty had financed the *Aeronautic Journal*, of which Ledeboer was editor, and at some time not specified, Beatty had been made chairman of the Pneumatic Tube Company, London Wall Buildings.

During the war Beatty's name was repeatedly brought up in connection with accusations of treacherous conduct. In September Bjorklund, a Swede and former pupil of Beatty's at Hendon, returned to Sweden with his aeroplane. MO5 ascertained that the aeroplane had been inspected at Hendon on mobilisation and reported useless and was moreover considered dangerous.

Beatty's Flying School continued its work during the war and Beatty trained officers for the Allied armies. He did not always give satisfaction. Two pupils (Scholart, a Belgian, and Branford) complained. The accusation was that Beatty deliberately held back the pupils; restricted flying; used unsafe machines; sent men up with engines set at half power. Moreover, the enemy knew about the de Haviland machines and where they were being built. Beatty, it was rumoured at the Royal Aero Club, had been offered a large sum to cross to Germany. MI-1c forwarded this report to MI5. Whether any action was taken does not appear.

In October 1918, in consequence of a report that G. W. Beatty (American Air Service), Manager of the Handley Page Works, was giving information to the Germans, wholesale enquiry was made about him. The informant seemed to know nothing of Beatty's first visit to England but he supplied certain details and gave information which led to an interview with a man who knew Beatty intimately. From the informant and this friend the following was ascertained:

Beatty was born in New Jersey on 28 August 1987. He came to England in January 1914 and occupied various addresses. He quarrelled with his wife and separated from her and hid his address so that she should not find him. He was governor and sole director of Beatty's School of Flying Ltd, Cricklewood, and a contractor for Handley Page Co., Ltd and for the Aircraft Manufacturing Co. His private character was bad and he was a bad payer, but he had an account with the London & Provincial Bank and his income was derived from the two firms mentioned above. He had done good work for the company and would certainly not betray secrets.

The enquirer was careful to suppress the names of his informants but internal evidence shows that Beatty's intimate friend was very probably Handley Page himself and if this is so the enquiry had gone round in a circle. MO5, it is to be presumed, had satisfied themselves as to Handley Page's integrity in the course of their enquiry in 1914, but as it stands incompletely recorded in the file it is a singularly unsatisfying case from the point of view of G work.

★

Formerly an Engineer Lieutenant in the German Navy, which he joined in 1899, Carl Meyer was appointed Marine Engineer in October 1910 and placed on the Retired List on 14 December 1912. The reason for this order was the adverse finding of a court martial to which Meyer had been subjected for having improperly communicated with a matrimonial agency.

Meyer came to England in July 1912 and travelled in the west, visiting Bristol, Newport and Exeter. He wrote letters to Herr Fagel, Hotel Stadt, Konigsberg, in which he referred to some vague business saying that he would face risks if he were well paid. Intercepted communications showed that, for the month of January, he received allowances amounting to 401 marks 67, that his pension was 180 marks a month, and that, for February and March, he received allowances amounting to 206.67.

Meyer was watched and it was ascertained that he had tried to start in different ways of business and eventually it became known that he and his wife had opened a shop at 199 Regent Street. This was the International Corset Company which was formed on 2 September 1912, and of which the directors, Paul Rosenberg and Hermann Hertz, lived at Cologne. A HOW for the Regent Street address was taken out from 7 April to 20 April 1914.

Meyer was arrested and searched on 8 August but there was nothing incriminating and no evidence against him. He was interned and at one time it was proposed to send him to Germany to counteract the German press campaign against atrocities to prisoners of war, but MI5 stopped this. Eventually he was released on grounds of ill-health. Madame Meyer continued the business till July 1916, when she left Regent Street and want to work as a blouse-maker. Carl Meyer was repatriated in January 1918 and on his way home, he despatched a telegram to his wife. This was the occasion of fresh instructions dealing with communications of released prisoners of war.

★

Robert Arthur Blackburn, of 37 Jenkinson Street, Liverpool, was born in 1896. Early in 1914 he made one trip as an ordinary seaman on a steamer of the Elder-Dempster Line. Then he was employed by his father to help in managing a common lodging-house at 121 Islington.

He seems to have been an impressionable youth, who excited his imagination with reading. As a result he wrote offering his services to the German embassy in London and received in reply a letter from Berlin, signed Leo Sirius, enclosing questions about defences and ship-building on the Mersey. These he answered and was paid £2 and received a further letter in July. His attempts at spying had not given satisfaction to his employers. The letter of June had been posted via Klunder, so

HOWs were taken out for correspondence to Blackburn and Sirius. It was ascertained that Blackburn had never been in Cammell Laird's employ.

Blackburn was arrested on 10 August and charged with having sent valuable information concerning the Mersey defences to a German in Berlin. He was committed for trial and the case came up on 28 October. Blackburn pleaded guilty and described how he had entered into relations with the Germans but declared that he had given them no information that was not in some way or other accessible to the public. He was sentenced to two years' confinement in a borstal institution.

While Blackburn was awaiting trial, the Liverpool Post Office intercepted a letter that came for him from Belfast and was couched in terms that showed the writer had tried to get secret information about ship-building in that port. In connection with this letter the Royal Irish Constabulary arrested a man named George Hopley and handwriting tests justified their action. But although enquiry in England brought evidence that Hopley had been in touch with persons at Liverpool and Manchester, there was no proof beyond the existence of the letter that he had been conspiring with Blackburn; Hopley was therefore merely charged with having communicated notes calculated to be useful to an enemy. As there is no record of what happened, it is probable the charge was either dropped or not proved.

Almost at the same time information was received from a supposed friendly German in America that there must be a big gang of German spies at Preston and that any correspondence marked Sirius was suspect. The Chief Constable of Preston could obtain no verification of the existence of such a gang and the postmaster reported that no article marked Sirius had passed through the post. In May 1916 a letter came for an Indian lodging at 121b Islington and at the suggestion of the postman, who remembered this had been a spy address, some enquiry was made. It was ascertained that twenty-one Indians, formerly ship's firemen but at that time engaged at the Oil Cake Mills, were living in the lodging-house, but the police found no cause for suspicion.

After Blackburn's release he joined the Royal Army Medical Corps. MI5, on consultation, had left the decision to the recruiting authorities;

they would have preferred, however, that Blackburn should have joined the labour battalion. A report from his commanding officer was asked for but does not seem to have been sent.

★

Frederic Sukowski was unknown to MO5 until 23 July 1914 when he was arrested on the afternoon of 3 August 1914 for suspicious movements in the neighbourhood of shipbuilding yards in Newcastle. He was making notes on a map. He had in his possession a map of England giving distances by road, rail and air, two measuring gauges, a paper with the names of shipbuilding firms in Newcastle and district, South Shields, Sunderland, Hartlepool, Hull, etc.

MO5 were informed of the arrest and telegraphed that the Attorney-General's fiat was to be applied for. The man was remanded and there the file ends. A note made by Major Drake in his file states that he was held under a Deportation Order.

★

August Reichwald was Krupp's general agent in England. On 31 July, Herr Frielinghuis, one of the directors of Krupp's, came to London on business, possibly to arrange with his agent some telegraphic code, whereby information could be sent without arousing suspicion.

Reichwald was arrested on the outbreak of war and search of his premises was made without result, so he was liberated, on about 17 August. He had a son serving in the Indian Army, as Assistant Military Secretary and interpreter to the Commander-in-Chief India. Captain Reichwald changed his name to Blaker. He was attached to the headquarters staff of the Indian Cavalry Corps in France as GSO for Intelligence.

The file is one long record of information laid against August Reichwald, who was an old man, and naturalised British, and his son Captain Blaker, who was an able officer and had done good service in intelligence work. August had a son, A. W. Reichwald, a general merchant of Newcastle-on-Tyne. In November 1914, instructions were given that A. W. Reichwald's correspondence should be watched. Any communications the contents of which showed, or gave presumption, that Reichwald was: trading with a foreign country; sending letters via a neutral country to an enemy country; supplying merchandise that would be useful to an enemy; collecting information of use to an enemy country; showing hostile sentiments; or showing connection with enemy alien residing in prohibited area, were to be submitted to Investigation Branch, GPO.

The correspondence showed that Reichwald had some engagement with the Essen, Rheinhausen and Stahlworks, Verband, and was in touch with Mr Peters of Barcelona and also with the Credit Reform in Berlin. In January 1915 a supervisor was appointed to the firm. In May 1915 W. F. Blaker (late Reichwald), Royal Horse Artillery himself wrote suggesting the internment of the many Germans who were then at large in England. At the same time came the report that the firm of Reichwald were also trading as the Celtol Supply Company and selling their manufactures to Irish farmers. Then Major Reichwald (alias Blaker) was sent home from the Front and attached to a battery here. His father interceded on Major Reichwald's behalf to get him reinstated with the Indian Cavalry Corps.

Nothing was ever proved against any member of the family but the feeling of the general community was so strong that when August Waldemar Reichwald applied for a passport to France, MI5E did not oppose the issue on personal grounds, but suggested reference to the French authorities first as their granting of the visa was doubtful. Dr Max Balsar Reichwald asked for a definite assurance that if he took a commission in the RAMC the minister responsible for the grant would state that after full enquiry he was satisfied as to Reichwald's bonafides. This could not be given and there was some doubt as to whether in the man's own interest, it was advisable to endorse the grant of the commission.

Of the other sons, one, Victor Reichwald, served in IW Battalion

(30th and 31st Middlesex) and another Edward was employed as an 'outside clerk' under the Intelligence Department of the Air Board. Concerning a third, Fritz Bernard, who was said to make model aeroplanes etc. MI5 made no enquiry.

The case is interesting as illustrating the difficulty of dealing with the families of naturalised Germans who had yet kept up connection with German commercial concerns that were of immense importance to the Imperial government.

★

The declaration of war on 4 August 1914 immediately increased the work and activity of G Branch, then the Preventive or B Section of MO5. Plans had been drawn up in July 1914 for some re-organisation of the bureau in the event of hostilities. The staff was to consist of the Director of Intelligence Police, three Assistant Directors, Captain Drake, Captain Holt-Wilson, Captain Haldane, and two intelligence officers. Each of the Assistant Directors and one of the intelligence officers was to take it in turn to work at the War Office MO5G, his duties being to sift the papers and questions brought to him, to deal himself with the minor questions and to use his discretion in transmitting the remainder to the bureau urgently or in normal course. In November 1914, the Preventive Division or B Section and the Detective or A Section were organised as separate branches.

Towards the end of the year it became known that Germany expected to maintain easy communication by post with her spies in the United Kingdom, has commerce destroyers would keep in touch with German residents in the United States by means of wireless. Floating mines would be laid to prevent food supplies from reaching our shores and missionaries in India would stir up sedition among the natives. In its main lines the work of investigation was carried on by the same methods as before the war. The chief agents continued to be the police, officials of the post office and special agents employed by the bureau. Owing to the great increase in the number of suspected persons, there was a noticeable increase in the number of HOWs taken out.

In his report for November and December 1914, Major Drake mentions various types of investigation:

General Inquiries: with regard to the bona-fides of persons who had been and continued to be in receipt of regular payments through German banks in this country with a view to detecting possible agents; search of all telegrams sent to certain countries since the outbreak of war.

Special Inquiries: with regard to records obtained and action taken with regard to certain persons holding commissions who were unfit for such posts; bona-fides of certain Belgians; foreign business firms and a hotel supposed to be under German management; attempts to re-establish the German spy organisations.

Other enquiries related to firms and cases of suspected of espionage. The two General Enquiries mentioned above illustrate the enlargement of scope conferred upon the bureau by the publicity and necessitated the war. The investigation of bank accounts and the search of telegrams were pre-war methods used in individual cases but now raised to universal application and carried out either by specially appointed persons as in the case of the banks, or by the ordinary channel of a great public service.

# I. German banks

The great German banks stood foremost among enemy organisations in this country. The German banks formed a highly centralised system, which, it may he noted en passant, was copied here when the policy was adopted of tightening up the links between the German clubs in London.

The four chief German banks, the Deutsche, Dresdner, Disconto and Darmstädter, combined in a group which dominated the economic life of Germany. The Deutsche Bank itself controlled twelve other important banks and had representatives who sometimes occupied such important posts as chairman or vice-chairman, on the directorate of 118 firms belonging to industry, commerce, insurance, and transport. Moreover, the banks had interests in a number of foreign railways, electrical companies and banks. With these German banks, G Branch was concerned only with regard to their agencies, possible use as agencies for: 1. Transmitting money for espionage and hostile purposes; 2. Conveying information disguised under business messages; 3. The collection of information by members of their staffs.

Under the Trading with the Enemy Act the Board of Trade had appointed chartered accountants to supervise the business of foreign companies and it was through these supervisors that MO5 instituted enquiries as to the regular payments of small sums which had been made through German and Austrian banks to private individuals in this country. In November 1914, the supervisors of four banks sent in returns identifying their payees.

It was the custom at the Deutsche Bank not to enter the address or description of the payee on the current card and the labour of supplying these data from other documents in the bank would have been too great; MO5, however, from their own records were able to supply the addresses of ninety-three persons. Enquiries were made in the vast majority of cases; the following various police authorities are noted in the files, and there are probably others which have escaped special record. Enquiries through the Metropolitan Police, sixty-four; City of London Police, fifteen; provincial police constables, sixteen, making a total of ninety-five.

Of the names received from the Anglo-Austrian Bank, one, Otto Teumark, and of those received from the Deutsche Bank, three, Percy Ernst Becker, Fraü E. Schuter, Bernhard Moses Biedermann, at a later date became the subject of special enquiry. Three of the clients of the Deutsche Bank were already known to the police and of these one had been searched as a suspect early in November, but without result, and one had been fined for possessing arms and a camera.

At Salford an enemy client of the Anglo-Austrian bank named Breuhne, who was in the employ of the Griesheim-Electro Company, had been arrested and interned on 25 October. But for detection purposes the enquiry hardly gave satisfactory results since either the recipient could be traced, when he always gave a good account of himself and was whitewashed by the police or he could not be traced and the enquiry proceeded no further. An instance of the latter type occurs in the case of Enoch Constantine, who up until July 1914 had been in receipt of monthly payments of pension money in sums of £8 6s. 11d.; enquiries about the address given at Gateshead, Newcastle or Felling-on-Tyne failed to establish the existence in those regions of any alien of the name of Constantine. These enquiries had reference only to pre-war payments, for with the transfer of the banks to British supervision it seemed unlikely that they would be used as remitting agencies to German spies.

## II. Search of telegrams by the GPO

On 9 August arrangements were made with the GPO to submit inland telegrams sent from ports and military stations with a view to ascertaining the address of possible spies. On 11 and 18 August, these lists were sent in as well as a number of other telegrams despatched from London and the country. Certain of these telegrams were picked out as possibly suspect but the vast majority were harmless and it was decided to place restrictions only upon messages sent from the Continent. Thereafter many telegrams from Gothenburg and Copenhagen to northern ports were submitted to MO5; some were stopped, others were partly erased and sent forward; on two enquiries were made. In this last category was a telegram from Baku containing details of payments amounting to more than £600 made in various countries; the addressee could not be traced.

## III. German consuls

The cases of two ex-German consuls, Franz Rahtkens at Middlesbrough, and Nicholas Emil Ahlers at Sunderland, are of interest. Rahtkens, who was arrested on suspicion by the Chief Constable of Middlesbrough, was a British subject, having naturalised in 1882, he was also a ship-owner. In this double capacity he had been receiving confidential and secret Admiralty documents such as trade routes during the war, instructions to vessels plying between various ports, which had been issued with a view to the safe passage of merchant ships past our minefields, etc. Among his papers were also found instructions from the German consul-general, dated 31 July 1914, to destroy 'all really secret affairs' in case of danger and to warn German vessels that diplomatic relations between Germany and Great Britain might be broken off. Rahtkens had also furthered the visits of German government engineers to British ports and harbours, and he had helped Germans to return to their country at the outbreak of war.

Major Drake concluded that the means whereby Germany had obtained information of the position of our minefields had been established, and that Admiralty Secret Instructions must not in future be allowed to fall into the hands of any person of German birth. He laid down as an axiom that all ex-German consuls of German origin, whether naturalised or not, must be regarded as dangerous enemy subjects, and he drew attention to the necessity for reconsidering the position of the whole class of naturalised British subjects of German origin, without regard to the date of their naturalisation.

Information regarding U-boat methods was obtained through an agent posted in an internment camp and working among the crew of a German submarine. A similar attempt made in an officers' camp failed owing partly to the inefficient agent employed.

On the outbreak of war the Central Censorship was established for the examination of mails between the United Kingdom and Germany with Austria-Hungary; it was extended to mails with Turkey when that power came into the war. But experience soon proved that such scope was insufficient and the system was extended as follows:

—  29 August 1914. To mails to and from Holland, Denmark and Norway.
—  19 September 1914. To mails to and from Sweden.
—  14 October 1914. To mails to and from Switzerland.
—  7 November 1914. To mails to and from Italy.
—  17 December 1914. To mails to and from Spain, Portugal and Romania.

Home Office Warrants had, however, been issued to the Central
Censorship on the outbreak of war for checking all correspondence to
certain addresses in neutral and Allied countries. The examination of
parcels to neutral countries was begun at the end of November 1914.
Letters to PoWs were despatched in separate bags through the Dutch
Postal Administration. Letters were sorted into four categories with
sub-divisions as follows:

*Dangerous:*
(i)   Containing definite political, naval or military information.
(ii)  Addressed to persons on the Black List.
(iii) Offering service to the enemy.
(iv)  Containing ciphers and codes.

*Suspicious:*
(i)   Indicating unusual relations between persons resident in the UK and
      abroad.
(ii)  Indicating payments made to or demanded by persons in the UK
      without mention of corresponding business.
(iii) Expressing intention of Germans to join the British Red Cross or
      similar organisations.

*Indiscreet:*
Expressing pessimistic views; letters from or concerning Germans or
Austrians liable to military service. All letters and telegrams to or from
neutral countries in connection with trading with enemy countries
and ordinary trade telegrams from and to any place were submitted
to the Home Office and duplicates were sent to the Foreign Office;
all letters and telegrams other than above mentioned and especially
those connected with diplomatic, consular, political, military and naval
arrangements were sent to MO5. However, it was expressly stated that
correspondence dealing with banking and finance were to be sent to
the Treasury, certain trade papers to C3, and correspondence dealing
with naval matters to the DID.

In addition to the Central Censorship, the competent military authority of a district had power to ask the postmaster to stop specific letters and telegrams, and at the ports papers carried by passengers might be seized by officers stationed there by MO5.

In examining letters submitted (1) by the Censor, (2) by the port officers, and (3) examining advertisements of the agony columns of the newspapers three codes, which were supposed to have been used by enemy agents, were employed. Special arrangements were made in the branch to carry out the work and a plant was established for testing letters by chemical means.

A special check was placed on cables to Smith, German consul at Rotterdam, with a view to ascertaining the names and addresses of suspects here. Of the names submitted, for example, one Sloman, father of Mrs Gould, was doubtful, and two, Blassneck and the German consul Menke, were well-known suspects. Very soon methods of evading the Central Censorship became known to MO5. Censor labels were removed from old envelopes and pasted on to fresh ones; messages were sent abroad in bundles of newspapers; letters were carried by smugglers to and from enemy-occupied territory or posted via intermediaries in neutral countries.

The methods of the Censor developed with experience aided by the suggestions of MO5. Thus in December 1914, Major Drake reported that it was known that German agents were sending information out of the country written in invisible ink on the margins of newspapers, magazines and pamphlets; however, no specific instance had come to light and it was desirable to take action with regard to printed matter passing through the post. An order had been issued in April 1916 that printed matter addressed to neutral countries should be delayed for forty-eight hours unless it were despatched by newsagents or publishers, the sending of all such matter to enemy countries was prohibited to all but certain publishers and newsagents, and by July private persons had been forbidden to post newspapers to Holland and a delay of a fortnight was imposed on press matter addressed to other neutral countries. Further, Major Drake, early in January 1915, desired that the Censorship should cover all mails to countries within five days journey of the United Kingdom. This was carried out in May 1915 when mails to Bulgaria and Greece were censored. At the same time a warrant for censoring the American mail (North and South) was obtained and put into force, intermittently at first. The question of mails in transit between France and northern neutral countries, including Holland, had for some time engaged attention. In April 1915 also mails in transit through the UK were made subject to censorship.

A weak point was found in the system of submitting to MO5 a précis only of interesting letters for, owing to this, evidence that would have served to convict a German agent was allowed to go through. The system was therefore altered; letters of interest were submitted attached to the précis of contents and MO5 made special arrangements for dealing with these letters. Investigation had been made of eight foreign businesses and of one hotel, the Ritz-Carlton, which had come under suspicion either of trading with the enemy or of being concerned in espionage. The establishment of Siemens & Co. was searched on several occasions and special examination made for wireless, and for some time a police officer was established on the premises to keep check. As regards the firm of Hugo Stinnes, coal merchants, with branches at several ports, MO5's officers at Cardiff were keeping special watch on their shipments of coal and one of the managers, Mr Fergusson, who had met Stinnes in Holland since the outbreak of war, was not again allowed to leave the country. Steps had been taken to remove from all vulnerable points and ports the tranches of Goldstuck Hainze & Co., grain merchants, a business largely managed by and employing a number of foreigners, which had reorganised itself into an absolutely British firm with suspicious alacrity.

The Admiralty was notified of the foreign composition of a firm with which it had large contracts and in the case of a similar firm dealing with the War Office, arrangements were made to prevent profits going to alien enemies.

The premises of Isenthal & Co., manufacturers of wireless telegraphy apparatus, were searched and measures suggested to safeguard public security while enabling the firm to carry on its government contracts.

Vickers Ltd had been warned against an emissary of the Irish-German-American element, who was seeking employment there, and the man himself was placed under police supervision. As regards London hotels, enemy members of the staffs who were of military age had been interned. Among the twenty-one cases of individual suspects mentioned some five or six are organisations of special interest as proving the efforts of the Germans to re-establish their Secret Service here. Major Ostertag was reported to be actively engaged in this work and a British citizen 'G-8' had been signalled from Rotterdam as being a friend of Ostertag, very pro-German, and an agent for journalistic pro-German propaganda in the United States. Adolf Becker, a partner of Becker & Wirth, Brussels, well-known as having supplied an accommodation address for Frederick Gould's correspondence, who had come to England, was interned after interrogation; Paul Esser and Kampe proved to be acting as connecting links in the system of German espionage in this country and were interned under a deportation order; a man named Huitket, who was going to Paris from Blankenberg carrying money, as it was presumed, for the payment of German agents, was intercepted at Folkestone and detained here.

★

Baron von Hettlebladt, who had been suspected of acting for Germany in South Africa in 1904 and 1905 and had afterwards come under suspicion in Canada, was interned in September 1914. He had married an Englishwoman, had settled at Cranbrook in Kent, and had influential friends who procured his release. The Chief Constable of Kent protested and he was detained by request of the Home Office.

A search made at his premises brought documentary proof of his having been formerly in the employ of the German Secret Service. Hettlebladt was interned finally in November.

★

On 6 November 1914, Carl Hans Lody, the first spy to be tried by court martial since the outbreak of war, was shot at the Tower. Lody was a lieutenant in the 2nd German Naval Reserve known as the Seewehr and a travelling agent in the employ of the Hamburg-Amerika Line. He used the cover of a genuine American emergency passport belonging to Charles A. Inglis who had deposited it for a visa at the Berlin Foreign Office, where it disappeared. Lody came to England via Denmark and Bergen, procuring there a certificate of American nationality. Arriving at Newcastle on 27 August 1914, he went straight to Edinburgh where he stayed a month with occasional absences of a night. One of these trips was to London, another to Peebles. From Edinburgh he went to Liverpool and then crossed to Ireland. He was arrested at Killarney. In the course of his travels he managed to dispose of a small hand-bag which was never traced.

Lody carried about £200 in banknotes, English gold and German gold. Some of the notes were traced to a South American named Kinkelin who left England on 1 August. Besides sending reports, Lody collected quantities of newspapers representing different opinions and classes of the community. Twenty-two different journals are represented in his collection. Generally speaking he seems to have protected himself by cultivating chance acquaintances and making trips in their company. Lody communicated with Stockholm in a telegraphic code and sent under cover to the same address letters in German containing spy reports *en clair* and directed to Stammer, Courbierestrasse, Berlin, and also to other addresses.

He used the signatures Charles, Lody and Nazi. His mission seems to have been a general one but he was to stay in England until after the first battle when he was to report British naval losses and then proceed to America.

Since 4 August all mails from the United Kingdom to Norway and Sweden had been brought to London and examined for letters to certain suspect addresses. Lody wired to the spy address at Stockholm on 20 August and having to endorse the telegram with his name wrote 'Charles Inglis'. His first letter, posted on 4 September was read, photographed and forwarded and others that followed were similarly treated in the hope of learning more. Eventually a letter came through to Charles A. Inglis c/o Thomas Cook, Edinburgh, dated 8 September 1914. This Inglis never called for. At what precise moment the traveller Inglis was connected with the writer of the letters does not appear, but two long reports signed 'Nazi' of 27 and 30 September were retained and orders issued for Lody's arrest, which took place on 2 October. Various addresses and a telegram were found on him. At the trial it was learned that such harmless words as 'shall' and 'leave' had code meaning. As a result of the trial special enquiries were made at King's Lynn as to the steps taken to guard against the arrival of undesirable aliens. Some uncorroborated evidence was adduced to the effect that Lody had been there in June and in the early part of July and had received telegrams under the name of Inglis and of Sideface. The details of Lody's American passport may prove this statement to be false.

The emergency passport issued to Charles A. Inglis on 4 August 1914 was sent to the United States for examination and returned afterwards to MI5. Through enquiries made by MO5 the name of the agent in Stockholm with whom Lody was in communication, K. Leipziger, was established.

# CHAPTER III

# 1915 and 1916

BEFORE the outbreak of war the bureau had worked mainly through the agency of the police. With the organisation of huge new forces in 1914 counter-espionage might expect a great accession of strength from the work of intelligence officers appointed to the armies. With a view to securing uniformity of procedure the following set of instructions for the guidance of officers in dealing with suspects whether alien or British was issued to the General Officer, Commanding-in-Chief; the GOC London District; the GOC Aldershot Training Centre; the GOC Aldershot Station; the GOCs of the Channel Islands.

1. Indications of espionage instructions were to be reported at once to Commanding Officers for transmission to the intelligence officer, or if urgent, the intelligence officer was to be informed direct.
2. The intelligence officer was usually to consult the Chief Constable with a view to discreet enquiry being made.
3. If the investigation showed serious reason for believing espionage was being practised, the competent military authority was to be informed and he would decide whether to refer the matter to the War Office.
4. If he decided upon getting an internment or removal order he must refer to the War Office for particulars concerning the individual in question.
5. Such reference was to be addressed to MO5G.
6. When the help of the police was involved the enquiry was as a rule to be left in their hands.

7.   In cases of emergency the competent military authority or intelligence
     officer would use his own discretion.

Thus the tradition of the bureau was imparted to the military officers
distributed throughout the country and at the same time the bureau
kept in touch with all genuine cases of espionage. Besides tracking
undesirables in the country, a considerable part of the ports' defence
consisted of keeping them out, hence it was decided that any Home
Defence Intelligence concerning ports and the coast of the United
Kingdom should be handed on to MO5G which would warn the Chief
Constables concerned, the Home Office for the Aliens Officers, and
Scotland Yard for the approved ports or other police matters.

Moreover, since September 1914, an officer of MO5G had been
stationed at Folkestone for the special purpose of watching the influx of
Belgian refugees, with a view to taking action in the case of undesirables.
A similar measure was adopted at Gravesend in February 1915 and at
Southampton a little later. In the two-fold work of distributing information
with regard to espionage and investigating reported spy cases MO5G
established contacts with the Metropolitan Police, MO5G officers at
Folkestone, Tilbury and Liverpool; intelligence officers in fortresses and
commands; city police at Hull, Newcastle and Liverpool; special police
officers in the Admiralty coalfields (through local Chief Constable); the
police at Southampton (through the Metropolitan Police); the Diplomatic
and Consular Services (through the Foreign Office); ports, aliens, customs
officers (through the Home Office); the Permit Office, Admiralty, Scottish
Office, the Local Government Board, the Board of Trade, the Registrar-
General, the Labour Exchanges and the Belgian Relief Committees.

The thirteenth monthly report which was issued in April 1915, laid
stress on the fact that although the Special Intelligence Bureau employed
a certain number of persons on direct enquiry, yet, on the whole, its
functions were administrative, advisory and co-ordinative rather than
executive. 'It gathers information from all sources on subjects bearing
on espionage, sees that this information is placed at the disposal of the
executive authorities concerned, and supervises enquiries and their

results'. The circulation of information was part of the work of the officers of A Branch (investigation).

In April information was received through the Foreign Office that a school had been established at Stockholm to train neutral spies to act as commercial travellers in the United Kingdom and Allied countries and it was afterwards learned that the German Secret Service had established its headquarters at the Strand Hotel, Stockholm.

The growth of the work in G Branch can be gauged from this table which shows, as far as is obtainable, the increase in certain classes of investigation from April to August.

| Figures taken from the monthly reports, April to August 1915 inclusive, which give an idea of certain classes of investigation and of the growth of the work of the branch during these months | | | | | |
|---|---|---|---|---|---|
| | April | May | June | July | August |
| General suspects | 158 | 251 | 449 | 763 | 852 |
| Persons of hostile origin reported | 118 | 76 | 113 | 175 | |
| Friendly and neutral aliens | 29 | 40 | 56 | 62 | 80 |
| Americans | 15 | 2 | 18 | 27 | 25 |
| Easterns | 5 | 6 | 4 | 8 | 16 |
| Suspects in public offices | 12 | 9 | 8 | 14 | 14 |
| Connected with the Army and Navy | 37 | 37 | 32 | 48 | 60 |
| Dockyards, shipping and aviation | 18 | 17 | 8 | 25 | |
| Suspects abroad and coming to England | 39 | 105 | 124 | 256 | 241 |
| Alien clubs and resorts | 1 | 4 | 3 | | |
| Letter agencies | 10 | 9 | 19 | | |
| Carriers | 16 | 13 | 11 | | |
| Passport permits | 19 | 33 | 24 | 32 | 43 |
| Press | 8 | 29 | 8 | 6 | 8 |

Correspondence submitted:

Letters, 730, 1006, 969, 979. Telegrams, 273, 376, 728, 616.

A few cases of some interest may be quoted. A case of mistaken civil status; the wife of a British subject living with a German whose name she had taken by Deed Poll: under observation. An Austrian woman in a London flat having a telephone, found to be the mistress of a retired ex-naval officer in a ship-building firm: deported. A German engaged in anti-recruiting: interned. The German manager of a firm of city chemists, who was allowed to go to Rotterdam to superintend the packing of medical stores intended for the army, wrote to his wife in Hamburg that he hoped to visit her. An attempted evasion of any order which might be passed for the confiscation of German property, a German at Middlesbrough asked his landlady to declare he owed her a debt of £81.

### Friendly aliens and neutrals

Two Swedish officers, who said they were going to Vancouver, had come to join the British Army: not allowed. A Frenchwoman travelled frequently between Paris and London on the pretext that she was interested in the estate of a person lost in the *Lusitania*: description circulated.

Two fresh types of offence are classified in May, e.g. illicit motor traffic and indiscretion, and the following occasions for suspicion seem worthy of note:

1.  Conduct: persons interesting themselves in soldiers or military affairs; women intimate with officers or soldiers; pro-German women.
2.  Friendly neutrals: Swiss waiters, because Germans might seek to pass as Swiss, and also German-Swiss would be of hostile sympathies; a Danish wireless-telegraphy expert entered an agricultural college.

### Connected with Army and Navy

One case of opposing recruiting. Press: a London newspaper had on several occasions used a military telephone to ask for information. An enemy agent had in his possession a document proving that he was to communicate by means of advertisements in newspapers.

In addition, four cases of American journalists or agents for newspaper syndicates came under suspicion; one of these had arranged for a source of military news from the Front.

A map of England divided into large districts had been found in the effects of the late German vice-consul at Newcastle; charts of the Irish coast and Bristol Channel had been intercepted on their way to Genoa; charts of the Persian Gulf and maps of coal mines in the north of England and Scotland had been asked for from Norway.

MO5 suggested that the maps and charts asked for should not be sent and by adding maps to the list of contraband goods the export of such publications was stopped. But the vast majority of cases proved of little interest. Where there was definite ground for dissatisfaction with the suspect but not sufficient ground for a trial it was possible to choose one of the following penalties according to the nature of the case:

1.  Internment if the suspect was an enemy subject.
2.  Restriction as to residence and movements involving a daily or weekly report to the police.
3.  Prohibition from leaving the Kingdom.
4.  Deportation.
5.  Leave to go abroad with a no-return permit.

The immense extension of the work in May led to an expansion and to some reorganisation of the branch. The duties were more precisely defined indicating not so much new developments as the increasing importance attaching to special features of the work. The importance of Irish affairs is proved by the formation of a section to deal entirely with them.

*Definition of duties of G Branch*
1.  Investigation of all cases of suspected espionage, sedition or treachery by individuals.
2.  Co-ordination and organisation of auxiliary action by government departments, naval and military authorities, and police for the above purposes.

3.  Preparation of the cases of persons arrested at the instance of the bureau for prosecution by the military or civil authorities.
4.  Examination of censored or intercepted correspondence and communications as submitted by the Central Censorship and Investigation Branch, GPO, and decisions as to the disposal of such papers.
5.  Classification of the methods employed by espionage agents.
6.  Recommendations for amendments to legislation and regulations for the purpose of preventing espionage, sedition or treachery, or of impeding the activities of naval or military spies and agents.
7.  Employment of the Intelligence Police personnel and provincial agencies, except with the Expeditionary Force.
8.  Recommendations for first appointments of personnel to G Branch.
9.  Semi-official correspondence and first draft official letters on the above subjects.

*Staff and distribution of duties*

Eight section officers and four secretaries were employed under Major Drake. Captain Carter and Commander Henderson carried out the work of A1 (cases arising in the London area).

A2 was reconstituted and three officers, P. W. Marsh ICS, R. Nathan CSI ICS, Captain H. S. Gladstone, 5th Bn. KOSB., dealt with all cases arising in Great Britain, without the Metropolitan area.

To A3, Major F. Hall, General Staff, all cases of suspected espionage, sedition or treachery in Ireland were allotted. Fresh duties were entrusted to A4, H. Hawkins Turner and Lieutenant W. E. H. Cooke examined, censored or intercepted correspondence. Miss S. Holmes, Miss M. E. Haldane, Miss M. C. Robson, Miss B. Hodgson divided the secretarial duties.

In order to check the influx of aliens into this country, in April 1915 amendments were added to the Aliens Restriction Order enacting that:

1.  Every alien landing or embarking in the United Kingdom or entering a prohibited area should carry a passport issued by the authorities of his own country not more than two years previously and, to this passport, his photograph was to be attached.

2. At all hotels and boarding houses a list of alien visitors should be kept. This second measure was made applicable to British subjects also in the following June.

These passports and lists proved of great value in identifying and tracing the movements of German agents sent to this country. At the same time the extension of prohibited areas so as to include a strip round the whole coast as well as some other tracts of country was under consideration. In May the government had decided upon the policy of interning or repatriating according to age all male enemy aliens who could not show cause why they should be left at liberty, and all female enemy aliens, with the exception of those held during deportation, might be repatriated. This was followed up by a measure enabling the authorities to intern dangerous persons of hostile origin and association.

The competent military and naval authorities, including MO5G, could send a recommendation to the Home Secretary for an order of internment to be directed against any person under these categories; that person had the right to appeal against the order to an Advisory Committee. All appeals of this nature had to pass through MO5G.

The measure proved of infinite value to the Investigation Branch in dealing with suspects against whom there was not sufficient evidence to bring them to trial. Indeed Major Drake wished to bring under the penalty of internment neutrals convicted of contraventions of DRR but against whom hostile association could not be proved. An instance in point is the case of Nideroest who had offered for publication in New York an illustrated article on the boom from Calais to Dover. He suffered merely a term of three months' imprisonment, and the Red Cross employee who had taken photographs for him merely a fine of £25.

During this year, much was learned as regards the German methods, spy centres, agencies, and steps were taken accordingly to counteract them. During the second quarter of 1915, the bureau learned of the existence of Hilmar Dierks' recruiting agency at Rotterdam and The Hague, who was also known as Richard Sanderson and was said to have 150 agents working in England, in July.

Dierks sent all his recruits to the Antwerp Adrniralstab Zweigstelle, 38 Chaussee de Malines there to be trained and to receive their instructions. Through the great spy cases reported lower down, and through the treachery of some of the Dutch agents employed, a good deal of information was acquired about the personnel and methods of the bureau.

Ernest Melin's confession revealed the existence of a bureau at Wesel, which acted independently of, and it would seem in rivalry with, the bureau at Antwerp.

In April 1915 a Dutchman told of the 'camouflage' of an air-ship shed near Brussels; of the dogging of travellers from England by German spies; of propaganda among Dutch firms connected with German toy businesses. German newspapers in quantities proportionate to the number of employees were despatched to these firms daily and Dutch versions were sent once a week. Regarding espionage proper, the Dutchman reported that spies were using double passports, one of which had to be given up at the last station before entering Holland; that fifty or sixty German firms were doing business in London and sending information in false business telegrams piecemeal to different centres to be afterwards patched together and forwarded to Antwerp.

Already in December 1914 it was reported that Belgian women were being sent via Folkestone to spy in France and the order was issued that such persons were to be allowed to come in but not to leave the United Kingdom.

With the object of destroying Admiralty mines, the Germans were reported to be intending to send over spies disguised as Belgian miners and to be stealing Belgian miners' books to provide identity papers for the purpose. Soon after, the report came that Germans were being brought in as coal-heavers.

In April 1915, the Germans were buying the services of Dutch agents who were to live in London and Paris and report from there. The British consul at Rotterdam stated that not only was a number of Dutchmen coming to England but many Germans were being encouraged to spend the summer in Holland.

From Washington came the report that in order to warn the U-boats of vessels carrying important stores for the Allies, Germans were taking situations with shipping companies in the United States and Canada.

A British ship's captain learned from a Belgian pilot of a scheme by which Belgians in England joined their army in France, then deserted, went as stowaways on a cheese-boat to Rotterdam and there consorted with Germans.

A German named Carl Haasters, head of a firm exploiting iron ores in Holland, required his manager to sign a certificate to the effect that a person, whose name he refused to give, proceeding from Spain but at that moment in Holland and known to the North German Lloyd company at Amsterdam, was a representative of the Iron Ore Company. As this company had in former years had dealings with the Gas Light & Coke Company the manager believed that Haasters intended to send over a hostile agent under guise of doing business with the British company and accordingly informed a representative of Scotland Yard. The ports were warned.

From Lausanne came the warning that about twenty young persons claiming Polish nationality and with papers in order were coming from Switzerland to England and then to America as dancers of Russian ballet. The ports were warned Washington also, and in February 1916 the Russian troupe, numbering seventy-three members, arrived at Washington. Nothing further transpired.

The following miscellaneous ways of carrying messages were reported at different dates: on gramophone records; sewn in the handle of a travelling bag, etc; in the soles of boots; in pills swallowed and recovered; under a false coating of fur covering a dog.

Owing to the delays occasioned by Postal Censorship, the practice grew up of firms sending their correspondence abroad by a clerk who travelled regularly to and fro. An officer at Tilbury reported that an immense traffic of this kind was in progress and that one courier would carry as many as one hundred letters. By regulation, the captains of neutral ships were entitled to carry 'ship-owner' letters and the same officer at Tilbury sent in a report incriminating the director and an officer of the Zeeland Steamship Company.

This complaint echoed one sent in by 'a traveller' in February 1915, who declared the measures taken with regard to travellers at Whitehall, Victoria and the ports to be insufficient; letters and telegrams could be sent from the steamers; clerks and journalists carrying letters for their principals were not supervised and no control was exercised over the crews of neutral vessels although there was much German capital invested in Dutch liners. As a result of Mr Barker's report the Zeeland Steamship Company was specially warned against including private correspondence in the Captain's box, a measure which had some effect, for in August, illicit carrying by small trading vessels was far commoner than by ordinary passenger boat. This traffic was conducted by the simple expedient of addressing letters to persons on board the ship lying in port.

During 1915 the system of port control was gradually elaborated. Its early beginnings at Folkestone, Gravesend and Southampton have already been mentioned. The influx of undesirables and persistent illegal carrying of letters caused MO5G to make formal complaint of the divided responsibility at the ports and to procure the appointment of special representatives at Hull, Newcastle, Liverpool, Bergen and Rotterdam in order to watch the traffic carefully and suggest improvements in applying preventive methods. These officers had no executive power; it rested with the aliens Officers to prevent an undesirable from landing or to admit him and with the police to arrest and search him. Accordingly circulars indicating the line of action required in the case of an individual were issued by E Branch at the request of the Investigating Branch to the Home Office as well as to the Port Officer. But the Port Officer acted as general adviser and supervisor in these cases. By means of this control the Investigating Branch could arrange for an undesirable to be kept out or admitted, to be most carefully searched, watched, his papers sent to Scotland Yard for investigation, or to have the man arrested and sent up to Scotland Yard. Equally important was the work done in stopping an undesirable from leaving the country or from making too frequent journeys to and from the Continent.

★

On 26 January a Belgian refugee living at Rotterdam wrote to the War Office stating that F. Leibacher of 1 Zwaanensteeg, Rotterdam, was a German agent who received letters containing messages in secret ink and forwarded them to their proper quarters. In the course of February three men, Anton Küpferle, Carl Muller and John Hahn, were found to be in communication with this address.

Anton Küpferle, alias Anthony Copperlee, was a German who became a naturalised American in 1913. He had been educated in the United States. At the end of 1911 he is said to have set up as a woollen draper at 1665 de Kalb Avenue, Brooklyn, New York, and to have failed in 1913. It is certain that he was employed as a salesman by two clothing firms between 1907 and 1913.

From passages in a letter and his last confession he would seem to have served at the Front between August 1914 and January 1915, in the capacity of a German officer. On 14 January 1915, he received $100 from Franz von Papen; an American passport was issued to him on the 25th, and he sailed for Liverpool on 4 February. On 17 and 18 February, two letters were intercepted addressed to Leibacher and written on paper headed A. Küpferle & Co., Importer of Woollens, 1665 de Kalb Avenue, Brooklyn. These letters contained messages in secret ink. From the text it appeared that Küpferle was in Liverpool on the 15th, in Dublin on the 16th, and expected to be in Queenstown on the 18th.

The bureau wired to Dublin and Liverpool police that Küpferle was to be arrested. Dublin replied giving a description of Küpferle and stating that he had left Kingdom for Holyhead on the 17th. He was supposed to be returning to America via Liverpool, The description and name were circulated to the ports and to Chief Constable Liverpool with instructions to arrest. But as the police report did not agree with Küpferle's written statement, Dublin and Liverpool were informed that he might still be in Ireland. Search, however, was made in London in the hotels in the neighbourhood of Euston and it was ascertained that Küpferle had spent the night of the 17th in one of them. He had left for

Victoria on the morning of the 18th. On the 18th, the boats for Flushing were held up owing to the German blockade and on the 19th a letter was intercepted which showed that Küpferle was awaiting further supplies of money at the Wilton Hotel. He was arrested that day. Evidence of his connection with Leibacher was found in Dublin and in London as well as materials for secret writing.

Küpferle's movements were traced in Liverpool. The information he had sent abroad was found to be mostly incorrect. Enquiries were set on foot in America to ascertain his nationality and business, and the American consulate were kept informed as to the case. As with regard to the postbox used, so also with regard to the judicial proceedings here, there is connection between the case of Küpferle and that of Muller and Hahn, which must now be recounted.

John Hahn was a British subject, the son of a German who naturalised as a British subject in 1897 and returned to Germany about 1905, there to end his days. Hahn spent the two years from 1901 to 1903 learning his trade as a baker and confectioner in Germany. From 1903 to 1910 he worked as a journeyman baker in London and Dublin in which places he spent two years. In September 1910 he bought a baker's shop at 111 High Street, Deptford, became a bankrupt at the end of 1913, and leased the shop to his wife in January 1914. It was raided by the mob in November and the business failed utterly in consequence of the war. Hahn had married in May 1912, Christine, the daughter of Richard Dorst, a German residing at 4 Osy Straat, Antwerp.

Carl F. H. Muller, a Russian, said to have been born at Libau of German parents, had lived at Antwerp for at least eleven years. He occupied a room in the house of Richard Dorst. He combined the occupation of check-weigher of cargoes on German steamers with other employment. He was for six months in Kattendyke's Engineering Works, Antwerp, and afterwards he was agent for a German firm dealing in motor-winches. Before the siege of Antwerp, Richard Dorst left with his family for Holland. Muller stayed behind and took charge of Dorst's property.

Muller had a daughter who is said to have lived in Hamburg and

Bremen: she was married to a German who perished in the battle of the Falkland Islands. By his own admission Muller was on friendly terms with German officers at Antwerp.

Muller arrived at Sunderland on 18 January 1915. He carried Russian papers and stated that he had just been released from a German prison, where he had been brutally treated. He called at the house of some English people with whom he had a slight acquaintance. They did what they could for him but Sunderland was at that time a prohibited area to all aliens and the police expelled him. He came to London to 38 Guildford Street, W.C. on the 13th and immediately got in touch with Hahn. On the 17th he left, returning to Guildford Street on the 21st. He went away almost immediately but came back on the 28th. He had been in Rotterdam and Roosendaal on the Belgian frontier. On 5 February he again went to Rotterdam, procured there a fresh passport, and returned to Guildford Street on the 13th. On 15 February he was signalled from Rotterdam as a German agent for the German GOC, Brussels. He was said to be receiving letters in London either poste restante or post office box addressed to the name of Leidec. Meanwhile, under the check on F. Leibacher (other forms Laibacher and Laybaker) letters had been intercepted of 3 and 4 February containing interlinear secret messages referring to military matters, signed AEIII and posted in the W.C. district.

The signature seemed to confirm previous reports received by the bureau of a book containing the record of German agents directed against England in which each agent was entered by a number corresponding to the order of his enrolment. On receipt of the first letter, enquiries were made at the address given in the *en clair* message, but without result. As, however, the handwriting faintly resembled that of a German who lived at the address, it was resolved to search the house for further evidence. Before this could be done, the second letter giving a different name and address was intercepted. On receipt of the message incriminating Muller, the police were sent to Guildford Street. Muller was interviewed on 16 February without much result. A check was put on the name Leidec. This resulted in the intercepting of two letters dated 20 and 21 February

addressed to Mr Lybecq, Postbox 447, Rotterdam, and posted in the
W.C. district. Each contained a secret message signed AEIII written on
the back of the letter. The writer mentioned that he was shortly going
to Sunderland. The letter of the 21st was written on a peculiar kind of
paper and the *en clair* message was in another hand. The bureau deduced
that AEIII was probably living in the Bloomsbury district; as he always
used a two pence stamp, the stamps of this value issued to a Branch office
were specially marked and enquiries with regard to the notepaper were
set on foot in the district.

Then came a letter dated 24 February written on the same kind
of note-paper as the fourth, containing a secret message beginning; 'In
the absence of AE' signed Hahn. The letter was posted in Deptford. The
bureau concluded that this second agent would be using his own name
and posting in his own district. Reference to the Aliens Register brought
to light the existence of John Hahn. The shop was raided and evidence
connecting Hahn with the writing of the two last letters was found.
Hahn was arrested on 24 February and gave a reference to Muller. The
next day Hahn's wife called at Scotland Yard, gave Muller's address, and
said he might be connected with the trouble.

Muller was arrested on 25 February and much incriminating evidence
was found in his rooms. Four of the marked stamps were found on him.
In May, Hahn made a written confession of some value to the bureau.
Muller, he said, had received a fortnight's instruction at Antwerp; by
means of photographs he had been taught to recognise the silhouettes of
British ships, and he had had to learn his code by heart. His chief object
in coming to England was to obtain precise details of Lord Kitchener's
armies. His repeated visits to Rotterdam were made with a view to
learning the course followed by steamers, and to give information
concerning the ships, etc. met with at sea.

Muller's cover was business in the tinned goods line; he got Hahn
to write two letters so that his own handwriting should not appear too
frequently. He offered Hahn a post in the German service and told
Hahn that the password 'Have you seen Matilda?' would get him past
any sentry in the German Army. Muller had been promised German

nationality; he had received 2,000 francs for some special service and his life had been insured for 16,000 marks.

The Special Intelligence Bureau ascertained that Muller had sent abroad information correct on the whole and applied to no fewer than eight different authorities for testimony as to the value of his information. The arrest of three German agents had been carried out within a space of six days. It was eminently desirable to suppress all notice of the arrests until after a certain date; the Cable Censor was warned to stop any mention of them in the press cables to America and the British press received like warnings. On 1 March, it was arranged to transfer the three prisoners to the Tower of London for greater secrecy.

The question of how to try the cases caused difficulty. At first it was decided to try them by court martial but the nationality of Küpferle, an American, and of Hahn, technically British and with the immemorial rights of a British subject, caused difficulty, political in the one case, judicial in the other. The case of Muller could not be separated from that of Hahn. On 16 March, however, the Defence of the Realm Act was amended to give the civil court power to inflict such punishment as might have been inflicted had the case been tried by court martial; to recognise the right of a British subject to trial by jury. And on 23 March, Regulation 56A was issued giving effect to the amendment. The three prisoners were therefore treated as British subjects and tried in the civil court under DRR 56A. The charge against all three was that of attempting to communicate information with a view to helping the enemy. Part of the evidence was taken in camera but the cases generally were tried and the sentences were by law promulgated in open court.

Küpferle's defence was that he had been asked by an American named Reilly (real name Ruehle) to collect information for the press and to forward it to Leibacher. An attempt had been made to get Leibacher and Ruehle to come over and give evidence in Küpferle's favour but they refused. Instead, three affidavits attesting to Küpferle's innocence were received from Holland from Leibacher, W. H. Muller and Verfuerden. Küpferle was tried on 18 and 19 May, but he committed suicide (before the trial was completed) on the 20th after making a written confession that he had spied on behalf of the Fatherland.

Muller and Hahn were tried on 2 June. Hahn was condemned to seven years' imprisonment. Muller was sentenced to be shot; his appeal was dismissed and the judges upheld the sentence which was carried out on 22 June. Mrs Hahn was not allowed to leave the country until December 1915. On 13 April 1915 a communique had been issued to the press stating briefly some of the facts regarding Küpferle, Muller and Hahn and thanking the press for its loyal co-operation in suppressing all mention of the arrests. At the same time special facilities had been granted to an American newspaper correspondent, who had been helpful with the case of Küpferle, enabling him to send his copy to America in time to show that he was not indebted for it to the British press.

Thus the names of the prisoners were known to the world and subsequently the sentences. But Muller being a very common name, it is possible that he was not identified by the Germans for at least one attempt was made, later on from America to ascertain clearly which Muller had suffered the penalty.

★

On 6 February 1915, among a number of Dutch postboxes used by German agents in England, were Richard Sanderson, Postbox 417 in Rotterdam, and Dr Brandt, in Dordrecht. These addresses were put on check on 9 February and on 27 February it was reported from Holland that a Mrs Schwartz, 38 Coptic Street, London, and a Mrs Wertheim of Hampstead, exact address unknown, lodged German agents, and on 10 May it was said that Mrs Wertheim was visiting Mrs Schwartz.

On 28 May 1915 Ernest Maxse, the British consul-general in Rotterdam, forwarded to the Foreign Office a report supplied by the French military attaché coupling Sanderson, of 72 Provenierstraat in Rotterdam, with W. Muller, of the Hotel Weber in Antwerp, H. Blanken, Wolfshoek 7b in Rotterdam, and Brandwijk & Co, 106a Bingleystraat, Rotterdam.

Sanderson, who represented the tea merchants Bjarks & Leming, was engaging young Dutchmen to travel in tea and sending them to Southampton, London, Cardiff and Hull to obtain news of the sailings of ships. Letters were to be addressed to Blanken and to Brandwijk: wires were to be sent in a certain code. Brandwijk's connection with Sanderson (alias Hilmar Dierks, alias de Boer) of Loosduinschekade in The Hague, was confirmed by Marius Hoogendyk, a Dutch sailor who gave the address Ipers Schiedamschedyk 33, as the postbox for letters.

Mr Maxse's report was the ultimate source through which, suitable detective methods having been applied, several German agents were arrested in England.

In all, fifteen people were dealt with in this double group of cases: seven men were executed as spies, one woman was sentenced to many years' imprisonment; three men and one woman were interned under DRR 14B; one man was imprisoned for a long term; another for six months; one was sentenced to three months' prison and eventually deported.

Haicke Marinus Petrus Janssen, aged thirty-two, landed at Hull on 13 May 1915. He carried a passport issued on 1 April and on arrival he wired to Hilmar Dierks for funds. He spent a week in Hull, then went to London and on the 23rd arrived at Southampton, whence he despatched five telegrams purporting to order different kinds of cigars, but in reality conveying information re the movements of ships, to Dierks & Co., from 24 to 28 May inclusive. After Janssen's arrest it was discovered that he had come to England in February to receive a medal for lifesaving at sea, and that he had visited Cardiff, Hull and Edinburgh besides.

Willem Johannes Roos, a sailor who had served in the Dutch Navy, landed at Tilbury on 14 May with a passport dated 13 April, went to Newcastle on the 15th, and thence to Edinburgh. He wired to Dierks & Co. from Edinburgh on 17, 18 and 30 May. Orders were issued for his arrest and he was traced to Aberdeen and Inverness, and was arrested in London on 2 June.

A search of telegraphic money orders brought to light payments of £10 and £20 made to Haicke Janssen on 19 and 31 May respectively and of £35 made to W. J. Roos on 25 May, the remitter in each case being Dierks & Co. These were found in the search of Janssen's room: various telegrams to and from Dierks & Co.; a communication from Dierks & Co. dated 9 March 1915; green and white trade cards issued by the firm; a descriptive trade-book of Dierks & Co.; a price list of the brands of cigars supplied by Dierks & Co., this list contained some letters and figures which were interpreted as code; a copy of *Jane's Fighting Ships* 1915; samples of different brands of cigars; eau de Cologne and custard powder and a bottle of liquid gum; various pens, nibs and a mapping pen.

There was besides a list of the addresses of various firms of tobacconists in Southsea and Portsmouth supplied by Stubbs & Co. Mercantile Offices in Gresham Street, and a letter from the same firm introducing Janssen to their branch at Plymouth.

Found in the search of the effects of Willem Roos were a cigar stocklist signed Dierks & Co.; a cigar stock list with printed heading Louis Dobbelmann, 106 Hoogstraat, Rotterdam; a number of plain memorandums and letter headings printed in the name of Dierks & Co.; a copy of *Pearson's Magazine* for May 1915 containing an article by Fred T. Jane, illustrated with photographs of different types of British warships and the names of several of His Majesty's ships written in pencil in the margin; various hotel bills showing the itinerary of Roos; a box of custard powders; a pen and seven nibs; a few cigars but no samples of different brands; and a communication from Janssen giving the address of the hotel at Hull from which Janssen was writing.

A comparison of the two cigar lists supplied by Dierks & Co. to Janssen and Roos showed that they were practically identical except that the one in the possession of Roos was fuller; it contained under the heading Mexico, code letters for a number of British ports on the eastern and north-eastern coasts. These were appropriately missing in Janssen's code. Roos admitted that he had been a sailor in the Dutch Navy. The pretext given by both men was that they were travelling for a firm of cigar merchants. It was ascertained that neither of them had called on any tobacconists in the places where they had stayed.

Willem Roos, in registering, had declared that he was travelling for the firm of Mr L. Dobbelmann, cigar merchants of Rotterdam. This was a genuine firm. Being interrogated, he did not mention the firm of Dobbelmann, but stated that he was in the employ of Dierks & Co., cigar and provision merchants, who gave him £35 to come to England. He admitted knowing Janssen quite well, who he said had no connection with Dierks. Janssen, on the other hand, stated that he was the only traveller employed by Dierks, and denied that he knew Roos. Being confronted with Roos he recanted partially. Both Janssen and Roos wrote from prison to their wives to apply for help to 38 Mechelsche Steenweg (Chaussee de Malines) and it was afterwards learned that Madame Roos, who lived in Ghent, had received a pension which was paid by the Discontogeselleschaft through the Algemeine Import and Export Bank of The Hague.

The papers found on the men were submitted for testing to a chemical expert. His tests brought up secret writing on the cigar lists. These had an odour of scent and the writing flashed up in a manner characteristic of scent. Gradually the expert reached the conviction that a fixative in the form of talc powder had been used with the scent.

Janssen was tried on the charge of having collected and communicated on various dates to Dierks & Co. at Den Haag information regarding the disposition of certain of HM ships and the movement of certain of HM's forces at or from Southampton. Willem Roos was tried on the charge of having collected and communicated information of a like nature regarding ships and forces respectively lying in the Firth of Forth and stationed near Edinburgh. Major Drake gave evidence as to the code and interpretation of the telegrams. Evidence of experts in the cigar trade proved that Dierks & Co.'s price lists were unintelligible or at least unusual. Per contra expert naval evidence proved that the information sent abroad by both men was approximately correct and most valuable to the enemy. They were found guilty and sentenced to be shot. The sentence was carried out on 30 July.

After the court martial and before the sentence had been confirmed, Janssen gave some information with regard to spy methods. All the addresses that he gave were however, already known to the bureau. He stated that the British had failed to discover two of the codes and that telegrams and letters of interest passed the Censor daily. Further he said that one method of smuggling messages was by slipping them down the back of a book between the binding and the leaves. Janssen also cautioned the British against women spies.

★

Georg Breckow (or Breeckow) was born in Germany in 1884, son of a Russian landowner who had failed and gone to live at Stettin. Breckow at some time of his existence served in the Cuirassiers. For three years he was employed in a big export business and then went to America where he earned a living as a pianist. He never became naturalised in America and in June 1914 he returned to Germany.

In March 1915 he was engaged by the German Naval Intelligence Bureau at Antwerp to act as imperial courier between Germany and America, but he was sent first to England with messages. Captain Schnitzer or Schmitzer gave him a forged passport made out in the name of Reginald Rowland from the particulars of the passport belonging to a man of that name. The real Reginald Rowland had in March deposited his passport a few hours with the police in Berlin.

Breckow was given an address for his correspondence and told to sign his letters George T. Parker. He was sent in to Holland and there Dierks supplied him with papers and cards of the firm of Norton B. Smith, New York. A genuine firm dealing in scrap-iron and other metals existed at New York under the name of Morton B. Smith. Breckow also received £45 for delivery to Mrs Wertheim and a letter from Mrs Hohwedell, the wife of a photographer in Stettin, for delivery to Robert Carter, an Englishman, residing at Southampton.

Rowland landed at Tilbury on 11 May, came to London and got in touch with Mrs Wertheim. On 20 May he went to Southampton and saw Carter and tried to induce him to return to Germany apparently under cover of an American passport. Both Carter and his landlady suspected

Rowland's motives and after some exchange of letters Carter broke off relations. Rowland then joined Mrs Wertheim and together they stayed at Bournemouth from 22 to 25 May. He went to Ramsgate with a Dr Tullidge from 28 to 31 May. From Bournemouth and Ramsgate he sent information to the Germans.

Under the check on Dierks & Co. the Censor forwarded from Holland a telegram of 30 May 1915, announcing the despatch to Reginald Rowland, c/o Societé Generale, Regent Street, London, of £30 on account of Norton B. Smith & Co., New York. Rowland was arrested on 4 June. By his German accent he had aroused suspicion on two occasions; owing to his handwriting and correspondence, his letters were stopped by the Postal Censor, who submitted a letter dated 25 May and a second dated 2 June, on the grounds that they appeared to emanate from a German who wished to live on the coast and to take photographs.

The letters were signed George T. Parker and posted in London. After Rowland's arrest they were identified by the handwriting as being his work. They were then tested and found to contain naval and military information, some of it concerning Scotland, references to Bournemouth, to a lady accomplice and to 'Lizzie' in secret writing. A batch of newspapers which was intercepted after Rowland's arrest contained a reference to a journey in the north.

Among other articles in Rowland's possession there was found a receipt for a registered letter addressed to L. Wertheim, Inverness. This apparently on 9 June, was connected with the references to 'Lizzie' which had at first been interpreted as a code name for the *Queen Elizabeth*. The Chief Constable of Inverness was wired to – he had already sent in a report regarding the lady to the Metropolitan Police – and replied that she had returned to London. She was arrested on the evening of 9 June. Also among Rowland's effects were found hotel bills establishing part of his movements; cards of Norton B. Smith and a letter showing that he represented the firm; *Jane's Fleets of the World*, 1915; a phial of lemon-juice; pens and a tin of talc powder: a code resembling in its general features one used by Haicke Janssen and Willem Roos. This code was written on a sheet of rice paper and concealed in the case of Rowland's shaving brush. He explained the lemon-juice by saying that he used it after shaving – an excuse which was also put forward by Ernest Melin. Rowland had received in all £110 from the Germans.

★

Louise Emily Wertheim, whose maiden name was Klitzke, was by birth a German Pole, and became by her marriage with Bruno Wertheim a British subject. For three years separated from her husband, she was in England when war broke out and procured with the aid of a relative at Hampstead and of a Hampstead doctor a passport to enable her to visit her mother in Berlin. She did not however leave until October when she went on visits to Amsterdam and there met an old friend named Dr Brandt. She returned to London in November and put up in Coptic Street.

In December 1914 Mrs Wertheim again went to Amsterdam to nurse the wife of an old friend named Moritz Lietzau. While there she arranged with Dr Brandt to correspond with him in a kind of family code. She returned to London at the end of January and introduced herself to Miss Gertrud Elizabeth Brandes.

Miss Brandes, of 62 Hammersmith Road, was the sister of Mrs Lietzau, and thence forward Mrs Wetheim made her headquarters at that house. But she would frequently go away for two or three days together without giving an address. Subsequently it was ascertained that she had visited Folkestone, Margate, the Isle of Man, Fishguard and probably Ireland and Holland during these absences.

In about Whitsuntide she called on an American lady named Miss Knowles – Macy at 33 Regent's Park Road – and induced her to go with her to Scotland. On 28 May they reached Edinburgh and Miss Knowles having no passport was told to get one and returned for good to London. Mrs Wertheim went to Dundee from 28 to 31 May and on 30 May drove to Carnoustie and Arbroath. She spent from 1 to 3 June in Inverness and there aroused suspicion by ordering a motor to drive to Cromarty. The Chief Constable was warned; he called at the hotel and noted irregularities in Mrs Wertheim's signature, interviewed her and practically obliged her to return to London. On 3 June he reported the matter to the Metropolitan Police. Mrs Wertheim returned on the 3rd and next day deposited her Scottish luggage with Miss Knowles.

On 7 June Miss Brandes turned Mrs Wertheim out and she then went to Miss Knowles for two nights. She was arrested in Miss Knowles' house. When the police went to search her room, she entered the maid's room, tore up a letter from George T. Parker and threw it out of the window. Among her papers, besides evidence showing that she had been recently in Berlin and had been communicating with German PoWs, there were found the address of Netta, wife of Dr Brandt; that of Althuis, 166 Loosduinschekade and letters of 7 and 18 May signed 'Mother' and 'Suzette' but written from Loosduischekade and by the same hand, which was that of Dr Brandt; letters from George T. Parker; an envelope addressed to R. Rowland; an Irish railway guide and Irish money; £115 in banknotes; a letter showing that she had applied to a Mrs Ausems for £50 to be sent in the name of her mother. This letter to which was attached Rowland's visiting card, seemed to have been used as a letter of introduction. She had besides a bottle of scent and a tin of talcum powder.

An examination of telegrams showed that on 1 May, Wertheim had sent a conventional message to a known spy-address in Holland. In examination Rowland lied freely. He denied that he had ever been in the army but sprang to attention at the word of command. Eventually he made some sort of confession the gist of which, as regards German methods, was given above.

On preparing the case it was discovered by chemical examination that his passport was forged and a photograph of the genuine passport was obtained from America. The Germans had altered the age to suit Breckow's appearance. Enquiries were made in America with regard to the firm of Morton B. Smith which denied all knowledge of Rowland. The news forwarded by Rowland was verified and that sent to him by Wertheim was carefully verified in its relation to her movements and the actual facts. The information of Rowland and of Wertheim was found to be correct. The enquiry involved a great deal of correspondence with

Chief Constables in Scotland. Wertheim's movements were fully proved but Rowland was never traced in Scotland, it seems unlikely that he ever went there.

Rowland and Wertheim were tried together in the civil court for Wertheim claimed her rights as a British subject. They were found guilty; Rowland was sentenced to be shot. He appealed, but the sentence was upheld, and it was carried out in October. Wertheim was sentenced to a long term of imprisonment.

★

Fernando Buschman was a Brazilian subject of German origin. His mother lived in Vienna, his wife at Dresden. He had been in partnership with a man named Marcelino Bello in Las Palmas. The firm Buschman & Bello traded as general merchants and importers, and Buschman who was an engineer, dealt with the engineering branch of the trade. At some time not specified, but presumably on the outbreak of war, Buschman severed his connection with the firm, which then became known as M. Bello & Company.

On 26 August 1914, Buschman left Las Palmas and went via Barcelona and Genoa to Dresden and thence to Hamburg. He wrote to Bello from Hamburg. He returned to Genoa and wired thence to Bello for money on 18 March; from Barcelona he wired again on 26 March. A small sum was sent which Buschman promised to repay as he had obtained a post at the Brazilian legation in London.

Buschman landed at Folkestone on 14 April 1915. His passport, which had been issued at the Brazilian consulate in June 1913, bore visas issued in Las Palmas, 26 August 1914; Barcelona, 5 September 1914; Madrid, 3 April 1915; Paris, 13 April 1915, and Boulogne, 13 April 1915.

Thus there was no trace of his journey to Dresden and Hamburg which became known only through a letter from the British Bank of West Africa dated 6 July 1915.

In London, Buschman stayed at various hotels. He made a rapid friendship with a naturalised British subject of Romanian origin named

Emile Franco, with whom he proposed to set up a commission agency for the sale of cheese, butter in tins, cotton, blankets, and soft soap to be imported from Holland, where Buschman stated that he had business. He also proposed to import cloth for the French armies from Spain. While in London, Buschman visited various firms with the ostensible object of renewing trade relations with the firm of M. Bello. He explained the change of style as necessary owing to loss of trade occasioned by the false belief that he, Buschman, was a German.

Entries in Buschman's diary show that on 23 and 24 April he went to Southampton returning by Portsmouth. Emile Franco saw him buy his ticket; Franco and the head porter at the Piccadilly Hotel also deposed that Buschman had intended to visit firms of banana importers at Liverpool. On 5 May, Buschman crossed to Rotterdam, visited various towns in Holland and returned on the 16th. Soon after he went to live with Emile Franco and the two men took a flat together in Harrington Gardens. Immediately after Buschman's first landing in England he had entered into telegraphic communication with H. Flores, Hilmar Dierks' partner in Rotterdam, to whom he wired repeatedly for money. The money was sent at least twice through the Brazilian legation in London.

Buschman had also wired to Bello in Las Palmas for money. On 4 June a telegram from Dierks asking Buschman to return and confer with Flores was intercepted and Buschman was arrested. He was interviewed and denied having done any business with Dierks, against whom he had been put on his guard by von Staa, of the firm of Ivers & von Staa. He stated that Flores was engaged in selling guns to the French and he, Buschman, was dealing in picric acid, rifles and cloth. The investigation that followed Buschman's equipment showed that Buschman had concluded no business in England, that on the other hand he was well equipped to act as a spy. He was a first rate mechanic, possessed a French authorisation to use the aviation ground at Issy, issued in 1910; he carried a French passport issued in Madrid on 9 April 1915. His papers, newspapers and music were covered with minute figures in secret ink and on a telegraph form there was a microscopic map in the same medium giving the positions of the headquarters of the British armies, corps and divisions in France during April 1915. A search of his papers and of old telegraph forms at the GPO gave proof of Buschman's connection with Flores, with an address formerly occupied by Colonel von Ostertag, German military attaché at The Hague, and a leader in espionage, and also with a man named H. Grund who had written to Buschman making an appointment for a meeting in Holland. A letter signed Chr. J. Mulder referring to deals in cheese and surgical rubber wares, which was thought to be in code, also contained a reference to Grund and a promising deal in bananas.

The case against Buschman was one of great difficulty. As the telegram of 4 June had not been delivered it could not be produced in evidence, and corroborative evidence of the visits to Southampton and Portsmouth could not be obtained. There was no proof that the secret writing, which Buschman denied absolutely, had been done by him and the map was apparently also an unsatisfactory piece of evidence.

On the other hand there was abundant proof that Buschman had been in the pay of Flores, who was well-known from the evidence of other spy cases. In addition to the earlier evidence, the financial manager of the American Express Company had received an order to pay Buschman £50 on account of H. Flores.

For the purposes of prosecution it was important to establish the identity of Grund. During July 1915, the bureau obtained some evidence of proof that Grund was a German agent; while he was said to have recruited John de Heer for Antwerp it was certain that the spy Augusto Roggen had written to him from Scotland. Enquiries made in Holland showed that Grund was a German, an inspector of a German navigation company, who had no fixed address but lived on a tramp steamer in the harbour, and received his letters at the office of Ivers and von Staa. Von Staa was an officer of the German Reserve. Grund's connection with the German Secret Service was attested by de Heer but it was evidence of a kind that could not be produced in court. The summary of evidence was taken on 18 August.

Buschman was tried on 28 September. He was charged on four counts under DRR 48 and found guilty of three of the charges, of committing preparatory acts to collecting and communicating information in contravention of DRR 18. The charge of attempting to elicit information was not proved. He was sentenced to be shot and was executed on 19 October 1915. Shortly after Buschman's arrest Regulation 18A was promulgated.

★

Alfredo Augusto Roggen was a Uruguayan, whose permanent residence was stated to be Montevideo, landed at Gravesend on 30 May 1915, and from London despatched a telegram to Flores asking for funds. Roggen travelled as a farmer and approached a London firm with a view to buying horses to the value of £3,600, and a firm in Lincoln on the subject of agricultural machinery for importation into Uruguay after the war. But he had no letters of introduction and did not pursue the business after his one call. He was in Lincoln on the night of 4 June; on 5 he reached Edinburgh and put up at the Carlton Hotel, where Mrs Wertheim had been on 28 May. He went to the police to register on 6 June, spent the whole of Monday touring the Trossachs, and completed his registration at Edinburgh on 8 June. He went to the Tarbet Hotel on the 9th meaning to stay for eight or nine days, his excuse being health and a desire for quiet fishing. Tarbet lies within two miles of Loch Long, which was then in use as a torpedo station and a prohibited area. On the evening of 8 June, Roggen had posted two cards in Edinburgh, one addressed to Flores, the other to Grund. He announced that he had found a pretty place for fishing and walking in the mountains and to Grund he gave his address as Tarbet Hotel, Loch Lomond. Each card contained a message for 'his girl'. The cards were intercepted and Roggen was arrested five hours after reaching Tarbet.

He was interviewed and gave an unsatisfactory account of his relations with Flores, whom he described as a friend of his partner in South America. The addresses found in a note-book of Roggen show refinements of precaution: 127 Binnemveg was half crossed out and written so close beneath the words 'Consulado del Uruguay' as to seem to be the address of the consulate in Amsterdam, the incorrect form. Ipers and von Staa was written immediately below a bogus address in Gainsborough. On a sheet of blotting paper was found a partly legible name which was taken to be G. Breckow. Connection between Breckow and Roggen was never established but it is to be noted that Roggen had stayed at the Bonnington Hotel and within easy reach of Breckow, who was then at the Ivanhoe Hotel, London. And in Edinburgh, Roggen had put up in the hotel visited by Mrs Wertheim.

A scent bottle and antiseptic talc powder were found among Roggen's effects and secret writing was developed on several of his papers. But most important of all was a map of the North Sea torn from a Dutch railway guide, on which some minute characters, words and figures were detected, as well as stains of oil. The tester however, pointed out the difficulty of obtaining results that would satisfy the untrained eye that such marks were anything other than stains in the fibre and added that the Germans had probably relied upon this effect in choosing the method.

But to satisfy the strictest requirements of proof the expert carried out his test in the presence of other witnesses, and also carried out negative tests that proved similar reactions would not be obtained by treating the unmarked fibre of the paper in the same manner.

Roggen was tried by court martial on four charges: (i) of coming to England on 30 May; (ii) of going from Edinburgh to Tarbet on 9 June; (iii) and (iv) of writing to Flores and of writing to Grund which were preparatory acts to the collecting and communicating of information with intent to help the enemy. He was shot in the Tower on 17 September 1915. Concerning his identity, it may be remarked that his passport was issued on 11 May 1915 by the Uruguayan consul at The Hague. It was not called in question here, but the Minister of Uruguay who knew members of the rich and well-esteemed family of the Roggens, did not know Alfredo Augusto, and subsequently declared that both he himself and the Roggens thought Alfredo Augusto a thief and a liar and would take no part in his defence. One of Roggen's methods was to represent that he had come through Switzerland and, had had great trouble with the German authorities.

★

A Peruvian, Ludovico Hurwitz y Zender went in December 1914 from Peru to New York whence he sailed for Christiania on 16 February 1915. He landed at Newcastle on 11 April, reached Glasgow on the 12th, and on the 13th took up residence at Duncan's Temperance Hotel. On the 20th he spent the night at Aberdeen and from the 21st to the 24th, stayed at Inverness returning to Glasgow on 24 April. On 25 May he left Glasgow and sailed for Bergen from Newcastle on the 28th. In Glasgow he is reported to have led a very quiet life, walking the golf links with the manager of the hotel, going twice down the Clyde on a Sunday, but not appearing to have any business or friends.

Early in June the bureau caused a scrutiny to be made of all telegrams sent during May from certain ports in the United Kingdom. Five telegrams sent by Ludovico Hurwitz from Glasgow between 15 and 24 May to August Brockner (or Brochner), 11 Todboldgatan, Christiania, attracted the notice of code experts. Ostensibly they were orders for different classes of tinned fish-goods, but the wording of the messages varied suspiciously and in a manner that resembled the arbitrary codes used by Roos and Janssen.

From the Chief Constable of Glasgow it was learned that Hurwitz y Zender had left the country meaning to return in a few weeks. The bureau having obtained a description of Hurwitz y Zender circulated it to the ports with orders for his arrest and rigorous search, adding that it was essential that the utmost secrecy should be observed. Neither the public nor press were to know of the arrest. On 2 July, Hurwitz attempted to land at Newcastle, was arrested and brought to Scotland Yard. Among other papers was a hotel bill showing that he had been to Copenhagen and a catalogue and price list of tinned fish and several tins of samples of these goods; he carried £84 in notes and £5 in gold. He had, among other objects, twelve new handkerchiefs and a bottle of medicine. Hurwitz declared he was travelling for the firm of T. Vidal, general importers of Lima, and that through the general agent, August Brockner, he had bought fish on their behalf. He was to have purchased handkerchiefs at Glasgow and various kinds of goods at Sheffield but he had done no business in England owing to the lack of specific instructions which he had expected but had not received by post. An agent sent to Christiania to ascertain the facts about Brockner, shadowed the man and saw him deliver a large envelope at the private house of the German ambassador, Brockner was also said to be in daily touch with the German consulate and to be organising German counter-espionage in Christiania.

The firm of T. Vidal in Lima did exist, but it had no standing or credit and was connected with the Germans. It imported goods through travellers from Manchester and the Continent. Eventually the whole correspondence between Hurwitz and Brockner was obtained, as also were five earlier telegrams sent from Glasgow to Aberdeen in April and early May. This correspondence was submitted to the destructive criticism of an expert in the fish trade. Hurwitz was ordering and Brockner transmitting his orders for fish out of season, in wrong quantities and packings. A summary of evidence had been taken in August but the trial was delayed owing to the necessity of getting documents from Peru.

Hurwitz was tried by court martial on 20, 21 and 23 March 1916, and condemned to death on four charges under DRR 48, of having twice committed a preparatory act in coming to England on 11 April and 2 July, and of having twice attempted to communicate information by sending a telegram on 15 and on 20 May. These two telegrams having been satisfactorily deciphered contained true information with regard to ships in the Firth of Forth. Hurwitz was shot on 11 April.

Three points are worth noticing: the general agent, Brockner, had in his office at Christiania only one class of goods, actually ties. Hurwitz carried one dozen new handkerchiefs and a bottle of medicine which was afterwards found to be Protargol. In the course of 1916, it became known that Protargol was a medium for secret writing and that ties and handkerchiefs were used by the Germans as vehicles for certain of these mediums.

★

Kurt Harlot de Rysbach, known as Kenneth de Rysbach (alias Charles Courtenay, alias Jack Cummings) was a British subject who came to England via Switzerland and France on 27 June. He sent abroad sheets of music covered with invisible writing, twenty-four newspapers, eight letters and two telegrams. In order to do this work he had been released from a German prison for civilians. He established himself in rooms with an Englishwoman who was a trick cyclist and procured an engagement which was to begin on 2 August in a Glasgow music-hall. On 9 July, de Rysbach wrote to Mr J. Cords at the spy address used by Zender. In a secret message he stated that he had a brother on HMS *Commonwealth* who would furnish information and that he himself would soon get a post as interpreter in the War Office. A comparison of the handwriting of the letter with that of recent applications for interpreterships produced nothing, but from a check on letters to the crew of the Commonwealth, the brother of the writer was identified and also exonerated. De Rysbach who had given various pseudonyms, was traced by a letter to his brother in which he gave his address and stage-name and also his photograph. He was arrested on 26 July, as also the girl with whom he was living. Materials for secret writing were found in his rooms.

He was tried by the civil court on 20 September, the jury disagreed as to their verdict and he was remanded. On the second occasion, the jury found him guilty and he was sentenced to imprisonment for life. De Rysbach's defence was that he came to England and promised to serve the Germans in order to obtain his liberty, and he had no intention to assist the enemy. Apparently that defence had some weight with the jury in the first trial. After his conviction he gave full details of his connection with the German Secret Service. He told how he had received instructions from German agents in Berlin and had been supplied with materials to be used for writing in invisible ink and addresses to which his communications were to be sent.

★

The identity of the spy who was arrested and suffered death under the name of Irving Guy Ries was not satisfactorily cleared up till after his sentence. The real person of that name received a passport from the Department of State, Washington, on 10 March 1915 he was to visit Holland, Austria, Germany, Switzerland, Italy, France and Great Britain. His mission was to take photographs for the Newspaper Enterprise Association in Chicago.

Ries was impersonated by a man named Paul Hensel who landed at Liverpool on 4 July with a forged passport dated 30 March to travel in Holland and Denmark; his ostensible mission was to collect new clients in Great Britain and elsewhere for three American firms, two of which dealt in hay and corn. He registered at Liverpool, stating he was going to London. Instead of this he went to Newcastle, Glasgow and Edinburgh, returned to Liverpool and thence reached London on 28 July. Between the 28th and 31st he went to Brighton, returning afterwards to town.

On his tour in the north, he visited only three or four firms, and he approached a few others by letter after leaving the localities in which they were situated. In no case did he do any business. On 8 August, he booked a passage from Hull to Copenhagen and approached the American consulate for a visa to get his permit. The American consulate discovered the forgery and impounded the passport. Ries then would seem to have destroyed incriminating documents in expectation of his arrest which took place on 10 August.

Meanwhile he had been the object of enquiry since 5 August. On the 3rd, the GPO had reported that he had received £20 by telegraphic money order from a Madame Cleton in Rotterdam, and the sum was suspect. This news was followed by news from Rotterdam to the effect that a telephone message passing between German GHQ Wesel and the German consulate in Rotterdam had been tapped and decoded. It conveyed instructions to pay Madame Cleton, 70 Provenierstraat, Rotterdam, certain sums of money for the mission of Irwin Guy Ries, Hotel Cecil, and to continue to pay a tenth of this sum weekly.

Seventy-two Provenierstraat was a known accommodation address of the agent Sanderson, alias Dierks, and had been on check since

May 1915. Madame Cleton was a name assumed by Sanderson's wife when her husband was taken into custody by the Dutch. No doubt existed as to Ries' connections and the wording of the message induced the belief that he was responsible for the destruction of the Ardeer Factory which blew up on 30/31 July 1915. After his arrest the bureau traced his connections in the States.

Of the three firms mentioned by him two were genuine but he did not represent either of them although he had applied to do so. A partner in one of these firms showed nervousness when he was interviewed. The third firm of Wackerow-Belcher did not exist but a man named Richard Wackerow was traced. This man stated that he had been American consul in Austria for eleven years and admitted knowing Ries, who was in the grain, wheat and flour business in Chicago, but refused to say more and avoided an office interview which he himself had arranged. Money orders received by and for Ries were as follows:

- 10 July £40; 31 July £20; 3 August £20 (before his arrest)
- 16 August £40; 21 August, £30; 21 August £39.10s (after arrest)

Ries was charged with: 1. Committing an act preparatory to collecting without lawful authority information, etc.; 2. Having been in communication with a spy; 3. Being found in possession of a false passport; 4. Having falsely represented himself to be a person to whom a passport had been duly issued.

He was tried by court martial and sentenced to be shot on 5 October. The sentence was carried out on 27 October. In proving the charges it was thought necessary to show that Ries had not done any genuine business but the evidence showed that he was competent to open business negotiations. Subsequently it was learned that the State Department at Washington had been unable to procure evidence of Wackerow's connection with Hensel, but owing to his having admitted that he knew Hensel he was arrested and interned in April 1917. Wackerow had been the US vice-consul at Breslau from 1902 to 1911.

★

On 9 June, the British consul-general at Rotterdam reported that David Stad had come over on the 1st and that Cornolis Marinus den Braber was shortly coming to this country. Both were Dutch seamen, purporting to act as representatives of von Brandwijk & Company for the sale of a custard powder. The firm was supposed to have a branch at 18 Lindley Street; Stad had a sister named Liebfreund, whose address was not known. Orders were issued that these two men were to be watched and their movements reported. They were traced to the house of his sister, Mrs Liebfreund, 16 Lindley Street, and den Braben to the house of a Russian named Carlishe or Kalische, 18 Lindley Street.

Stad had wired to Brandwijk for money and £7 was sent to den Braber by Ipers on the 26th. Stad had arrived on 9 June, bringing business cards of von Brandwijk; Braber arrived on the 18th. Neither of the men had done any business.

The police searched their rooms, found dummy cases of custard powder but no samples, and ordered the men to report daily to the police station. On the 23rd Stad and den Braber were arrested for having neglected to give proper particulars to their landlords, and Liebfreund and Carlishe were arrested for having failed to keep a proper register of their lodgers. The charge against Stad and den Braber failed on a technical point and they were liberated on 14 July 1915. There was, however, no doubt they had come over to spy and they were interned under DRR 14B. Meanwhile the ports had been warned to arrest and search any persons travelling for von Brandwijk.

The case against Liebfreund and Carlishe resulted in a fine of £5 for Carlishe, and in six months' hard labour for Liebfreund. Liebfreund was a Russian tailor who came to England in November 1914, married Anna Stad on 2 May 1915, and found Carlishe's lodging for den Braber. Moreover, letters referring to D. Stad's business in England were sent directed to Liebfreund from the address of M. Stad.

The bureau had no doubt that Liebfreund had come to England for the purpose of helping the German Secret Service and on the expiry of his sentence procured an order for his internment. The Advisory Committee, however, refused to sanction the order. In 1917, Liebfreund returned to Russia to serve as a soldier and his wife went back to Holland with a no return permit. Den Braber was deported in October 1919. There is no record that Stad was deported.

★

In July van Zwol, chief officer of the SS *Caledonia* was reported to be associating with German agents and bringing over information to Volbrath. On the 25th he was said to be carrying information by means of marks on apples and pears. The full story was not known until October 1917, but as it explains some of van Zwol's action in England it is worth inserting here.

In June 1915 the Dutch authorities summoned Hochenholz on suspicion of his having enlisted Dutch seamen for espionage in England. He confessed to having several Dutchmen in his employ and the police discovered that J. van Zwol was one of them. Van Zwol was arrested on 24 August and confessed that he had given information about the British fleet to Hochenholz; his cabin was searched and in it were discovered a slip of paper bearing the names of several British men of war, and apples and pears marked with ciphers and letters. Van Zwol was allowed to go but photographs of the slip of paper and of the apples were forwarded to England.

On receipt of the report from Rotterdam dated 25 August, orders were issued to arrest van Zwol on his arrival at Hull. This was done and his cabin searched; apples and pears were found in it but nothing incriminating. Van Zwol, however, in his interrogation at Scotland Yard admitted that he had been approached by Hochenholz who asked him for information saying that it was required for publication in a newspaper. Van Zwol stated that he had once told Hochenholz the number of ships in the Humber and for this had received 24 gulden. He admitted his connection, with Harry Vanderberg, his nephew, who had been signalled as a spy on 30 January, and with Valkenburg, a publican who had served a term of three months' imprisonment on suspicion of espionage for Germany.

There was no evidence that van Zwol had committed an offence on British territory; he was therefore interned under DRR 14B on the grounds of hostile association and ordered for deportation in October 1919.

★

The third group of enemy spies dealt with by the bureau in 1915 consists of a number of agents who were sent out apparently by the Berlin centre, or by some centre not identified. These were Robert Rosenthal, Ernest W. Melin, Josef Marks and Albert Meyer.

Simultaneously with the letters written by Meyer to Goedhardt, certain letters signed Johanesco and Erikssen, addressed to Goedhardt, containing secret writing and posted in northern ports were intercepted. The writer was never traced with certainty, but as a result of investigation and of some information received from Holland, a Swedish sailor named Per Gustav Erikson was interned under DRR 14B (in November 1915) and a Danish sailor, W. H. Möller, was deported.

Robert Rosenthal, a German, made three journeys to England on behalf of Captain von Prieger, Chief of the Admiralty Secret Service in Berlin. It is very probable that this was the Berger whose presence became known to the branch owing to their enquiry as to cheques paid into the German banks from abroad. In the middle of November 1914 he came to London via The Hague and Folkestone with orders to go to Plymouth, Portsmouth, Weymouth, Dover, Grimsby and Newcastle. From London he despatched on 19 and 23 November telegrams giving information with regard to ships at Edinburgh and Portsmouth. He embarked for Holland at Folkestone on 11 December after staying at Portsmouth from 4 to 7 December 1914.

On 9 January 1915 he arrived at Hull from Copenhagen, and wired on the 9th and 11th news about His Majesty's ships. From Hull he went to Newcastle and Liverpool, where he embarked on the 16th and went via Cardiff to Spain and Italy, and so to Germany.

For these two journeys he used the cover-address George Haeffner, Christiania, Kirkegatan 30.

A third journey took place in mid-April again via Copenhagen and Hull. He went to London, Birmingham, Glasgow and Edinburgh sending wires to Salomon, Vestervoldgade 10, Copenhagen, from those cities on 22 April, 5 May and 11 May respectively and letters on 9, 10 and 11 May. The story of Rosenthal's passports is complicated. From 1908 to 1913 Rosenthal was in the United States, having left Germany on account of forgery. He returned to Germany in November 1913. In June 1914 Rosenthal had urgent reasons for wishing to leave Germany and with the connivance of a friend he obtained at Hamburg a consular certificate of American nationality. With this he obtained an emergency passport in Berlin, where for a time he worked for the Relief Commission. In October he was sent to The Hague to get a genuine American passport, but was given instead a consular certificate and an affidavit to say he had lost his passport in Berlin. He was given a new emergency passport and with this he made his two first journeys to England but on the second occasion it seems to have aroused suspicion at Newcastle and he was frightened out of the country. For the third journey he procured a passport issued at Washington on 26 January 1915. Von Prieger had shown him apparatus for fabricating American documents and had offered him a passport and a birth certificate, but these he had refused.

Rosenthal's ostensible reason for coming in November and January was to dispose of a patent with regard to smoking. His arrest on the third journey was due to a happy accident. On 8 April, Rosenthal wrote from the Hotel Bristol, Copenhagen, to Franz Kulbe, Berlin Schöneberg, Belzigerstrasse 10, a letter containing a secret message to the effect that he was going to start work in England under the pretext of selling a patent gas-lighter. He signed his letter Robert Rosenthal. Through some mis-sort the letter came to England; the censor thought the *en clair* message suspicious, tested the letter and found the secret message. The letter was submitted to MO5, the head of which section handed it on to MO5G on 3 May. The address of Franz Kulbe was already known to the bureau as that of Captain von Prieger and orders were at once issued for the arrest

of any traveller in a patent gas-lighter. Late at night on 11 May he was
arrested in the act of embarking at Newcastle for Bergen.

Being interrogated and led to admit the facts of his passage at
Copenhagen, he was then confronted with his letter when he immediately
gave up the fight and confessed his true nationality and mission. Among
Rosenthal's effects were found *Fleets of the World* 1915; a new map of
Glasgow; a Scotch road book; field glasses; some flags; eau de Cologne
and violet powder. He had been given 2,500 marks to last till the middle
of May. Of this £100 was in gold.

Five of Rosenthal's telegrams dated 19, 23 November, 9 and 11
January, and 16 April, were produced in evidence and proved to contain
substantially accurate information. He was court martialled on 6 July and
hanged on the 16th.

★

Josef Marks carried an American emergency passport which had been
issued in Berlin on 1 February 1915, without the production of any
identification papers but on the personal identification of the American
consul Thompson and the vice-consul Heinrich Guadflieg both of Aix-
la-Chapelle. The passport bore visas from the Aachen police, 13 February
1915; the German consulate in Rotterdam, 15 June 1915, object: journey
to Germany; the American Legation in The Hague, 21 June 1915; object:
journey to England; the British consulate in The Hague, 15 July 1915;
object: business with the Safety Chemical Company, 1 Eagle Street,
High Holborn.

The American minister at The Hague believed the passport to be
a forgery and warned the British consulate and on 25 June, Rotterdam
reported to the bureau that Marks was coming to England as an independent
spy sent out by GHQ Berlin. Orders were issued to the ports for the arrest,
search and conveyance to Scotland Yard of Josef Marks.

He was signaled as crossing on 15 July. Recognised and accosted
on the boat by PC Billett he at once asked to see an intelligence officer
to whom he would give important information. He added that he was

being shadowed by a German agent. In various interviews he gave the following story: he was born in Germany but was educated in the States and became an American citizen. He returned to Germany and married and set up in business there. In August 1914 he and his wife were arrested by the Germans and after pressure he entered the German Secret Service. He was trained by the Antwerp Bureau, had to make two trial trips in Holland and then was allowed a short holiday in Germany. He was coming to England to find out about munitions, was to use a book of stamps as code and received £45 for the trip. He made up his mind to give information to the British authorities and on the way over wrote a letter to the Minister of Munitions.

The letter was actually written on the ship's notepaper and was delivered up by Marks. The codebook and about £37 and letters that he had written from prison in Germany to the military authorities to complain of his treatment were found upon him; also a registration certificate proving that he was born at Munich and was a civil engineer. Investigation proved that Marks was in all probability a German subject, as he had once possessed American citizenship but had allowed it to lapse. Moreover he was identified as Multerer, the former fraudulent managing director of the Safety Chemical Co., who had lived in England as a German subject from 1911 to about June 1915 and had left owing many debts. While in residence here Multerer had business notepaper printed for his wife under the name of Marks. He would visit Germany two or three times a year. Marks was charged under DRR 18 and 46 with an act preparatory to committing an offence, embarking upon and voyaging to Tilbury by ship with the intention to act as a spy. The question was at what precise moment he abandoned that intention and whether he was sincere in his confession.

Two officers went to the prison but Marks then stated he thought the German espionage system was best and refused to give any information. A month later he offered to obtain the formulae for the new German gas and its re-agent. He was tried by court martial on 28 September 1915 and was sentenced to five years' imprisonment. In December 1919 he was deported.

★

Ernest Melin was a Swede, the son of a former managing owner of the Thule Steamship Company, and had been for many years manager of that company. He left it in 1906 and after some years of idleness obtained a post at Nikolaieff, which he was forced to leave on account of the war. He went to Hamburg, was recruited for the German Secret Service by Hilmar Dierks and was engaged by the Antwerp Bureau.

He came to England on about 15 January, spent a fortnight in London and returned to Holland on 29 January. The Antwerp Bureau insisted that he should make the rounds of the English and Scottish ports and this he refused to do. He was then taken on by the Wesel Bureau at a salary of £50 a month. He was sent to London on or about 26 February with instructions to report to Katie Smith, Huize St. Joseph, Lent near Nijmegen. His reports were made on the fifth page of a newspaper. Between 2 March and 12 June, he sent off twenty-nine such reports. He had also a telegraphic code in which the names of Dutch banks stood for various classes of ships. This he had to learn by heart. His salary was paid by cheques forwarded by Schwedersky & Company and drawn on the Union of London and Smith's Bank, on advice from the Rotterdamsche Bankvereeniging. These cheques were dated 15 March, 12 April, 22 May. Other cheques dated 15 June and 12 July were paid by the Banque Beige pour l'Etranger, acting for S. van Dantzig. The three first cheques were cashed by the British and Northern Shipping Agency at the request of Melin.

On 16 March, the bureau was informed that E. W. Melin, of 23 Upper Parkway in Hampstead, was attached to the German Secret Service. The check put on his name resulted in intercepting Schwedersky's cheque on 15 April. Enquiries were then made at Melin's address and it was ascertained that he was living at a boarding-house, was fond of drink, went to the City every day, and spent the afternoons at the Café Monico. On 12 June, two envelopes containing three letters signed Kate and addressed to Melin were intercepted. Between the lines of an affectionate family letter were questions about British ships in secret writing. The envelopes had been posted at Tilbury.

The house was searched, a bottle of lemon juice, a pen and toothpicks were found as well as a Baedeker, with the names of various British ports and hotels marked in pencil. Also between the pages of an English and Swedish dictionary was a slip of paper bearing the names of some regiments and other military terms; Melin also had four other dictionaries. Melin was arrested on the 14th; he was interviewed on the 15th and acknowledged having received money through Schwedersky of Rotterdam. Through the case of Trebitsch Lincoln, Schwedersky was already known to the bureau as a German agent. Efforts were made to trace Melin at the ports but without avail; he declared he had never left London. The letters of 12 June had not been delivered to him, but it was important that he should acknowledge they were for him. On 26 July, he was shown the envelopes of the letters containing the cheques of 15 June and 12 July. He asserted that he was expecting a cheque from Rotterdam, was then shown the envelopes and the signature of the three letters containing secret writing; these also he acknowledged as being meant for him. The letters were then unfolded and the secret writing which had been developed stood revealed. Melin confessed his connection with the German Secret Service and gave the details mentioned above. He signed a receipt for the cheques and the money was impounded by the War Office.

Melin was tried on the charges of having twice come to England with intent to collect information, of having in his possession lemon juice for the purpose of unlawful communication of naval and military information, and of having attempted to collect information by recording the names of units of His Majesty's Forces. The summary of evidence was taken on 4 August; he was tried by court martial on 20 and 21 August, found guilty and shot on 10 September 1915.

★

At the end of June 1915 the Censor took exception to a note written on one side of the sheet and referring vaguely to business and a journey that might take place in a fortnight's time. Posted in London, this letter was addressed to Mr B. Goedhardt, 147 von Blankenburgestraat, The Hague. The Censor ironed the back and discovered a secret message conveying information about the Thames defences, Chatham Dockyard and so forth. A 'first' letter was also referred to.

The address was put on check for letters and telegrams on 2 July; it was circulated to the ports with instructions to arrest any traveller on whom it was found. On 13 July, a postcard containing another secret message and addressed to the same street and house but to the name Niendecker, spelt also Niendieker and Niendikker, was intercepted. It was signed Lopez.

The signatures of the first letter, 'van Nordensund' and 'Sven Person' were interpreted: 'Your worker from the North', and the investigation started on the theory that the writer was a Scandinavian sailor. At the same time enquiries in Holland established the existence at the address of a man named T. Niendiker, and that Goedhardt was an alias. The clue of the signature proved to some extent false, but on the 20th another letter in the same handwriting and also containing information was intercepted. It was signed 'Belmonte' and bore the address 38 Greek Street. Both signature and address were false. Finally, a typewritten letter, headed 1 Margaret Street and signed 'Tommy' begging for a remittance of £50 resulted in tracing the writer. The police called at the address, discovered that a man and his wife lodging there had not yet filled up their registration form, gained access to the room and identified the handwriting on a label as that of the writer of the letters.

Albert Meyer and his wife Katherine were arrested 30 August. He was by a turn hotel-waiter, cook, tailor, commercial traveller, and was in all probability a German. He claimed to have been born in Constantinople of Danish parents, but the Danish embassy subsequently could find no trace of his birth. Everything about Meyer was false; in business and in the lodging he used the alias Marcelle, and for business purposes he gave an accommodation address, 96 Shaftesbury Avenue, at which place he called for his letters. Among his papers were found testimonials of his work as a waiter dating from September 1910 to August 1914, but these do not agree with the records of his movements as shown by the books of the Geneva Association. From these books it would appear that Meyer came to England from Hamburg on 25 August 1911, went on 14 March 1912 to Harrogate and returned on 22 August to London. On 17 October he took his membership book saying he was going to Spain and returned to London on 6 June 1914, saying he had come from Nice. On 24 July he took his book saying he was going to India, but it would appear he went instead to Blackpool. On 10 August he brought his book back but fetched it away again on 30 March 1915, saying he was going to Copenhagen. The testimonials in Meyer's possession contained no reference to his first visit to England but showed that he had been in Seville, Spain, from October 1911 to June 1913, and in Pamplona from July 1913 to May 1914.

These facts are certain: early in August, Meyer was stopped at Folkestone as he was trying to embark and detained as a German. He was interned until 25 or 29 September when he succeeded in convincing the authorities that he was an Ottoman subject. He came to London and with Katherine Gray took a room at 40 Albany Street. He stated then that he was receiving 30 shillings a week from his father.

In March he applied for a permit to go to work with his father who owned, he said, the Hotel Bristol, Copenhagen. He produced a birth certificate and the application was granted. But he never got further than Holland, whence he wrote postcards to Katherine Gray bidding her call for correspondence at some address in the Haymarket. She wrote to him on 14 April asking him to return. He came back on 13 May, married her on the 20th and was turned out of his lodging owing to their joint misconduct on the 26th. He then moved to 134 Albany Street, although he had stated he was going to Edinburgh as a waiter. On 20 July, the Meyers moved to 1 Margaret Street.

Meyer had registered under the National Registration Act giving his occupation as a traveller. Among his effects were found a letter of appointment as a picture vendor made out to J. Smith by a genuine firm of printers in Amsterdam; a letter of appointment as a cigar vendor together with other letters from the Amsterdamsche Sigarenfabrick of van Hulst; a letter from Siegfried Meyer, who purported to be his father, from the Hotel Bristol, Copenhagen; a catalogue of various brands of cigars; the blotting-paper which seemed to have been that used in writing the letter signed Tommy; scent; three pens, and a small bottle of green ink with a small brush. A search of receipts for money orders disclosed the fact that on 23 July, Meyer had received £10 by telegraphic order from van Yselmuide, 13 Sleephellingstr, The Hague, and after his arrest sums of £40, £10 and £50 were sent by Niendiker.

Meyer was charged on 5 November with having attempted to communicate information, with having used secret ink, and with having attempted to communicate with a spy. Meyer applied to be defended by Crussmann but this was not allowed.

At the trial, evidence was given that Meyer had sent correct information and that F. Niendiker was a wholesale tobacconist at Nieuwe Haven, Rotterdam, who resided at 147 van Blankenburgstraat, The Hague, and was in touch with The Hague Secret Service. As regards secret writing it would seem that Meyer confined himself to the use of lemon juice, but that he had the materials for developing another process which was doubtless the one in use by his employers.

He was found guilty on all the charges and sentenced to be shot. He was executed on 2 December. There was no evidence against Katherine Meyer, but she was a woman of bad morals and it was thought that Meyer had obtained some of his information through her associations. She had been released from prison before Meyer's trial, but as she failed to notify her change of address she was again arrested and sentenced to three weeks' imprisonment on 27 October 1915, and in December she was recommended for internment. The order was made in January 1916 and upheld by the Advisory Committee. Eventually she was removed to a lunatic asylum.

Of these agents Robert Rosenthal was in direct touch with Berlin, and Josef Marks was reported to have been sent out by Berlin. Ludovico Hurwitz y Zender and de Rysbach may have been recruited by Hilmar Dierks, who went frequently to Norway, to which country they sent their reports. Ernest Melin was one of Dierks' men but he had transferred to the Wesel Bureau. Carl Meyer is doubtful, as Niendiker, to whom he sent his reports, was, in 1915, working apparently for Antwerp and

Wesel and was connected with Frankfurt. Niendiker's name does not appear on the Antwerp list, but in May 1918 he undertook a confidential errand for the Antwerp branch. In August 1915, Niendiker seems to have replaced Dierks in Holland and to have been engaging spies on a pretext of having some translations made. As regards the activities of these men, Rosenthal was at work as early as November 1914.

Marks' previous history lays him open to great suspicion; and Meyer may very well have been a professional spy. His faked testimonials, his connection with the Hotel Bristol, Copenhagen, his knowledge of Crussmann all point to his having been a spy before the war. His methods in 1915, however, are those of the Antwerp school. It will be noted that he married after he had joined the Secret Service.

★

A fourth group of enemy agents consists of those spies or would-be spies whose cases either were handed over to the Belgian government to deal with or, although not in themselves of much importance, were interesting to the bureau for some feature of the enquiry. These are Adolphe and Charles Dittmar, and the two Scherers, both German, and their gang, nine in all, being a Tunisian, Israel Khlat, and two letter-carriers; an American of German origin who used the alias Kenneth Triest and Mahon; Abdon Jappe, a Dane; a Briton, May Higgs, and Edward Edwin, a Swede.

Advice received from Mr Webber and Captain Beliard that a Belgian refugee named Pervost, formerly lock-keeper at Boesinghe, was suspect led to the arrest of this man and his two daughters at Folkestone. They carried documents proving that espionage had been going on behind the Allied lines, and they confessed to being in touch with a German agent named Dittmar. In consequence Adolphe Dittmar and his brother Charles, and two brothers named Frederick and Otto Scherer were arrested at the Christian Waiters' Home, 48 Charlotte Street, in Soho. These Germans had come over at the outbreak of war from Belgium on the pretext of avoiding German military service; all had been placed under some restriction and one of the Dittmars had been interned for a short time and then liberated.

Grupe and Madame Fontaine, who were also connected with the Dittmars, were arrested and the whole gang was handed over to the Belgian authorities and deported for trial abroad on 4 April 1915.

A Belgian who was in communication with a German espionage agent named van Lodz, denounced a Tunisian Jew named Israel Khiat and indicated a source of further information about him. Khiat could not be induced to come to England but two letter-carriers Mrs Schletien and Charles Craserts, and Maurice Dupriez, all of whom had been connected with Khiat, were arrested. Information about Mrs Schletien had been received from the port officer.

A private citizen of Cardiff received advice from a friend in America that a German, passing under the name of Lathom Mahon, had enlisted in the Naval Division and was stationed at the Crystal Palace. This was reported to the Chief Constable at Cardiff who communicated with MI5. Lathom Ramsey Mahon was found to be the assumed name of Kenneth Gustav Triest, a boy of nineteen, son of an American of German origin. He was arrested, interrogated and released, but he wrote to Baron von Schroeder offering services on behalf of Germany and the Baron handed in the letter to the authorities.

He was re-arrested and it was proposed to try him by naval court martial. The American ambassador intervened. Triest was found to be not quite sane and was handed over to his father who took him back to America.

On about 20 May 1915 a detective of the intelligence office, Plymouth Garrison, got in touch with Abdon Jappe, a Danish electrician, and by pretending to be contemplating illicit traffic in copper induced the man to show his hand. Jappe was arrested by order of the competent military authorities and handed over to civil custody on 29 May 1915, He carried two codes. He was sentenced to three years' imprisonment on 2 November 1915. The action of the detectives had forestalled the bureau and improper methods of detection having been pursued, evidence of hostile association was not procurable, hence when the Home Office wished to shorten Jappe's sentence, he could not be interned under DRR 14B. Eventually he seems to have been deported.

★

In July 1915 the Censor intercepted a letter from May Higgs, a British subject, addressed to her mother in Holland, through whom Higgs offered her services to the Germans. Three difficulties were encountered in dealing with this case: (1) the question of sex, (2) the question of mixed parentage, (3) want of co-ordination between various departments of government and between the various branches of the bureau itself.

May Higgs was eventually found to be not a suitable subject for trial. Restriction under DRR 14B was adopted and she was entrusted to the care of relatives. Then she applied to go abroad and as it was impossible owing to her nationality to issue a no return permit, arrangements were in making to watch her and otherwise hinder her return, but before these were completed, she slipped abroad on a provisional pass from the Home Office at the end of 1916, In a very few weeks she returned, and was then interned under DRR 14B. Eventually she was sent to a convent for the duration of the war.

★

Edward Edwin, a Swedish masseur, was engaged to treat wounded soldiers at the Duke of York's School, Dover, on 27 March 1915. For this purpose he had left a private practice which he had carried on in conjunction with Nurse A. M. Humphreys from 39 Beauchamp Road, Lavender Hill, their joint home in south-west London.

Edwin was brought to the notice of the bureau by the intelligence officer at Dover, who had received independent statements from two wounded soldiers, Private Phillips and Private MacNaught, to the effect that Edwin had asked specific questions as to the number, organisation, etc. of British troops in Belgium and France. Edwin also wished to ascertain the position of minefields in the Channel and the measures taken to protect hospital-ships. He incited the men to desert and promised to get them out of the country if they did.

Edwin was much interested in the sale of an ointment, Vetterim, and alleged that it would irritate a wound and so retard recovery. Wishing to advertise the ointment in the Dover Standard, he became abusive and uttered pro-German sentiments when told the advertisement could not be inserted that week.

Edwin was arrested on a charge of espionage on 5 August but the case presented some difficulty as neither of the witnesses against him had a completely clean record. Afterwards it was discovered that Edwin had been arrested early in April for examining certain military works near Dover and that towards the end of March he had put specific questions as to the numbers and training of recruits going to France. He was tried by court martial on 2 October, found guilty on three counts of attempting to elicit information and sentenced to seven days' imprisonment with hard labour and deportation on the expiry of his sentence. He left the United Kingdom voluntarily.

Nurse Humphreys was allowed to go to Sweden in December 1915 but she returned destitute in September 1916, and then made ineffectual efforts to procure reconsideration of Edwin's case.

★

In his report on the work of the Admiralstab Zweigstelle at Antwerp, Hans Eils declared that Mrs Lizzie Wertheim was the first spy sent out by that branch. It is almost certain she is the 'Mrs Wertheimer' alluded to in the February report and in that case her activities had begun probably in November. Mrs Wertheim's connection with Miss Brandes forms a link between the pre-war and the war organisation of the German Secret Service, for in February 1913, Miss Brandes had been in close touch with Heddy Glauer, wife of Heinrich Grosse, and Heddy Glauer in making this confession insinuated that Miss Brandes and her sister, Mrs Claassen, were at that time engaged in espionage. In 1915, however, the Special Bureau knew nothing of such contacts, but they rightly esteemed Miss Brandes to be a dangerous agent. It is interesting to note that Miss Brandes was then working for Baron Bruno von Schroeder in connection with his charitable efforts and consequently must have been in daily contact with Adolf Evers.

Eils also declares that Georg Breckow came to England in December 1914, which is of course possible, although there is no hint of it in the file. Other agents of the Antwerp branch who came early to England were Ernest Melin who was here from 13 to 29 January, and Haicke Janssen who came probably at the end of January. Melin afterwards transferred to the Wesel branch, but Janssen's visit is specially interesting since it seems to have marked a turning-point in the development of German methods. Up until May 1915, Lizzie Wertheim worked for a man called Dr Brandt, who is reported as living at Dordrecht, and concerning whom nothing more seems to be known except that early in May, he wrote to her from 166 Loosduinschekade, The Hague, which connects him with Hilmar Dierks, Heinrich Grund, Hochenholz, Jan van Brandwijk, Vollrath and Cark Ritzkey. Of these men only four, Grund, who was German, Carl Ritzkey, a Russian, van Brandwijk, Dutch, and Heinrich Flores, another German, appear on the Antwerp list and are listed respectively as agents A-1, A-19, A-51 and A-68. But Richard Sanderson, alias Dierks, may possibly be connected with A-2, Carl Schroeder, a German confidential agent in Hamburg, who is described as very intelligent, energetic and the introducer of many agents and confidential agents. Even in 1915 Dierks was frequently in Hamburg and introduced many agents to the service.

Hilmar Dierks first appears in our records in February under the name of Sanderson. Janssen came over to England on a genuine pretext, namely to receive a medal for saving life at sea. This was given to him at Liverpool on 13 February. He then visited several British ports and presumably returned to report at Antwerp. On 9 March he received a communication from 'Hilmar Dierks' and on the 30th the two men signed an agreement establishing a bogus firm of export and commission agents at Loosduinschekade, in The Hague. They went to live there en pension and a waiter named Olthuis took care of the rooms occupied by them. Janssen was continually away on journeys but Dierks' part was to recruit and equip the agents sent out and to maintain correspondence with them.

From early April 1915 onwards, telegraphic money orders seem to have been sent by Dierks. Dierks was arrested by the Dutch government in June and his wife carried on the work of paymaster under the name of Madame Cleton. In May Heinrich Flores seems to have joined the business. He was a teacher in the German school at Rotterdam, a war invalid who had returned to his pre-war occupation. Later on he is said to have taken the alias Frank and to have lived at Zwaardecroonstraat. He was in daily touch with the German consulate at Rotterdam.

Heinrich Grund became known to MO5G through his connection with Fernando Buschman and Augusto Roggen, and through John de Heer's confession, Grund's connection with the Admiralstab Zweigstelle in Antwerp, became known. Grund, who had lived in Antwerp before the war, was entered on the Antwerp roll as A-1, with the note that he was a very reliable, successful and clever worker. His special mission was to place his agents on ships coming to England and to examine them as to what they had seen on the journey. He also kept watch on the shipping in Rotterdam harbour and reported the movements of shipping off the Dutch coast by wireless to Hamburg. He is said by this means to have brought about the capture of the SS *Brussels*. In 1916, Grund moved to Utrecht and opened a motor business there.

Hochenholz was also was interested in shipping. He was known to Janssen and van Zwolj. His name does not appear on the Antwerp roll but possibly he may be identical with A-31, Emil Gleichmann, described as engaged in an enquiry service in Rotterdam, and captain in the Mercantile Marine, educated, reliable and very capable.

Jan van Brandwijk was entered as A-51, and was a Dutch casual labourer who had met with an accident and had been compensated by the Dutch government. His entry on the roll gives the following note: enquiry service at Rotterdam. Uneducated but very diligent. Good connections in shipping circles, mostly among the employees. Very pro-German.

The Dierks-Hochenholz gang was broken up by the Dutch

Government in the autumn of 1915. Sanderson, alias Dierks, who in August had been acquitted of the charge of endangering Dutch neutrality by inciting young men to do espionage and other services for the German Army and Navy was in October found guilty by the Court of Appeal at The Hague and sentenced to one year's imprisonment, but in the meantime he had disappeared from Holland. In June 1917, it was reported that he was coming regularly to the United Kingdom on behalf of Germany, and he was signaled to the ports for arrest, but nothing further was heard of him.

Dierks was succeeded by de Snoek (alias Patent, alias Schwaebsch) who had been in partnership with Haasbroeck in the business of German counter-espionage and Haasbroeck, an underling of Dierks, engaged the spies Schell and Pierre Verdun, one of whom was said to have had a share in the *Lusitania* outrage, the other in the torpedoing of the cruisers HMS *Aboukir*, *Cressy* and *Hogue* by the U-9 on 22 September 1914. Haasbroeck betrayed the Belgian spy Pierre Rotheudt, an agent of the Germans, to the French and lost the confidence of the Germans about July 1915.

Hans Eils states that the Antwerp branch directed the work of spies coming to England from America and Holland, and it is quite possible that the agents who communicated with Norway were also Dierks' men, as they certainly used his methods. It is worth noting the method of approach of these spies: Anton Küpferle from America, although he had been fighting in the German Army; Fernando Buschman via Spain and France but coming from Germany; Haicke Janssen, who was to spy in the south, landed at Hull; Willem Roos who went north, landed in London. It is elementary that care was taken to replace passports which contained inconvenient records and no doubt a spy avoided encountering the same port officers more than was necessary.

Another point which was carefully dealt with in a report on the Dierks agents is that of the arrangement of the spies' itineraries, so as to ensure that spies should pass through important places in regular succession. Willem Roos, Lizzie Wertheim and Roggen passed through Edinburgh between 15 May and 8 June 1915, and were possibly to be succeeded by

Reginald Rowland who was to leave town when Wertheim returned. Buschman, Rowland, and Janssen passed through Southampton between 13 April and 29 May. Between the visits of Buschman and Rowland other agents must have gone there.

On arrival in England the spy wired to his base giving his address and asking for funds. Wherever possible a spy tried to get into some private house. Carl Muller, Wertheim and Roos either scraped an acquaintance or used a pre-war acquaintance as cover, the obvious reason being to avoid hotel registration. As regards the Aliens Registration Order all the spies conformed. Other spies tried to settle down with a companion in a flat or furnished rooms: Buschman forced a rapid friendship with Emile Franco; Georg Breckow meant to establish himself with Wertheim; Albert Meyer, who had a companion, married her no doubt for greater convenience. The fixed quarters and companion, whether accomplice or not, enabled a person to escape notice, to get their letters regularly, and if need be to have a companion for their excursions. This, it is clear from Breckow's letters, the agent considered important but the employer sometimes objected on the score of expense.

As regards Breckow, it seems clear that he was to occupy an outstanding position; he brought money and orders to Mrs Wertheim, he was to work with her and to forward her reports, he was to recruit a fixed agent at Southampton and probably he was to keep touch with Roggen.

As regards payment, Dierks seems to have sent it by telegraphic money order and by telegraphic orders on banks. Berlin seems to have paid by cheque or to have supplied funds to the spy before his departure.

The regular paraphernalia for a German agent's equipment consisted in two kinds of materials for secret writing: lemon-juice, and scent used with powder as a fixative, and very fine pens; a book to help them identify types of warships; and business documents purporting to establish their bona-fides. In connection with these it is worth noting the progress made in passing from bogus names of firms through names closely resembling those of genuine businesses to genuine businesses and addresses as in the case of Albert Meyer and finally to the completion of genuine business as in the case of Frank Greite.

In the use of their business cover the spies were remarkably ineffective. Haicke Janssen and Irving Ries collected names of firms to call on here but Janssen went no further and Ries merely wrote to the firms. Fernando Buschman also collected names of firms at Liverpool but never went there. In no case was any business concluded, and it was often a simple matter to prove by means of experts that the travellers had no understanding of the business they were engaged upon. Breckow (alias Rowland), indeed, was so sensible of this that he proposed to drop his agency and revert to his own profession as a pianist under cover of which he could visit the places he needed to see. Kenneth de Rysbach was a music-hall artist and in this struck a fresh note.

Towards the end of the period the spies seem to have adopted confession of being in German pay as cover to their practices, or possibly as a mode of getting into the United Kingdom. Josef Marks may have been a forerunner of the double agents of 1916. John de Heer, Marius Hoogendyk and Charles van Ekeren were willing to assume that role in 1915.

Generally speaking, the spy adapted his communication to his supposed business but in some cases there were alternative codes. It is noticeable that the monthly report for April 1915 mentions only fifteen unimportant cases of the use of code and ciphers. By the end of the summer the codes had multiplied. In addition to the four codes known to have been used by German agents before the war, the following codes seem to have been in use at various dates between November 1914 and December 1915:

A German agent in Copenhagen wiring to a centre in the United Kingdom a message to be forwarded to the Minister of Marine in Berlin used surnames or Christian names to indicate the names of countries, towns, bays, channels, etc., mention of illness, etc. to indicate operations, and prices to indicate dates.

In February, a German communicating with Rotterdam and the German consul at Rotterdam were using family codes: relationships indicated military or naval units (eg. Father = Dreadnought); names of towns indicated harbours; numbers of ships were indicated by terms of endearment or by alphabetical Christian name code; latitude and longitude by names of Dutch towns; a nation by some special Christian name.

In the corset code supplied by German Headquarters at Antwerp to an agent in England, places in the United Kingdom were indicated by prices; places on the Continent by business terms; countries by colours; military and naval terms by descriptive words.

A man named Pearson cabled from Holland to New York orders for ammunition for Germany. He used a typewriting code which passed our Censor.

Writing daily from the United Kingdom to Christiania, a German agent used a code in which any letter out of the line counted.

In April Dutchmen sent to England communicated with Rotterdam in commercial telegraphic cipher and code; a three figure group indicated warships of different tonnage; a two figure group merchant vessels; one figure indicated transports. The place mentioned in the telegram indicated the port of departure, the date was ascertained by deducting two days from the date mentioned in the body of the telegram.

Robert Rosenthal used a telegraphic code which the Germans thought could not be paraphrased and also a postal stamp code; Abdon Jappe's book-code used the Testament and also a letter code; the cigar code of Willem Roos and Haicke Janssen used names of foreign ports and brands of cigars indicated vessels and ports of the United Kingdom.

Reginald Rowland (the alias adopted by Georg Breckow) used a musical code in which ships and ports were indicated by the name of some selection or piece, the two first letters or else some punning meaning indicating the word intended.

Secret signs were also in use in letters sent through the Esperanto Association and on maps of microscopic dimensions carried by spies. Augusto Roggen used a fruit code in which the words 'potatoes' and 'bananas' were supposed to indicate various types of ship. Ludovico Hurwitz y Zender used terms which would appear to relate to business in butter, cheese and goods. Another code consisted of pin–holes, dots, spots and tears on printed documents. Communications were also made by means of advertisements in the public press.

Charles van Ekeren supplied further particulars about methods in use at Antwerp. He mentioned two codes somewhat resembling some already known and a cipher. This was founded on a combination of letters to indicate military units and numbers. Messages were written in lemon juice on the inside of envelopes or between the lines of satirical postcards about the Kaiser; letter-groups would be marked in an *en clair* message, but so faintly as not to damage the fibre of the paper.

Copies of the code were sent to the Chief Censor with the request that all such telegrams should be forwarded to MO5G without previous reference to the sender.

To communicate with Antwerp and Wesel, Ernest Melin used a banking code in which classes of ships were indicated by the names of well-known Dutch banks; the number of ships by a sum of money in pounds, which sum had to be divided by five; the names of ports by the names of Dutch hotels; the dates and nature of movement by commercial phrases. The Wesel bureau would occasionally vary the names of the firms and hotels. The increase in the use or detection of code appears in the fact that whereas fifteen cases, mostly harmless, were reported in April, seventy-three were reported in August 1915.

To sum up, use was made, in turn or in combination, of Christian names, surnames, terms of relationship, names of countries, cities and firms, dates, prices, figures, and every kind of merchandise, coupled with ordinary words and word combinations to which a conventional meaning was attached. The examples given below illustrate the methods.

On 10 June 1915 DRR 22A prohibiting the use, unlawful possession of, or refusal to disclose the key of any cipher or code or other means adapted for secretly communicating naval, military or air-force information was issued.

On 28 June 1915 Ernest Maxse supplied a copy of the German translation code on which Haicke Janssen was subsequently detected, and a copy was passed to the Telegraphic Censorship and to the GPO.

★

It was known as early as November 1914 that secret writing was being used by German agents. In February 1915, Carl Muller and John Hahn were using lemon juice, while Anton Küpferle had a mixture of lemon juice and formalin for secret writing, and German Secret Service agents were overheard agreeing that interlinear writing in secret ink passed the Censor.

Reginald Rowland and Lizzie Wertheim used lemon juice and also probably colourless scent, such as eau de Cologne, with talc powder to fix it. Willem Roos and Haicke Janssen used scent and wrote in a microscopic hand on the margins of newspapers and books. They despatched from six to ten newspapers or books daily and always sent a postcard to notify that a message was on the way. The frequent use of music for recording information should also be noted. Besides the mediums used by arrested spies others were discovered in the course of the summer.

Medicines containing essential oils were sent to PoWs who used them together with code, such as a dot to indicate a place, or a corner slightly turned down or a tear in the margin. Preparations of powders, pomades, soap, hair-lotion, dentifrice, labelled with the genuine labels of Parisian firms, were also pressed into service. Soap and ferro-cyanide of potassium was another mixture used on slightly tinted paper. Agents in Switzerland used Oja-paste, a yellowish paste diluted with water and scented with rose, on unglazed yellow paper. Ten parts of acetate of lead to fifty of water; alum, milk, thin well-boiled starch water are also mentioned as mediums. When soap was used it required much dilution with water or a faint trace was noticeable on the paper.

Augusto Roggen used oil of peppermint and talc powder, and Fernando Buschman used scent, writing minute figures on old bills, letters, pages of a Spanish newspaper, railway time tables, envelopes, Censor's labels and music. Our chemist reported that a message written in a scent like eau de Cologne when used with talc powder should last for three weeks to a month.

The Rotterdam Post Office called attention to the use of secret writing along the gummed edges of the flaps of envelopes; one such envelope had passed sealed with five seals. After the arrest of Küpferle, Muller and Hahn, DRR 24A prohibiting the use of secret means of communication was issued.

From the point of view of investigation the source of information leading to detection is of primary importance. Analysis of these sources, with regard to the spy cases from November 1914 to early September 1916, gives the following results:

| | |
|---|---|
| Check on spy addresses | 10 |
| Scrutiny of telegrams to the Continent | 3 |
| Scrutiny of telegraphic money orders from the Continent | 1 |
| Postal Censorship acting freely | 3 |
| Intelligence officers | 3 |
| Information from British agent in Holland | 4 |
| Information given by American Minister to British consul-general, Rotterdam | 1 |
| Belgian Counter-espionage Service (on one denunciation) | 9 |
| Belgian (private, on one denunciation) | 3 |
| American (private) | 1 |
| Dutch (editor of Telegraaf) | 1 |
| TOTAL | 39 |

Certain of these cases, Irving Ries and Josef Marks for instance, might be grouped under two categories and a third case might be credited to the Postal Censorship if their discovery of George T. Parker (Georg Breckow) were treated as an independent case.

It is obvious that the check on a spy address is not in the first instance an ultimate cause, but it becomes one when established by a case. Of the main sources for such checks, the principal four were the reports of agents abroad; communications to and from German agents here; addresses found in their possession; and Postal Censorship.

The first and second were by far the most important. The skill of the branch in handling such information needs no comment: experience, imagination, resourcefulness and patience were all brought to bear on turning it to the proper use and in choosing out of the treasury of old methods and new protective measures those most apt for the purpose in view. The general search of telegrams sent from certain ports is an instance of an enlargement and fresh adaptation of an old method – and it led to the detection of three spies each in a different port. The tracking down of Muller and Wertheim furnish brilliant examples of intuition correcting false deductions. The first also illustrates the need for patience in awaiting the right moment to strike. Had a search been made of Muller's rooms when the police visited him first the chances are that he could never have been connected with Hahn and proof of his guilt obtained. Some of the cases demanded a long watchfulness but, in general, arrest followed with amazing rapidity on the first alarm, a rapidity which demonstrates the officers' skill in handling detective methods. Incidentally, too, the value of the new measures, the aliens restriction orders, the hotels registration order, the prohibited areas, the watch at the ports, the Postal Censorship was amply proved.

After arrest, proof was built up by verification of the spy's contacts, movements, business, information. This involved much labour and correspondence, and in certain cases it became necessary for the officers to cajole, of course after the necessary warnings, the victim into admitting the genuineness of documents proving his own guilt – a very disagreeable task.

As regards the preparation of a case, the principle was strictly adhered to, to bring forward only such evidence as was strictly necessary to obtain a conviction – thus economising labour, time and money. The benefit of legal advice in each case enabled the officers to concentrate on useful points and to avoid technical errors. During the course of these investigations the officers tested the weak points of the DRR. In June 1915 DRR 18 was made absolute by forbidding the collection etc. of any information for communication to the enemy. Experience showed that not only in the filiation of cases but also as a means of obtaining proof against agents, their 'contacts' were of immense value in the earlier cases. Much effort was expended upon proving the truth and value of the information sent and in verifying the nature and business of the persons with whom the spy was in communication abroad, and during June and July it was established by direct enquiry that Dierks and his gang had no genuine business, or concurrently that they were in direct contact with Germans.

But then arose cases, such as those of Robert Rosenthal, Josef Marks, David Stad and Cornolis den Braben where no overt act in this country could be proved against the agent, although it was certain he had come to spy – and either the agent had to be convicted on his own confession, or sentence of a much lighter nature than the offence warranted was passed upon him. At the request of MI5G therefore, Regulation 18A was passed making it an offence to communicate or attempt to communicate with a spy, and defining the terms 'communication', 'spy' and 'spy address'.

The knowledge of spy addresses was also put to a preventive use on 3 June. Orders were issued to the ports to arrest any traveller found carrying the address of Hilmar Dierks and similar orders were issued on the 10th with regard to Heinrich Flores, and at the end of the month with regard to Jan van Brandwijk.

All the spies carried *Jane's Fighting Fleets of the World*; under DRR 18 recent editions of naval annuals were ordered to be withheld from sale.

It was evidently of the utmost importance to keep the German government in ignorance of the arrest of their spies for as long as possible. Not only therefore were the names of arrested spies kept secret, as well as all details of the cases, but steps were taken to continue furnishing reports to the German employers. The method followed seems to have been to copy the first letters intercepted, either altering or so writing the second reports as to render them harmless. The copies were then sent on and the originals kept. After the arrest of the writer, faked letters containing reports were sent abroad and were paid for by the Germans. As a result of the experience gained in the cases of these spies, the attempt to trace spies by means of remittances paid to them was renewed. Success had rewarded such efforts in the case of Irving Ries and from September onwards a watch was kept on all incoming telegraphic orders of £10 upwards emanating from Holland, Denmark, Norway and Sweden and Switzerland. The lists sent in by the GPO at regular intervals were carefully collated with the records; if there was a personal file of the recipient the remittance was noted in it. If there was no file, enquiry was made of the appropriate police authority, and, if necessary, the recipient himself was asked to explain. The same difficulty arose in these cases as has already been noted with regard to bank remittances; a number of persons could not be traced even by the Special Intelligence Police, and the enquiry stopped short just when it seemed most promising. Nevertheless, enquiries in both types of case acted as a useful check.

After the case of Fernando Buschman special measures were also taken with regard to incoming remittances made through banks and especially through the American Express Company, which was at that time receiving many payments for German clients.

Much of the secret writing was supposed to have been done in scent. Experience gained in testing this and certain specimens which were the work of submarine prisoners led to action being taken to deal specially with the letters of prisoners of war. As regards the secret writing done in scent, the methods of developing were then imperfect and produced results so uncertain as to be not always of value for purposes of trial. Hence where possible they were not emphasised in court.

In the preparation of the cases, great care was taken to keep the representatives of the government whose nationals were under accusation in touch with progress of the case and a representative was always present at the trial.

One result of the branch's many successes was to rouse the Dutch government to take action to protect its subjects from the machinations of German recruiting agents. Dierks was arrested on 29 June but subsequently released; on the 8 August van Brandwijk ostensibly retired from business and in the end of the month the Dutch obtained proof of the connection of Dierks, van Brandwijk, Titzky, Hochenholz, and Vollrath with the German Secret Service, and of their meeting in conclave at 118a Claes de Voreslaan. Hochenholz and Dierks managed to escape; the others were arrested and the gang was broken up. Another result was that the Germans multiplied and incessantly changed their accommodation addresses in Holland. The measures taken by the

German counter-espionage service during 1915 and 1916 give a criterion of the success of our methods.

In Holland the Germans were photographing Dutch travellers to England and refusing them passports for Belgium; they were shadowing persons going from Belgium to England and it was even said that they were snap-shotting the travellers on board the Zeeland boats with a view to identifying persons who had been granted passports from Belgium to Holland on condition they went no further. Such photography was strictly forbidden by the Dutch government and the Port Officer declared that it was not done on board tile boats.

The most careful steps also were taken at Antwerp to prevent recruited spies from meeting each other or from being seen on their way to and from the spy headquarters.

★

Re-organisation of the Special Intelligence Bureau took place again in August 1915 when the name of MO5's A Branch was changed to MO5G. The definition of duties marks an advance in the status of the Special Intelligence Bureau and G Branch, as well as closer co-operation with other departments and defence organisations. To Clause 1 were added the words: 'Issue of orders to police, military and other authorities for arrest, search or observation of such persons (e.g. spies and suspects) and scrutiny of their correspondence'. Moreover, it was found convenient to appoint Mr Cousins of the GPO to act as a connecting link between MO5G and the GPO. He was given a post as Secretary in MO5G for the special purpose of examining letters stopped under the Home Office Warrants.

The fresh definition includes also the work of co-operating with the GOC's GHQ and the Allies' counter-espionage, and responsibility for the whole of the official and semi-official correspondence on all the subjects dealt with in the detection of espionage. Such an increase of duties involved an increase of staff: two section officers, Captain Carter and Lieutenant G. C. Peevor, with four secretaries, supported Major

Drake in the general work. Three officers, Major V. Ferguson, R. of O., Commander Henderson RN, Mr P. W. Marsh, with three secretaries formed the personnel of G1 which took over the duties formerly alloted to A1.

Four officers, Mr R. Nathan CSI, CIE, Captain H. S. Gladstone, Major S. C. Welchman and Captain G. de C. Glover, both of the South Staffordshire regiment, and six secretaries formed the personnel of G2 which corresponded to the former A2. In G3 Major Hall with the help of one secretary continued the work he had done in A3 and added to it the examination of reports on enemy agents in foreign countries except Scandinavia, Holland and Denmark, and belligerent territory on the continent of Europe. A4 simply became G4 with no change of personnel or duty.

The G2(a) staff was Commander Henderson, Major F. S. Reeves, Mr P. W. Marsh, Lieutenant Taylor, Lieutenant G. N. Wakefield, and took over the work of the former G2, the preliminary investigation of cases of espionage in Great Britain. At G2(b) Mr H. L. Stephenson dealt with cases of sedition among Indians and Egyptians in the United Kingdom, and cooperated with police and counter-espionage services in India and Egypt in cases of all types falling under G1 and G2(a). G2 and the two sub-sections had a clerical staff of twelve. In G5 Major Hall, with the help of Major Welchman and two secretaries, conducted similar investigations with regard to Ireland, and co-operated with counter-espionage services in the Overseas Dominions, Crown Colonies and Protectorates, with the exception of Egypt. A third officer, Lieutenant M. Bremer, went to G4 which added to the examination of intercepted correspondence that of the documents of suspected persona after arrest.

To G5 Lieutenant G. C. Peevor and Mr B. Westell fell the preparation of cases of persons arrested at the instance of the bureau for prosecution by the military or civil authorities.

G Branch was then organised in five sections and two sub-sections and the distribution of duties was made on the two principles of geographical areas and race. Major Drake, with one section officer and four clerical staff, kept the general direction and dealt specially with methods of known or suspected enemy agents.

To G1 under Major V. Ferguson and Major H. B. Matthews, with two secretaries, was allotted the preliminary investigations of fomentation of strikes, sabotage and peace propaganda. G3 under Mr R. Nathan, dealt presumably with all cases of espionage, treachery and sedition arising in London, duties formerly allotted to G1.

In April 1916, a re-arrangement took place. G2 then absorbed the duties of the sub-section formerly known as G2(a), cases of espionage in Great Britain, which disappeared, and a fresh section, known as G6, Mr H. L. Stephenson and Mr S. Newey, with six secretaries, took over the work formerly allotted to G2(b), cases of sedition among Indians and Egyptians, etc.

G2 then had a staff of seven officers, Mr H. B. Clayton, Commander Henderson RN, Mr P. Marsh, Major Welchman, Major Reeves, Major Anson, Captain Sassoon, and seven secretaries.

In September 1916 the work in Ireland and in the Dominions had grown to such dimensions that G3 was constituted into an independent branch known as D.

G5 dealing with the preparation of cases of persons arrested at the instance of the bureau, was absorbed presumably by the direction of G and G6, dealing with sedition among Indian and Egyptians in co-operation with Indian and Egyptian services, became known as G5.

In September 1916 by the formation of the Standing Advisory Committee closer contact between the branches was ensured. Besides the head of G Branch, ex-officio, Major Anson was nominated as one of the two extra members.

In November 1916 the photograph and handwriting books were given into the keeping of H2, and the work requiring translation was sent to the Military Translation Bureau, MI7(c). It was then arranged that, should it become necessary for a case to be transferred from one branch to another, any further action must be decided by consultation and agreement between the branch officers concerned in the investigation.

In December 1916 a fresh sub-division took place. The enquiries necessitated by intercepted correspondence (formerly G4) were delegated to G2(a) and the remaining work of G2. Other cases of espionage in Great Britain was allotted to sub-section G2(b). The change was effected on 18 December.

In dealing with the work within the branch, from time to time restrictions had to be made so as to ensure uniformity and discretion in the conduct of business. Officers were not to order arrests without reference to the head of the branch or his chief section officer, or the heads of H and F, or the Director of Intelligence Police. Moreover, cases which might become important were to be brought up in their early stages.

With regard to records and circulars, G officers were responsible for marking for inclusion on the Black List (remodeled in 1916) the names of all persons reasonably suspected of being enemy agents or in connection with such; for due care and restraint in circulating the names and addresses of suspects and information with regard to enemy methods, so as to ensure that the recipient of the circular had only such information as was of use to him, and that pending investigation was not compromised.

Major Drake reserved for himself or his section officer the decision in cases of suspected sabotage; 'munitions offences' and cases affecting munitions works and factories had to be referred to the Ministry of Munitions before any action could be taken; prosecution for press offences was left to MO7(a).

The immense extension of government services and consequent modification of methods due to the war appears in a memorandum instructing officers to start an investigation on the easiest line of enquiry by referring to the office or department likely to have precise knowledge of the suspect, rather than to ask for police enquiry.

It was also important to reserve the special agents for special work, and to avoid employing them in any way which would necessitate their appearance in court. The data concerning travellers as such which E Branch collected at the ports, permit offices and foreign controls, were of material assistance to the branch in tracing the journeys from the United Kingdom to find persons under suspicion.

On the other hand, it was the duty of G2 officers to bring to the notice of E officers new information entailing the amendment and cancellation of E Circulars, etc., the promulgation of new circulars, and also the return of suspects' papers after they had been confiscated at the port of entry and passed to G3 for examination.

The list of offices to which the circulars of MO5 might be despatched shows the following connections in November 1915: Bureau Central Interallié, Paris; GHQ I(b), France; MO6(c); British vice-consul, Le Havre; Belgian Intelligence Service, Folkestone; French Intelligence Service, Folkestone; French consulate, London; Civil Permit Office, Downing Street; Military Permit Office; Assistant Commissioner, CID Scotland Yard; HM Inspector under Aliens Act; IO Edinburgh who communicated with Leith, Granton, Burntisland, Methilt Leven, Dysart, Kirkcaldy; IO Falmouth; MCO Folkestone, Hull, Bristol, Tilbury, Newcastle, Southampton, Liverpool; and Captain Lamb, Inspector-General of Communications at the British Expeditionary Force (IGC).

Late in September 1916 the scheme for the interchange of counter-espionage information between MI5 and GHQ Intelligence B on the one hand and between MI5 and IGC Intelligence on the other hand was carefully worked out and MI5 was to send two copies to GHQ Intelligence of all information concerning German espionage or counter-espionage methods which might be of utility to intelligence officers in France, and GHQ Intelligence and IGC Intelligence was to send to MI5 as well as to BCI all information about German methods other than that of purely local interest. Similarly, MI5 was to send a copy to GHQ I(b) and IGC Intelligence of reports dealing with suspects who might be likely to enter the Zone of the Armies in France or Belgium and with firms suspected of espionage who were likely to send agents into those zones. GHQ I(b) and IGC Intelligence were to notify MI5 of suspect individuals having dealings with the United Kingdom. An interchange of suspected addresses and letters agencies was also to take place. In forwarding information a list was also to be sent of the offices notified.

When the Bureau Central Interallié was omitted from the distribution list, the information sent by MI5 was to be regarded as undesirable for communication to the Allies. It was the duty of E Branch to notify the French Section of Control in London of suspects entering France.

In February 1915 officers had been appointed at Le Havre, Boulogne and Calais for special intelligence work with a view to stopping leakage of information. Similar appointments were made to the ports of Rouen, Marseilles and Dieppe in June of the same year. Subsequently correspondence between the Intelligence Service on the Line of CHQ, IGC, GHQ and the War Office was divided into Normal and Urgent. Urgent communication, telegrams or information about suspects and their movements was to be carried on directly between MO5 and the port officers on the Line of Communication and these would communicate with GHQ and UK ports.

In October 1915 it was laid down that intelligence officers of the Home Defence Directorate were to send in weekly summaries to their directorate; cases of action taken under Regulation 14, 14A, and all cases in which aliens as such were concerned were not to be included in the summary, but forwarded to the War Office as secret documents, the inner envelope being marked 'MO5 Aliens'. Telegrams on such subjects were to be addressed to MO5's telegraphic address. By this order G Branch was affected only in so far as these returns would call for further investigation of individual cases.

A further gap in the co-ordination of home defence was filled by the institution of district intelligence officers to link up the armies in the United Kingdom with the Directorate. These officers, who were trained by MO5G, received instructions with regard to alleged cases of espionage like those issued to intelligence officers in January. So early as January 1915 measures had been concerted by the French, Belgian and British representatives with regard to passports, letter-carrying, and the elimination of suspects from Red Cross organisations. Belgian and, as already reported, British officers had been attached to Northern French ports, and French officers to southern ports in England.

In the autumn of 1915 the co-ordination of Allied services engaged in counter-espionage was achieved by the formation of the Bureau Central Interallié which had its headquarters at Paris. The Bureau Central Interallié was to act as a clearing-house for intelligence other than that dealing with military operations.

The British Mission at first communicated directly with the Military Control Officers abroad and in cases of urgency would send the names of suspects to British representatives abroad and answer their enquiries. Soon after the institution of the BCI the Black List was remodeled and it became the duty of G officers to mark and pass to G Section all papers dealing with persons suitable for inclusion in this List; such were all persons reasonably suspected of being enemy agents or connected with any enemy activities. It was, however, expressly laid down that certain limitations should be observed in circulating lists of names to officers or bureaux outside MI5; the names on the lists were to be selected according to the interests and needs of the recipients and these names were not to 'be circulated until the enquiries were completed; moreover some information regarding enemy methods or agents was not to IDS circulated at all and in these cases the papers were to be marked: "Hot to be circulated without reference to..."'

In the spring of 1916 the BCI complained of the roundabout way in which intelligence from MI5 (the name by which the bureau was then known) was reaching them. In May special arrangements were made to communicate all important counter-espionage news dealing with German espionage, and also the Black List which was communicated to the Bureau Central Interallié, to Captain Ladoux of the Ministere de la Guerre via Commandant Wallner at Folkestone. The British Mission in Paris then began active operations on its own account and this led to considerable confusion and difficulty of which Major Drake complained in July 1916. Hence in August the British Mission was restricted, except in cases of the utmost urgency, to direct communication with London, GHQ, BEF, and IGC, while MI5G undertook the distribution of counter-espionage lists to all other organisations.

★

Our counter-espionage in Petrograd first sent in news of a spy centre in Stockholm in December 1915, together with four suspect addresses in that city. In the following March, the German naval attaché at Stockholm was said to be employing seven persons indoors and fourteen outside; the consulate-general employed nine persons, his special work being connected with trade licenses; and a man named Freiwald had been moved from Aachen, where he had been engaged in catching Dutch spies, to take charge of German counter-espionage in Stockholm with the object of getting rid of nests of foreign spies. In April, May, June and December, reports were received from 'N' in Copenhagen, the French War Office and the Russian Admiralty giving long lists of names and particulars of German agents in Sweden. Many of these men were journalists. The head of the naval section directed against England had an office in Stockholm but lived at Goteborg and received the bulk of his correspondence via Goteborg under cover to the addresses of women.

In November reports were received that Christiania was a centre for information with regard to the United Kingdom. Although it was not realised at the time, there were two German Secret Service centres in Antwerp – one for military, the other for naval news, but as has been already seen from the spy cases the two sometimes overlapped.

In December 1914 *The Times* had published some account of a spy centre at Lorrach and in September 1915 a report of a similar organisation at Antwerp placed both institutions on an equal footing; subsequently one of our agents visited the military school at Antwerp and furnished a detailed account of the locality and methods used. The centre at Antwerp was situated at 10 rue de la Pepiniere, and went through to the rue de l'Hannonie. The head of it seems to have been a woman known as 'la femme blonde', 'Barone Jeanne', 'Madame Slaghmulder', Frau or Fraulein Doktor.

Agents were recruited among Belgians, soldiers and women in Holland. The men were sent to join the Belgian Army on the pretext that they had escaped from internment in Holland. They were to obtain their information and if necessary to desert in order to bring in their reports. They were sent mostly via Holland to France, sometimes however they passed through Switzerland, but never through Lorrach. The spy was expected to return within eight or twelve days. Agents were also sent to Paris, Orleans and Bordeaux. The spy had to memorise questions about the coast from Havre to Boulogne and about French and British military and naval affairs. He was to wire news in a commercial code, to use interlinear writing in secret ink in his letters, and to send picture postcards to certain addresses in Switzerland or Holland as a sign that information was on its way. The instructions given to one agent in April 1915 were that he was to stop in Calais, Boulogne or Havre, or else in Amiens or Abbeville and always in a place where he could himself learn something. He was to stay in France as long as possible and, if taken as a soldier, to get a post as chauffeur and cover as much ground as he could. He was to supply information on very precise questions grouped under seven different headings and dealings with naval and military matters (only seven questions were devoted to the British Army), and the method to be followed in this case was direct interrogation of the officers and men. The naval questions concerned the warships stationed at the French ports, armoured merchantmen and neutral ships, and the cargoes carried by both classes of ships.

In February 1916 news was received of a spy school at Brussels which recruited agents in Lille and Brussels. The spies left for Holland via Esschen and then on foot to Roozendaal; they went to Switzerland via Aix-la-Chapelle and Fribourg. Letters were sent to hotels to be forwarded by the porter or manager to the German consul who would send them on to Antwerp. It was expressly stated that owing to the British counter-espionage measures the Germans had modified their methods and were interviewing their agents in Berne and Zurich to avoid their being marked down in Belgium. Moreover the agent who visited the Antwerp school reported that it was in April more difficult to pass via Holland than via Switzerland. In July the centre at Zurich was shifted to the neighbourhood of Lucerne.

About this time, too, came in a report of German espionage at Strasburg with centres at Constance, Singen and Lindau. The agents employed were unknown to each other; they were neutrals and preferably Swiss. They received a numbered paper of identification which was given up before crossing the frontier into France or Italy. They had to obtain news of a simple character and they delivered it by inserting commercial advertisements in a paper previously agreed upon, or by a message on a postcard, 'Am sending or offering you 150 boxes of sardines' which would moan '150 regiments of infantry stationed where I write'.

*The Times* of 5 May 1916 contained a report that the German system in Holland had been reorganised and was employing 162 men and sixty-eight women agents at Rotterdam. The Central Defence System was quartered at The Hague; it included branches for ordinary spying extraordinary spying, and the creation of discontent and suspicion of England. This information came from the *Telegraaf*.

In Copenhagen, too, was a school where agents would be trained for a fortnight and after being tested by other agents they would be sent to England wearing English clothing and with instructions to return in two weeks at most. About twenty agents would be sent every week to different towns in England.

A description of the organisation and methods in use in Southern Germany came to hand in June 1916. The school at Lorrach was recruited from an office at Frankfurt where the former head of a Swiss station buffet engaged waiters who were out of work and from an office at Fribourg under the management of an ex-commissioner of police.

The spies travelled to and fro under the protection of a workman's pass, which was issued by a German officer after the first journey had been made under cover of a proper passport duly stamped and visa'd. The existence of the Lorrach centre had been known at least since March 1915 when the Chief Censor reported that letters issued through this office could be posted in France and be delivered in England uncensored.

At Munich another spy centre was established at the headquarters of the Central Police Division 16. Here neutral travellers, and also employees, musicians, governesses of French or Italian nationality who had been caught in Germany by this war, were pressed into service. On pretext of some flaw in their papers neutral travellers would be taken to the office and interrogated and, if they showed a friendly disposition, they would be told they could add considerably to their earnings; if they refused to answer Germany was closed to them; persons of French or Italian nationality were offered permission to go and see their families in their native country and, if they accepted, faked papers were given to them and 60 marks a day for expenses.

Reports of May and June 1916 deal with the organisation in Spain which was located chiefly in Madrid and Barcelona. Much correspondence was received at the offices of Roeb, a patents agent, and officer of reserve of the German Army. In June it was reported that the Germans were trying to get hold of French men and women in order to send them over the frontier with false papers. Women of Italian nationality were also enrolled for this purpose. Press propaganda was carried on at Barcelona and the German consulate was said to be in direct wireless communication with Germany. At this city there was also a depot for every sort of chemical used in sabotage of munitions, etc., and in secret writing. The convents were said to be meeting places for spies and also stations for wireless telegraphy.

In the winter of 1915-16 the Swiss took action against the spies in their midst and imprisoned agents of both sides, but the reports received show strong pro-German bias in Swiss governing circles. An agent who declared he was acting on behalf of Germany was shut up with German and Austrian prisoners and learned much from them. One German trick was to get an agent imprisoned for a few days on a trumpery charge of contraband in order that he might obtain the reports of more important agents who were in prison for some time.

Sub-Lieutenant Wright, who may have been responsible for the report mentioned, was in prison with German agents and sent in a useful account of their methods coupled with suggestions for the use of our service. He pointed out that the Germane used their disabled and unfit men as spies in neutral countries and that all spying was done under cover of contraband trade. The advantages of this method were that information and goods were brought in at the same time, excuse was provided for travelling and a defence for the German employer when charged with spying.

The Germans made use of Switzerland as a place of receipt for apparently innocent letters conveying information of value to Germany, such correspondence taking place on an enormous scale and unchecked by the Swiss authorities. Switzerland was also a place of arrival for Jewish German Americans who travelled in England, France and Italy and brought goods and news for Germany. It was also the recruiting ground for spies who were sent into France to buy raw materials or to sell German goods; recruiting was carried out by means of advertisement in the local papers. Such a case was reported in December 1916, when a Wurtemburg lady was condemned to three months' prison. As counter-measures, Lieutenant Wright suggested that any individual coming from abroad who had made only a short stay in England should be looked on as a suspect and, before granting him a permit to leave, he should be required to make a signed declaration of his itinerary during the past two months and this itinerary should be checked; and that a press-cutting agency should be started in Switzerland to watch the advertisement columns and answer suspicious offers of employment.

Another method used by the German agents was that of naturalisation. As early as January 1915 reports had been received of the immense number of Germans who were taking out papers of naturalisation in Spain; in February 1916 Germans were carrying out the same policy in Switzerland and, as the Swiss passport did not state whether the holder's nationality was by right of birth or acquired the suggestion was made that before granting a visa the British consular authority in Switzerland should insist on the production of a certificate of Swiss birth signed by the mayor of the locality in which the applicant resided.

The same informant declared the German legation in Berne to be a centre of espionage; Geneva and Lausanne to be overrun by Turko-Egyptian spies; German-Swiss to be carrying on propaganda in Egypt and Salonica, where Greek spies and Jews were also at work. He suggested that the German-Swiss in Egypt should be carefully watched; that no neutrals should be allowed to leave Salonica, and that all neutrals going to Switzerland should be carefully searched.

Through France came the news that many of the Swiss military were either the sons of Germans naturalised in Switzerland or closely connected with leading German families and that some former German officials were then in Swiss pay or that former Swiss officials were then in the German service, and that the Germans were masters of the banking world.

Besides espionage Switzerland was also a centre for German propaganda. Libellous pamphlets were printed at Zurich to be scattered among neutral nations.

★

Germans were said to be obtaining information through English-speaking spies who conversed with British invalided officers in Switzerland. In August 1915 an agent at Geneva reported that the Germans were trying to get in touch with French families and so to obtain access to France through the medium of a bureau for supplying information gratis to the families of PoWs or missing men. The bureau was advertised in the press, its address was that of the German consul at Geneva. A similar case, that of an individual named Whiting, had occurred in England. Warnings were issued to GHQ I(c), the War Office, intelligence officers and Scotland Yard.

The Italian Mission declared that an Austrian was recruiting café-concert artistes and ladies of good social position as spies and that these sent messages on scraps of paper twisted in the stalks of artificial flowers which they mingled with real flowers in bouquets. Again it was said that messages were being sent into Italy from France concealed in flowers from the Riviera and that agents were passing from France to a place near Genoa under pretest of seeking a cure.

Another method of carrying letters was reported from Switzerland, sometimes by committing them to the servants of wagon-lits and restaurant cars. It was proposed to stop the running of through trains and to make the passengers go on in a fresh train, near which the officials of the first were not allowed to go.

In April a horoscope agent at The Hague named Roxroy was getting in touch with soldiers by advertising horoscopes in *Le Matin* and *Le Rire*. He was thus said to be gaining information about the armies, the places in which they were stationed, their movements and moral. Among the methods reported from Holland and Belgium were examples of a Dutch officer who collected all information of military value which came from behind the Front to men interned at Heerlen and forwarded it to Germany; men on leave returning from England to Groningen internment camp and Belgians returning from England would be cross-examined for information as to the position of camps, fortifications, munitions factories and other matters.

Another way of obtaining information was to allow a large number of letters to pass from Brussels to England and wait for the replies, picking out items of interest when they came and then forwarding them to destinations.

Towards the end of 1915 it became known that German agents were writing to various British government departments offering information, particularly about munitions and explosives in the hope of getting an official reply that would cover them in their efforts to procure information about such matters. If they succeeded they would travel as businessmen or commercial travellers, show the letter to the police, conform with all regulations, get the required knowledge and leave.

MO5 stated these facts in a circular distributed to the Director of Trench Warfare, GPO, Admiralty, Home Office, Scottish Office, Irish Office, India Office, Colonial Office, Foreign Office, Treasury, Ministry of Munitions and Inventions Committee, Local Government Board, Board of Trade, Customs and Excise, Board of Agriculture, and the Port of London Authority, mentioning that four such cases had occurred recently in which either the German agent had been arrested or had got out of the country under cover of a letter from some department or office.

In February 1916 it was made an offence under DRR 45 for a person to speak or act in such a manner as to convey the false impression that he was employed in a government department. About this time the port officer at Hull sent warning that telephones were probably being tapped, and a difficulty of control arose in the fact that certain of the employees were not under the GPO but under the corporation. The suggestion was made by MI5G that the character of the Hull telephone employees should be investigated.

The Assistant Provost-Marshal was warned of a system of collecting the visiting cards of army and navy officers with the object of selling them to men of all nationalities who might thereby locate military and naval units. A valuable haul of letters concealed in a tray of muscatels disclosed the fact that German firms were trading in Spain under assumed Spanish names and were urging their correspondents in Germany also to take cover. A number of names and cover names were thus obtained.

In August 1915, as a result of several proved cases of spying, a circular was issued to the effect that all commercial travellers coming into England for the first time since the war were to be looked upon with suspicion, and that Swedes in particular were acting as spies and engaged in procuring goods for Germany. In the same month special suspicions were being attached to the German-speaking Swiss and measures were under consideration for restricting the travel of Germans who had acquired Swiss nationality since the war. One German agent who entered the country by Folkestone and left by Hull had travelled as an officer of the Norwegian Naval Reserve, hence a circular was issued that all naval officers of neutral nationality were to be regarded as suspect and signaled to MO5.

In view of the fact that the Germans were recruiting agents among Dutch diamond workers, it was suggested that such persons should produce a guarantee from the Dutch Diamond Workers' Union and should be allowed to settle in the United Kingdom during the war. The number of such persons was to be kept to the lowest possible. In November 1915 G Branch had cause to suspect South American and North American travellers coming into the country from Holland, Denmark, Norway and Sweden on neutral ships, and a list of suspicious circumstances in connection with such travellers was drawn up for circulars to the ports. It included the inability of South Americans to speak Spanish on the plea that since infancy they had inhabited North

America; passports issued by the British vice-consuls of obscure places in the Argentine, Brazil or Uruguay. Other suspicious travellers were people going to Switzerland who said that their relations were dead; second class passengers on neutral ships; and neutrals volunteering information against German fellow passengers.

Other counter-espionage measures suggested by the Special Intelligence Bureau were the refusal of visas to all persons coming from Belgium: to order that special attention should be paid to all repatriated or escaped Belgian PoWs; and to check the passage of hostile agents under the guise of soldiers by ordering that all leave-men should carry identity cards bearing their photograph as well as their leave certificate.

On other accounts it was proposed to make the possession of a certificate of identity compulsory for aliens. In order that the sender of a bogus telegram should be traced, such certificate of identity was to be produced at the post office by the sender of the telegram and it was also suggested to prohibit the despatch of picture postcards to Holland and Sweden. Experience had shown that the Germans were employing Germans over age or militarily unfit to collect information, or to act as paymasters, organisers of espionage or messengers. Such men were also believed to be organising sabotage of various kinds, peace-propaganda, and strikes, and in native territories, sedition. By the regulations in force, Germans of this class travelling on neutral ships could not be touched; four such persons who had made use of false passports had been tried and shot but a fifth, a German officer of the Reserve, a man named Gulden who travelled as Captain Frederick Dunbar, could not be brought to trial owing to lack of suitable legislation, and MO5 wished the law to be altered.

It was proposed that all enemy subjects should be removed from neutral ships and detained until it was proved that they were not engaged 'actually or potentially' in any form of war endeavour prohibited by international law.

It seems to have been falsely reported in March 1916 that the Germans had transferred the headquarters of their spy organisation against England to Stavanger in Norway and to be sending agents to England under cover of Norwegian passports on torpedo-boats transferring them to British trawlers mid-ocean. It was also said that German agents were procuring employment on Allied ships by producing Dutch certificates. Young Germans returned safely to Germany carrying Peruvian papers. In August two agencies for fabricating passports had been discovered in Rotterdam.

In March the majority of suspects seemed to be coming from Spain and Greece, but a few still came from Holland and France. Measures were under consideration for limiting the number of British consuls abroad who had power to grant visas, and for keeping direct touch with these consuls so that all intending travellers to England might be dealt with on uniform lines. In this we would be copying the German system.

An agent from Christiania reported that the Germans were providing excellent cover for their spies who were conducting genuine business in the fish trade, had proper bank accounts, were acknowledged and protected by the German Minister and could not be turned out by the police. The agent suggested that the British might adopt certain of the so methods, a plan that was agreed to by MI5 and a certain importer of Norwegian canned goods went to Norway for a time on their behalf.

The Germans attempted to send in an agent as representative of a Swedish firm; this was met by a refusal to grant a visa unless the British firm wrote to say they desired a visit from the representative of the foreign house. But this they did not.

★

In June 1916, after the battle of Jutland, it was anticipated that German agents would he coming to this country to ascertain the damage done to His Majesty's ships. A special warning was therefore issued to the police through the Home Office instructing them to interrogate severely all commercial travellers of alien origin arriving in any police jurisdiction with a view to obtaining precise particulars as to their business, length of service, pay, orders received, execution of such orders, etc., and if possible their answers were to be verified by reference to the firms which they had visited. In July 1916 MO5G caused a circular to be issued that the German government were recruiting circus-riders, music-hall artists and actors of the regular stage as agents, and asked that special attention should be paid to such persons and particularly at naval centres. In case of suspicion the strictest enquiry could be made under DRR 53 and if insufficient evidence was found to justify arrest under DRR 53, the particulars were to be reported and papers sent to the War Office; if the suspect moved, the Chief Constable of the district to which he was going was to be informed and asked to keep him under observation.

Among the types of agents mentioned in the second half of 1916 was the case of an employee of the Putilow Powder Works at Petrograd who is alleged to have been in Hull during the battle of the North Sea and to have gone thence to Stockholm, where he gave to the correspondent of the *Deutsche Allgemeine Zeitung* all the information he had collected in England. There were other agents masquerading as nurses and supplied with Belgian nursing diplomas. Also, refugees from Belgium and Northern France, Belgians supplied with French papers and French with Belgian papers, and German agents masquerading as the crews of tramp steamers.

In connection with this latter class of agent, the Foreign Office had issued a circular to the diplomatic representatives of neutral states calling attention to the negligence of consuls in granting certificates of nationality to alien seamen.

In August 1916 a German agent of the Russian Secret Service reported that a special bureau was established at Rotterdam with the object of making detailed enquiries of all officers and members of crews of neutral ships. In order to obtain accurate reports of the damage done by Zeppelin attacks, neutral businessmen and engineers would be sent over two or three days before a raid to do genuine business in the part selected for the attack. On being referred to, 'T' had no knowledge of the bureau but stated that just before the last raid he had had to deal with a number of persons who wanted to go to England. These persons claimed to have been approached by German agents and to be willing to betray their employers without payment provided the visa for the journey were granted, and he suggested that in future persons of the class described should be held until enquiry could be made about them. In

October the Germans did try to send in agents in preparation for a raid which did not come off and the question arose of holding up traffic from Holland and Scandinavia for twenty-four hours. It was however decided that the precautions already existing were sufficient.

In Spain, the Germans were said to be collecting information with regard to the movements of ships and cargoes from insurance agents. Letters were received from North and South America written with a view to localising military units or to identifying military censor stamps for future reference. Such missives would appear quite harmless: either the address of an officer would be asked for or a friendly letter would be addressed by some group of schoolchildren to men at the Front. The policy followed with regard to letters about officers' addresses was to wait for the answers and then after submission to DSI, either to retain them or return them to sender with an enquiry as to the bona-fides of the writer.

DRR 22B had been issued requiring every person who makes a business of receiving for reward letters, telegrams, postal packets of any kind to register the address of his business and to keep a record of all packets so received. This register was to be open to inspection by the police.

★

In February 1915 all telegrams from the United Kingdom to neutral countries in Europe were being delayed twenty-four hours, yet spy messages were going through.

In answer to a question from MO5A, it was stated that the basic principle of Cable Censorship was the withholding of facilities for trading with the enemy. MO5G then (presumably) pointed out that nearly all spy messages by letter or wire were couched in trade terms and that, in concentrating upon blocking commercial relations with the enemy the trade section of the Censorship had lost sight of the more important question of espionage. At this time the Dierks gang's activities were under investigation and MO5A asked for drastic restriction of cables to America and to the Continent, but the interests of trade prevailed and in the end it was arranged merely to subject cables to North and South America to the same delay as those to the Continent.

MO5 had failed in October 1914 to stop transmission of all cables not bearing the name and address of the sender, and in January 1915 to procure the name and address of the senders of all cablegrams submitted. But in June 1915 it was arranged that the A. forms of telegrams from certain post offices should be examined at the GPO's investigation branch by persons with a knowledge of code and particular handwritings.

The advantages claimed for this method were greater secrecy and power to judge the genuineness of a message from knowledge of national peculiarities in handwriting. Messages which the Chief Censor believed to defy detection as spy production were picked out by the GPO and their senders were put on trial.

During 1916, the Postal Censorship was extended at home and abroad. Besides the inclusion of countries in south-east Europe already noted, which took place in April 1915, a warrant for the examination of mails to and from the United States and the states of South America was obtained in May and, as regards the United States, regular examination of the mails was enforced in December 1915 at the most urgent request of MO5G.

Letters to and from PoWs were brought under regular examination in November, in which month also mails carried on neutral ships which voluntarily entered British ports became subject to examination. As previously noted, transit mails had been under examination since April 1915 and in October of that year it was stated that only in the transit mail did the enemy frankly and fully reveal the details of his business. Between 20 June and 8 October more than a hundred letters had been noted or photographed for containing codes for the evasion of Cable Censorship or other similar information. In April 1916 incoming mail to South and Central America was made subject to censorship and a warrant was obtained for the Japanese mail. In March 1916 the Cabinet authorised the examination of letter mails carried by neutral ships which had been ordered into port from the high seas.

The letters submitted to MO5G during this year belonged to the categories of peace propaganda; Independent Labour Party pamphlets, seditious literature; letters relating to possible enemy agents; letters infringing DRR 18B, such as those dealing with patent specifications, and inventions were also submitted from December onwards.

Early in 1916 MO5G directed that all indiscreet letters containing useful information, with the exception of those that were suppressed or returned to sender, should be submitted, and also all letters in the American mail indicating the locality, movements or activities of German agents. So large a number of worthless letters had been received that it was necessary to define strictly what was of value; on the other hand in censoring the Irish mail it became evident that evasion was taking place since no letters for persons on the general Black List were intercepted.

In June 1915 under DRR 22A it was made an offence to possess codes and ciphers unless the possessor could prove they were harmless; he was also to produce the key on requisition.

The sending of picture postcards etc., was prohibited as also the despatch of newspapers except by newsagents and publishers under license. Arrangements were made with *The Times* that the names and addresses of all advertisers should be given and that any doubtful cases should be reported to Scotland Yard, and a recommendation was submitted that similar precautions should be taken in the case of other newspapers. MO5G noted that no spies had been detected under these measures but many advertisements had been refused or else referred to the police for enquiry.

In connection with the seizure of official reports sent to directors of the Zeeland Company, G suggested that official reports or debates on topics of military interest should not be sold during the war or that indiscreet speeches in the House should be censored before publication. The use of invisible ink or of secret means of communication was made illegal and subsequently the use of all code was prohibited.

In July 1915 it was arranged that the Censor's Office should carry out all tests for secret writing and code and thus decide whether action by MO5 was necessary. As a rule letters containing code or secret writing were to be photographed but in case of emergency the missive was to be transmitted at once to MO5. In testing, factors regarded as suspicious were blank sheets of paper, blank postcards, unduly large spaces between the lines, arrangement of postal stamps, marks, crosses, dots indicating that a secret or code message is involved.

Drastic methods were employed to discover scratches and damage done to the surface of the paper. At that Censor's request, G Branch agreed to keep that department informed of the value attached to the letters submitted. No differentiation was to be made on the lists but in really secret cases the Censor was to receive a separate warning.

In July and August 1915, special measures were adopted with regard to the PoW correspondence with a view to prevent their sending messages in secret ink. Instead they were to use only highly glazed paper, soft pencil and ungummed envelopes; the despatch of picture postcards, drawings and embellishments of any kind was prohibited. Outgoing parcels from PoWs were delayed so that they could not reach the nearest German agent within a week of their despatch.

Special measures were taken with regard to envelopes stamped 'On His Majesty's Service'. Such envelopes were never forwarded by post but always by Foreign Office bag, yet some had been seen in the office of the German consul-general at Rotterdam. Censors were therefore instructed to open all such letters. It may be noted that various attempts were made to obtain envelopes stamped by Allied governments. The mails to Holland, Denmark and Norway were of chief importance from the point of view of counter-espionage. Writing about the Scandinavian mail, MO5 stated that six convicted spies had corresponded with Norway and Sweden and that, as Holland had been rendered less suitable as a German espionage centre, it was to be expected that Scandinavia would play a greater part. In a general report on the value of the Postal Censorship, MO5G said that it had assisted directly or indirectly in ten out of twenty cases of enemy agents dealt with since the outbreak of war; it had prevented leakage of information, supplied links between suspected persons, thrown light by German propaganda, and helped to locate enemy agents in foreign countries.

The whole question of how to prevent information being conveyed out of the country was discussed in a G paper of January 1916. Messages were conveyed by post, wire or persons: as regards letters, it was not considered probable that much use would be made of so slow and risky a method, although code might readily escape detection by an inexpert censor. On the other hand, while nearly all the wires submitted looked suspicious, it was unlikely that really dangerous messages would give this impression. The difficulty of detecting code in wires diminished greatly when the address was a known spy address, but in other cases, knowledge of the address and status of sender and addressee did not suffice, the only safeguard was to investigate the bona-fides of the sender before despatching the wire. Other possibly fruitful methods were to scrutinise wires to neutral countries bearing addresses of more than usual length or addressed to firms and individuals whose names did not appear in directories, and all wires to a particular town on a particular day.

The report's author considered that insufficient measures had been taken with regard to carriers. Carriers would either report verbally or convey documents secretly. Regarding carriers of verbal messages, it was suggested that thorough enquiry be made about all persons constantly crossing the sea; and in all suspicious cases co-operation be maintained with a British 'C' agent in Rotterdam; also, more thorough investigation be made by MO5G before granting the permit; and, as regarding carriers of documents, that a more thorough search be made of constant travellers and great care be exercised in case of a find so as to collect evidence that would convince a judge and jury.

Various methods of conveying information out of the country came to light in the winter of 1915-16. Spies were sending messages in invisible ink enclosed in envelopes addressed to Belgian and English PoWs and marked in some way recognisable by the German Censor who forwarded them to the proper quarter.

The British Postal Censor was asked to test letters addressed to British PoWs in Germany with the same stringency as was applied to ordinary correspondence. It was reported from an unguaranteed source that letters of a harmless nature would be posted in England for the United States of America, there steamed open, fresh messages inserted, and the envelope posted back to the original sender. In 1917 the Censor carefully examined all returned letters from the United States of America.

Parcels of suspiciously marked 'magazines' were being sent to PoWs and the opinion was expressed that old books should not be allowed through to enemy countries without careful enquiry into the bona-fides of the senders, as documents and papers of an undesirable nature were being sent abroad. From a Dutch newspaper, the *Telegraaf*, it was already known that code advertisements containing news of the movements of British ships were being inserted in the 'Servants Wanted' columns of the press, and these were wired to Berlin as soon as the English papers reached Holland. News was carried abroad by various methods, sometimes on a slip of paper inserted between the sides of a matchbox and on the back of the paper covering the box; in books, periodicals, newspapers and on banknotes – these things being carried ostensibly for use of the journey; in shaving brushes with screw-tops; stamped on the skin of a Belgian woman; on toys carved by German PoWs; concealed in slabs of chocolate, etc. Other means employed were messages on gramophone records concealed in a case marked 'Glass' directed to a cover address, but destined for a former Belgian official, Joseph de Bueger; concealed on board a ship with the connivance of the mate.

In July 1916, owing to a report from Copenhagen, a system was discovered of smuggling goods and letters from Germany to America and vice versa. The smuggling agents were a checker on the piers and a landing agent at New York. They received £20 per packet of mail delivered in New York or Copenhagen. Hugo Schmidt, the representative of the Deutsche Bank in America, received the letters in New York.

Messages were said to be carried in the following ways: hollow sticks carried by repatriated prisoners of war; the backs of luggage and hotel labels; every article of clothing and adornment; parts of the body and mock wounds, bandages, etc.; fountain pens, cigars, pipes; articles of food; invisible writing on wrappings of parcels and linen; mnemonic notes on printed matter carried for the journey; photographic plates and films not developed; gramophone and phonograph records; and carrier pigeons. The methods of countering such illicit carrying were restrictions on travel and careful searches at the ports, but in practice this was difficult unless the person had been signalled in advance. Even the ordinary search of correspondence and papers carried by passengers necessitating the scrutiny of small bits of paper, scribbled notes, addresses and figures on the margin of business papers took so much time that the Home Office suggested carrying out the examination in London – a stop which would completely have nullified all efforts to stop letter carrying.

Papers might also be conccaled in heavy luggage which would escape search at the ports. The difficulty of meeting this danger was to find an authority that had both time and power to conduct the search. Another much used method was by abuse of diplomatic privilege. During July 1916 the right to carry diplomatic despatches under privilege was restricted to official couriers of the diplomatic service, and unofficial persons carrying despatches were subjected to the same inspection as ordinary passengers. But diplomatic official couriers themselves were so suspect that in October the French government agreed to present them from travelling by the Folkestone and Boulogne route.

Moreover, Danes and Spaniards were getting their letters sent in legation bags. In July 1915, Regulation 24, prohibiting illicit letter carrying had been amended so as to cover persons at the ports who ordinarily came in contact with the crews of vessels, and in June 1916, shipping-agents were instructed to forward for censorship in London all letters addressed to persons on board ships sailing for a port not in an Allied country. Only three classes of letters were excepted, and they were letters from the owner to the captain of the ship; letters relating to charter; and letters relating to cargo.

Still reports came in of letter-smuggling by ships' crews and G4 commenting on the report of our inspecting officer indicated five possible methods of evading the regulation and declared the only complete solution to be in cutting off all intercourse between the crews and the shore. There remained for consideration the censoring of seamen's correspondence. After much debate the work of censoring all correspondence addressed to the captain and crews of vessels trading to neutral countries was transferred to the military control officers who forwarded anything they did not understand or considered suspicious to MI5G or to the Censor for translation or comment.

DRR 24B was issued in November prohibiting the conveyance of any written or printed matter to any enemy or neutral country except under special permit and with the exception of the following classes of letters: ships' papers; patent specifications authorised for export; letters, etc., carried by the GPO.

Early in April 1916, it was known that evasion of the censorship on mail to the United States was carried out by posting letters to intermediaries in Canada. A test censoring of Canadian letters was made in April and letters passing between Ireland and Canada were censored for a while. After, the Irish rebellion censorship was reimposed in August, and in September a warrant was obtained for the occasional examination of the mail to Canada.

In June censorship of the South and Central American mail was extended to outgoing correspondence, and in September, after the discovery of the new German secret ink, MI5 urged that the whole of the American mail should be censored. In November a test censoring of the French mail was carried out.

In dealing with outgoing mails the great weapon was delay – delay sometimes inevitable under pressure of work or German attack, in special cases, however, deliberately imposed. In June 1916 it was estimated that no letter could reach Rotterdam within forty-eight hours and that no wire could reach the German authorities within about fifty-four hours. The result was beneficial in other ways; it was considered possible to restrict censorship on the inward terminal mail to that correspondence of persons on the German Black List, to abrogate the delay on outgoing letters to British prisoners of war, and to remit censorship on incoming letters from PoWs with the exception of those sent by the so-called Irish Brigade at Zossen and Limburg.

Owing to the discovery that Joseph King MP was corresponding with Otto Gaupp, a suspect German journalist at The Hague, the privilege which projected outgoing letters from the House of Commons was withdrawn. The regulation prohibiting the use of secret ink was extended to cover mechanical means of transmission such as concealing a letter in the binding of a book or between the pages of a pamphlet gummed together. Indiscreet persons had reported facts and speeches made in a secret session of the House and certain reports were published. Two copies of these having been found in envelopes addressed to persons connected with a Dutch shipping company, it was made illegal to publish any report of or reference to, a secret session of either House of Parliament or of Cabinet proceedings. In August the export to enemy countries of any kind of printed matter had been prohibited, as also all correspondence with book-makers, lottery-agents, fortune-tellers and pseudo-scientific institutions. This order was specially aimed at institutions in touch with the Rozroy Agency which prepared horoscopes for soldiers, and concerning which Steinhauer had made special enquiry in pre-war days.

It was in the power of MO5 to make arrangements for secret censorship for a limited period in any particular town and, in February 1916, a report on the secret censorship begun at Inverness in July 1915 showed that good work had been done in preventing strikes, disorder and leakage of information. On the other hand, an inland censorship for Chatham imposed in September 1915 ran for one month only as it had proved valueless. Suspicious telegrams from ports were referred by the port officer to the Censor's department and arrangements could be made for overhearing telephone messages from any suspected call-box or telephone office. A record was kept in such a case of the suspected person's connections and the conversations were submitted periodically to this bureau.

An instance in point is the case of George Spicer of the *Dover Standard*, who telephoned information about the movements of troops. Spicer had been prosecuted in the civil court in connection with some information sent by telephone which had been overheard by arrangement with the GPO. The magistrates dismissed the case on the grounds that it was a press offence which had not been referred to the DPP, and as it had not had his sanction the action must fail. Mr Moresby, MO6G's legal adviser, considered that it was not a press case as there was no evidence to show that the information was intended for publication. But the GPO raised the question of legality; the regulation forbidding alien enemies to have telephone lines, except with the consent of the police, was administered by the police. In twelve cases, however, by arrangement with MO5, the GPO kept observation on lines which might be used for enemy purposes. This was a special precautionary measure not based on any regulation but justified by the exceptional circumstances. The GPO however, objected strongly to any proposed extension of the system. In replying to the GPO, Major Clayton stated that MO5 had asked that calls from a certain number at Dover should be censored and the results had been very valuable and he wished to continue the present arrangements, promising that no requests for the interception of telephone messages would be made except when there were strong grounds to expect important results.

The action could be covered by principles of common law and, if any case were brought into court, the overhearing of a conversation could be proved in camera which was a safer way from a preventive point of view than promulgating a new regulation to legalise the deed. The position was accepted by the GPO, with the warning however, that identification and proof in London would be a very different matter from proof in a small locality.

★

Reports received from various sources between April and December 1915 disclosed three kinds of traffic involving money. Repatriated PoWs or people returning from the Continent were carrying British, French and Belgian gold and notes, involving in some cases considerable sums of money. The Germans were having quantities of Russian notes bought for their account in London, it was supposed for espionage purposes, possibly also to gain a hold over businessmen. It was expected that one of the conditions of peace would be the transfer into German hands of the French holdings of Russian securities. Traffic in copper coins was suspected.

Taking the last point first, in September a dearth of copper coin was noticed in Devon and soon after the shortage of such coin became acute in Ireland. Silver coinage also began to fail. Various reasons for this shortage were put forward by the Mint and other authorities. Then the trouble spread to Sweden. In October the Swedish government prohibited travellers from carrying more than one Krona's worth of copper out of the country and at the same time it became known that the Germans were requisitioning Belgian copper money and sending it to Germany. Whether the German demand was responsible for the shortage in other countries was never clearly established.

As early as April 1915 passengers were reported to be carrying abroad gold coins sewn into their linen or hidden in boxes of cigarettes or in cloth buttons. MO5 warned the port officers of such practices, and also of the traffic in Russian notes. In August 1915, in order to place some restriction on the export of British and Allied currency, MO5 made arrangements at the ports to exchange such gold and notes into German currency if the traveller was bound for Germany or German-occupied territory; moreover the Treasury was warned of the practice.

The Treasury, however, declined to press for a regulation limiting the export of notes and specie, on the grounds that such action might impair the national credit, so MO5 subsequently attempted to extend the system of exchange at the ports to all currency being conveyed out of the country in considerable amounts without regard to the ultimate destination of the traveller. In February 1916 it became known that German financial agents in New York were buying English sovereigns for the South American Exchange and were refusing to buy other gold coins or bar gold. Moreover English gold coinage was being carried to the Continent by the crews of South American boats. Certain Belgians at Flushing were said to be collecting all the British and French gold they could and selling it to the German authorities at Brussels; in August of the same year a Spanish woman was sent into France via Italy to buy up French gold and soon after the Banco Hispano-Americana was seeking to import into Spain gold supplies from a firm in Glasgow.

On 5 December 1916 DRR 30E was issued prohibiting the melting down or using of gold coin of British or foreign currency for any purpose except currency, and a further regulation, 41B, was drawn up restricting the remittance of money to countries in German occupation except under license.

★

It is not possible to enter into the special work done by Section G1 but one set of enquiries had so important a bearing on the future conduct of the war that it sails for notice. During the latter end of 1915 and the whole of 1916 G Branch had investigated the cases of the Diamond Reign public-house, and the Communist Club at 107 Charlotte Street.

After the closing of various German clubs on the outbreak of war, the Diamond Reign became a meeting-place for bitterly hostile British citizens of German birth and enquiry showed that close touch was maintained between some of its habitués and those of the Communist Club, which boasted such members as Georgi Chicherin, Maxim Litvinov and Artur Zummermann.

The Communist Club kept in touch with German PoWs, intrigued with the Labour Party to stop the arrest of 'peaceful' alien enemies, fomented strikes on the Clyde and spread revolutionary doctrine among Russian seamen, through the Russian Seamen's Union which maintained close connection with the International Transport Workers' Union in Berlin. The Russian Seamen's Union had its centre at the Seamen's and Firemen's Union in Commercial Road.

Between September 1915 and April 1916 ten Germans and nine naturalised British subjects of German birth, all of them frequenters of the Diamond Reign, were interned, and in November 1916, the Communist Club was raided and twenty-two persons of various nationalities were recommended for internment. The Home Office sanctioned the internment of seventeen, and three were freed as the case against them was weak, and two, Chicherin and Sandelevitch, were offered the choice of internment or deportation on the charge of hindering recruiting and fomenting labour trouble. Chicherin was interned for months and after the Russian Revolution was allowed to return home with many other Russian communists.

The action of the police in these cases and, particularly with regard to the Communist Club, calls for comment. The Germans were confident they could bribe the police, and the favourable reports always sent in about the Communist Club were not adequately explained by the excuse that it was convenient for the police to keep the anarchists and communists undisturbed in one centre; of this the police strike of a later date affords abundant proof. It is probable that the unwillingness of the police hampered the Special Intelligence Bureau considerably in procuring adequate punishment for these men; the work of informers had to be relied upon and this had a notable effect after the war when the question of denaturalising disloyal subjects came before the Advisory Committee.

The following instances taken from the report for September 1915 give a general idea of the work of the branch. All the cases, it must be remembered, would not come under the cognisance of the branch but only those in which investigation was required.

- Prosecuted: the pro-German wife of a clergyman at Darlington. Offence: enquiry about munitions factories. Punishment: month's imprisonment.
- Ordered for arrest: conditionally on proving identity with a pre-war German spy, a man who had applied for a permit to go to Holland.
- Signalled not to be allowed to leave the United Kingdom: a man suspected of illicit trading in munitions.
- Under observation: five, among these a nurse on the east coast who had spent most of her youth in Antwerp, Germany and Russia.
- Check on correspondence: a house which had been the rendezvous of German immigrants studying textile machinery.

F Branch dealt with cases of internment under DRR 14D but all enquiry was carried out by G Branch. Interned: a Roman Catholic priest, ex-officer of the Landsturm, officially allowed to visit Belgian wounded soldiers in Northumberland; a German who had posed as a naturalised British subject for over twenty years, and had special knowledge of the Tyne river; a German posing as a Luxemburg citizen; a naturalised British subject who had served in the Prussian Guard and was in the habit of visiting the concentration camp at Frimby; a German managing director of a company for synchronising clocks all over London, in a position to do mischief by sending a high voltage current along the wires, twice convicted of minor offences under the ARO.

Recommended for internment: seven, of whom four were persons sentenced to various terms of imprisonment for false declarations under ARO, and a fifth was to be prosecuted for the same offence. One of these offenders was a former German consular official who had obtained employment in munitions works.

—  Recommended for deferred internment: one, a man who when drunk uttered pro-German sentiments.
—  Removed or recommended for removal from ports or other places: three women, two men of whom one was in a position to damage the Leeds waterworks.
—  Under orders for arrest: one, the son of a naturalised Frenchman of Polish origin and a German mother, evaded service in the French Army and went to Sweden.
—  Recommended for deportation: after imprisonment of six weeks, a woman who entered a prohibited area and failed to register under ARO.
—  Repatriated or recommended for repatriation: four women, two of whom lived on the English coast, one at Londonderry, and the fourth was engaged to a British officer.
—  Not to be allowed to return: one German woman who posed as a Swiss, went frequently to Folkestone, made friends with officers, and left for Germany before proceedings could be taken.

Among other aliens the following G cases are reported: a Dutchman, who offered, his services as a Secret Service agent and was kept under observation; a Belgian sub-agent employed to recruit Belgians for munitions work in England and on whom incriminating documents had been found in Holland was arrested under DRR 55 and interned; a Belgian who had been twice to Germany since the outbreak of war and had tampered with his passport.

- Suspected cases in the army: eighty, and, of these, four were G cases; a sergeant was arrested at Chatham as he could give no satisfactory proof of his nationality (it was proposed to discharge him as undesirable and leave him to the police to be dealt with under ARO); an intelligence officer with the army in France married to a German lady residing at The Hague and friendly with a well-known German agent (GHQ informed and checks placed on the correspondence of the officer and his wife); two other less interesting cases.
- Suspects on account of their correspondence: seventy-eight.
- Intercepted telegrams: from Liverpool to an address supposed to be a spy address, telling a German prostitute to get leave to go to New York; prolix telegram from Newcastle to Amsterdam sent by a man of the same name as a would-be informer against the Germans in 1909: from London to Stockholm asking for money: from Amsterdam to Leghorn sent by a man bearing the name of an enemy agent at Rotterdam. Several other telegrams satisfactorily solved.
- Observation: six cases, of these a person writing from Scheveningen to one employed in munitions works at Sheffield suggested that letters could be sent by the Foreign Office bag to avoid censorship. No explanation could be given by the Foreign Office.
- Check on correspondence: two, of these a person writing from Geneva to south London asked to be paid for forwarding letters and squaring the Secret Police to keep silence.

- Censor Department informed: one, an officer in a well-known regiment was found to be corresponding with a woman reported to be dangerous and living at Frankfurt.
- Severe caution: one, forwarding old photographs of submarines to America.
- Warning: a lady in London who was to act as intermediary for German correspondence between Hankow and Germany.
- Eastern suspects: nineteen, in May there had been five such cases. Barcelona was found to be a meeting-place for Indians of whom one travelled on some unexplained business between points in Spain, Paris and America; Grimsby was said to be a port whence Pan-Islamic literature was despatched to India; and seditious Indian publications were reported to be coming into England from America; a Swiss woman married to a Persian was reported to be coming to this country as a German spy; a number of Indian revolutionaries were found, or suspected to be, in touch with Indian revolutionary leaders who were acting as German agents in Switzerland: of the Indians in England one had been interned, another had been searched and interrogated and proceedings under DRR 14B were in contemplation; the others had not been arrested but their cases were still under investigation. An Indian and his wife of German origin were arrested at Hull and Liverpool respectively; and a Hindu, a mystic, was arrested on the 4 September, pending extradition. Other suspects were of Egyptian origin.
- General Cases: 154.
- Proposed internment under DRR 14B: a man with an Irish name, deserted in 1914; cases associated with Indian seditionists, contributed articles to the *Indian Sociologist*, corresponded with Krishnavarma, who became a German agent.
- Correspondence: fifty. Blueprints of the Royal Aircraft Factory were returned from America through the Dead Letter Office. Conclusion: the censorship of American mails en bloc is essential.

- Enemy Aliens: 196.
- Refusal to endorse application for release from internment: a Czech, formerly chauffeur to General Officer Commanding Cromarty defences.
- Easterns: thirty-five cases, showing that the extremist section of the Indian Revolutionary Party had fallen largely under German influence and were being used by the Germans for their own purposes; an Oriental Literary Society, an offshoot of the Anglo-Ottoman Society was reported to be hostile to Great Britain and interested in peace propaganda.
- Alien Europeans other than Belgians: compelled to reside in a definite area under DRR 14, a man suspected of espionage but against whom there was no definite proof.
- Government offices: twenty.
- Dismissed: lady employed in Postal Censorship living among pro-Germans.
- Munition works: twenty-eight.
- Description circulated and Ministry of Munition informed: a man employed in three high-explosive factories since July, in each case left suddenly and then disappeared.
- Press: fifteen.
- Restrictions under DRR 14: a man who posed as a correspondent of *The Daily Telegraph* and pretending to be an American tried to get a permit to enter the Zone of the Armies.
- Suspects abroad: 192.
- From October onward MO6(c) dealt with these cases, the action of MO5 being restricted to precautionary measures against their landing in British Dominions.
- Circulated for search and information to be sent to MO5: a German consul in Spain; a British subject of German origin; a merchant and director of a mining and water company.
- Description circulated: a man arrested for supposed espionage in Switzerland and released for want of evidence, reported to be going to spy in France.

| Statistics showing the growth of the office work between July and December 1915 | | | |
|---|---|---|---|
| | July | December | Total for six months |
| Personal dossiers | 1,097 | 1,274 | 7,543 |
| Telegrams | 728 | 287 | 3,559 |
| Letters | 649 | 1,435 | 7,690 |
| Suspects circulated | 334 | 415 | 2,980 |
| Internments recommended | 25 | 7 | 81 |
| Internments sanctioned | | | 70 |
| Deferred internment and alien restriction | 5 | 2 | 30 |
| Sanctioned | | | 30 |
| Permit | September 28–30 | | |
| Applications | 598 | 1,396 | 4,874 (for three months and one week) |

| Statistics for 1916 | | | | | |
|---|---|---|---|---|---|
| | January | December | Jan–June | June–Dec | Totals Jan–Dec |
| Personal dossiers | 1,173 | 732 | 5,893 | 4,764 | 10,657 |
| Telegrams | 308 | 472 | 2,541 | 3,329 | 5,870 |
| Letters | 2,129 | 2,201 | 15,410 | 17,847 | 33,257 |
| Irish American | 358 | 342 | 2,992 | 2,559 | 5,551 |
| Peace letters | 161 | 314 | 1,225 | 1,512 | 2,737 |
| Disloyalty | 367 | 250 | 66 | 1,900 | 1,966 |
| Suspects circulated | 221 | 386 | 1,327 | 1,847 | 3,174 |
| Internments recommended | | | | | 4 |
| Sanctioned | | | | | 3 |
| Permit applications | 1,381 | 2,783 | 9,324 | 15,595 | 24,919 |
| Inland passes | Total for six months: 192 | | | | |

★

Jonkheer Johan Jakob Calkoen came to England to promote some company to trade in coconuts. He stayed at the Savoy Hotel from 14 May to 7 June 1915 when, under pressure from the Dutch consul he was allowed to leave the United Kingdom against the advice of the police. He was given a no return permit. In July he was known to be working for Klein, alias Cremer, the officer in charge of the German espionage centre at The Hague, and a search of telegraphic money orders showed that he had received £40 and £10 from N. Cleyton, Rotterdam, in May. Subsequent reports connected him with Pompe van Meerlevvoort, also a German agent, and with the agent Reichmann who had supplied the funds for the Calkoen-Reichmann Bank to further contraband dealings in stolen securities. Calkoen was also reported to be conducting questionable money operations in Switzerland. Finally it was known that Reichmann, Calkoen and Kinzler were intimate friends and all engaged in making money as best they could.

Calkoen appears on the Antwerp List of 1917 as A-3. His task was to manipulate Dutch firms connected with England. He was described as educated, reliable and with good connections but unable to return to England where he had previously worked for the Zweigstelle. Calkoen had been the subject of two circulars to the ports: in the first dated 31 August instructions were given to search him and signal his arrival to Scotland Yard but not to alarm him and not to arrest him unless the necessary evidence were found on him. In the second, dated 29 April 1916, orders were given to take his papers at the port and to send him up to Scotland Yard.

H. F. P. Kinzler was seen at Scotland Yard on 24 May and confessed to having received instruction as a spy against England. He was deported and orders were given that he was not to be allowed to re-enter the United Kingdom.

Pauline Slager and Georgine Ulrich (Ulricht or Ullrich) landed at Tilbury on 29 July; they were searched, their passports were taken from them and they were told to call at Scotland Yard. There they stated that,

after performing at various places in Italy, they had come to England
to earn their living as music-hall artists, and that if they succeeded in
obtaining a contract they would settle in a flat. They were told that as
soon as they notified their permanent address their passports would be
returned to them. However, on 11 August, without notifying the police,
they went to Glasgow and on 14 August to Edinburgh. They there
aroused some suspicion by putting up at the best hotel and by presenting
themselves for registration without producing passports. In consequence,
the Chief Constable referred to the Metropolitan Police. Meanwhile
two wires sent from the Victoria Hotel, London, to Adolf Carre,
Zwaardecroonstraat 41a, Rotterdam, and to Van Straalen, Binnenamatel
42, Amsterdam, were answered by van Straalen wiring £40 to Slager.
A third wire was sent from Edinburgh on 19 August and £40 came in
reply from Van Straalen on 20 August. The Metropolitan Police had
been deceived by Slager's half-truths, but the bureau telephoned on 19
August to the Chief Constable of Edinburgh repeating her message to
van Straalen and asking for a full enquiry. As a result the women were
detained at Edinburgh on a charge of entering a prohibited area without
the necessary identification papers; they were admonished in the Sheriff's
Court, sent back to London, and left the United Kingdom on 25 August
with a no return permit.

Pauline Slager was half-sister to Kinzler. She beguiled the police by
giving worthless information against Mrs Helene Schurmann. As soon
as the women had left, information began to come in against them and
from Belgian and French sources the following details were ascertained:
Ulrich used the alias D'Aumont or Dumont and was associated with the
German spies Droesse and Dr Reichmann.

A photograph of Slager was sent to the bureau with the information
that she and Ulrich were coming again in October; a letter to her, which
was intercepted in Holland, showed that negotiations were proceeding
for buying her a horse and that she was to tour Glasgow, Inverness,
Edinburgh and then the southern and eastern ports.

Her photograph was circulated to the ports with instructions to allow
her and her friend to land but to keep in touch with her and to inform

the bureau, and the Metropolitan and local police. She did not come in October. In December she was again reported to be coming but did not appear. In December 1915, a troupe consisting of Mrs R. A. Madigan, Swedish circus-rider, Miss E. M. Ojers, Dutch circus-rider, Hendrik Hinsmau, a Dutchman, and Vittorio Corini, an Italian stableman in charge of Adolphe Carre's circus-horses landed at Hull and went through to Liverpool on 20 December. They returned to Rotterdam on 16 February. Corini was afterwards reported to have been intimately connected with Pauline and her half-sister Eleanore Dezentie, née Kinzler.

It was not till January 1917, when he was reported to be going to America with elephants, that Corini was signalled as a suspect, or till March 1917 that this former journey to Liverpool seems to have become known to the bureau and then, in reporting it, the British agent explained that in the absence of definite cause for suspicion visas had been grafted to the troupe though unwillingly. Orders were issued to arrest Corini on board any ship. At the end of the year 1917, the British consulate supplied details of Pauline's family: her mother Catherine Donkers had married first Henry Slager and secondly Henry Kinzler and of her numerous family four at least were proved spies or suspects. These were Marguerite, married to Hermann Droesse; Pauline mentioned above; Eleonora Dezentie, and Henry Kinzler. Catherine herself collected the reports sent in by her children and forwarded them to the Germans. During 1916 and 1917, Pauline and Eleonora were repeatedly said to be travelling in Italy for espionage purposes. They were also said to be in touch with Karpesteyn, a Dutch circus-rider who acted for the Austrian legation, and with Suzanne van Damme. On the Antwerp List of 1917, Slager figures as A-54.

Task: establishment of relations with suitable persons in artists circles with a view to their going to England. Characteristics: artiste, clever.

According to Hans Eils, she did offer to come to England again after the 1915 fiasco but was not allowed. It is worth noting that repeatedly rumours were set afloat that a spy who had been in trouble with the authorities here was returning to this country, but the Germans never did send them back. Hence the rumour may have been a German method to divert attention from the person whom they really were sending. On leaving the United Kingdom in August 1915 the two women had given their address in Holland, at 69 Baendelstraat in The Hague, which was the address of Pauline's mother.

An Indian named Sopher, who had been a dresser and then a clerk in the Indian hospital at Brighton and had incurred suspicion for wearing his uniform after his discharge, applied in February 1916 for a permit to go to visit Mrs D'Aumont at 69 Daendeletraat in The Hague. On being interviewed, he at first lied asserting that D'Aumont was a journalist but, on being shown his error, he dropped all pretence and admitted a very cursory acquaintance with D'Aumont and De Regals (Ulrich and Pauline Slager), whose addresses were found on him. A prosecution under DRR 16A for carrying a spy address was not considered advisable; it would have involved one of the officers who had interrogated Sopher going into the witness box to prove the man's lies and consequent guilty knowledge of the nature of the address, and it was not certain that, if convicted, Sopher would be detained for the duration of the war. He was interned on the grounds of his hostile associations and attempt to renew a dangerous connection, and the order was upheld by the Advisory Committee. Other persons whom the bureau watched in connection with the case of Pauline Slager were her brother, Wilhelm Cornelis Slager, a musician and refugee in London, and his wife and first cousin Maria Juliana née Dronkers who, after spending some months in London, went in July 1915 to live at 69 Baendelstraat in The Hague. Their correspondence was undoubtedly suspicious, but nothing was proved against them. By agreement with the Belgian authorities, Wilhelm Slager was not to be allowed to leave the country but he never attempted to do so. On the other hand, when his wife wished to return to him in London, she was kept out of the country for some ten months and when she at last got a visa to come, she was interrogated at Scotland Yard and all her effects were examined but without result.

★

Eva de Bournonville, aged forty-one, was by birth a Dane, but became a naturalised Swede, was employed as a shorthand clerk and typist at the Danish legation in Stockholm. She procured a passport to come to England 'for recreation' on 30 August 1915. She left Stockholm on 20 September and travelling via Christiania, Bergen and Newcastle, reached London on 24 September spending the night at the Kenilworth Hotel. Next day she went to live at 7 Kensington Crescent, moved on 9 October to a residential ladies club at 11 St George's Square, and on 16 October to the Whitehall Hotel, 15-16 Bedford Place. She gave the Danish legation at 29 Pont Street as her address and her letters were forwarded from there, enclosed in envelopes bearing the legation crest.

Miss de Bournonville had satisfied the Aliens Officer at Newcastle as to her bona-fides: she carried letters of introduction from the secretary of the Danish legation at Stockholm to Count E. Reventlow, secretary to the Danish legation in London and from the Danish minister in Stockholm to the Danish legation in London. Miss de Bournonville is said to have been a friend of Dr Sven Hedin.

Since 1903 Miss de Bournonville had known and corresponded intermittently with Miss Jeanie Snall Johnstone, a schoolteacher who in 1915 resided at 63 High Street, Dumbarton. Early in October, de Bournonville wrote to Miss Johnstone and received from her an introduction to that lady's brother, William Johnstone, a steel and iron traveller who lived at Hackney. Miss de Bournonville called upon Mr and Miss Johnstone three times and on the last occasion roused their suspicion by her conversation. She asked where the new anti-aircraft guns were fixed; she stated that she was applying for a post at the Censorship and asked Mrs Johnstone to answer any questions set by the War Office, adding: 'We must both tell the same tale'.

Miss de Bournonville spoke Swedish, Danish, French, English and German. On coming to London, she immediately got in touch with the PoW Help Committee. Between 25 September and 1 November, she wrote twelve letters to an address in Stockholm recording the letters on the back of her writing block.

All these letters were signed with fictitious names, the signature changing with every letter; the name of the addressee also varied but the address remained always: 35/37 Birger Jarlsgatan in Stockholm. In these letters she referred vaguely to persons whom she was actually meeting or writing to in England, taking care to disguise their names. It was the vagueness and lack of interest of these letters, no doubt, which first aroused the suspicion of the postal examiner, who on 2 October intercepted the third letter of the series. It was tested and found to contain a secret message about the falling off of recruiting and a sorrowful admission of failure on the writer's part.

A message in the fifth letter showed that the writer had a correspondent in Dumbarton and had some thought of attempting to get into the War Office. In the sixth, the spy was trying to get in touch with officers and using 'charity' as a means to this end. Reports followed of the damage by the Zeppelins at Croydon, of airships under construction, of air defences in and about London, of the impossibility of sending newspapers except through newsagents owing to the fact that the British counter-espionage had found out the use made of them by the German spies.

A duplicate of this last report, numbered eleven and addressed to Major Charles Hohlay, Belgian PoW, Interned at Blankenburg (Mark) Germany etc., was intercepted by the Censor who found the *en clair* message unusual and the signature incorrect. The Censor intercepted ten letters in all. The bureau endeavoured without success to trace the writer through clues contained in the letters; she was identified towards the end of the month by her handwriting on a telegram despatched on 20 October to an address in Stockholm. The first step taken was to ensure that she should not slip out of the country by asking that the permit office should refer to the bureau any application made by Miss de Bournonville. Observation was kept upon her and she was followed to Mr Johnstone's house who was interviewed by the police. One of the agents employed by the bureau put up at the Whitehall Hotel, and supplied Miss de Bournonville with incorrect information which she duly sent on to her employers. Meanwhile, a Lieutenant Holmes, who was staying at the hotel with his mother, Lady Holmes, had noticed that the police were watching the hotel and realised their object. He told the officer that de Bournonville had asked some curious questions about barracks in England. De Bournonville was arrested on 5 November. Among her papers were found the writing-block mentioned above, a picture postcard addressed to Captain Maclean of Ardgour, a PoW at Blankenburg, Germany, an envelope addressed to Major Horlay, and three copies of instructions regarding communication with PoWs abroad.

Other documents showed that she had made great efforts to obtain a post in the Censorship and that, although Count Reventlow refused officially to give her a reference, unofficially he had helped her to the best of his ability. Moreover, she had used her connection with Danish diplomats for furthering her private correspondence and for placing certain addresses and medical prescriptions in safety. She possessed materials for secret writing including tablets of soap impregnated with potassium ferro-cyanide, also a strong magnifying-glass which may have been used either for deciphering or writing secret messages.

In her examination at Scotland Yard, de Bournonville confessed her activities as soon as she was confronted with her letters and she admitted that she had received money sent from the German legation through a bank in Stockholm. The German military attaché at Stockholm and another person who had come to Sweden from Germany had made the arrangements. It was ascertained that the money was paid in cheques drawn on the London City & Midland Bank, made payable to Miss Eva Bournonville, Danish legation and endorsed E. Reventlow, secretary to the legation. Miss de Bournonville received cheques for £15 dated 15 and 23 October and one for £30 dated 3 November. She banked the money with Count Reventlow who from time to time sent her small sums. She also deposited £12 at Lloyd's Bank.

On 12 October the bureau had learned that the address in Sweden to which de Bournonville had posted her letters was a German Secret Service bureau under the direction of a Baron von Oppel, who was almost certainly identical with a former secretary of the German military attaché in London; also that direct communication was maintained between spies in England by means of letters addressed to PoWs and marked with some sign known to the German Censor. The date of this information shows that it preceded the discovery of de Bournonville's communications through the addresses of PoWs.

De Bournonville was tried on 18 and 19 January 1916. The originals of her letters were produced in court and, although she laid stress on the fact that she had reported only what the man in the street could find out unaided, the jury found her guilty of attempting to communicate information which might be useful to the enemy with intent to assist him. She was sentenced to death and the sentence was commuted to imprisonment for life.

In court Eva de Bournonville stated that she had been recruited for the Germans by a man named Schmidt, whom she had known in 1912. She met him in a restaurant in July 1916, and being pressed by debt, she accepted work at a remuneration of £1 a day. He instructed her in the use of ink and gave her the three names to which she addressed letters to 35/37 Birger Jarlsgatan, Stockholm, and the two names of British PoWs.

★

Johan Christian Zahle Lassen aged fifty, married and father of three children, had been a tobacco-planter in Sumatra and afterwards employed in the iron, steel and machinery business in Copenhagen, had twice started ventures on his own account and failed, and in 1911 had gone to Panama. There he worked first in American steamship companies and then in the Panama Banking Company. Owing to ill-health he left Panama in December 1914 and returned via New York, Liverpool and Hull to Copenhagen, which he reached on 1 January 1915. On the passage to England, he made friends with a Mr Challoner, agent for Messrs Sandeman, wine merchants of Pall Mall, and with Miss M. A. Pole of Wallasey, to whom he suggested marriage. He entered into correspondence with Challoner from Copenhagen hoping to obtain work in England as a linguist.

Mr Challoner is said to have applied for a post in the Censorship on behalf of Lassen, who knew Danish, Dutch, German, English and some French and Spanish. As there was no vacancy in the Censorship, Mr Challoner mooted the question of Lassen taking up an agency for Messrs Sandeman, and Lassen came to England via Bergen, to continue negotiations. He landed at Newcastle on 9 September and was met at King's Cross by Challoner, who accompanied him on the 10th to the Home Office. The port officer had doubts about Lassen's passport, which had been issued on 2 September and endorsed by the British consul 'to London to visit Mr Challoner on a personal matter of business'. Lassen saw Mr Haldane Porter, satisfied him as to his credentials and received back his passport. On 11 September he went to Liverpool and called upon Mr Richard Watson, brother-in-law of Mr Challoner. He also saw Miss Pole on that evening and spent Sunday and part of Monday with her, returning to town on 13 September. Before the journey to England, Lassen had spent twenty-four tours in Berlin at the request of his friend Dr Katz who wished Lassen to buy food for Germany in Denmark. This Lassen refused to do. Mr Challoner thought Lassen's information would be interesting, so the two men called at the Foreign Office where Lassen made a statement of no particular value. Lassen being anxious to return quickly to Denmark, applied for a special permit at the Home Office, called there and gave some further information with regard to affairs in Germany and offered his services to England. He then got his passport from the Foreign Office and sailed for Copenhagen on 20 September. He had ordered and paid for five dozen bottles of whiskey which he intended to dispose of in samples to private persons. He had also expressed the wish to get a post in the Foreign Office or Home Office. From Copenhagen Lassen wrote to Challoner on 3 and 27 October and on 2 November 1915, on which date he ordered twelve dozen bottles of whiskey. In every letter he spoke of returning to England for a short visit and asked Challoner to obtain travelling facilities from the Home Office; in the third letter he showed a desire to come over immediately without prejudice to yet another visit at some future date. He also communicated with another firm about ordering consignments of cigarettes.

Lassen landed at Hull on 12 November and stated afterwards that he had written from Hull to Mr Haldane Porter asking for permission to leave the country again in a very few days but Captain Haldane Porter never received the letter.

Lassen had been signalled as a spy from Copenhagen on 9 November and orders were issued to watch and report his movements and to have him taken to Scotland Yard. He was met at King's Cross, interviewed at Scotland Yard, searched and detained in custody. He carried about £90. In his interview he made no mention of his connection with Germans. Then, after three days in prison, he made a voluntary statement regarding his visit to Dr Katz of Berlin, a man known to the bureau as the recruiting agent and organiser of espionage directed against this country from Sweden, Denmark and Norway.

Two days later Lassen insisted that he had important information to give. Two officers from MI5 saw him and he stated that before and after his visit to England in September he had seen Count Ranzow, German ambassador at Copenhagen, that he had told the Count his impressions of England and that the Count had said that a great Zeppelin raid was to take place over London on a particular date. Lassen stoutly denied that he was a spy saying that he had come over to give this information but his story did not stand cross-examination.

Verifications were made of some of the addresses found on Lassen. One of these, R. Emmecee & Co., Gothersgade 91, Kobenhavn, was that of a firm dealing in agricultural machinery, provisions, groceries, and doing a large trade with Germany. Two other addresses on slips of paper were identified by a censor as addresses in Copenhagen but, in contrast to procedure followed in the case of Dutch addresses, no enquiries were made in Copenhagen itself.

A search of telegrams showed that, in September, Lassen had wired the day of his departure and ship and had asked for news to be wired c/o the Danish consulate at Hull; in November he had wired the date of his arrival. Both these wires had been sent to Lassen's permanent address. Nothing more resulted from the enquiry prosecuted through the GPO. No trace could be found of Challoner's application to the authorities for a post to be given to Lassen in the Censorship. Equally unsatisfactory was the examination of various scents and medicaments in Lassen's possession. They were identified indeed by the expert, but he made no suggestion that they could be used as secret ink.

It may be worth noting that on the back of a letter from Percy Robinson, the solicitor employed in Lassen's defence, there is a draft in Lassen's handwriting of a series of six telegrams, all dealing with the same journey in variants suggestive of code. A summary of evidence was taken on 16 December and Lassen was tried on 27 January 1916 on two counts under DRR 48 and 18 of having come to England on 9 September and on 12 November 1915 for the purpose of collecting information etc., with the intent to assist the enemy. He was acquitted and sent back to Denmark with a no return permit. He returned to Copenhagen on 30 January and his description with orders that he was not to be allowed to re-enter the United Kingdom was circulated a few days after. Meanwhile from Copenhagen came the news that Lassen was a German spy and had been to Caen several times via Holland. A few days later, Mr Challoner sought advice as to whether he should have any further dealings with Lassen and was recommended not to do so.

Then Lassen was reported to be coming to England again and to be boasting that he had learned all he wanted from the officer in whose charge he was. Finally Lassen, who had made acquaintance with officials at four government offices and the inside of a British prison, wrote asking for compensation for his imprisonment and loss of business, and suggesting that he should be put into communication with some 'trusted agent' of Major Drake in Copenhagen.

★

Emil Brugman, a partner of van Spanje and Visser, dealers in motor trucks and lorries, landed in England on 14 October 1915 for the ostensible purpose of laying before the Minister of Munitions a process for making gun-cotton from raw material plentiful in Russia. Accompanied by a

Russian engineer named de Mazia, to whom Brugman carried a letter of introduction from the Russian military attaché at The Hague, Brugman called at the War Office, saw the Director of Military Operations, who sent him to the Superintendent of Research at Woolwich, where he was referred to the Ministry of Munitions.

Brugman received two letters from Lord Moulton dated 18 and 26 October. Lord Moulton stated that the government would consider the process and asked for samples. With Lord Moulton's letter, Brugman obtained a permit to go to Holland to fetch samples and returned to England on 26 October. No licence to trade in munitions had been given to him. On both visits he had spent some days at Woolwich. Through some error, when Brugman first landed in England, his papers were sent direct to the Ministry of Munitions and not as they should have been to MO5E or Scotland Yard.

In November Brugman was reported to the bureau as associating with German agents, travelling frequently to England and carrying a letter from Lloyd George. He was also said to be passing contraband rubber into Germany together with van Haestert, J. Rutlin and de Brugge. Enquiries made by the bureau failed to establish that any letter to Brugman had been written by or on behalf of Lloyd George. In the following March Richard Tinsley reported that Brugman, who was known to have been engaged in smuggling goods for Germany, was coming to England and might be using letters written by Mr Lloyd George.

A British agent 'R', acting as double agent in Holland, then met Brugman in London accidentally and reported him to the bureau as a friend of Alexander Blok, adding that he had been sent to England against the wish of G. Elte and in all probability to ascertain whether 'R' had come to England. Brugman and 'R' had recognised each other but had not spoken. Soon after this, Visser wired to England to ascertain whether Brugman were still at the same address.

Brugman was at once arrested; in his possession were found three tall-pointed nibs, permanganate of potash and various other toilet accessories, and his luggage showed that he had travelled extensively in Germany. He admitted knowing Blok and Ekte. 'R', who was asked for particulars regarding Brugman's character and financial status, his dealings with Blok and Blok's nationality, his connections with van Spamje, and with Germans, was unable to discover anything definite about Brugman's business, but his character was no better than that of his associates van Spanje, L. H. A. Visser, Willem van Baleu, Van dem Hucht, Rutten and van Suchtelen, and van den Haere. Moreover, Brugman had relations with Blok, Philip Dikker, Frank Greite and Helene de Lemaitre. Van Bale (not Baalen), had with Blok engaged the spies de Bie, Pannebakker and Peter Steunebrink.

Meanwhile, the police ascertained that a pass for the Ministry of Munitions, carried by Brugman and dated 16 October 1915, was in all probability a forgery, and that de Mazia might very well be his accomplice. De Mazia had come to England from Brussels in August 1914 and had possessed two passes allowing him to leave the country without examination. One of these had been recovered, the second, dated 25 August 1915, he had retained until 11 May 1916 when he called at Scotland Yard to find out why Cohen was on the Black List. De Mazia was signalled with instructions that he was not to be allowed to leave the country.

One of Brugman and Cohen's guarantors was a David Mayer Cohen, a somewhat shady character who had been intimate with John Hahn of the Carl Muller and Hahn case. Brugman himself wrote from prison suggesting that he should be allowed to go to Holland for a few days with a sergeant and promising to obtain there information of the greatest importance. No satisfactory medium of secret writing could be made from any materials in Brugman's possession and there was no direct evidence against him. MI6(d), the department engaged in countering illicit traffic in munitions, might have prosecuted him under DRR 30A for offering to deal in munitions without a license, but in view of Lord Moulton's letters and the encouragement the men had received from the Ministry of Munitions, it was unlikely that conviction would be secured, therefore it was decided to deport Brugman and de Mazia. Tinsley's reports showed that Brugman's friends abroad were anxious about him and attributed his arrest to the action of an enemy whom they declined to name. They may have been referring to Elte, it was however possible that 'R' was indicated. In order to safeguard 'R', Brugman was told that he was suspected of having traded with the enemy and 'R' was sent back to Holland some fourteen days before Brugman in order to discredit Brugman. It was arranged that he should be specially searched at the port and rumours of his intended betrayal of the Germans set afloat. Yet after this Brugman was noted on the Antwerp List as A-32 for renewed employment.

★

Adolfo Guerrero was the son of a Spaniard of good position and a Philippine, brought up by an uncle. He was educated partly in Switzerland and there imbibed German sympathies. He qualified for the bar but never practised and soon dissipated his fortune in riotous living. In 1909 he was teaching dancing in Paris, afterwards he may have attempted some journalism in Spain. For some years he had lived with Ramona Amondarain (this is the form which she herself used), a Spanish dancer known on the stage as Aurora de Bilbao. She had obtained her parents' consent to their marriage but there was opposition on the part of Guerrero's mother. From June to September 1915 the pair stayed together in a hotel at 8 rue Fromentin, Paris, and there earned a bad character. Then for a while they separated. In October they were in Spain, Guerrero going there from Bayonne, and they spent from 24 to 27 January 1916 in the Hotel Barcelona at Madrid. On the 28th and 29th they travelled together to Paris, via San Sebastian, and there asked for visas for England. Guerrero obtained his without difficulty, Amondarain's was refused as she was not his wife, and she was told that to procure a visa she must produce a certificate that she had work to come to here.

Guerrero landed at Folkestone on 1 February. On 30 January the Admiralty had telephoned to the bureau that in all probability Spanish journalists would be coming to act as German spies. This warning was issued to Folkestone, Southampton and Falmouth on the 31st. Accordingly the port officer at Folkestone signalled the arrival of Adolfo Guerrero, correspondent for *El Literal*, and bound for the Regent Palace Hotel. A specimen of Guerrero's handwriting was obtained.

Comprehensive checks were put on all letters and telegrams to and from Guerrero, and the Censor was asked to keep special watch on all letters coming from Spain with a view to detecting secret writing. Guerrero was also kept under close observation, and the police made arrangements to see his correspondence before it reached him. They supplied particulars of two addresses to which Guerrero had written and the information that on 3 February he had rented the offices of F. Palan, cork importers, Woodman's Yard, Minories. Guerrero moved to 23 Lisle Street on 5 February. Between 2 and 8 February inclusive Guerrero wrote six letters to as many different addressees. The sixth was addressed to Don Antonio Arregui, Calle de Velasquez, Madrid, and was followed by a postcard giving the number as '66'. In this last letter, Guerrero stated that he had written two letters to 'our friend Louis' and another two to 'Frederic', and he asked the addressee to tell his manager to order his banker to send money between 27 and 30 February. All these letters were tested for secret ink without result, but certain marks before certain initials were noticed. The letters were photographed and sent on and the addresses were recorded. Guerrero on 14 February moved again to 24 Charlotte Street. Five more letters written by Guerrero were intercepted, one of these being a letter to the bank of Spanish America asking for a draft of £30. He was arrested on 18 February and in his papers was found a slip of paper bearing three addresses; Sr. Don Luis de Riquer Juan Luque 12, Madrid; Frederick Skjellas, Minde Bergensbanen, Norway; Guanta 154, Spain.

Frederick Skjellas had been known to the bureau since 26 January 1916 as a spy address, and consequently these addresses were correctly interpreted as representing the two centres to which Guerrero's reports were to go, and his own spy denomination. As early as 5 February a Postal Censorship examiner was prepared to make an affidavit that Skjellas, an ex-German consul, was currently talked of in Norway as a German spy, and was in constant contact by telephone with Bauermeister, who was known to be a German spy.

Another damning document in Guerrero's possession was a forged identity card, his 'piece de justification' as correspondent of the *Liberal*. Guerrero had landed in England not knowing a word of the language, a hindrance indeed to a foreign correspondent but also to a spy. Guerrero made the most of this point in his defence. In his second interrogation, Guerrero was accused of having received a letter from Hans von Krohn, head of the German organisation in Spain. This he strenuously denied. He asserted that he knew Skjellas 'a Frenchman' but denied having written to him. One Nainanoto who had written from Madrid he stated to be a dancer. Enquiries made of Ramona Amondarain and Palan seemed to prove that Guerrero himself had tampered with Palan's letter engaging Amondarain, and the editor of the *Liberal* at Madrid denied all association with Guerrero. It was decided to try him and the necessary verifications were made in London as a spy and in Spain. The most interesting of his associations in London was Paul Gil, a waiter at the Spanish Club in Charlotte Street, and formerly coachman to Guerrero at Santander. Paul Gil, who had induced Guerreo to become a member of the Spanish Club, had seen Guerrero on the morning before his arrest. Guerrero's rooms had already been searched and he had been told to present himself at Scotland Yard. Anticipating the worst Guerrero begged Gil to write and inform Arregui in case arrest should follow. Gil carried out his request but the letter was intercepted. The police procured and submitted a complete list of the members of the Spanish Club in Whitefield Street, Soho. Sergeant Tausley was sent to Spain to verify persons and facts with regard to Guerrero's case. His report was damning. There were two Luis Riquers. The younger Riquer admitted having received a postcard from Guerrero (date disappeared) but stated that he had dropped acquaintance some time before owing to Guerrero's way of living. The elder Riquer was pro-German but had sold copper both to France and Germany. Antonio Arregui, engineer, had been brought up in Germany, had visited Germany repeatedly since the war, had spent a fortnight there in April, and had up to 1 April occupied besides the room in his mother's house, one in a flat at Fortuny 3, which flat was undoubtedly a spy address. Guerrero's account in the Spanish American Bank showed that Arregui had paid him £24 at Lisbon on 23 July 1915. But all the money in Guerrero's account had been paid in by himself. Tausley produced evidence that Guerrero had never been connected with the Liberal, which was pro-Ally, and demonstrated how the identification card had been forged by Guerrero himself. Guerrero however had in January arranged to send articles to the pro-German paper *La Accion* but he had not sent any articles. On the other hand, one of Guerrero's relatives said that he had been to Norway some eighteen or twenty months previously. Further evidence was required as to Guerrero's previous history and as to the personality and associates of Arregui, who was said to be an associate of Hans von Krohn, the German naval attaché. This information was asked of the French Service.

A most interesting report came from France connecting a German named Janker with a dancing academy at 4 Boulevard de Clichy and the Abbaye de Thelme restaurant, Place Pigalle, which was frequented by the dancer Amondarain. Between 15 and 20 January 1916 a Spanish dancing master of the Academy had met Janker in Madrid and had been recruited by him to spy in Paris. On leaving the building where the dancing-master had been interviewed by the Germans he met Adolfo Guerrero coming out. The address of the building was Calle Fortuno 5 (or 3). In a statement of November 1916 Guerrero corroborated this meeting but with some change of detail. The French were thanked and asked whether they could induce the Spanish dancing-master to come and give evidence at Guerrero's trial, and also to find a witness who knew Arregui and had seen him in the company of von Krohn. But the Spanish dancing-master had been sent to Spain on some mission and had not returned.

Guerrero was tried on 13 July 1916 on the charges of having come to England to collect information and of having on or about 18 February communicated with a spy named Frederick Skjellas and he was sentenced to death. This sentence was commuted to ten years' imprisonment.

Ramona Amondarain was deported on 22 September 1916. She replaced Guerrero promptly and tried to force the Germans to employ her by stating that Guerrero had given her a tube of secret ink. She got hold of a French agent and took him to the German centre after having offered to procure good agents to work in France and England. The French Service was warned against her.

In September Guerrero confessed that he had been sent over by Arregui, whom he had visited once or twice at Calle Fortuny 5, von Krohn was present and the room contained a great number of maps and shipping lists. Guerrero was to have gone to Glasgow and Falmouth. He was to have communicated by letter using well-known phrases as code. He had written twice to Spain using the name Victor Guantas. Subsequently he gave information with regard to the secret ink used by the Germans. He carried in his pocketbook a piece of blotting paper about two inches square, this was impregnated with some salt, and a piece the size of a postage stamp, steeped in a very little water, would give the solution required. This ink had to be developed like a photographic plate. The Germans had substituted letters with messages in secret ink for newspapers marked in pencil, since so many of them were lost. The message was signed with the spy's number and name. Guerrero had used the ink twice – in Paris to announce the arrival of Zippo, in London to announce his own arrival. The ink business he said was a new development.

Another way of packing the ink was to put the crystals in a metal tube. The British authorities had mistaken such tubes for 606 cologne. Guerrero had had one tube but had managed to dispose of it.

Letters were sent in duplicate, one to Scandinavia and one to Spain and they were checked against each other. Information was paid for separately according to its value, expenses were paid at the rate of £50 to £75 a month. Guerrero was compelled to open an account at Madrid and the Germans paid the money into it. The bank would send a cheque from Madrid and he would cash it at any bank which had an agent in Madrid.

In this second interview, Guerrero stated that he had no knowledge of code, the Censors detected it and it was too risky. Soon after he declared that he had written three or four letters to Madrid containing this code. It is a question whether these letters were written in arbitrary code or in secret ink. Guerrero also stated that the Germans meant to send over in February a number of demi-mondaines who were to get in touch with soldiers. He also knew of two or three Spanish agents who were coming, and some Germans in London frequented the Spanish Club which was pro-German. He had been told to rent a safe-deposit and to keep useful documents there. Three months after leaving Madrid he was to go to San Sebastian.

Guerrero had stated that he was the 154th spy to come to England during the war but he seems to have confused his serial number with the number of those who came.

★

Frank L. Theodore Greite (alias Greitl, alias Greibe) claimed American citizenship but the embassy of the United States in London did not admit his claim. He stated that he was born at Brooklyn of a Dutch father and Danish mother. When war broke out he was in Germany. In April 1915 he was in Hamburg and registered with the police as a Prussian subject, nevertheless he obtained in Berlin an emergency passport as an American citizen and returned to the United States.

Early in July he got in touch with the French Oil Mill Machinery Company in Liqua, Ohio, and then came to Europe as their representative. He landed at Bordeaux in August, transacted genuine business on behalf of the company in France, and then came to England using introductions supplied by Mr French, an American and president of Robbe Freres, Paris.

Greite took a flat at 57 Connaught Street and settled there with Suzanne Dupont, a Frenchwoman who was engaged to a French officer then at the Front. Owing to information received from Charles van Ekeren, the bureau was expecting the arrival of one Theodore Greitl, a ship's captain who would come via Rotterdam en route to the United States of America and would sign his telegrams Frank Greitl. On 8 October 1915 orders were issued to Hull, Folkestone and Tilbury for the arrest of this man on landing. The following day the vice-consul at Le Havre signalled that Frank L. T. Greibe, an American traveller in the oil-cake business, had crossed on 8 October 1915 and was bound for Hull.

Frank Greite applied on 13 October for a permit to go to Holland, at the suggestion of the bureau he was put off for a few days while arrangements were made for his arrest and interrogation at Scotland Yard. He was seen by the assistant commissioner on the 23rd, proved plausible and convincing, and was given a permit with the intimation that if he went to Germany he would not be allowed to return to England.

Greite returned to the United Kingdom on 2 December to open an office at 57 Connaught Street, Hyde Park; he went again to France on 4 January 1916 and returned ten days later via Dieppe and Folkestone, where he was held up but eventually allowed to proceed. An account of his journeys was furnished by the base commandant at Dieppe. The registry then suggested that Frank L. T. Greite was identical with the alleged spy, Theodore Greitl, but this was not admitted by G Branch. Again in February when he made a second application for a permit to go to Holland it was pointed out that he was travelling too much and that to restrict his travels to Holland was of no practical value. G2 considered that the man was harmless, and that his threat if he was long delayed to go to the United States of America and sail thence to Holland would just suit the bureau. Greite went to Holland on 15 March and returned on 25 March. Meanwhile several things had happened to call attention to him:.On 16 March the Censor submitted a curious telegram signed Suzanne Greite recalling him on business; on 22 March the port officer sent in an urgent report about his frequent travels; on 23 March the consul-general in Rotterdam wired to the Foreign Office that Frank Theodore Greitl, who had been reported as a spy last October and was probably a German agent, was returning to England.

On receipt of this message G Branch decided that he was to be well searched each time that he travelled, and detained if he could not produce evidence of doing genuine business. Thereupon the port officer detained Greitl and sent him to Scotland Yard. On interrogation

Greite admitted that he had spent five years at school in Berlin, and then served as a ship's boy and afterwards as a steward. He readily signed an authority for the examination of his banking account. This account did not seem to support his admitted expenditure of £100 per month, and it bore entries of cheques for £98 deposited in December and for £150 deposited in January 1916 without any details as to the source of payment. Greite declared that the sums represented money which he owned in Germany and which had been transmitted through a bank in Holland.

Greite was arrested and a search of his effects showed that he had in his possession the addresses of Christian Mulder and of Dikker, l'Oudeshaus, Amsterdam, apparently a dealer in old clothes. Mulder was a known German agent who had communication with Fernando Buschman and Peter Steunebrink.

As regards Dikker, letters from him to Greite's address were found to be addressed to the names of the two companies whom Greite represented. In one of these, dated 2 January 1916, J. Dikker instructed Greite in carefully veiled terms to write his secret messages across the open message and not between the lines; in another dated 23 February 1916, Dikker summoned him to Holland on the pretext of arranging for the sale of machinery there. Enquiry showed that Greite was the accredited agent of the two firms in America and that he had been to Liverpool and Hull on genuine business. The case against him depended upon obtaining proof of a criminal connection with Mulder and upon what could be ascertained with regard to Dikker. Richard Tinsley was set to work in Holland. Mulder, twice visited, denied all knowledge of Greite but wrote to Greite to warn him of the visits. Thereupon Suzanne Dupont returned to sender an old letter written by Mulder on 23 December 1915 which referred to the despatch of Netherlands Overseas Trust Circulars. Then Mulder wrote again asking for enquiries about this letter.

Interviewed by Richard Tinsley's agent, Dikker stated that he knew Greite as a traveller for a well-known American firm. Dikker also wrote to Greite on 12 and 30 April complaining of the non-arrival of letters and hinting that pay would be stopped. The Rotterdamsche Bankvereeniging could give no clue as to the cheque for £58 except that it had been bought over the counter by a stranger. In May Greite himself supplied a clue. He promised one fellow-prisoner named Behan a large sum of money to procure his escape, and begged another fellow-prisoner named Wilhelmi, who seemed likely to be released, to go to Dikker and get him to invent an explanation of the two cheques that came from Germany. Wilhelmi, having completed this errand was to write to Greite using the password 'Remember Helene'.

Acting on this information, one of Tinsley's agents interviewed Dikker repeatedly; Dikker thereupon declared and also wrote letters to Greite to the effect that the two cheques represented payments for the sale of machinery on behalf of a third person, whose name however, he declined to give; Helene, he said, was a mutual girlfriend. Tinsley, who was then engaged on research into Brugman's character and connections, of whom the principal was Alexander Blok, learned from van Spanje that Brugman had met a demi-mondaine named Helene Lemaitre with Blok at some restaurant and had there been asked to do some errand for Blok. Tinsley thereupon identified Greite's Helen with Helene Lemaitre and pursued the clue. On being questioned Dikker acknowledged that he had introduced Greite to Blok, who was a buyer of foodstuffs for Germany, but denied that Blok was a spy or that he had had business relations with Greite. Van Spanje, however, who was seen talking to Blok, stated that Blok was a buyer for Germany and Dikker, who was Blok's clerk, had sold two machines for the oil-press man, meaning Greite; Blok had then sent Greite a commission.

The solicitor undertaking Greite's defence wrote, without consulting MI5, to Dikker in terms which conveyed the explanation given by Greite in examination as to the source of the two cheques. This was that they had been paid by his father-in-law Scheidemantel. The solicitor's letter escaped notice in the post. In reply, Dikker forwarded in support of Greite's defence two letters purporting to have been written by Scheidemantel. These documents, which arrived too late for the trial, furnished additional proof against Greite.

Before the evidence with regard to Greite's connection with Dikker and the sending of the cheques was obtained, Sir Archibald Bodkin had pointed out that previous to two of the interrogations, Greite had not received the necessary caution, therefore his answers could not be used in evidence, and that the case was complicated further because he had done genuine business and the rules of evidence would exclude 'grounds of suspicion' only against Greite, except such grounds as fall within Regulation 18a. The case depended therefore upon proving that Mulder was a spy and his address a spy address, and for this purpose his communications with Buschman's could be proved in evidence.

Accordingly, Sergeant Hubert Ginhoven proved the facts with regard to Mulder's business which was a retail druggist's store where all manner of Red Cross appliances were sold. Major Carter gave evidence with regard to Mulder and stated concerning Dikker's cheques that the Germans had recently altered their method of paying their spies, sending banker's drafts instead of, as formerly, postal and telegraphic orders. Wilhelmi's account of Greite's connection with Dikker and Beham's story of the plot for Greite's escape completed the evidence. An attempt to bring over Helene Lemaitre and the informant who had squeezed Dikker to give evidence at the trial failed through the action of the Dutch police who arrested the witnesses as they were embarking.

Greite was tried on 11 and 12 July 1916 and sentenced to ten years' imprisonment for doing an act preparatory to collecting information calculated to be useful to the enemy and for being in communication with a spy. Greite had confessed to his solicitors that the man who financed the German spy agencies in Holland and Copenhagen was Alexander Blok, a Dutchman of Klosterstrasse, Hamburg. He employed two runners who interviewed all the spies, 'Wilhelm' of a Hamburg coffee firm and Schulz, a proprietor of boats at Hamburg. These men put up at the Victoria Hotel, Amsterdam.

The Germans, who believed he had been shot, paid a pension to his reputed widow. Suzanne Dupont, who was invited to leave the United

Kingdom under penalty of deportation should she refuse to go. She left on 8 August 1916.

★

Early in May 1916 Richard Tinsley reported that Leopold Vieyra, alias Pickard, was coming to England and suggested that the man's statement should he verified. Some time previously the Censor had submitted a letter from Leo Pickard enclosing three photographs which he had sent to a Mrs Anny Pickard Fletcher asking that they should be endorsed to the effect that they were portraits of himself and returned to Rotterdam, adding that his name was Vieyra as well as Pickard.

Vieyra landed on 6 May with a passport issued at The Hague on 16 April 1916. He was searched and interrogated and sent on to Scotland Yard. Vieyra had first come to England in 1904 and from that date until 1911 had managed the affairs of a company of players known as 'the Midgets'. Then he went to Brussels and the United States and returned to this country in 1912. In May 1914 he went to Holland to sell films which he had bought here. His object in coming over was to buy more films to sell abroad. Since 1909 Pickard had been on intimate terms with a widow named Mrs Fletcher who managed a boarding-house at Acton owned by him. She passed as his wife, and helped him with the film business when he was absent in Holland. Vieyra was informed that he could not travel backwards and forwards during the war and he chose to remain in England. He procured an identity book as he wished to travel beyond the 5-mile radius.

Tinsley wired from Rotterdam and reported also in writing that Vieyra was said to be a German agent. He had been denounced by Logeher, brother-in-law to Elte, who was engaged in recruiting spies for the Germans. Vieyra had received 2,500 florins before sailing; his expenses for one month were calculated at £2.10s per diem, and payments to him in England were to be effected through Blydenstein's Bank, Threadneedle Street. Another 2,500 florins were to be deposited in a bank in Holland for Vieyra's disposal on his return after an interval of two months. Vieyra was said to have a mistress named Josephine Jensen and to be in touch with Heinrich Voltmann, a German. This was followed by a report implicating Vieyra and Elte with a gang of German agents, among them Alexander Blok, Moses van Leeuwen, Andries Bloemenhoofer and Logeher, Elte's mother-in-law and the informant. The usual checks were put on and Pickard was found to be communicating with Josephine Jensen at Hemonystraat 1 in Amsterdam. Frank at 33 Regulierbreestraat in Amsterdam, and S. Blom at 26 Pretorierstraat, also in Amsterdam, about a film business in terms which showed that the three people were cognisant of the same deal. Several of Vieyra's letters were treated for secret writing without result. The majority of the letters were sent on. An immense correspondence passed and in June both Vieyra and his employers complained of delay in delivery even exchanging telegrams on the subject. On 26 June S. Blom wrote enclosing copies of letters on 9 and 19 June. From this batch of letters it appeared that Pickard had transferred his account with Blyderstein to the London City and Midland Bank; that S. Blom had sent one remittance to Blyderstein's and another to the London City and Midland Bank and that if the London dealers were too sharp Vieyra was to try the provinces. These letters were seen on 11 July. Meanwhile it had been ascertained that Frank was probably a genuine dealer in films. It afterwards appeared that Vieyra had bought some second-hand films but was finding unexpected obstacles in shipping them to Holland. On 17 July the bureau asked Tinsley for information regarding S. Blom and heard in reply that at 28 Pretorlerstraat there was no such person but that Sophia, wife of Simon Dikker and sister-in-law to Philip Dikker of the Greite case, might be intended as her maiden name was Blom. Directly after S. Blom wrote warning Vieyra that some mysterious person had called to enquire about the film business. Meanwhile Pickard had applied for a permit to leave the country, thus once more confirming Tinsley's earlier reports and the War Trade Department suggested to the bureau that he might be worth while searching. The Censor was therefore requested to submit all letters addressed to S. Blom even though they might appear to be about trade only. S. Blom's warning letter of 26 July was seen by the bureau on 5 August and finally Mr Fletcher received a letter from a soldier in France, complaining of the censorship as a check on his pen and saying he would get a green envelope.

On 24 August Pickard was arrested. A mass of correspondence was found among his effects, ammonia and a packet of cotton wool, also a bottle of an unknown liquid somewhat resembling water, and a box of ball-point pens.

In his interrogation Vieyra stated that he had bought films to the amount of £164 since coming to England in May, and had sold them at a profit of £80. He could however give no reasonable account of his business dealings with S. Blom, 'his partner'. He denied knowing Dikker or Schultz but said he had some years before been introduced to Voltmann by Schmidt. He had brought to England a draft for £125 bought in the name of Leo Pickard from the Twentsche Bankvereeniging, E. W. Blydenstein and Company, Amsterdam; this was cashed by a film dealer and with it he opened an account with the London City and Midland Bank. Remittances for £100 and £121.9s.7d. followed, paid through Dutch banks to their correspondents here. The last payment was entered to the account of S. Blom.

Further efforts were made in Holland to get precise details regarding Blom, but were ineffectual. Josepha Jenson, Mrs S. Dikker and Philip Dikker maintained silence. Sergeant Ginhoven was then sent over.

Exhaustive analysis of the bottle of unknown liquid found in Vieyra's possession showed that it contained salts of an uncommon substance in such minute quantity that ordinary methods could not touch it. Eventually a threefold process of development was discovered and to this a letter of Vieyra's dated 14 July 1916 and addressed to Blom which had been detained and previously tested without result was submitted. The test was successful and a secret message about sailors, the calling up of Belgian soldiers, munitions, and the transport of troops was revealed. The *en clair* message acknowledged receipt of Blom's letter of the 26th; the secret message which was imperfectly developed mentioned Plymouth, Newcastle and Glasgow, and matters of naval interest.

The case till then had been singularly weak as it rested entirely upon

Vieyra's relations with Blom whose identity had not been satisfactorily established. It may be interesting to note the work required by the lawyers for bolstering up the case as it presented itself, before the final proof was obtained. Proof of handwriting; proof of Vieyra's first interrogation compared with his application for permit to go to Holland; a statement from Blydenstein's bank and a copy of the account; a statement from the London City and Midland Bank; tracing as complete as possible of all the money paid by Blom to Vieyra; first-hand evidence as to the occupier of 28 Pretoriusstraat, the names and relationships of those persons, and a certified extract from the Dutch Marriage Register of Simon Dikker to Sophia Blom; evidence given about Dikker in the case of Greite could be repeated in this case and a comparison of the letters from Dikker to Greite with those from S. Blom to Vieyra might be useful; the description of S. Blom given by Vieyra might be compared with the appearance of Simon Dikker, if Sergeant Ginhoven could succeed in interviewing the man; particulars of Frank, Voltmann, Schmidt and Schultz would be useful should cross-examination be necessary; particulars also of Vieyra's bona-fide business transactions were to be obtained. This necessitated the sorting of the enormous mass of correspondence into files under the names of the addressees.

Hubert Ginhoven, who was sent to Holland, discovered that there was no dealer in gold and silver, or dealer in films named S. Blom in 28 Pretoriusstraat, but a year previously Simon Dikker had been running a pawn-shop in the name of his wife S. Blom. Dikker admitted having furnished an accommodation of Vieyra's correspondence and that Vieyra had written to and received money from S. Blom but denied knowing Blom's present address.

Ginhoven also furnished particulars about Philip Dikker, whom he overheard talking to Frank, 33 Regulierbreestraat, about the case of Pickard. Frank stated that he had received fifty-five packets of films from Pickard and a list of another set of films which would follow if Frank sent the necessary certificate from the Netherland Oversea Trust. Frank had not paid for the films, had not given Pickard any money and knew no one named S. Blom in the film business. Josephine Jensen admitted going with Vieyra to Rotterdam to see Elte, who gave Vieyra some money; but to another agent she stated that the interview had taken place at The Hague. Elte admitted knowing Pickard but denied having given him any commission in England, and denied all knowledge of S. Blom.

Ginhoven's report was corroborated by the Amsterdam police to whom the Dutch consul-general had referred after some correspondence with S. Blom. Proof was given by dealers in films and the Secretary of the British Board of Film Censors whom Vieyra had seen in the course of business, that he had never once mentioned S. Blom although he had spoken of his partner; on the other hand the evidence of employees of the London City and Midland Bank showed that £121 9s. 7d. had been paid to his account by order of S. Blom, 28 Pretoriusstraat, Amsterdam, and the Twentsche Bankvereeniging admitted having made a payment on behalf of S. Blom on 26 May.

Further evidence showed that Pickard had been in communication with a dancer of German birth, a woman who had between August and October 1914 entered various prohibited areas. Evidence was also given of the testing of the letter of 14 July, in July, without result and again in September after receipt of the bottle of colourless liquid which was found in Vieyra's possession. A letter from S. Blom to Pickard dated 26 July was also included among the exhibits.

Major Drake gave evidence of the warnings received about Vieyra from Tinsley, of the intercepted letters to and from Blom, and of enquiries made with regard to Blom in Holland, also of the information possessed by the bureau concerning the spy Dikker.

Meanwhile, the Dutch consulate had been communicating with S. Blom, presumably through the legation bag since the letters were not stopped by the censor, and S. Blom answered and complained of the annoying visits of mysterious persons who wanted to know all about his partner.

Vieyra's trial by court martial began on 14 November; on the 15th he confessed. He told of his having been asked to go to England by Elte in the presence of van Leeuwen and Frank; of his subsequent engagement and journey to Antwerp, where he saw Schultz and received orders to go to Newcastle, Glasgow, Portsmouth, Plymouth, Hull, Harwich and Sheerness; his special quest at Newcastle being to obtain information re ship-building and repairing. Vieyra was to write to S. Blom, whom he never met, neither had he ever met Philip or Simon Dikker. Schultz instructed him in the use of secret ink, and gave him a bottle of the liquid and three handkerchiefs impregnated with it. Vieyra sent from seven to ten letters in secret ink to S. Blom, his reports being drawn from imagination, from the newspapers, and from what he saw in the streets. He never received any code message from Blom.

Vieyra was charged under DRR section 24A with attempting to send abroad a message written in a secret medium, dated 14 July 1916; under section 18 with attempting to communicate information on the same date under section 18A with having been in communication with a spy, namely S. Blom. Vieyra was sentenced to be shot having been found guilty on all three charges. The sentence was commuted to imprisonment for life.

★

Adolpho Guerrero had declared that the Germans were seeking to engage North Americans as spies and the truth of this statement was proved in the case of George Bacon and his friends. Bacon, however, belongs to the group of persons connected with the spy address of Meisner-Denis, 53 Rokin, Amsterdam, and of these the first in order of date is Jacobus Johannes van Zurk who was brought to notice on 31 May 1916.

In various interviews he gave Richard Tinsley the information that he had been engaged by the Germans to visit Glasgow, Newcastle and Cardiff, but he was not to go to Liverpool, since a Dutchman stationed there furnished excellent reports, that his (van Zurk's) reports were to be directed to van der Hucht and to Meisner-Denis, 68 Rokin, Amsterdam, that in a silver-mounted scent-bottle he carried secret ink made up as toilet water, that his *en clair* messages were to concern insurance business. Van Zurk supplied the British with a specimen of his ink.

Van Zurk, accompanied by his mistress Elsie Scott, came to England and was made use of to write to van der Hucht, but not to Meisner-Denis, and at the end of July £77 was deposited for van Zurk at Blydenstein's Bank on behalf of the Germans. He proved not only unsatisfactory but dangerous; Elsie Scott after contriving a quarrel with him went to live with her mother at 39 Pyke Road, Barry Dock, and, with her mother denounced van Zurk to the police there.

The bureau shipped van Zurk back to Holland with a no return permit. The check on his correspondence showed that he kept up affectionate relations with Elsie Scott and that she was hoping to rejoin him in Holland. She was not allowed to go nor was van Zurk allowed to come and fetch her, and in March 1917 Tinsley was warned to have nothing more to do with van Zurk.

The checks on the various addresses were cancelled in the course of 1917. Then, in 1918, information received from the Americans caused Elsie Scott again to be regarded with suspicion. Her complicated family relationships were thoroughly investigated and orders were issued that neither she nor her mother were to be allowed to leave the United Kingdom.

The discovery of the Antwerp roll of spies threw further light on this case; Jakobus van Zurk (A-40) on returning to Holland had again applied for work with the Germans; his task was to investigate conditions in the Bristol Channel, Edinburgh, Glasgow and Ireland, and a report was expected from his wife (Elsie Scott) on her return from England.

A check had been placed on Meisner's address on 10 June 1916, and on 13 July, a letter addressed to Denis, 53 Rokin, Amsterdam, written by Mrs Albertine Stanaway, 63 Sandgate Road, Folkestone, was intercepted. It is impossible to understand Mrs Stanaway's case without an intimate acquaintance with that of Pierre Rotheudt, which dates back to the earliest days of 1915.

On 27 January 1915 the Foreign Office was informed by Rotterdam that Pierre A. Rotheudt, a Belgian grain merchant of German parentage and sympathies, was coming to England as a German agent, and going to the address of J. Williams, Lennock House, Boutflower Road, Clapham

Junction. The information was circulated to the Director of Intelligence Department, MO5G and Criminal Investigation Department. As the port control was not then built up into efficient service, Rotheudt slipped past unnoticed by the bureau.

The police, however, acting independently, called at Williams' house and ascertained that Rotheudt had arrived on the 28th, and had been sent by Williams to the Shaftesbury Hotel, whence he had gone to Folkestone to the house of a Mrs Stanaway. Mrs Stanaway was asked to give up any letters which might be addressed to Rotheudt at her house but she had none. Rotheudt was interviewed at Scotland Yard and allowed to go. Rotheudt stated that he was a corporal of the 8th Regiment of the Line in the Belgian Army; had escaped from Namur, and renewed acquaintance with his old schoolfellow, Williams, in Paris on 25 August; he had been invalided and had been living at Roosendael with a man named van Melle; he had come over to England on business but was expecting shortly to rejoin the army.

Rotheudt went back to the Front; was wounded, and after being in hospital at La Panne, went to Folkestone on 12 July, and again put up with Mrs Stanaway of 84 Cheriton Road. At the same time he hired another room in a house opposite the French consulate and so situated that he could see everyone who went into the consulate. Soon after the Germans shot a number of French agents on their appearance in German territory. It was supposed that Rotheudt had furnished information leading to such action for, by 26 July, the French Intelligence Service had evidence that Rotheudt was in communication with Haasbroeck, a sub-agent of Hilmar Dierks, alias Sanderson, and addressing letters to Corn-Winterberg, Rywielhandel, 16 Bierambachstraat, Rotterdam. Rotheudt was also expecting to receive letters through Williams at the Shaftesbury Hotel.

Rotheudt, who arrived from France on 12 July 1915, was arrested and closely examined by Captain Dillon but he managed to clear himself. The Belgians, however, watched him; they gave him some small post in the Belgian consulate. Then a Belgian gendarme named Dumont ascertained that Rotheudt had telegraphed to and received postal orders of £5 and £10 from 'Hector', 132 Prins Hendrikkade, Rotterdam and Rotheudt was arrested by the Belgian authorities between the 23 and 30 August on a charge of high treason.

The details of the case were for long unknown to the bureau which had confined action to Hebden communicating the French report about Rotheudt and the verifications obtained from the Folkestone police, to Commandant Mage. Commandant Mage replied, giving the bare facts of Rotheudt's arrest and asking for enquiry with regard to Williams and a woman named 'Ebden' with whom Rotheudt was said to be intimately acquainted.

The police in enquiring for Williams of the Shaftesbury Hotel got on to the wrong track; but the woman was identified as Mrs Selma Hebden of 34 Broadmead Road, Folkestone, a German, British by marriage and well-connected. She stated that she did not know Rotheudt but that through Mrs Stanaway, her dressmaker, she had procured Rotheudt's services to get a travelling trunk belonging to her from Aix-la-Chapelle. On the outbreak of war Mrs Hebden and her husband, who were staying at Aix-la-Chapelle, had been obliged to leave at two hours' notice. Rotheudt proposed to recover her box through 'von Millais' with whom Mrs Hebden had entered into communication.

The bureau instituted further enquiries about Mrs Hebden and at last on 16 October a report was received from the Chief Constable of Folkestone corroborating the information given above and enclosing two postcards from 'Vancellelle' Borgeshout 16, Roosendael, about Mrs Hebden's box. Late in September, Commandant Mage asked for and was granted a full warrant for all correspondence addressed to Mrs Stanaway, who admitted having received and answered letters from Rotheudt's friends and also having received £3 from van Melle of Roosendael to pay for Rotheudt's defence. This money had been posted in London. It is obvious that 'von Millais' and 'Vancellelle' represented misreadings of 'van Melle's' name. At the request of Commandant Mage the originals of the telegrams sent to 'Hector' by Rotheudt on 17 and 21 August were produced; in the second Rotheudt had asked that, a reply should be sent to Hebden's address which he gave. 'Hector' sent £10 on 23 August, but to Mrs Stanaway's address, this apparently explains a request which came from the Rotterdam Post Office on 23 August that their telegram of advice wrongly sent to Folkestone should be returned. It was decided that the originals of the telegrams and orders must in no case leave the United Kingdom. Independent enquiry was made by the Paris General Post Office as to a postal order for 20 francs which had been sent to Rotheudt by 'Vancellelle' of Roosendael. Rotheudt had told a Belgian agent that he was in correspondence with van Melle and received 50 francs a month from him.

Van Melle and his wife and Rotheudt were all questioned as to their relations with each other; Rotheudt stated that the money had been left for him with van Melle by his parents, who had been expelled from Antwerp early in October 1914 and had then come to Holland; Mrs van Melle admitted that she had lodged with Rotheudt's parents but denied having accepted any deposit for their son; van Melle denied that he knew Rotheudt at all. Commandant Mage sent this information to the bureau in January 1917, for the purposes of their investigation only into the case of Mrs Stanaway.

Rotheudt was tried by court martial in France, and sentenced to death on 11 December 1916, but the sentence was commuted to imprisonment for life. He was shut up in Fresnes Prison.

Mrs Stanaway had been sharing a house with Madame Grouillet, who went to Calais to give evidence at the trial. On her return Madame Grouillet turned Mrs Stanaway out of the house because she was an object of suspicion to the police.

From prison Rotheudt, through an illicit channel, sent to Mrs Stanaway a long account of the court martial, which she destroyed, but she kept a letter in which he stated that he had been tried for espionage. Through the gendarme Dumont, who was a principal witness, she obtained Lieutenant Michiel's version of the trial – this she copied, although it was addressed to Dumony, and alleged afterwards that she had destroyed the original. In September she sent Rotheudt £5, received from van Melle; in January 1916, she sent him a 20 franc Belgian note. Through Stanaway, Rotheudt communicated as he wished with the outer world. He wrote to her on 27 March, 5, 10 and 23 April, and 8 May enclosing fabricated receipts to prove that 'Hector's' remittances were in reality a loan, and he also sent three letters in April for Stanaway to forward with the receipts to the Orsbach family in Amsterdam. One of these was a draft of a letter purporting to come from his parents. This draft bolstered up the story of the loan; it was to be copied and returned to Rotheudt with the receipts through Stanaway. At the same time, Rotheudt corresponded with the Orsbach family once a month through the regular prison channels and Stanaway wrote simple straightforward notes about him to Miss Emmy Orsbach (also known as Durbac). But she forwarded the forged receipts and the illicit letters to the Orsbach family on 29 April 1916, and in May Rodolphe Orsbach wrote out a letter in the sense desired by Rotheudt.

In May or June Albertine Stanaway heard from Meisner–Denis, but there is no record of the contents of that letter. On the intercepted on 13 July, she wrote to Meisner–Denis giving him her new address, 63 Sandgate Road, and stating that Pierre was still in France. On 11 August, she wrote again acknowledging receipt of a letter of 28 July, thanking him for its contents which she would forward to the 'unfortunate one' and hoping he had received a registered letter which she had posted to Meisner–Denis on 9 August. This was a letter written by Mrs Stanaway on paper belonging to the Charing Cross Hotel, signed 'R. Valravens, Chaplain' and addressed: 'Dear Madame'. The gist of it was that 'Mr P. R.' could no longer write to her or receive her letters but she might still forward money and the eye-glasses. On 13 August, Rotheudt resumed his correspondence with Orsbach, writing this time in Flemish and forwarding his letter by an illicit channel. This letter is not extant but he followed it up with a letter in French written on 1 September and obviously despatched by some other intermediary than Mrs Stanaway. He explains to Orsbach that Mrs Stanaway had suppressed his April letters to Orsbach, that two months had passed before Rotheudt heard of it, that she had sent him money (20 francs) from van Melle in August and that he suspected her of embezzling his supplies.

He told Orsbach that he was writing by the same post to 'Hector' of

Rotterdam and he bade Orsbach tell his parents to go and enlist the help of one Laarsen, at an address given vaguely but indicating the naval spy centre at Antwerp. Rotheudt wrote again on 10 and 30 September (on which date he also wrote to Stanaway) and on 12 November he expressed his astonishment at having received no reply to his letter of the 13 August. The reply came at last in December, when another 20 francs was sent.

Summing up the facts it is clear that Mrs Stanaway, knowing that Rotheudt had been condemned as a spy, aided and abetted in passing forged documents to his friends in Holland. She received money from Meisner-Denis, just about the time when she forwarded 20 francs to Rotheudt, and either she herself or someone writing in Flemish but posting via Mrs Stanaway told Rotheudt falsely that she had suppressed his April letters. The chaplain's letter to her was either dictated by Rotheudt in his indignation, or else written as the result of action taken by the prison authorities. For at some date not mentioned they discovered Pierre Rotheudt's illicit correspondence and re-opened his case. It may be that the Germans wished to wash their hands of Rotheudt and either bribed Mrs Stanaway to deceive Rotheudt or used her as an unconscious tool.

At the end of September, even while a fresh investigation into Rotheudt's case was in progress, he had found means to continue and extend his illicit correspondence, giving in the letters of August to October proof that he expected from the Admiralstab-Zweigstelle at Antwerp help to secure either a revision of his case or his escape from prison. These letters, which also furnish presumptive evidence against the Orsbach family, came to knowledge only at the end of January 1917, in connection with the investigation into the case of Mrs Albertine Stanaway.

It was Stanaway's correspondence with Meisner-Denis in July and August 1916, that brought her to the notice of the bureau. By 18 July the writer had been identified and steps taken to keep her in view. Subsequently it was established that she had written and posted the letter signed 'Valravens' at the Charing Cross Hotel on 9 August, that it was a copy was not known until much later. It was also known that Stanaway was remarkably intimate with the Hebdens, and Commandant Mage wrote that she had kept up communications with Rotheudt through an illicit channel. Afterwards he supplied information as to Rotheudt's connection with Mrs Hebden, 'Hector' and van Melle.

Van Melle was said to be in touch with a German spy named Walter Yzenberg and with the head of the German Kriminalpolizei at Rotterdam; he had photographed refugees from Belgium and had handed the photographs to the German police.

Then the bureau went further back in their enquiries, they identified 'Williams' and procured the original police documents referring to him and caused him to be looked up. He was then and had been for some months living in France. It was thought too late to put a check upon the addresses of Winterberg, 'Hector' and van Melle.

It was decided to arrest Mrs Stanaway and a Special Branch detective inspector was sent down to help the local police in the search of her rooms. At the same time, Tinsley was asked to have Meisner–Denis, at 53 Rokin in Amsterdam, carefully watched in connection with the cases of Stanaway and George Bacon. Mrs Stanaway was arrested on 9 December. A number of Rotheudt's letters were found in her rooms as well as a copy of Lieutenant Michiel's letter to Dumont about the trial of Rotheudt and Valravens letter to herself. Mrs Stanaway, when interrogated, lied about her knowledge of the charge on which Rotheudt was convicted and also as to her communication with him in prison, she denied having received money from Meisner–Denis but gave what seems to be a true account of Valraven's letter. She admitted having written to van Melle and Madame Orsbach in order to keep Rotheudt in touch with his friends.

A check was placed on Mrs Hebden's address and a specimen of her handwriting obtained. On 2 January 1917, a circular was issued that Mrs Hebden was not to be allowed to leave the United Kingdom. Mrs Stanaway was interrogated again on 28 December. Her account of her relations with Rotheudt and Dumont were substantially true, she was however unable to explain why she had copied Michiel's letter to Dumont, but denied that it was for the purpose of sending it abroad. She stated that she had destroyed the original.

The police meanwhile verified her history. Albertine Regnier, French, had come to Folkestone from Liverpool in December 1911 and was employed as a dressmaker by Messrs Gordon Bros, at 16 and 18 Cheriton Place. Soon after she married Frederick Stanaway, ship's steward, who in September 1914 joined the Kent Cyclists Corps and was sent to India.

She made the acquaintance of Pierre Rotheudt in September 1914 and when he returned in January 1915, he went to her house for three nights (1 to 3 February) afterwards bringing her to London and introducing her to his friends. Three other men, all Belgian soldiers, were devoted to Mrs Stanaway. The French authorities were informed of the correspondence between Stanaway and Rotheudt and their attention was drawn to those four persons on French soil, e.g. Valravens, Williams, Geens, and Janssens, who were intimately connected either with Rotheudt or Stanaway.

Copies of documents relating to Rotheudt's trial were procured from the Belgian authorities but upon the whole these documents tended to prove Mrs Stanaway's innocence in July 1915. In spite of all efforts the only charge which could be formulated against Mrs Stanaway was that of communicating with Meisner-Denis on three occasions, but Meisner-Denis cleverly avoided supplying proof of his connection with the German Secret Service, and the Orsbach family declared that the money sent by van Melle came from Rotheudt's parents in Antwerp. Then the family produced first the letters which Rotheudt had written to them in September 1915 and afterwards Rudolphe Orsbach's written statement that he had connived in Rotheudt's scheme for procuring his liberation, together with the letters and original draft which Rotheudt had sent via Stanaway in April and her covering letter dated 29 April 1916. With these were sent photographs of Pierre Rotheudt's receipts for money advanced him by 'Hector'. Rotheudt was thrown to the wolves.

On 31 January 1917, A. M. van Melle wrote to Stanaway enclosing a letter from Rotheudt's parents, this letter was censored by the Dutch but not by the English censor. The bureau however, discarded the Belgian evidence against van Melle: it was impossible to prove that van Melle's remittances emanated from an enemy agent, although as shown above there is some doubt as to the remittance of 28 July mentioned in Mrs Stanaway's letter of 11 August. There is a report that the post office check on Stanaway had failed completely and coupling this with the fact that Rotheudt explicitly mentioned receiving Belgian notes, it seems probable that all money transactions passed in notes and not in money orders. As the case against Stanaway rested solely upon three letters, in themselves innocent, although addressed to Meisner-Denis, Sir Archibald Bodkin advised against prosecution but suggested that Mrs Stanaway should be interned. Accordingly an order was obtained under DRR 14B on the grounds of her association with the spy Rotheudt and of her correspondence with another German agent.

A second case which arose out of the check on Meisner-Denis was for some time thought to be connected with Mrs Stanaway. This was the case of George Vaux Bacon, an American journalist and correspondent of the Central Press Association of New York City who landed at Liverpool and came to London on 5 September. On 20 September 1916 Bacon wrote to Meisner-Denis announcing his approaching journey to Holland on business for the Central Press Association and for the discussion of Louis Joseph Vance's new photoplay. The letter was intercepted by the censor on 29 September and dealt with by Major Carter on 9 October. Owing to this delay Major Carter did not forward the letter, a circumstance that had big consequences. It was ascertained that Bacon had gone to Holland on or about 22 September.

Richard Tinsley was then set to work in Holland, and after having been asked for information about Meisner-Denis, was asked for details with regard to Bacon. His agent approached Bacon somewhat clumsily and Bacon, who knew that Meisner-Denis had not received his letter of 20 September, suspected that the British authorities were on his tracks. He admitted knowing Meisner-Denis, but made no further statement and avoided further contact with the agent.

Orders had been issued that Bacon was to be searched on his return, but not alarmed. Bacon arrived in England on 2 November, but nothing suspicious was found on him nor did the interrogation yield much. But he told the officer at the port that Mauritz Hyman, a Dutch Jew, had been trying to get information from him at Amsterdam.

Tinsley, meanwhile, had reported Bacon's departure and that he had been seen off by Mr Peter J. Cribben and an American journalist, Rutledge Rutherford. He added that Cribben believed that their mail was held up in England.

At this stage a fresh informant comes into the picture. A metal merchant named Frederick George Graff had been placed on the British Black List, and had suffered monetary loss in consequence. In order to get his name removed from the Black List, he gave Tinsley information about his mission to a branch which the Antwerp Admiralty Zweigstelle had established in America with which it maintained communication through messengers. These men carried instructions in secret writing on what appeared to be blank sheets of paper. Graff produced two such sheets which he was to deliver to A. A. Sander, 876 East 15th Street, Brooklyn, and the War Film Office, 115 Nassau Street, New York. He was told on the way out to make observations on the south and south-east coast of England, and on the way back to stop in the country and procure the answers to two lists of questions. One of these ran: 'Where is the English end of a submarine cable from Alexandrowski on the White Sea?'

Graff carried a bottle of secret ink, shoe-laces and a cashmere sock impregnated with the same. The ink was made by steeping a piece of the material in an ordinary glassful of lukewarm water previously boiled. The secret instructions carried by Graff are dated 14 October 1916. By 23 November the sheets had been developed and the message photographed and translated. The instructions make mention of two kinds of secret ink. The first was a method of acknowledging receipt of the instructions by cablegram addressed to Philip in Copenhagen. The second was a duplicate of the instructions which was to be carried over by Symonds at the end of the month; two other carriers, Stieg and Baer, the latter of whom was returning to England; and a financial agent named 'Pas'.

The secret instructions also refer to an 'affair with David' which had gone wrong (it is interesting to note that the British Censor had stopped a cablegram from 'Davis War Film, 150 Nassauer Street' to Arthur Philipson, Skideregade 51, Copenhagen, on 2 September). The instructions mention payments which are to be made to Mrs Ruil and directing that all 'Charlie's' letters are to be addressed to Ruil, 47 Pieber Bothstraat, The Hague, and no other address used. Both were found afterwards to be identical with Rutherford.

Upon this information a search of cablegrams was made; at first only the intercepted message to Philipson was discovered, subsequently a wire to Gaston Blom on 17 December 1916 at the Hotel Bristol in Copenhagen, acknowledging receipt of a report was investigated; eventually a message dated 22 November 1916 to Kankratz in Hamburg, from Dr Wilberlaurer of Patterson, New Jersey, announcing the arrest of 'Robert' and adding 'Charles and everything fine' was unearthed and explained. A search of radiograms fell through owing to the labour and expense involved. The War Film Company, Stieg, Symonds and Baer were signalled to the ports, and instructions issued to hold up Baer. Home Office Warrants were taken cut for A. A. Sander and Rutl, and Tinsley was asked to identify Rutl, while a similar request was sent to New York with regard to Davis and Sander.

On 1 December 1916 a circular was issued to the ports and to the capitals of Europe that New York had become a spy centre and that particular attention should be paid to neutrals or persons who journeyed to the United Kingdom from the United States by indirect routes. Bacon, meanwhile, was being watched in England. He had on 3 November deposited a draft for £200 with the American Express Company, he spent some days in Worcestershire and then returned to town, where he went to the Coburg Court Hotel, Bayswater. On 21 November an article which Bacon posted to Virgil V. McNutt of the Central Press Association, New York, was stopped by the Press Censor, and the same day a letter from Bacon to Rutledge Rutherford mentioning Pete Cribben was submitted. It seemed harmless and the bureau sent it on, but decided to have Bacon interviewed at Scotland Yard and frightened out of the country. Meanwhile Bacon had given the police the slip and had gone to Ireland on 25 November. He visited Dublin, Cork, Killarney and Belfast, and on 8

December returned to London via Dublin. On his return he found a letter from the assistant commissioner, Basil Thomson, inviting him to call at Scotland Yard, which he did on 9 December. He admitted his connection with Meisner–Denis and was detained pending further search.

About this time the bureau received through an intercepted letter and an informant, further information of the utmost importance. Kuno Meyer wrote on 23 November to Schiemann of Berlin announcing the arrival of the *Deutschland* in America and mentioning that reports satisfactory in the highest degree had been received from three sources in Ireland. The informant had arrived in England on 2 December. Early in November he had been approached in New York by A. A. Sander, had acquainted British agents with the fact, and at their bidding had carried on. On the 11 December he came to Scotland Yard and gave an account of his engagement and of the instructions he had received. The informant's story bore out what was already known through Graff and added many other particulars. The newest German method consisted in despatching American journalists to work in couples, one to collect information in England and forward it in secret writing to the other, who was sent to Holland to supply the accommodation address and to forward German instructions to the spy in England. The informant's correspondent was to be Charles B. Hastings of the Maas Hotel in Rotterdam. If communication was cut between him and Hastings, the informant was to report at once to the German consul at The Hague and say: 'I am from Wilhelm, Admiralty staff Antwerp'. If anything happened to Hastings, [XXXXXX] was to write in duplicate to the Meisner–Denis address.

Presumably, the latter course was to be taken if [XXXXX] was unable to leave the country. [XXXXX]'s secret ink was a gonorrhea mixture packed in a tin and impregnated in a black sock. [XXXXX] and Hastings had to agree upon a code the name 'Joe Brady' or 'Brady' signified a journey to Holland. In a letter from Hastings, this name was a summons to [XXXXX] to come to Holland; in a letter from [XXXXX] it would mean that he was going over to Holland. [XXXXX]'s revelations were afterwards confirmed by Charles Hastings who added the information that the word 'Gertie' occurring in a letter would mean that it was a spy communication.

Charles Hastings, a disreputable American journalist, was in May and June engaged in publicity work for the Germans in New York, and in almost daily contact with Albert Sander. In August, Sander told him about the new secret ink which was despatched from Germany in small phials used for salvassen and costly drugs. On 13 November Sander enlisted Hastings to come over to Europe as a German agent and he sailed on 22 November, touched at Falmouth where some examination of his effects took place, and landed at Rotterdam on 9 December. Hastings' mission was to register at the Haas Hotel in Rotterdam where he was to receive and forward letters addressed to him there by [XXXXXXX]. On landing, he was to deposit his credentials, a sheet of 'Old Hampshire Vellum' bearing a communication in secret ink, with the German consul, and ask to be put in touch with Wilhelm of the Admiralty staff in Antwerp. Alfred Schultze interviewed Hastings at Rotterdam on 13 December and introduced him to Wilhelm Duell. Both men seem to have expected Hastings to return to America by the next boat, but Sander had given him the option of returning at once or getting touch with English journalists in Holland, and he chose the second course. Schultze then sent him to Amsterdam where he acted under the orders of Duell, who lived on the Rokin, nearly opposite Meisner-Denis, and lent his rooms to Schultze for interviewing German agents. Hastings stated that Duell called to fetch letters sent by [XXXXX] but that reports supplied by Hastings himself were posted to Schultze under cover to consul Cremer. On the other hand, Richard Tinsley reported that German agents collected Hastings' correspondence at the Haas Hotel in Rotterdam, and let him have only what they chose; and that Rutherford was at one time impersonating Hastings at the Haas Hotel, and Tinsley's reports are confirmed by Hastings' admission that after a time Duell ceased to call for letters.

Meanwhile, the enquiry with regard to George Bacon was proceeding upon the usual lines. The police found a trunk belonging to him deposited with the American Express Company and a letter addressed to him from Rutledge Rutherford at the same place. Among Bacon's possessions there were other letters from Rutherford, a packet of ball-pointed pens, a bottle of Argyrol and a pair of black socks impregnated with that solution. There was also a pocket-book with the addresses of Meisner-Denis and van der Kolk in thick pencil. Van der Kolk had been known as a spy address since 25 September 1915. In Ireland, Bacon had met a Sinn Feiner at Cork and a sympathiser with victims of the Rebellion at Belfast. He had also made friends with various officers and persons of another class. Besides mentioning Hastings, [XXXXX] had stated that an American journalist, whose name began with R – it might be Rutherford – had been in England for some time. Since 11 November Rutherford had been known to the bureau as a friend of Bacon. Another suspect was Peter J. Cribben, said to be the American representative of a shipping firm. Bacon stated that he was arranging for the import into Holland of certain cargoes of foodstuffs from America, and, on behalf of Cribben, Bacon had offered an invalided British officer £2,000 a year to handle the stuff at Dover.

The bureau asked Tinsley for definite information with regard to Meisner-Denis, Rutherford, Hastings and Cribben. Tinsley replied identifying Rutherford with the Rutl of Graff's instructions, and this was corroborated by a letter in which Mrs Rutherford informed her husband that she had received $200 dollars on a particular date.

Cribben was a tobacco and motorcar dealer who put up at the Maas Hotel in Rotterdam. By the end of 1916 therefore, the bureau could piece together the information supplied by Graff and [XXXXX] and, applying it to the case of Bacon, deduce that a spy centre subordinate to Antwerp existed at New York under the direction of Albert A. Sander. This correspondence was conducted by 'Charlie' who had been writing to Meisner-Denis, but in October the Germans, having discovered through Bacon's experiences that the British were on the track of Meisner-Denis, replaced him by Rutledge Rutherford, who thenceforth would stand in the same relation to Bacon as Hastings to [XXXXXX]. Moreover all this gang of American spies used the same arbitrary code and secret ink.

Rutherford was signalled to the ports for arrest, Hastings and Cribben for search and shadowing. If Hastings was met with on a ship going to

America, he was to be sent to London. Enquiries set on foot in England resulted in establishing certain facts concerning Rutherford.

Rutledge Rutherford, an American journalist, landed in England on 3 April 1916 with a passport issued in Washington on 16 March. He applied for a permit to go to Holland and gave Amsterdam and The Hague as his destination, his object being to study with a view to publication in the American press the food supplies of the armies and food shipments to and from Holland, as also the work of the Belgian Relief Commission in Holland. On 13 April he had procured a letter to Mr Young, the Commission's representative at Rotterdam. As references Rutherford gave Frederick Wile of the *Daily Mail*, and C. Hermann Senn, also connected with the press.

Rutherford, who had known Senn before the war, called upon him in London and asked him for information as to the food supply in England and Europe, and also as to the War Office. He promised to send articles to Senn from Holland but did not do so. Rutherford left for Holland on or about 19 April, but there was no trace of his journey at Gravesend. In Holland, Rutherford met Charles Edward Russell, a Socialist American journalist employed by the Newspaper Enterprise Association who had come over to England with his wife on 26 June and had left for Holland on 5 July to enquire about foodstuffs and wages in that country. Russell returned to England on 15 July and went to Dublin on the 25th, returned to London on the 26th and left for France en route to the United States on 4 August. On account of these journeys and of his connection with Rutherford, the bureau looked upon Russell with suspicion. The French police gave him a good character but he published an article in America on the suppression of the Irish Rebellion of a distinctly hostile tendency to Great Britain. When America came into the war, Russell took part in vigorous propaganda for the Allies, and is said to have left the Socialist party because it was pro-German. On the other hand, he himself wrote that the Socialists had turned him out of their party while he was in Russia on a mission for President Wilson and that he went willingly. Eighteen months later his wife wrote a letter praising the Bolsheviks and saying, 'Ed is a real

Bolshevist.' This puts a different complexion on Russell's break with the Socialists.

From Holland, Rutherford sent articles to the *Pittsburgh Bulletin* in Pittsburgh, and the *Forecast* and the *Standard* in New York. Rutherford also contributed articles to the *New York American*. On 24 August 1916 he warned the editor of the *Daily News* in London of the approaching submarine blockade of England and on 10 November he wrote to the *Pittsburgh Bulletin* that interruption of food supplies would prove England's ruin. A replica of this, as well as other articles of a like nature, were stopped on 26 December. Enquiries made in America established the fact that A. A. Sander, another contributor to the *New York American*, was the manager of the C. P. Watt, or Central Powers War Film Exchange, and had as his associate a man named Charles Wunnenberg.

Meisner-Denis and Rutherford observed such caution that Tinsley could obtain no proof of their connection with the German Secret Service, but early in February the proofs were supplied by Frederick Graff, who handed in two more sheets of undeveloped secret instructions for New York. These were dated 28 and 29 October, and referred to Mrs Rutherford's pension, and to steps which New York must be taken to recover letters addressed to Meisner-Denis. Orders were to be given that Bacon would no longer be paid from Holland, but a monthly remittance was to be sent in the name of Mr W. T. Mc.N. (Virgil V. McNutt, of the Central Press Association) through the American Express Company. Letters to Rutledge were to have an *en clair* message about the presidential election and a message in secret ink on the back. Letters of that kind arrived well and regularly.

The bureau received the developed sheets on 9 February 1917 and on the same day Bacon made what seems to be a full confession. He had been recruited for service by a Bohemian named Posselt, had been introduced to Albert Sander, and finally engaged to go to spy in England by Charles Wunnenberg, alias Robert Davis. This was the 'Charlie' referred to in the secret instructions. In order to obtain his passport Bacon induced Virgil V. McNutt to engage him as unpaid correspondent to the Central Press Association. Wunnenberg then gave Bacon instructions in the use of the secret ink, which could be developed only at Antwerp. Reports were to be sent to Rutherford at the Hotel Maas in Rotterdam, who would forward them via Berlin to Antwerp, but in case of urgency Bacon was to write to Meisner-Denis or van der Kolk. From London he sent two reports to Rutherford during September. He wrote to Meisner-Denis as money was running short and getting no reply, he went to Holland and there saw Rutherford and Schultze, who was much interested in the details of his journey from America. He was paid some £200, with which he bought a draft on the American Express Company in London. Soon after returning to England, Bacon went to Ireland and from Dublin posted to Rutherford a letter containing a secret message. This was not intercepted.

Bacon was tried by court martial, found guilty and condemned to death on 26 February. The sentence was commuted to life imprisonment, but, at the request of the American authorities, he was released by the Home Office, which granted a licence under the Imprisonment Act and went back to America to give evidence against Albert Sander and Charles Wunnenberg, who had been arrested at the end of February. After a drastic bill against espionage had been passed by the Senate on 20 February, Sander and Wunnenberg were condemned to two years' imprisonment and a fine for conspiring to spy upon a government with which the United States was at peace. Eventually Wunnenberg made a confession, and Bacon was sentenced to a year's imprisonment in the United States.

Albert A. Sander, formerly employed by William Randolph Hearst on a German newspaper, and Charles Wunnenberg, a naturalised American of German birth and by profession an engineer, carried on their activities as German agents under cover of a film company. At the address of the company they set up the German American Literary Defence Committee with the object of fomenting sedition in Ireland and India.

In the spring of 1915, Wunnenberg had been introduced to Dr Passe of Cologne who had sent him to New York to recruit journalists as spies. After getting in touch with Sander, Posselt and Ford who were on the staff of the Irish paper, Wunnenberg returned to Passe and was then introduced to 'Wilhelm' and Schultze of the Antwerp bureau. He want to Antwerp, learned the use of a secret ink, the information that was required, and then went back to America with instructions that his agents were to write to Meissner-Denis and to Philipson, at Skidergade 21, Copenhagen, who would forward the reports to Germany. Wunnenberg recruited Rutherford, sent him to England and Holland, and then was wired for himself. Wunnenberg sailed for Europe on 18 May, picking up Rutherford and took him to Hamburg and Berlin. From Berlin, Rutherford went to Antwerp and Wunnenberg to Wilhelmshaven, where he was instructed in the use of bombs for blowing up ships. Afterwards he went to Copenhagen and concerted measures with Russian naval and military officers for betraying ships carrying stores from America to Russia into the hands of the Germans. Wunnenberg found the man Wreslauer who could give shipping facilities to the Russian buyer. Wunnenberg also recruited Sidney Lush, who carried despatches to Denmark for Germany about the importation of war films into America for propaganda purposes. His cover for the importation of these war films made a contract with the Central Powers to market all the films which the Central Powers could supply.

In order to finance the press scheme, drafts were drawn upon Adolph Pass of the Pass Kramer Hatband Company in New York by Charles Wunnenberg in his own name and $1,200 was drawn in two cheques on Philipson in Copenhagen. Some of this sum was sent to New York in the name of Robert Davis, the real Davis having allowed Wunnenberg to conceal his German name by the use of that alias. Afterwards Wunnenberg stated that all wireless messages were addressed to Mankratz in Hamburg, afterwards identified as Eugen Wilhelm, Philipson in Copenhagen, and Meisner-Denis at The Hague. Agents were sent out to work up the Irish and the Hearst Press against Great Britain, and in February 1917 an agent was sent to America for propaganda purposes and to enlist men who were to enter the British Navy and place bombs on ships. Bansof, who was buying for the Russian government, acted as buyer for Great Britain also and sent reports from London to 'Wilhelm' at Antwerp.

After arresting Albert Sander and Charles Wunnenberg, the Americans tried to get hold of Charles Hastings and Rutledge Rutherford. Hastings, who had lost the confidence of the Germans, left Holland willingly with the American emissary, was interrogated at Scotland Yard on 14 and 15 March, returned to America on 31 March, and was tried and sentenced to a year's imprisonment. Rutherford, more deeply compromised, fled to Antwerp and was sent to Stockholm where he stayed for a few days. He then returned to Germany and worked in Hamburg for the *Continental Times*. His private letters were despatched to America through the agency of Heinrich Grund. At one time Rutherford used the postal address of Mahler. An attempt made by the Germans to send him to Switzerland failed as the Swiss legation would not grant him a passport. The Antwerp roll notes that in 1916 Rutherford had done good service in England and later on in Holland, where he obtained general information from English journalists and sent serviceable reports from Holland regularly, and that in 1917 he was compromised in Holland and Scandinavia and could not return to America owing to the watch kept by England.

Hans Eils declared that Rutherford recruited the spy Rothardt, who came to England for four weeks and wrote six or seven letters from Hull, Edinburgh, London and South Shields. This presumably was J. C. Roodhardt, designated A-93, who accepted German pay but applied for work to the British Service. He lay hidden in Holland and was eventually dismissed by both services in 1917. Rutherford therefore stands foremost among American journalists who are known to have supplied information to the Germans.

Three others who took an interest in Irish affairs were watched at the instance of the bureau. Of these Charles Russell, mentioned above, was known to Rutherford. Robert Mountsier, who travelled with a lady companion, and went to Penzance and Ireland, knew Bacon. Arthur Gleason of the *New York Tribune*, with which Rutherford was also said to be connected, went to Ireland with a recommendation from the Foreign Office. The Under Secretary for Ireland, being warned by the bureau, handled Mountsier and Gleason carefully. The other American, Peter Cribben, who knew George Bacon and was seen off to America from

Holland by Rutherford in November 1916, there can be little doubt. In 1915 Cribben was working as a mechanic in a garage. Then the Tomplerman Steamship Company sent him to Holland about the cargo of the SS *Virginian*. While there, Cribben placed orders in the United States for large quantities of goods including apples and pig-iron. He was a man of no character and Major Carter believed him to be a spy and warned the US Army's Intelligence Department.

The agents mentioned connected to this case who appeared on the Antwerp List were: A-82 Meisner-Denis, Lieutenant of the Landwehr (retired); A-42 Arthur van Graff; A-58 George Vaux Bacon; A-30 Rutledge Rutherford; A-77 Wilhelm Duell, alias Thuringsen; A-13 Charles Wunnenberg; A-105 Adolph Pass, supply officer of the Rhenish District; A-93J C. Roodhardt, alias Rothardt; A-107 Georg Mahler, who worked with Ground and transmitted reports with regard to Dutch shipping.

To these must be admitted [XXXXXX] and Charles E. Hastings, whose names are not quoted in the copies of the Antwerp List supplied to the bureau.

It was alleged that Rutledge Rutherford had become a member of the London Press Club, a report that was neither contradicted nor corroborated, but the fact remains that he satisfied the Germans, and the case of Anthony Spalding affords a good illustration of how this could be achieved.

Spalding was a journalist of twenty years' standing and of some position. He had been for three years assistant editor of the *Bombay Gazette*, then six years on the Manchester staff of the *Daily Mail* and after chief sub-editor of the *Daily News* in Manchester. At the end of August 1914 he was appointed an assistant censor in the Press Bureau, on the recommendation of the president of the Newspaper Owners Federation. Spalding was engaged in the cable room of the Press Bureau and it was his duty to enter in a notebook all decisions taken by the presiding chairman of censors with regard to the circulation or stopping of specific items of information and to guide the other censors in their work by the light of these notes.

From March 1915 until February 1917, Spalding wrote some twenty-five letters to one Charles Stead, a colour merchant in Manchester, which contained specific news relating to naval and military movements, new inventions, damage done by air raids, foreign alliances, and the private and public affairs of government officials in high places. Stead and Spalding were intimate friends and the letters were written for the information of Stead only. He, however, communicated them to other persons, in particular to Charles Richmond Way, a traffic assistant at the Manchester Ship Canal Company, and also had some of the most important letters typed by his female clerk.

On 23 February 1917 Way showed these letters to William Goodman, a merchant of Manchester, and Goodman who was a special constable communicated with the police. The police saw Way who promptly handed over copies of some of the letters and gave the name of Charles A. Stead who, when interviewed, prevaricated but finally under pressure admitted that the letters had been written by Spalding and produced the whole bundle of them. Stead and Way were arrested on 27 February, and charged under DRR 18. From their statements it was clear they were aware that it was dangerous to be in possession of such letters. The case was at once reported to MI5 by the Chief Constable of Manchester who sent an inspector up to town with the letters. After due verification Spalding was arrested quickly at the Press Bureau on 28 February and his house was searched and particulars of his bank account obtained.

No evidence of hostile connection was found and the three men were admitted to bail; Spalding however was kept under observation. It was proposed to try the three men by court martial. It was accordingly arranged that Stead and Way should be withdrawn from the jurisdiction of the magistrate, re-arrested and admitted to bail and bound over to appear in London for a summary of evidence to be taken on 24 March. At the same time the opportunity was to be given them to claim their right of trial in a civil court. The necessary notices were issued by the London District. Meanwhile an attempt to trace the information to its source showed that some of it could not have come from the Press Bureau but might possibly have been gathered from the staff of

*The Times.* The information was ascertained to be substantially correct, at the same time Spalding's dealings with stockbrokers showed that he had not made correct use of his professional opportunities. Spalding, Way and Stead all claimed their right to be tried in the civil court and at the DPP's suggestion it was decided that as there was no evidence of hostile intent or corruption against any of the accused, Stead and Way, who had been merely receivers of information should be dealt with in a court of summary jurisdiction and they appeared at Clerkenwell Police Court on 19 April to be fined £100 and £60 respectively with £20 costs each.

Spalding was committed for trial in the civil court and his case was heard on 26 April before Mr Justice Low. Counsel for the defence had reckoned on being able to meet a charge of collecting and communicating information likely to be useful to an enemy, hence Spalding at first pleaded not guilty, but the indictment was so drawn that of the seventeen counts of receiving, collecting and communicating information, only four were coupled with the clause alleging utility to the enemy, and in face of the documentary evidence it was not possible to deny the more general charge. Hence, at counsel's suggestion, Spalding withdrew his former plea and pleaded guilty to fifteen out of the seventeen counts. He was put into the witness box and in his cross-examination he admitted and expressed sorrow for his indiscretion but defended himself by stating that two of his slips were mere records for purposes of his work as assistant censor and that as regards the letters he had obtained his information either from gossip in the press club, or in conversation with other members of the Press Bureau, and not directly from the cables and other documents to which his work gave him access; that moreover these outside sources often supplied much more detailed information than official sources.

In face of the very reason for which a Press Censorship was established such a defence was inadmissible, and the judge sentenced Spalding to three years' imprisonment. Spalding appealed and the sentence was reduced to twelve months' hard labour. One of the most secret pieces of information Spalding stated he had received from Mr Acland, editor of the weekly edition of *The Times*. Mr Acland was summoned to Scotland Yard and in examination gave the impression that he was concealing something from the authorities. Further action was contemplated but the efforts of the editor of *The Times* and lack of evidence on which to base a prosecution caused the matter to be dropped. During the case Mr Justice Low commented on the absence of any specific regulation in the Defence of the Realm Act making it an offence for a censor to divulge any matter whether of a public or private character which had come to his knowledge in the exercise of his duty and pointed out that some of Spalding's worst offences could not be dealt at all under the regulations and he laid down the principle that disclosure of any information, whether significant or insignificant, obtained in the course of duty was a breach of faith and should be punished severely as such. Further, he recommended that persons employed as censors should avoid the society of journalists and the purlieus of press clubs.

★

It was manifest that, by the middle of July 1915, British counter-espionage had smashed the German organisation painfully built up by the Admiralty Zweigstelle and their system of employing bogus commercial travellers had failed. Accordingly, between July 1915 and May 1916, three new types of travelling agent appear: as artistes, persons of better education with business experience and a social backing, and genuine businessmen or agents. These persons were chosen carefully with a view to the object of their mission. A new objective arose: in addition to naval and military espionage, information was required about the government offices, old and new, and semi-public services. There was besides, evidence of manipulation of commerce afforded by the mission of Jonkheer Calkoen and possibly also of Leopold Vieyra, and there were also signs of the existence of permanent agents stationed at the ports and in London.

Regarding the travelling agents there was abundant evidence that the information they could pick up en route was of first-class importance. Therefore they arranged to travel backwards and forwards as often as possible between Holland and England, and Copenhagen and England. Emil Brugman had to fetch samples from Holland which an ordinary man would have brought with him; Johan Lassen, for a very small amount of business, make two journeys and contemplated a third in the immediate future. Frank Greite, the cleverest of them all, travelled repeatedly between France and England and Holland.

The feeblest of these spies appear to be the circus-riders, Pauline Slager and Georgine Ulrich. They were travelling in search of employment, which, even in wartime, seems an unlikely pretext, at any rate as they carried it out. The Germans themselves realised this and sent over, for it is practically certain that Vittorio Corini was a spy, a whole unit of the Adolphe Carré troupe. Hans Eils states that a horse worth £500 was bought for Slager, who never came again: it is probable that Corini brought it over in December. The troupe stayed at Liverpool from December to February 1916. Those agents whose object it was either to gain access to or a footing in government departments travelled singly and came with excellent introductions from diplomatists or from accredited agents of well-known business firms. Eva de Bournonville, Lassen and Brugman were all connected in some way with diplomatists. In this work, Josef Marks was the forerunner. He invented the method, which characterises the men's work, of giving information for cover and in order to obtain more. (It will be recalled that in January 1915 Trebitsch Lincoln had attempted to use this method, and had failed.)

Between them they obtained access to the Home Office, the Foreign Office, the Censorship, the Department of Munitions, Woolwich Arsenal and the PoW Help Committee's office. Lassen wired on his arrival in England, but to his wife; otherwise both he and Brugman made their journeys so short that there was no need to communicate with their base. In consequence there was no proof of communication against either man; Lassen had given some information to both the Home Office and Foreign Office, and although Brugman's spy associations in Holland were well known, he had some authorisation for his action in the two genuine letters from the Ministry of Munitions, and could not be touched. This achievement reaches the high-water mark of cover for German agents.

De Bournonville's method of writing to the address of a British or Belgian prisoner of war and putting a special mark on the envelope was also a good discovery, though she spoiled her work by the inanity of her letters.

Regarding the recruiting of these spies, de Bournonville had known the agent Schmidt since 1912, and Lassen's whole behaviour gives some reason to think he returned from Panama for the purpose of espionage. Brugman seems to have been recruited by Alexander Blok, the regular agent in Holland of the Antwerp Zweigstelle.

In the third group of agents, a setback, perhaps more apparent than real, is to be noted in the engagement of Adolpho Guerrero. He was not really a journalist but was immersed in a disreputable world of dancers, and he knew no English. The event showed, however, that he had an accurate knowledge of German intentions: he predicted that they would be sending over demi-mondaines and Americans. The officers of G Branch believed that he was keeping back something. Guerrero declared that he had deceived the Germans by pretending he knew English. This is barely credible. Guerrero frequented the pro-German Spanish Club, his woman companion was a dancer. There is clear evidence that the Germans expected the two to come together for Guerrero actually wrote as if both were on the spot when Ramona Amondarain was still held up in Paris by the refusal of a visa. Hence it may be that the dancer was to be the spy and to get in touch with educated persons who knew foreign languages while Guerrero had some mission of manipulating commerce or sabotage among compatriots.

Greite and Vieyra were both businessmen: Greite being the accredited agent of American firms, and Vieyra having lived in England and become a dealer in second-hand films. Vieyra had a home and female friend established here as well as connections in the theatrical and business world. Greite brought over a mistress and good business introductions from France. Greite was probably the best agent the Germans sent over during the war, therefore, it is worth noting the strong and weak points of the methods employed by, and with regard to, him. These are the long and careful preparations for his work and the circuitous route to this country: he left Hamburg for America in 1915, by July he had become the representative of two well-known American firms, he landed at Bordeaux in September, did some business in France, and produced introductions to English firms from the American head of a good French firm; his use of genuine business as a cover to his movements and his correspondence; spy letters for him were addressed to the name of firms he represented and there is some suggestion that instructions were conveyed in secret-writing on business circulars. Greite's own letters must have reached Philip Dikker through two intermediary addresses, the first of which was the address of a well-known Dutch firm; his domestic arrangements, which gave him a stable address and an aide in conducting correspondence while he himself was moving about the country. Moreover his nationality disarmed suspicion.

The weak points were Greite's German accent and a personality that inspired distrust. The choice of oil-pressing machinery to travel in was not altogether happy because to offer it, as Greite did, in Holland was like carrying coals to Newcastle. Equally, the choice of films as an object of trade in Vieyra's case was unfortunate if genuine business was to be carried through for cover.

Pauline Slager was stopped on her telegram to Holland for money which was sent by money order; accordingly, with Eva de Bournonville the Germans reverted to payment by bankers' drafts, and, as in the case of Fernando Buschman, forwarded them through the legation of a neutral country. No doubt the country represented protested. Greite was paid also by bankers' drafts which paid a great part in the enquiry in Holland and at the trial. The Germans took warning and Vieyra who came next received a month's pay in advance and expenses for one month were sent by banker's draft. The second month's pay was kept in Holland. This system of pre-paying Dutch agents, together with raised rates of pay, led to a remarkable collapse in the summer of 1916. The risks being great and the pay good, many men took the work but never left the Dutch shores. The recruiting agents, Alexander Blok, G. Elte and others, levied commissions on the pay of recruits and finally, either winked at their not leaving the country, or contrived to make a further profit by causing the departing agent to be betrayed to the British authorities. Vieyra and Jacobus van Zurk (the latter was however a willing victim) are the classic instances of this combination. After this debacle of the German service, rumour told of some low haunt in Holland where spies of either camp bought and sold news with a view to their employers' respective requirements.

With Jacobus van Zurk, we enter upon the group of spy cases in 1916. His importance as a spy was nil, but he and Elsie Scott contrived to hoodwink the British officer in charge of the case. By a put-up quarrel, Elsie Scott got off to Cardiff where she was in a position to get some of the information required, while van Zurk after remaining virtually a prisoner in London, was shipped back to Holland where he also contrived to hoodwink the Germans. It was fatal to their scheme that he should have given away the Meisner-Denis address.

Regarding Mrs Albertine Stanaway, there is no certainty except that she seems to have really loved Pierre Rotheudt and risked much for him. But her power of communication with him in prison, the documents regarding his trial which she had either kept or disposed of, and her possession of Meisner-Denis' address gave grounds for strong suspicion against her. In aiding a spy she did more than either Suzanne Dupont or Mrs Fletcher Pickard.

With George Bacon we come to a fourth type of German agent, the professional journalist, and to a great development of German policy with regard to Ireland. At the time when Bacon was under suspicion, proof came to the bureau that the Germans were well-satisfied about the results of their system of communication with Ireland. Bacon frequented Sinn Feiners and lied as to his instructions, which definitely included espionage in Ireland. This period, between June and December 1916, includes perhaps the highest achievement of G Branch, if the importance of results rather than the number of spies arrested be considered. And these results are due partly to some carelessness and lack of judgement on the part of the Germans, and partly to ill luck. After the Hilmar Dierks business it was careless to allow one spy address to run on from early June to late September, it was perhaps ill judged to recruit the spy [XXXXX] of British origin, without more precaution. It was a mistake to recruit the Dutchman Frederick Graff whose business depended on standing well with the British. But it was genuine ill luck that just the information given almost simultaneously by [XXXXX] and Graff should bear directly and in the most illuminating fashion upon the spy who was making use of that cover address, and the spy habit of giving information when in a really tight place did the rest. An organisation in New York, but subsidiary to the Antwerp centre, and in constant touch with it by means of messengers who carried instructions in secret-writing and materials for secret-writing from Europe to America, stood revealed. A new type of spy – the American journalist; new methods of spying and spy communication e.g. from the journalist in England to the cover-address of his 'pair' in Holland, and new forms of code, came to light. The information of many American subjects led the American authorities to take drastic action, with the result that the German centre in New York was destroyed. In course of the proceedings, a vast conspiracy under the leadership of A. Sander and Charles Wunnenberg, for the prosecution of espionage, sabotage of ships and buildings, and capture of Allied food-ships at sea was laid bare. This last object involved the cooperation of a very important Russian official.

Certain points in the Axel Grebst case raised some doubt as to whether he was not involved in the same business.

★

The principles of the German system were summarised by the Special Intelligence Bureau as follows:

> Each agent must act independently; he is not to know other agents in his locality, nor is he to look up old acquaintance in the service; he is to travel alone and keep to himself. From what has been said already on the evidence of German spy cases in England, the instructions as to travelling alone refer evidently to the actual journey in search of information.
>
> On arrival at his destination he is to report to a Secret Service agent, who will direct him where to go next and will act as a link between him and the centre but will do no active work himself.

The agent is to write often and in detail and to confirm by a short resumé the information sent in a previous letter; he is to write in duplicate posting via different countries; he is to post as soon as the letter is written and in a different district from that in which he lives; he must use a false name and address and disguise his handwriting.

In letters containing interlinear notes the agent must choose an interesting subject for the text *en clair* (and, according to the Antwerp method, it must be a subject capable of development into a longish correspondence, such as a law-suit for instance).

The agent is to obtain information at first-hand, to frequent workmen and railway officials and, in the military zone, officers and men of the Army Service Corps, the wounded, bars and cafes frequented by soldiers, sailors and munitions workers. He must avoid cities like London and Paris, and take care not to get roped in as a soldier. He is to correspond if possible with soldiers at the Front and to note the movement of postal sectors. He is to travel as much as possible and to enlist the unconscious help of those he meets.

Having obtained anything of value he is to risk all in order to get back by one of several specified routes, but trivial information is to be sent in writing.

Before the agent starts on his mission he has committed everything to writing; at first he collects specified details which are pieced together abroad; then he may have to obtain plans, designs, etc-, and later on he may be given tiny wireless apparatus which will be sent to him piece-meal.

Agents sent to England are chosen from:

1. Persons already known in this country who will then escape suspicion.
2. Citizens of the United States of America who have a knowledge of English and business connections here.
3. Neutral sailors: e.g. Dutch and Danish sailors in Dutch ports.

Agents came to England via Holland, Scandinavia, Spain and America.

A favourite cover was that of shipping agent out of work. In the winter of 1915-1916, German agents communicated with Peter Steunebrink in business code referring to oriental carpets, with Frank Greite in code referring to oil-press machinery. Peter Steunebrink was to use picture postcards when his messages referred to ships, their station being indicated by the place of posting. The code was as follows:

- 'Postcard' 'letter' 'news' = 'There is not.'
- One number following mention of one of these words = 'There are no First Class Ships but there are so many Second Class Ships.'
- One number without mention of 'postcard' = 'There are so many First Class Ships.'

In January and February MI5's investigations resulted in discovering a fruit code used between Spaniards in France and the Balearic Isles. A Spanish woman had been shot at Marseilles for having in her possession a code which, under guise of placing orders for fruit, would enable her to give information about French and British regiments drafted to the East. A check placed on letters to a fruitseller at Soller produced nothing. Very soon after, an agent wrote from Copenhagen declaring that code was being used in business and press telegrams addressed to Danish papers, which the Germans were buying up in order to control the messages of their foreign correspondents. As remedies he suggested copying German methods and holding up wires for two days or more when important movements were in progress, and limiting press telegrams to exact quotations or extracts from newspapers published in England.

During 1916 repeated use was made of a code supplied by MI5, and known as C code, from ports in the north of England, and the Censor's fortnightly reports showed a growing number of undecipherable code messages. In March, a favourite method of code communication was by the despatch of cards of postage stamps sent openly and as though for the use of collectors. The message in return would be conveyed by stamps sent back as unsold. Ultimately the posting of stamps was limited to specially licensed firms.

Jacobus van Zurk was communicated with in a code in which the third syllable of lines containing an uneven number of words alone counted. Leopoldo Vieyra and Frederick Graff used variants of this form of code:

– Date = date of despatch or purchase.
– Time = time.
– The date and time = time cited.
– Degrees of longitude = the initials of the firm according to the fisheries chart.
– Minutes of longitude = number of herring barrels purchased.
– Minutes of latitude = purchase price in cents.
– Minutes of latitude = purchase price in gulden.
– Course = degrees of the compass card expressed in cases of eels reckoned from north round to the right.
– If not in motion, particulars as to the state of the market e.g. market firm or dull etc.

*Ship's class:*
– Dreadnought = cod with head
– Large cruiser = cod
– Light cruiser = haddock, large
– Auxiliary cruiser = haddock
– Destroyer = plaice
– Submarine = sole
– Monitor = smelt
– Troop transport = skate
– Net barrier = whiting
– Minefield = turbot

In November 1915 a secret ink was used which could be developed by perchloride of iron mixed with water so as to give a solution of the colour of cognac. 'Gloy', a preparation of gum, was also used.

The secret writing was frequently on tinted paper, and sometimes found inside envelopes lined with tissue paper, inside newspaper wrappers, under postage stamps and the folds of envelopes. The re-agents were heat; powdered oxide of copper; liquid colours, chief of these black ink; adhesive powders; gases or vapour, chiefly of iodine; tobacco smoke.

Early in the year, a method of writing with a chemical pencil, green with a white filling, on thick fibrous mauve-coloured paper, had come to light. The writing was absorbed by the paper but appeared clearly on attempting to burn it. Unglazed paper was also in use for writing in plain water with a new nib.

Agents sent out from Antwerp were given a phial of some liquid which resembled alcoholised water; a sponge and a handkerchief which had been steeped in some liquid and then dried. The sponge and handkerchief were to be soaked in water and would then produce the liquid contained in the phial. The paper was to be moistened with a sponge and written on in a longitudinal sense, then dried, then damped with ammonia and water, dried again, and the *en clair* message written in ordinary ink. Some pre-arranged message in the *en clair* text, for instance, an allusion to the illness of Henry, would indicate that the cover address was no longer in use.

The same process could be used with plain water for the secret message, and a word agreed upon beforehand was to be put in the text to show which liquid had been used. This method was followed by the British chemist, who discovered that iodine vapour would develop such writing. The paper was to have a smooth surface, and the writing done with a ball-pointed pen which would leave no mark.

The Antwerp school used ammonia and alcoholised water, the Brussels organisation, lemon-juice, urine, sympathetic ink in bottles marked Belladonna, and milky ink. Many photographs were to be taken, and messages written on the mounts under the photograph, or in the envelopes.

From time to time German agents would supply our officers with a bottle of secret ink. But it was always a question whether it was really the latest invention and not a plant.

As to the writing of secret messages, the instructions varied: Peter Steunebrink and Frank Greite were to write across the message *en clair* and on both pages so as to avoid attracting the attention of the Censor's eye by a blank page. Afterwards the messages had to be written on the back of the page containing the *en clair* letter. This letter must be interesting as the Censor would stop anything too uninteresting to be sent on.

During the period under review in every case but one the spy was detected on information received from the Intelligence Service abroad. From August 1915 to May 1916 the cases appeared isolated and there is no connecting link of spy addresses to help the detection branch. And as regards spy letters the secret ink used by the Germans was so good as to escape notice in censoring, provided the spy wrote a good *en clair* letter. Therefore, the lesson of these cases is the necessary dependence of passive upon active intelligence in time of war.

The principle has to be carried even further; the intelligence work abroad varied in quality so much that Scotland Yard, when requested to interrogate suspects signalled from foreign parts, asked for precise particulars as to the origin of the notices as a help in forming a judgement on the suspect, and the Censor asked for all particulars that could be given with regard to persons on his lists as a guide to his staff in examining correspondence.

During 1915, therefore, the work done by MI-1(c) officers acting in conjunction with the consular offices abroad and specially in Holland, Denmark and Norway, grew to be of prime importance for G Branch; the outer frontier was actually in the foreign port where a visa must be obtained as a preliminary step in coming to England.

With regard to outward bound passenger traffic, the permit system by which no person could leave the United Kingdom without stating where he was going, on what business and to what address, and without satisfying the authorities of his bona-fides, was inaugurated.

As a third measure of precaution, in the course of the same year, a system guarding the ports was developed by E Branch, which collected statistics of all travellers and eventually acted as a link between the Special Intelligence Bureau and the permit office on the one hand and the Special Intelligence Bureau and the British consuls on the other. Thus there were three fences through which the traveller had to pass satisfactorily and at each of these a record would be kept to which E Branch had access.

The value of these records in tracing the movements of undesirables needs no emphasis. But, as the cases previously recorded show, the frontier controls could be used in the most elastic way, to prevent spies from embarking in foreign ports, to allow them to embark subjecting them to thorough search at the ports, to take the papers from the suspects arriving in this country, forwarding them to Scotland Yard where the suspect could call to claim them and be subjected to examination by the police, or, in the case of known urgency, to arrest the spy on landing and send him under escort to Scotland Yard.

These are the four grades of frontier work recorded in the files and, according to the nature of the case, G Branch would select the method to be put into practice by the port officers. Again, the cases reported show how by the working of the permit systems and E Circulars to the ports, persons possessing inconvenient knowledge could be kept in the country, others who were allowed to leave would be especially searched for documents or addresses, and sometimes the search was, as it were, advertised so as to brand the traveller in the eyes of the Germans.

The second use in which MI-1(c) agents were put was to obtain evidence with regard to associates, employers and trading of reputed spies. A most important part of the evidence consisted in obtaining proof as to the veracity of a man's statements on these points. After the arrest of many spies in Holland and the issue of DRR 18A, the British agents found great difficulty in getting clear evidence of spy connections: Christian Mulder, Alexander Blok and Philip Dikker proved so intractable that Hubert Ginhoven, a Special Branch detective of Dutch birth, was sent over from England to see what he could do. The same man was sent to Spain to collect evidence against Adolpho Guerrero and great difficulty occurred in America in connection with the enquiry into Frank Greite's associates.

The fact that Greite and Vieyra did genuine business was also an obstacle to detection: it afforded cover for journeys and cover very difficult to remove in case of arrest. In Greite's case, delay could be and was imposed in spite of his bluster, but to stop him absolutely without proof of espionage was impossible. Vieyra was informed as soon as he arrived that he must either stay or go without return and undertook to stay. The difficulty in this case arose from the fact that trade letters, if genuine, could not be unreasonably delayed or spoiled by testing, and it was not until after his arrest that one of his letters was drastically treated as to develop secret writing.

The advisability of checking frequent journeys in wartime, even if the motive be genuine business and the inadequacy of limiting such journeys to neutral countries, is amply illustrated. The importance of an accurate memory for and accurate recording of names is illustrated in the case of Greite, as well as the necessity for allowing a liberal margin for mis-spelling them. Brilliant work was done by Tinsley in tracking the connection with Blok through linking up the password 'Remember Helen' with Helen Lemaitre.

Investigation in Albertine Stanaway's case was hampered by the facts that intelligence services of three Allied nations were involved: i.e. French, Belgian and British, and that the case was merely the continuation of that of Pierre Rotheudt. It seems clear that if the case of Rotheudt had come within the province of the British authorities, the bureau would have pulled out every stop in 1915. As it was, the bureau took only such steps as were asked for by the Belgians and neglected the most ordinary precautions: e.g. a check on Winterberg's address.

Secondly, when Mrs Stanaway's case was under consideration, it seems to have suffered from the fact of her association with Meisner-Denis: it was over-shadowed by the much more important George Vaux Bacon and Rutledge Rutherford investigations. The full import of the break, or apparent break, between Rotheudt and Stanaway does not seem to have been realised and there is no sign that she was questioned upon it. Her curious intimacy with Mrs Hebden, a woman who by marriage at least was in a totally different social position, was never explained.

Among the achievements of the year, the discovery of the new German secret ink ranks high. Hans Eils stated that Pickard (Vieyra's alias) was one of the first agents to use it. Pickard came over in May, the development of the ink was discovered in September and used on the apparently blank paper of instructions carried by Graff in December and February 1917 with results already described.

To other points of great interest to G Branch were the success of its efforts to limit the sending of news out of this country by limiting the despatch of newspapers and prohibiting the despatch of picture postcards.

Eva de Bournonville had a number of picture postcards of London in her possession and with secret marks on these she could easily have indicated the places where bombs had fallen during air-raids. The fact that after the discovery of the spy address at Stockholm only one letter escaped notice reflects great credit on the GPO and Postal Censorship.

In August 1915 the proposal that the bureau should be consulted in all important cases of contravention of DRR was approved. Power to search premises and seize prohibited documents had been conferred upon certain conditions and persons in July 1915; powers to arrest on suspicion that a person was carrying dangerous documents followed in February 1916.

DRR regulation 19 was amended by giving power to the competent military or naval authority to specify areas in which the taking of photographs was prohibited and by deleting the clause 'with intent to assist the enemy'. Finally by a regulation to prevent the misuse and loss of confidential documents, plans etc., it was considered that the counter-espionage legislation was made complete and the regulations 18, 18A, 19, and 19A supplemented by powers of search, interrogation and arrest under DRR 43, 51, 52, and 55 should form the basis of important amendments to the Official Secrets Act 1911.

Communication of information regarding the passage of a ship along the coast of the United Kingdom was restricted to Lloyds and the recognised owners and agents; and a regulation was added to guard against the publication etc. of new inventions and designs of value to the public safety.

Again this year, attention was drawn to the inadequate safe-guards obtaining with regard to neutrals who might infringe DRR repeatedly and yet, because no hostile association could be proved, would escape with a short term of imprisonment.

On the other hand, the action of MI5 in ordering that Rutherford should be taken off any ship wherever found and the arrest of Grebst on board a neutral ship in transit between one neutral country and another indicates a changed and stronger policy necessitated by the harder pressure of the war.

As the result of the Brugman, Lassen and de Bournonville cases, a clause was added to DRR 45 in November 1915 prohibiting false statements made with a view to obtain a pass, certificate, permit. Government departments also were warned that enemy agents were offering information about new inventions and other matters with a special view to espionage, and DRR 29A was issued. This regulation makes it an offence to trespass on factories, workshops etc. and provides for the issue of permits to authorised persons.

Attempts to procure entrance into government departments or munitions factories etc. were guarded against by making it an offence to speak or act in such a way as to cause the unwarranted belief that a person was employed in any government department. This was extended in March to include false representation with regard to employment by the government of any of His Majesty's Dominions or any foreign government. In October a clause was added to guard against the destruction, willful loss, unauthorised retention and loan to another person of passes, permits, certificates and licences.

In July 1916 the Chief Constable and especially those on the coast were warned against travelling artistes; this was followed up by arranging privately with the dramatic agencies in London to forward lists of all alien music-hall artistes and theatrical performers obtaining contracts through their agencies, and of the places at which they were to perform. By this means it would be possible to acquaint the police and military and naval authorities beforehand.

Subsequently, the Variety Artistes Federation asked the government to prohibit the entry of foreign music-hall artistes. Ramona de Amondarain had come into the country on false pretences through a bona-fide offer of work, and the decision to employ neutral workmen opened the door to a flood of applicants of a dangerous character; in August, consular authorities in Italy, Portugal, Scandinavia and Spain were warned not to consider applications for a visa unless the letters of engagement sent from Great Britain bore a police stamp.

In the spring of 1916, the cases of Adolpho Guerrero, Frank Greite and 'R' seemed to show that enemy agents were no longer being paid by telegraphic money orders but by notes through banks. To abandon the safeguard of the existing check on telegraphic orders was not possible, safety lay only in development of policy. To the data supplied regularly by the GPO it was proposed to add data of remittances paid through British banks on advice received from neutral banks abroad, the individuals of whom the British firms had no special knowledge.

In 1916 the bureau scarcely ventured to trust the Censorship to deal with a matter necessitating such absolute discretion, hence, with the help of Sir William Plender, a confidential circular to the managers of banks asking for the weekly returns of required information, was drawn up. It was never issued as the labour involved on the banks and on the bureau would have been stupendous. But from that time forward Sir William Plender supplied to MI5 monthly statistics of payments of from £15 upwards made to Germans here through the London agency of the Deutsche Bank. These lists were treated exactly as the previous lists of 1914; particulars were noted in the case of persons known to the bureau and fresh cases were enquired into at the rate of ten a day. Thus the enquiry initiated by Major Drake in 1914, was resumed with some modification in 1916, and for a time became a recognised detection method.

The general effort with regard to the banks was not altogether dropped, however, but through Mr Martin Holland, secretary to the Bankers' Clearing House, arrangements were made by which British bankers would report any suspicious payments of any kind which they might be called upon to make.

Meantime the ports had been notified that the Germans were discontinuing the practice of sending money payments to their agents here and it was supposed that agents would arrive in future furnished with adequate supplies; hence any person landing in this country and carrying sums of from £50 to £150 was to be notified to the bureau. There were thus three possible checks on incoming monies: on telegraphic orders, bankers' orders, and on money brought in at the ports.

In December 1916 the data concerning recipients of telegraphic orders was made more generally accessible for reference by being tabulated on an index kept by G2(c).

Under the ARO of April 1915 all aliens entering and leaving the United Kingdom were required to produce documents of identification. In November, under DRR 14C, the provisions of the order were extended to British subjects: all British subjects embarking in this country had to procure a permit; those entering the United Kingdom had to produce the same documents as aliens, a passport issued by a Secretary of State or a special permit. The permit system, which at first was enforced only for travellers to Scandinavia, Holland and France, was extended in August 1916 to all civilian travellers going to Spain, Portugal and South America. Power was conferred upon the competent military authority to remove all persons, aliens and British, who remained in prohibited areas in contravention of the regulations.

In January 1916, under the ARO:

1. Prohibited areas were extended so as to include all places within ten miles of the coast.
2. Non-resident aliens found in prohibited areas without a permit or an identity book might be expelled.
3. Every alien coming into the Metropolitan Police District after 14 February 1916, and every alien leaving the district to go and live elsewhere in the UK must register.
4. Registered aliens wishing to enter a prohibited area must provide themselves with an identity book of a prescribed form.

In June it was made an offence to attest particulars given in an identity book if the relevant particulars were not filled in. In May 1916, the principle of making special military areas had been adopted, and in July the powers so conferred were put into force in the district north of the Caledonian Canal transforming Inverness into something resembling a continental frontier station. In the same month the aliens registration order was extended to cover all Allied subjects, including French, Russian, Italian and Serbian.

In June compulsory registration of alien visitors to hotels, boarding-houses and lodging-houses, was extended to include all unfurnished rooms let to aliens. The registration of British visitors in hotels etc. had been made compulsory in January 1916. The effects of the Recruiting Act, and of German propaganda with regard to strikes, anti-recruiting and rebellion were seen in the Amendments.

The decision was taken to import foreign labour under conditions agreed upon by the government departments concerned. MI5 insisted upon and obtained the condition that the men must agree to stay for the duration of the war. The Germans then obstructed the recruiting of good workmen. Regulation 27 was extended so as to prohibit theatrical or cinema representations likely to prejudice recruiting etc. of HM's Forces. This was followed in July by an amendment making it penal to undermine public confidence in bank or currency notes. In order to enable the police to keep in touch with the strike-leaders deported from Glasgow, a paragraph was added to Regulation 55 enabling the police to take photographs and fingerprints of persons arrested under this Regulation.

In order to deal adequately with the Irish rebels interned in England, Regulation 14B was amended to make any person interned under the order subject to the same restrictions as a prisoner of war – unless specially exempted by the Secretary of War. Free passage to Ireland was restricted in August.

In consequence of the visit by the welfare campaigner of Miss Emily Hobhouse to the Ruhleben internment camp in Berlin, a section was added to the DRR making it an offence for a British subject voluntarily to enter enemy country or enemy occupied territory during the war except under special permit.

It has been convenient to summarise the cases of spies arrested or examined between August 1915 and December 1916; those of Pauline Slager and her friends which belong chronologically to May, June and July 1915. Slager's value to the Germans seems to have been greater after her journey to England than before and definite knowledge of her spy activities came to G Branch only in the autumn of 1915. In reviewing the four groups of cases mentioned, two main periods of German activity may be distinguished, from late July 1915 to early May 1916, and from June 1916 to December 1917.

The achievements of G Branch during these seventeen months were as follows:

–   More complete information about the personnel etc. of the Antwerp Marine Bureau; discovery of new recruiting system in Holland; discovery of subsidiary centres in Stockholm and Madrid.

- Sentence on four spies; many others, of whom two most important, checkmated permanently.
- Discovery and disruption of very big and dangerous centre in New York, subsidiary to Antwerp. Sentence on two spies in England and three in America. The internment of one possible spy.

When caught in the toils, the average spy either offered to give information against his employer or stated that the giving of such information had been his ulterior motive in coming to England. Certain it is that from June 1915 onwards an increasing number of Dutchmen accepted German service with the intention of betraying their employers; others like Charles van Ekeren, served them faithfully for a time and then quarrelled on a question of pay; others, like [XXXXX] had a patriotic motive; and a fourth class belonged to the race of double agents who served and betrayed both aides impartially.

The success of MO5G in catching German spies during the summer induced the Antwerp bureau to take special steps to discover what organisation lay behind such results, and in November they sent over Peter Age Christianus Steunebrink, apparently to enquire into British counter-espionage. There seems little doubt that Steunebrink gave the British more information than the Germans bargained for.

The usual method followed in such cases was for the double to offer his services to British officials abroad; the offer would be duly forwarded to MO5G which would request the British official to move warily and examine the man further. If the man seemed genuine, or sometimes it there seemed a good chance of gaining valuable information without too great a risk, he would be allowed to come over, would be interviewed, and finally sent back with a no return permit. This was the course taken in the case of Steunebrink.

From these various agents mentioned above very important information was obtained about the Antwerp bureau. This was supplemented in 1918 by the discovery of the Antwerp roll of spies for 1916 and 1917, and the statements of Hans Eils who had worked at that office since the latter end of 1915. Of these various statements the following summary may be made.

The bureau was established at 38 Chauseee de Malines (Mechelsche

Steenweg), Antwerp. All its dossiers were marked Admiralstab – Zweig Marine Nachrichtstelle, Antwerp; Aht. Berlin; Marine Korps, Brügge; Meldeamt Hord Wesel.

It would seem therefore that the Antwerp bureau worked in with Berlin in launching spies on England from Scandinavia, and that the Wesel branch was the collecting place for news.

The bureau was the centre from which agents were sent to England and America. It was founded by Ludwig Schnitzer, director of a firm of tobacconists at Rotterdam, who in 1914 was compelled to leave that town. Captain von Gorschen, who was head of the organisation, was born and brought up in England. Under him worked Rittmeister Eugen Wilhelm, known as the 'Coffee King of Hamburg', and Captain Alfred Schulyze.

These men interviewed and trained the spies, while Carl Schultz took charge of the secret inks and instructed the spies in the use of them.

The instruction of spies included the use of telegraphic and written codes, the silhouettes of different types of warships of differentiations, and the questions, which they were presumably to memorise. The spy was given two addresses to write to. These addresses were changed for his next visit to England. Charles van Ekeren's four addresses were:

– Heer W. Atzrott, c/o Firma Scharenberg, 52 Willem de Zwijgerlaan, Hague.
– A. Niendecker, 147 van Blankenburgstraat, Hague.
– Adolphe Carré, 41a Zwaarde Croonstraat, Rotterdam.
– Jan Hendriks, c/o Hotel Fleissig, 129 Warmoesstraat, Amsterdam.

It is to be noted that Heinrich Flores was said to have gone to live at Zwaarde Croonstraat and that the name Adolphe Carré may conceal that agent's personality. Charles van Ekeren also denounced Theodore, alias Frank Greite.

From Peter Steunebrink, MO5G learned of the recruiting agency which had grown up in succession to that of Hilmar Dierks, that of A-4, Alexander Blok, a Jewish ex-banker of Hamburg, whose business had been wrecked by the war, and of G. Elte. The spy cases of 1916 show the importance of this information. He also gave the cover addresses of Christian Mulder, 28b van der Taketraat, Rotterdam, and Ferdinand Grant, 139, Leeuwehaven, Rotterdam.

Steunebrink supplied a specimen of secret ink and the correct information that the message was written across and not between the lines. His instructions were never to ask any questions but to listen in clubs, public houses and popular resorts. He was to stay a month, to receive £75 a month and £15 for expenses. He was to furnish reports on ship-building in the different ports and on the results achieved by air-raids and other matters. Steunebrink returned to Holland and told the Germans that the British Secret Service knew all about the Antwerp centre. The Germans, realising that the movements of their agents crossing the frontier could be watched, gave up summoning recruits and spies to Antwerp and thenceforward conducted the training and interviews in Holland. Wilhelm and Schiltze then travelled regularly in Holland, putting up at the Vieux Doelen Hotel in The Hague, and the Victoria Hotel, Amsterdam. The Hotel Maas, Rotterdam, was also a spy centre and various of the spies on the Antwerp roll lent their rooms for the purposes of spy instruction and interviews. Such was the position of affairs in 1916.

In that year also the counter-espionage section at the Villa Arcadia, 106 Badhuisweg, Scheveningen, emerged into prominence and eventually grew to very great importance.

The names of some 136 agents were on the Antwerp books; of these, ninety-two figure in the extract in MI5's files, and MI5 had records and correct information of about sixty-six of these agents.

The notes attached to the spies' names on the rolls and information from other sources, show the following types of services required recruiting agents, covering address and confidential tasks; espionage in England – travelling and residential; espionage in Holland:

1. Interrogation of crews.
2. Interrogation of travellers from England, and especially journalists.
3. General look-out off the Dutch coast.
4. Special look-out for signs of a British landing.

5.  Watch on British legation and consulate.
6.  Manipulation of relations with the English and French services and with the Dutch police.
7.  Manipulation of Dutch telegraphists.
8.  Watch on travellers going to Germany.
9.  Manipulation of Dutch firms connected with English trade.
10. Financial and unpaid agents, e.g. German merchants.

The list shows the balance of espionage weighted heavily on the Dutch side and the consequent immense importance of our establishing our outer frontier in Holland.

Among these agents two seem to have filled residential posts in Great Britain. A-6, Harry Bekkers, was secretary to the Dutch consulate at Liverpool, who is said by Hans Eils to have sent, during 1915 and 1916, daily reports in secret ink through a lady at The Hague, and A-46, de Bie, who had a permanent post with a London firm and went to England in July 1916. In September of that year he was reporting from Glasgow and Edinburgh in letters addressed to his wife. Guerrero declared that a permanent German agent met all spies in England and gave them instructions, but that he himself had not been here long enough to see this man.

In January 1917 Colonel Drake left and on 15 January Major Carter took charge of the branch. G5 was constituted into a separate branch for Oriental affairs and G2 under Major Anson was split up into four sub-sections to deal respectively with: enquiries arising out of intercepted correspondence (G2(a) Mr Marsh, Commander Henderson, Captain Hordern, Captain Cookson); enquiries arising out of matters referred by the ports control (G2(b) Major Welchman, Captain Sassoon); enquiries arising out of matter referred by P (G2(c) Lieutenant Ripley, Lieutenant Fielding); enquiries arising from any other source (G2(d) Mr Clayton, Mr G. Streatfield, Lieutenant H. Lawes, Mr H. B. Goad).

In February 1917, a considerable change took place in G Branch. In the general specification of duties it was laid down that recommendations for amendments to legislation and regulations were to be made in consultation with G1.

The duties of Gl were restricted to investigation of cases of sedition and peace propaganda arising from enemy activities; G2 retained investigation of cases of suspected espionage in Great Britain; G4 resumed the investigation of intercepted correspondence taking it over from G3(a). On the other hand three new sections were constituted:

- G3: to deal with photography, chemistry and technical research.
- G5: for translation.
- G6: for procedure and investigation in special questions.

Note: E retained control of investigations in the cases of persons in transit through the United Kingdom.

Re-organisation took place in September and again in October 1917. While the general duties assigned to G remained the same, changes were made in the section B. Photography, chemistry and technical research, and translation dropped out; the duties of G2 were taken over and expanded by G3 under the fresh definition: 'Executive duties connected with investigation, arrest or trial of persons suspected of espionage'; to G2 were allotted general duties connected with enquiries into the bona-fides for questions connected with secret writing and correspondence.

In February 1917 the instructions issued to the police on the outbreak of war to forward to MO5G particulars with regard to any aliens who had served in any army, navy or police force were extended so as to include Chinese, Japanese, Siamese, Persians and Egyptians.

Subsequently Major Carter procured from Scotland Yard information with regard to certain members of the old Imperial Russian Secret Service who had been engaged in watching Russian exiles and revolutionaries in the capitals of Europe. Major Carter drew up a memorandum foreshadowing the adoption of special measures for watching agents of the new Russian government at work here and he proposed to gather information from Dutch and other sources. On the complaint of the General Officer Commanding at Chester that Manchester was a centre for aliens and that special preventive measures were required, an officer was sent up to investigate. He reported against taking special action but recommended that the competent military authorities should not institute or make investigations on their own account but refer all suspicious cases at once to MI5. Whether this plan was adopted does not appear but it is to be noted that such a plan involved a total change of principle from that obtaining hitherto, which was to work as far as possible through the ordinary channels e.g. the local constabulary.

Arrangements were made to keep GHQ GB(1) informed of all enquiries asked of MI5 by the commands and with this object all answers sent by MI5 were despatched in duplicate.

It was essential that in notifying GHQ I(b) of the departure of any person for France full particulars of the case should be given, and that when enquiries were made by GHQ I(b) of MI5 and no particulars were available special enquiries should be set on foot at once.

Equally it was important to maintain close co-operation with the assistants to the military attaché at the United States embassy.

In May instructions were issued that direct correspondence between MI5 and an intelligence officer attached to command headquarters was to cease and all cases involving disciplinary action against members of HM Forces were to be referred direct to GHQ HF(1).

With a view to closer co-operation it was arranged that all officers of the counter-espionage services in France should have a week's course of instruction at the office of MI5 and afterwards opportunities were made for counter-espionage officers abroad to study the methods and work of the Postal Censor.

In March 1917 it was known that subjects of Allied countries were seeking to evade military service by scraping an acquaintance with Dutch subjects, eliciting information with regard to their birth, family etc. and then writing giving these particulars to the burgomasters of Dutch cities with a request that papers of identification should be forwarded to the writer. MI5G met this by arranging with the censor to stop and submit all such letters.

Owing to a letter intercepted in the American mail to Holland and forwarded by MI5G to the American ambassador, that official wrote begging that his government should at once establish a Postal Censorship.

In the following month G4 sent to the US government a copy of the Cable Censor's Handbook.

In January 1917 a table was made of the results achieved by MO5 to December 1916. Entered on this record were only the certainties easily accessible from documents. This means that MO5 followed cases up to a certain point but received no information unless it were specially asked for as to whether or when the recommendation for deportation was carried out by the Home Secretary.

The numbers given were made up from reference to the old Black List.

| Disposal of persons known of likely to be engaged in activities prejudicial to the public safety or defence of the realm during the period October 1909 to 10 December 1916 | | | | | | | | |
|---|---|---|---|---|---|---|---|---|
| | Before war | | During war | | Totals | | | |
| DISPOSAL | M | w | M | F | M | F | Total | Remarks |
| 1. Sentenced to death | | | 13 | 1★ | 13 | 1 | 14 | ★prison |
| 2. Suicide | | | 1 | | 1 | – | 1★ | ★during trial |
| 3. Prison | | | 6★ | | 6 | 1 | 12 | ★Official Secrets Act |
| 4. Prison | | | 1 | | 1 | – | 1 | |
| 5. Interned | | | 136 | 21 | 136 | 21 | 157 | |
| 6. Deportation | | | 113 | 11 | 113 | 11 | 124 | |
| 7. Forbidden to re-enter UK | | | 195 | 73 | 195 | 73 | 288 | |
| 8. Prevented from leaving UK | | | 90 | 30 | 90 | 20 | 110 | |
| 9. Restricted by DRR 14B | | | 17 | 6 | 17 | 5 | 22 | |
| 10. Excluded under DRR 14 | | | 443 | 111 | 445 | 111 | 554 | |
| TOTAL | 6 | – | 1,015 | 243 | 1,021 | 243 | 1,264 | |

# CHAPTER IV
# 1917

DURING 1917 the news was circulated that all papers issued at Buenos Aires must be regarded as suspect and that Mexican passports and especially those issued in London belonged to the same category. Holders of Greek passports were to be examined for Ottoman subjects from Syria had been imported into France to work on munitions and as they had no identity papers the Greek Patriarch in Paris was supplying these. German agents were also said to be entering France under cover of false papers with the crowd of repatriated prisoners of war.

Another method of evading close enquiry was reported in an Italian book on espionage. It consisted of exchanging an original passport granted in the country of birth for one procured at a consulate in a foreign country, where enquiries could not be so precise.

In January 1917 a warning came from Christiania that Finnish sailors and passengers alike were to be viewed with suspicion. It was known that the Germans were experiencing difficulty in procuring Dutch agents with credentials sufficient to justify their prolonged stay in England.

The following secret methods or possible methods of communicating information were reported in 1917: handkerchiefs embroidered in Morse Code; imitations of Raphael Tuck's picture cards sold to Belgians interned at Harderwyk and sent by them to comrades at the Front or to refugees in France; religious books, psalters or leaflets containing prayers; newspapers sent in batches to enemy countries, the number of newspapers indicating the number of troops at a particular point, the colour of the ink in which the address was written indicating the arm of the service, notices were circulated to the port officers and other persons concerned. Other methods of communication were by phonographic records and by printed advertisements.

All importation into and export from this country of phonographic records was prohibited. As regards control of advertisements it was arranged that all advertisements must have a police visa before publication. It was suggested that provincial newspapers should have the option of sending advertisements to be censored in London but that ordinarily the local military authority should exercise supervision while direct police censorship should be arranged for large centres.

The question of how to stop leakage of news from the internment camp at Groningen was one of considerable difficulty; threat of court martial on the men's return to England was no use, removal for a space to Flushing would provide a pleasant change, the cells at Groningen would provide no remedy, while stopping all leave would be hard on the innocent.

A suggestion was made that smuggling of letters should be punished by a term of imprisonment extending beyond the original furlough granted by the Dutch government; it was however a question whether that government would allow the right to take such action.

In 1917 the following methods of evading censorship and search are mentioned: papers hidden in a diplomatist's cabin while search of the ship was in progress; letters carried on board at the last minute hidden in linen-baskets; messages hidden in vacuum flasks and hollow ten cent pieces; crews bribed to carry letters by Dutch soldiers offering drink on board the ship; abuse of Vickers White Bag from Russia; repatriated Russian Jews smuggled letters on incoming steamers; pro-Bolshevik articles transmitted to the *Manchester Guardian* through some channel unknown by a British MCO at Vladivostok.

In December 1916 restrictions had been put on the export through the port of printed or written matter including photographs, pictures etc., except under permit. The same restrictions were imposed upon parcels and samples. The three last examples of evasion quoted above and other changes made during 1917 in those regulations which govern the communication of news and information to and from foreign countries are significant of the immense development of certain aspects of the German attack and of some corresponding change of feeling within the country.

In January 1917 the press called attention to the smuggling abroad of peace propaganda literature, the circulation of which was prohibited in this country. Two pacifist Members of Parliament and others in high places were suspected of being concerned and the press insinuated that there was one law for the powerful and another for the humble. But the whole question was a very difficult one.

Since July 1916 passengers leaving the United Kingdom had been warned that any papers passengers other than those required for identification purposes were liable to seizure at the ports, but in practice it was found that much inconvenience was caused to the travellers by their being deprived at the ports of their personal documents. An attempt to limit the inconvenience was made by posting large notices warning travellers of the regulations and requesting them to despatch all those documents other than identification papers which they required abroad, by post abroad under cover to the Censorship. These notices of course were directed to honest people who had no motive for smuggling. There remained the other class of traveller to deal with.

The officers of MI5 pointed out that in practice it was impossible to use the full powers of search conferred under DRR 54, and therefore evidence against offenders was difficult to procure except by some happy accident. In certain cases it might be inadvisable to use powers of interrogation under DRR 53 but it might be possible where there was suspicion of smuggling for the competent military authority to order a search of the premises of the suspect under DRR 51.

In this sense, however, nothing was done, for the Home Secretary pointed out that there was no evidence that the smuggling had been carried out with the connivance of the authors of the pamphlets. But in November DRR 51 was amended to cover search of premises in cases where a leaflet had been printed in contravention of any regulation.

The case of Mrs Smith provided an illustration of two further dangers not met by the regulations. Mrs Smith was smuggling prohibited pro-

German literature to a PoW in a colony. When taxed with the offence she pointed out the newspapers of which she had sent cuttings had been passed into this country through the Press Censorship.

With regard to this point, the import into this country of literature of a dangerous character, both the Censor and the India Office had been pressing for legislation on account of the dangerous spread of Indian seditious or revolutionary publications, which were pouring into the country from America, Holland, Sweden and Switzerland. In June 1917 DRR 27B was issued prohibiting the importation of publications containing dangerous matter of which the publication and circulation in this country was forbidden under DRR 27.

On the same date, DRR 24 and 24B were redrafted: to DRR 24 was added a clause forbidding evasion of the Censorship with regard to printed or written matter, pictures, photographs; to DRR 4B a clause making it an offence to evade censorship through the post by sending letters by devious routes through countries where mails were not usually censored or by secreting letters in newspapers, parcels etc. and throwing on any person contravening the order the onus of proving that such letters were not intended for himself.

In July regulation 54 was amended so as to make it an offence to answer falsely a question with regard to the carrying of letters.

Another favourite method of evasion was by abuse of diplomatic and consular privilege. Between September 1916 and December 1918 129 cases of abuse of privilege were counted in the transit mails, and up until June 1918 eleven cases in the terminal mails. Practically every neutral country was at fault. The Censorship referred these cases to the Foreign Office but MI5G noted three of them (Rosenow, Pedro and Merry del Val; Patrocinio also furnishes an instance in point) and instituted an inquiry into the export of Gaelic League pamphlets from the United States to Switzerland via the United States embassy in Rome.

The consuls were the chief offenders; thirty one neutral consuls in neutral and enemy countries acted as intermediaries for commercial and private correspondence belonging to the enemy, whose custom it was to send four of every letter each by a different route. Their privilege was withdrawn from the consuls; it was ordered that the official correspondence of embassies and legations be sent under cover to the Chief Censor with a guarantee as to the official nature of the contents of the bag signed by the ambassador, minister or his deputy; private letters written by the ambassador, minister or secretary were to bear on the cover the signature of the writer. Later on, MI5 again considered the withdrawal of privilege from neutral missions but the Foreign Office ruled that the only course possible was to take official note of every case of abuse detected.

Another point with regard to correspondence by legation bag was raised by the fact that Germans sometimes paid their spies through a neutral legation. In such cases it was likely that the money would come by cable, the instructions with the name of the payee by letter, with the result that such payments could not be traced by the Censor or the GPO.

In 1916 GHQ I(b) had asked for the list of Dutch intermediaries suspected of being German agents, the names and addresses, however, changed incessantly, but few of the checks imposed were productive. Subsequently de Bueger, a Belgian official in the Remount Service attracted attention by forwarding letters to four different agencies, one of which was situated at Lille. At that time the Germans connived at smuggling letters, provided they saw the contents first, a system of which de Bueger would certainly have been aware, and our agents abroad pressed for the total abolition of intermediary letters. An attempt was made accordingly to restrict the traffic to one firm, Thomas Cook & Sons. A clamour arose from the Belgians in England; some modification was made but the problem was never satisfactorily solved.

With a view to detecting spies MI5 obtained returns of the names of persons corresponding daily with Holland, Denmark and Norway, but these were unproductive; on a list of thirty-nine persons writing to Norway, for instance, only one enquiry was made and that led to no action.

Equally fruitless were special tests of all correspondence written in red ink and an immense number of tests of letters on paper suitable for secret writing. Reference to the time of sailing of Dutch colliers was added to the list of indiscreet utterances.

In 1917 a series of questions regarding the respective delimitations and rights of MI5 and the Postal Censorship received solution. These concerned: the proper authority to deal with cases of evasion of censorship at the ports; the right to see and; the right to retain the originals of telegrams and letters.

The case of Sir Richard Cooper, head of a big chemical works at Berkhamsted, gave rise to important decisions about inter-departmental and intersectional procedure and also about interpretation. Cooper wrote to Dr Stokes in America explaining the unfair working of the Excess Profits Tax and propounding a scheme of evasion by setting up works in America.

He sent a copy of this letter to America in a sealed envelope carried by McKillop, an employee of the firm. McKillop, who was challenged at Liverpool, at first denied that he was carrying any letters and when the letter was discovered gave a false account of its contents. He was handed over to the police who did not immediately charge him; the letters were also given to the police.

The case was referred first to G and then to E Branch and both took action independently and in ignorance of each other's interest in the case. But under a previous ruling the originals of letters seized at the ports had to be sent to MI9. E's policy in dealing with such cases had been to treat them as summary offences and hand them over to the civil authorities; G Branch however, declared they were not summary offences and must therefore be referred to the competent military authority. Therefore the question arose as to which department and which branch was the proper authority to deal with a prosecution. The DPP ruled that a copy only of the letters seized on letter carriers should be submitted to the Censor; that the local competent military authority alone could decide on prosecution and settle the nature of the offence and that if he required the decision of a higher authority, he must refer to MI5 and G Branch would advise in the question of prosecution and category of the offence.

G Branch determined to prosecute and were frustrated by the Law Officers of the Crown on a question of interpretation. The Law Officers declared that in all previous decisions with regard to prosecution under DRR 34 the answer to the question whether or not the terms of the letter itself constituted an offence had been the determining principle and they declined to prosecute Sir Richard Cooper on the grounds that the terms of his letter did not constitute an offence.

The DSI protested against such a principle pointing out the probable consequences should it become generally known that a person might defy the regulations with impunity provided he wrote an innocent letter and that the Home Secretary took a grave view of the case under discussion. As a result, Regulation 54 was amended so as to make a false declaration about the carrying of letters an offence. Consequently the allocation of letters in cases of evasion was altered. Sixty-five cases of contravention had occurred in some four months, the greater number proving trivial offences. It was arranged, therefore, that the original letters should be sent to MI5G only in cases of evasion when there was evidence of sinister intent and in cases of intended evasion if there were already evidence incriminating the writer.

These cases were treated on their own merits: no action, a warning, circulation to the ports for thorough search and interrogation with check on the writer's correspondence are examples of the treatment accorded. Portuguese labourers returning home after being employed in the camps were specially warned, thoroughly searched and all letters had to be taken from them. When it was known that letters were being carried on small coasting steamers plying between Holland and Leith, rigorous search was carried out on board ship and all letters posted within a mile of the docks were examined.

The importance of seeing originals of telegrams and letters and the reluctance of other departments to submit them appears from the episodes connected with WT1D and the Postal Censorship. Early in 1917 the Admiralty wished to prohibit the despatch of foreign telegrams from any place north of Inverness and to restrict it from important ports in England and Wales to persons doing genuine business. But as both F and G Branch concurred in thinking that an enemy would always find means of sending a message through some licence-holder, the Admiralty accepted the existing arrangement whereby all outgoing telegrams were delayed for eighteen hours.

Then the WTID revived the question. Any commercial letters or cable which the Censor regarded as suspicious was submitted to the WTID and the chairman of that body expressed the belief that it was possible to convey military, naval and other information to the enemy in words pertinent to any genuine business in such a way as to defy detection; as existing safeguards ignored the character of the trader he suggested that the use of posts and cables should be restricted to alien traders holding permits whose bona-fides had been carefully scrutinised. No change however was made in the policy but Major Carter, after a vain attempt to get from the WTID the originals of suspect letters and telegrams, procured a list of small traders disliked indeed, but against whom that department had no definite suspicions.

Regarding trade letters, Major Drake had encountered difficulties since 1915, when testing for secret ink was transferred to the Censor's Department; the spies were using commercial code and secret ink and both were difficult of detection and in order to settle whether or not a letter should be tested it was necessary to handle the original. Certain letters, however, the Censor submitted in photograph under the impression that they were harmless trade letters and it was necessary to emphasise the fact that, of the firm on the General Black List, four were fraudulent and six were using genuine business as a cover for espionage. The question recurred in 1916 when the new chemical ink and re-agent were discovered. Thenceforward there were two possible tests, the Minor and the Major test. The Minor test was of little use for up-to-date German methods and its employment in the first instance prejudiced success in a subsequent Major test. On the other hand, the Major test destroyed the document and the Censor therefore hesitated to apply it in the case of a possibly harmless commercial letter and on other grounds. Major Drake pointed out that Frank Greite had made £1,000 in business, and that after many of Leopoldo Vieyra's letters containing secret ink had passed unscathed through the Minor test he was detected on the single original letter submitted to MI5 and subjected by their direction to the Major test.

The Major test indeed proved so valuable that in March 1917 all letters in the files of a date earlier than October 1916 were ordered to be subjected to it. Finally, it was arranged that letters not connected with persons on the General Black List but suspect because of the text or paper used should be submitted before testing to MI5G, which could then have a photograph made before the destructive process was carried out.

The Censor desired to retain the originals of stopped letters for his records, but MI5G successfully vindicated its title on the grounds that such letters might afford valuable evidence. If a personal file existed the letter was filed in it; if there was no personal file the original might yet serve to trace a suspect or change of address through identification of handwritings.

The linking-up of records was as important to the Censor as to MI5, hence it was arranged that when a new check was imposed on a person concerning whom Censor slips had already been received, the number of the last slip received should be quoted.

In 1917 the DSI laid down that whereas the Postal Censor acted as the agent of MI5, in regard to the messages of spies written in arbitrary language code or secret writing, MI5 was responsible for taking all necessary measures of counter-espionage. Although the list of checks supplied to the GPO and Censor were not identical, there was overlapping; accordingly certain classes of foreign mail letters formerly opened by the GPO were transferred to the Censor and the post office servants were instructed to act on the checks only after reference to MI5 unless the matter were urgent, in which case a special report was to be sent. Subsequently, in spite of the preponderating role of the Censor, the GPO check on foreign letters was retained and use of its great advantage in the matter of speed.

Arrangements were made, however, to keep the GPO and Censorship mutually informed as to the progress of their respective checks. In December MI5 agreed to forward to the Trade Censor all trade letters submitted by the GPO.

The GPO was accustomed to furnish monthly returns of such checks, but if they produced nothing lapsed automatically, at the end of three months or six months unless renewed by MI5. Early in 1917, MI5 asked for monthly returns of the names and addresses of persons corresponding with suspects, and a fortnight's notice of those checks that were made to lapse automatically. In June 1918, fortnightly returns were by the local postmasters of checks that had been quite unproductive during that time; weekly returns were now sent in by the London offices.

★

In October 1917, MI5 began to consider steps to procure the help of banks in checking possible remittances for propaganda, and chiefly that form of peace propaganda in Europe, known as Boloism. The history of Bolo as recorded in our files has an important bearing on the action of MI5 in this respect. In January 1915, information had been received through the Remount Department at Bayonne that a man named Paul Bolo, who styled himself counsellor and financier to the ex-Khedive, was living at Biarritz and appeared to have plenty of money, and that through some connection with the French politician, Joseph Caillaux, he had access to French government circles. As it was felt that Bolo should be watched the information was forwarded to GHQ France. Subsequently, the BCI reported that in 1916, the German government had financed peace intrigues, employing as their chief agent the ex-Khedive, who had appointed Bolo to organise the work. Bolo, however, had pocketed the two million entrusted to him but had done nothing in return. (In 1918 it became known that the Khedive had broken with Bolo in August 1916.) Meanwhile, on account of the ex-Khedive's negotiations with Germany and Austria with regard to the subsidising of the French press, a report from Sir Horace Rumbold emerged giving details of the money supplied to Bolo and connecting Cavallini with the affair. Rumbold declared moreover that Cavallini had acted as intermediary between the ex-Khedive and Joseph Caillaux, who was preparing to launch pacifist agitation on a big scale in France.

News of the arrest of Bolo appeared in the press on 5 September 1917 and, shortly after, it was stated that the arrest had taken place in consequence of the discovery made by the American police that during the course of 1916, Paul Bolo being then in Paris, had had sums amounting to £400,000 paid in his name into various American banks, and had had the greater part of the money remitted to him by transfers on French banks.

In October the bureau enquired whether any payments connected with Bolo Pasha had been found in the books of the Deutsche Bank, but Sir William Plender pointed out that no new business had been undertaken since the war and that he as Controller had had access only to pre-war books and records.

On 12 November, by direction of the Home Secretary and Secretary of State for War, a joint committee was appointed to investigate the activities of pacifist societies in Great Britain and to enquire to what extent, if at all, they were being financed by enemy money. During the month of November the work developed like a snowball. Between 12 and 23 November 1917 five pacifist centres were raided for the purpose of discovering how they received and disbursed their funds. A circular was sent through the Treasury to the Bankers' Clearing House for distribution to banks requiring monthly returns of all payments of sums of money of £800 or over made to private individuals since 15 October 1917 by order of Dutch, Scandinavian, Swiss, Spanish or Danish clients; and any payments of £25 or over to a private individual since 15 October 1917 by order of the above mentioned clients 'if these orders appear to come with regularity, e.g. once a month or twice a quarter'.

Payments that were obviously of a business character were not to be included. The circular was issued at the instance of Colonel Kell by the financial blockade section of the Treasury on 28 November. Later on the banks were asked to supply the names and addresses of the recipients, and if possible of the persons by whose order the payments were to be made, but owing to banking customs the names of the payee and remitter were not always known to the bankers here.

Of the 216 banks circularised, 113 had no returns to make. They were therefore released from the obligation on the understanding that if any payments of the required nature were made it was to be reported. Enquiry retrospective for the last five years had been ruled out as impracticable, but Sir William Plender was approached with a view to ascertaining particulars about the confidential books of German banks, Mr Bromley Martin of Martin's Bank having stated that it was practically impossible to discover suspect accounts from a bank ledger. The deed boxes and books of the Deutsche Bank were examined in February 1918.

Meanwhile, Sir William Plender had pointed out that drafts on London could be purchased in Germany and might pass through various hands before being collected through a bank in London; it was therefore impossible to trace enemy payments unless information was supplied as to the source of payment. Owing to these difficulties and to the enormous amount of labour involved, an extension of the scheme so as to include in the monthly returns of the banks all cheques and drafts drawn on the banks from abroad, was withdrawn at the request of MI5.

During November, the London branch of the Comptoir National d'Escompe de Paris received orders to pay £1,000 to each of three individuals, who up to 6 December had not claimed payment. G3(b) asked the bank to obtain from the payees a receipt bearing their signature and address should they call at the bank for the money, or should the cash be drawn through another branch or bank to submit at ones the name of that branch or bank. A reply was received to one of these remittances.

It was suggested in Parliament that German commercial houses were used as spy centres and that examination of their books would reveal suspect payments. A G Branch officer called upon the Comptroller of the Companies Department, who stated that the work of investigating all the more important German firms and banks was practically at an end and he had already notified anything that appeared suspect. In view of the above no general enquiry was made with regard to the staffs of the enemy banks. By the ARO provision had been made for the supervision of individuals and such of the enemy subjects as remained at work at the banks were more or less under observation of the British supervisors, From time to time, however, a question in Parliament or an outcry in the press is noticed in the files.

On one such occasion, in August 1916, the statement was made that eleven German or Austrian clerks had been discharged from the

Deutsche Bank and forbidden to take up other employment in England. Occasionally, however, an individual member of the staff would draw the attention of MI5. The following employees and officials of the Deutsche Bank became the subject of investigation: Count James Minotto and Dr Ernest Kuhn, both employees; Baron Maximilian Von Kapp, president; Otto Roese, Wilhelm Pannenborg, managers.

Minotto and Baron George von Seebeck, of the Die Kontogesellechaft, were friends of the German ambassador. In August 1914 Dr Ernest Kuhn had been imprisoned; he was released owing to the action of Minotto who got an official of the American embassy to intervene. Minotto was then carrying an Italian as well as a German passport. The three young men escaped to America at the end of August and procured employment in the Guaranty Trust Company. By the end of the year, Minotto was at Buenos Aires on a mission for the company but he was then in close touch with Count Luxburg. MI5 heard of him first from an intercepted letter to Baron von Rapp, which was sent to the Home Office by Mr Ernest Marshall of the *New York Times*. Some enquiry was made both as to Minotto and Rapp. Minotto was over here about September 1915 and MI5 heard of him again in March 1916 when he was reported to be a pro-German and travelling frequently between Germany, France, the United States and England. Action was taken to stop and search and keep in touch with him should he come again. In consequence of the arrest of Bolo, von Seebeck, Kuhn, and subsequently also Minotto were arrested in America. Minotto had been arrested previously in August 1917 and let out on bail. MI5 then learned all that was known to the American embassy and took the following steps: a circular was issued to all the ports, GHQ, Home Office, Scotland Yard, Director of Naval Intelligence, the Public Prosecutions Office, the Bureau Central Interallié, GHQ I(b), GS(1), HQ L of C Areas, and MI-1(c) for distribution in New York, Madrid, Rome, Berne, Copenhagen, Stockholm and Christiania D for Malta, informing these offices of the facts, cancelling the previous circular and stating that no visas were to be issued to James Minotto. Property belonging to von Seebeck and Kuhn that was stored in a depository was searched and Kuhn's correspondence was examined. The papers showed that Kuhn had handled a good deal of money in his financial deals, he had paid cheques for large amounts to Minotto but there was nothing to indicate direct association with the German government and no evidence of direct association with von Seebeck. The indications are that von Rapp and Otto Roese were in fairly close touch with Minotto. They were also in touch with Felix Aschert, who had organised a letter-carrying business. This Aschert was in 1916 reported to be engaging spies and acting as financial agent for Germany.

In spite of being the object of much suspicion von Rapp was exempted from repatriation as he was useful in winding up the affairs of the London agency, but in August 1918 his services having been dispensed with, he applied for repatriation which was granted. Meanwhile, various enquiries had been made of him with varying results he gave some information with regard to Richard Mayer Bacum, a suspect bank promoter who had formerly organised a Russian section for the Deutsche Bank in Berlin, but he would or could give no help about a quantity of papers belonging to the Deutsche Bank which it was thought might be connected with German espionage. He was interviewed with regard to certain circulars, alleged to have been issued by German ministers, and dealing with measures which were to be taken by German banks and other institutions for encouraging espionage in countries outside Germany; von Rapp denied having ever received these circulars.

Otto Roese was evidently an important man. Two attempts were made to procure his repatriation. The first took place in April 1915 through Aschert who communicated with Pannenborg on the subject in an obscure wire. Pannenborg having been interned in May the next attempt took place in July through the American embassy. In consultation with the Treasury, the Home Office had however decided that Roese was not to be allowed to return as he possessed important financial knowledge and in July he was debarred from visiting the city. He, however, contrived to get his wife back to Germany. He had lost two sons fighting in the German Army. In May 1916 he was repatriated; he then wrote to von Rapp from Berlin complaining of this country's action with regard to German banks and their personnel.

Wilhelm Pannenborg was repatriated at some date prior to March 1918, he and von Rapp were reported afterwards either as having lingered in Holland or as having visited that country after repatriation. Thus, although there was no direct proof against the officials of the London agency there were grounds for suspicion and in October 1917, when the Bolo transactions had become known, MI5 successfully opposed the nomination of Felix Aschert as intermediary for communications which were to pass between the official supervisor of the Deutsche Bank London agency and the head office in Berlin. They also opposed the nomination of the Rotterdamsche Vereeniging, an institution which had developed enormously during the war, which was closely associated with enemy interests and indeed suspected of being under German control.

Special enquiry into the position of the German and naturalised British staff of the Dresdner Bank was begun by G2(d) in March 1917. In consequence of information sent to Major Claude Dansey by the editorial department of the *Daily Mail*. Shortly after, in connection with the discovery that the Deutsche Orient Bank had been engaged in political propaganda in Egypt, and apparently also in connection with an article of the *Daily Mail*, Ml-1(c) asked the bureau for information about the German and Austrian staff of the Dresdner Bank.

With this bank the Khedive had an account into which, as was afterwards known, he had paid the large sum which was conveyed to Bolo by Cavallini. Out of a list of twenty-three names forwarded by MI-1(c) the bureau supplied particulars with regard to twenty-one persons: seventeen Germans had been interned between May 1915 and December 1916, one had gone to America, another had been repatriated, and the fate of the two others was still the subject of enquiry; yet another was a woman concerning whom enquiry would be made. None of these persons were known to have been engaged in espionage.

In October 1917 there came from Rotterdam a list of fifty-nine employees who had left the Dresdner Bank between January and August 1914 with a request for information about these individuals. The list was sent to Mr Bromley Martin who gave the following account of the pre-war terms of employment accepted by the staff of the bank:

The staff of the Dresdner Bank were engaged on a three years' contract and on a wholetime basis. Only a few of the senior men stayed beyond their contract time; most of the Germans used their time as an opportunity for business education and many of them, on expiry of their contract, stayed in this country and started businesses on their own account.

*

In May, the government decided upon the policy of interning or repatriating according to age, all male enemy aliens who could not show cause why they should be left at liberty; all female enemy aliens with the exception of those held during deportation, might be repatriated. This was followed up by a measure enabling the authorities to intern dangerous persons of hostile origin and association.

The competent military and naval authorities, including MO5G, could send in a recommendation to the Home Secretary for an order of internment to be directed to any person under these categories; that person had the right to appeal against the order to an advisory committee; all appeals of this nature had to pass through MO5G.

The measure proved of infinite value to the investigating branch in dealing with suspects against whom there was not sufficient evidence to bring them to trial. Indeed, Major Drake wished to extend the scope of its operation to neutrals convicted of contraventions of DRR but against whom hostile association could not be proved.

In March 1915, Mario Guell, aged forty-one, was recommended to Commandant Wallner of the French Secret Service, by a French agent who had worked with Quell in the automobile trade. In the course of 1915, Commandant Wallner sent him to Germany four times – from March to May, in June, in September, and in December. After his return in June, Guell said he had been arrested at Looerrach in September, he was offered work by Captain von Reschenberg of the German Secret Service in December; he accepted the offer and was sent to Antwerp for instructions. Of the two first trips he submitted reports of no great value, on the third trip in September he gave no report at all; concerning the fourth trip he told Commandant Wallner frankly about his trip to Antwerp. After some hesitation Commandant Wallner accepted him as a double agent and instructed him to write certain letters to an address which had been given to Guell in Antwerp, L. Florini, Entrepreneur, Hotel de l'Europe, Lugano.

Without mentioning these circumstances the address was given to the British authorities who put it on check, and a letter dated 18 January 1916, addressed to Florini, was intercepted and tested with iodine fumes. A secret message flashed up and disappeared after a few moments. The writer could not be traced.

After December 1915, Guell was of no further use to Commandant Wallner. Early in 1916, Guell told the Commandant that together with Jose Berges he was founding a factory of false pearls and that he had worked previously in a similar business run by the firm of Hsuach. Between January and July 1916, Guell went twice to Russia in connection with this new business. In August 1916 he was signalled to the Commandant as a pro-German and as possibly a German agent. He was then preparing for a third trip to Russia. Guell was brought to the notice of the bureau by Commandant Wallner who informed MI5E that two Spaniards formerly employed by the French Intelligence Service had lately undertaken to work for the Germans and were going to Russia; he asked that visas should be gleaned after a delay of six days and that their movements should be watched in Norway. If they went to Russia the Russian authorities were making arrangements to arrest them; if they went to Germany under pretext of working for the French, he suggested that the British authorities should arrest them on their way back.

The two men arrived and were kept under observation in England but they did nothing suspicious. From the Grosvenor Hotel, Guell despatched a telegram to Guell, Calle San Beltram 114, Barcelona, while Berges sent telegrams to: Marsans, Teatro Novedades, Barcelona and Iturmendi, Condal 2, Ohnica, Barcelona.

The wires announced the safe arrival of the two men. The three telegrams were in Guell's handwriting which Lieutenant Fetherston identified as that of the writer of the Florini letter mentioned earlier. Enquiries made in Spain showed that there was no Guell at the address given; Marsans, the son of a banker, was connected with a lady who was pro-German and greedy of money, Iturmendi was a doctor, and his clinic was a centre of pro-German intrigue in Barcelona.

Guell and Berges went through to Russia. Care had been taken at the British ports to do nothing to arouse the Spaniards' suspicions but in Norway they were seen conversing with Germans. The Germans noticed that the party was being watched and no doubt warned the Spaniards. In October it was thought that the men would return shortly. Towards the end of the month the French had news that they were returning from Germany in seven or eight days and would probably sail for Spain direct from Scandinavia. Guell and Berges were not arrested n Russia. They made several journeys from Petrograd to Rostov and went also to Vitebsk and Guell went to Petrozavodsk.

In Rostov they bought from an English firm 288 kilos of fish scales for the manufacture of false pearls, but the Russian government refused permission to ship this purchase. This was on 17 November but it was not till 7 January 1917 that the two men left Petrograd for Spain via England. Instructions were issued to Newcastle that they were to be sent under escort to Scotland Yard. Among Guell's papers were found the address of the proprietor of boats going direct from Bergen to Spain; the record of a telegram which he had despatched from Bergen; receipts for six telegrams and two registered letters sent direct from Russia to Spain, a pass-book showing a credit of more than £2,000 and no withdrawals in an account which he had opened with a Russian bank in 1916; a number of addresses but no letters, for he had torn them all up.

Berges had no addresses; he had a letter of credit on the Credit Lyonnais for £1,000, of which he had withdrawn only 1,000 francs for a draft on Paris. Both men carried a quantity of picture postcards, mostly of Russia, and some of these had been marked. Guell carried aspirin tablets, potassium bromide and a box of brown powder labelled Protargol Berges had tincture of iodine and throat tablets. These materials were sent for testing but the final report of the expert on secret writing is not in this file.

In examination, Berges asserted that he had written the two wires signed with his name and despatched from the Grosvenor Hotel, while Guell admitted that all the three telegrams were in his own handwriting. Berges explained that he was by profession an actor and the director of the Teatro Novedadis, but that he wished to retire from the profession and devote his energies to business, and take a partnership in the firm of Antonio Guell, the father of Mario Guell. Both men asserted that Antonio Guell was a maker of artificial pearls, and that Mario Guell was travelling for it. Guell declared that his father's business had been carried on at 14 Calle San Beltrani, Barcelona, until August or September of 1916, when he moved to a place called Bardalino (or Badalona) two miles from Barcelona. Guell's account of the Florini letter was confirmed by Commandant Wallner who added the information that Guell's father, Antonio, carried on the manufacture of paper bags and tinfoil at 14 Calle San Beltrani, Barcelona, and that in September 1916 Mario Guell had moved to 36 Calle Badalona, a little house in which there was no trace of any industrial undertaking. There he passed as a commercial traveller. Although Commandant Wallner had never quite trusted Guell he was unable to formulate any definite charge against the man.

Orders were given to search the GPO for any telegrams that Guell might have despatched from England on his various visits to this country. Meanwhile, the Spanish ambassador was pressing for a definite charge to be brought against the prisoners. As no direct evidence of espionage was found and neutrals could not be interned on the mere ground of hostile sympathies, the suspects were released on 30 January 1917 and sent to Spain on 10 February, and instructions were issued for their arrest should they attempt to return. After they had left, the originals of the telegrams they had despatched from Russia arrived in England; they were not considered suspicious.

The Director of Naval Intelligence had demurred to Guell's release on the grounds that he was the agent of the suspect firm of Heusch. Subsequently the French Intelligence Service supplied the information that the firm of Heusch, manufacturers of artificial pearls, had sent Mario Guell to Russia in 1918 to buy fish scales for them. In 1916 they used him for the same purpose, but instructed him to act as though for his own account and as he was without money or credit Mario had his business paper and cards stamped with the name of his brother's firm, Antonio Guell y Soler. Thanks to the help of the Spanish consul in Russia, Guell had contrived to procure fish scales for Heusch and was engaged in effects to get permission for their export. The credits standing to Guell's account in Russia represented funds belonging to Heusch.

In October 1917 GHQ I(b) discovered that an inhabitant of the British Zone was corresponding with M. M. Guell and Cie, 14 Calle San Beltrani, Barcelona.

★

Alfred Hagn, a Norwegian, applied for leave to come to this country as representative to England of the *Dagblad* and the *Ukens Hevy* on 29 September 1916, four days after obtaining a passport at Christiania. He landed in England on 9 October and spent six weeks in London, leaving again for Norway on 19 November. His application for a permit was submitted to MI5 who knew nothing against him. Early in January he applied for leave to come again as correspondent for the *Dagblad* and perhaps a Bergen and Stockholm paper. He expressed the intention of staying for the duration of the war and gave the Norwegian legation as a reference. So swift a return being undesirable, Major Dansey issued instructions that, unless eminently satisfactory in examination at the port, Hagn should be allowed to land only on condition of signing an undertaking to remain in England during the war. Hagn signed the undertaking and landed at Hull on 11 April, came to London and put up at 39 Tavistock Square. On 21 April he applied at the Foreign Office for permission to visit the Front. Mr Carnegie of the Information Department of the Foreign Office, instituted enquiries about Hagn among trustworthy Scandinavian journalists. As none of them would vouch for Hagn or recommend him in any way. Mr Carnegie referred to MI5 which drew attention to Hagn's signed undertaking but raised no objection to leave being granted. Mr Carnegie then required a recommendation from the Norwegian legation; this was immediately forthcoming.

On 7 May a report was received from MI-1(c) that Alfred Hagn was a German agent, but as the source of their information, the Christiania police, must be kept secret, the matter would require delicate handling. In consultation with Scotland Yard it was agreed that casual observation would be unsuitable and after verifying Hagn's address, Melville was sent for a few days to 39 Tavistock Square. Further, the case was signalled to the GPO, MI8, MI9, to the Home Office, permit office, ports, and military permit office. Major Carter also communicated with Mr Carnegie to arrange that, in order not to arouse Hagn's suspicions, he should be allowed to participate in some trip for foreign journalists. Hagn, having run short of money, applied to his vice-consul for help. The vice-consul lent him £5, and wired on his behalf for money to be sent care of the consulate. This telegram was addressed Synnoeve, Braaten, Loerenskog Station. Instructions were given to the GPO to forward the telegram and not to stop any reply to it but to send a copy to MI5. The wire was despatched on 14 May. Meanwhile, Melville had made friends with Hagn at the hotel, had ascertained that the *Dagblad* had another correspondent in London, that Hagn did a good deal of writing in his bedroom, left the hotel at 11 a.m. returning in time for dinner. By going out with him, Mr Melville had managed to let him be seen by three members of the special staff and agents were watching to see whether he posted any letters.

On 12 May, Melville had scoured from a glass-stoppered bottle in Hagn's bedroom some white liquid which on being tested proved to be F, in MI9 nomenclature.

Upon this report Major Carter obtained the GPO's authorisation for a detective of MI5 to go to the nearest post office and open a letter-box; warning of the gravity of the case was sent to the Telegraphic and Postal Censor and to the GPO, and the Censor kept special watch for communications going to the *Dagblad* and for money orders coming to the Norwegian consulate. On 14 May a letter was intercepted purporting to have been written by Hagn's mother to her son on the 7th, and this was followed by a letter from 'Syrmoeve' acknowledging receipt of a letter and card from Hagn and summoning him back to Norway at once on account of his mother's illness. The rendezvous was at the Hotel Norge, Bergen.

On 16 May, Hagn was seen to post some letters; the box was cleared and a letter addressed to Fru Julie Hagn, c/o Herr W. Erikson, Simonsairk pr Loxevacg, Bergen, was found. On the following day he posted a roll of papers to the address of an English lady in Paris. Other intercepted letters dated 18 and 17 May respectively show that Hagn had written on arrival a postcard to Halsen and three letters subsequently to 'Synnoeve', and that an article of his writing had appeared in the *Bergenstldende* but that with the exception of the letter from his mother he had received no news from Norway. Letters for Halsen were addressed Fröken Pauline Hall, c/o Herr Madssen, Tergenfrlnaton 36, Christiania. Hagn's letters were tested for secret writing but none was developed; however on the letter to his mother a shred of cotton wool was found.

Other letters and articles written by Hagn were intercepted and tested without result. It was known that he had been to Hampton Court, near which there were munitions factories, with a man named Prederloeen, and that he had noticed the theft of some of his secret ink. As it was thought that he might he using some medium unknown to us it was considered dangerous to leave him at large any longer and he was arrested on 24 May.

Major Carter, who was present at the arrest and search, appended a note to his report to the effect that an officer of the department thoroughly conversant with the ways of spies should always attend at the search of a suspect's rooms. F ink was found in a bottle marked edinol dentlfloe; in a bottle labelled 'gargle'; on a ball-pointed pen and impregnated in a sponge; three canvass collars and a scarf. Cotton wool, the use of which Hagn was unable to explain, was also found in the room. Hagn explained that he had written only three articles since his arrival and that he was to be paid £8 an article; he had come over with £5, had received no money from Norway but had borrowed £5 from the Norwegian consul and £3 from Mr Prederloeen. He denied that he had used secret ink but it was made clear to him that the whole process was known and after removal in custody he made a written confession admitting that he had secret ink in his possession. Hagn was seen once more and from the two interrogations the following account of his life may be drawn up:

Hagn was born in 1882; his father died early and at the age of eight his mother took him to be educated in America. In 1895 they returned to Norway, and after further study there Hagn became a jeweller's engraver. Some years later Hagn took up painting and literature. He went three times to Paris to study art, he published a book and wrote articles and stories for the *Dagblad*. In 1910 he came to England for the purpose of journalism only and his articles on the state of England attracted the attention of the Germans and, after some resistance on his part, they engaged him to work for them. They gave him a certain sum out of which he spared all he could for his mother, but he was delayed in Norway and spent most of what he had reserved for the journey. The Germans refused further supplies until he had worked for them. The two Germans with whom he was in touch were known as Laven and Leifholt. Synnoeve Braston, to whom his letters were to be sent was said to be an innocent girl.

The questions on which the Germans required information were:

- Was the damage done by the Zeppelins really so slight and did the population take things as calmly as was reported?
- Did the Press Bureau keep a lot of information from the public?
- Was it likely there would be strikes?
- Was there a shortage of food owing to the submarines and was there any likelihood of food riots?
- Do the British carry troops in hospital ships? (Confirmation wanted) Time and day of the week of the arrival and departure of these ships.

The Director of Naval Intelligence and Foreign Office were informed of the question regarding hospital ships and the peculiar insistence of the Germans with regard to this point. It was thought possible that they received false reports on the subject from their agents who were known to accept pay but to remain hidden in Holland and Denmark instead of proceeding to England.

Hagn applied subsequently for another interview and confessed that he had used secret ink three times, that he was to write to two addresses and that his real mission was a naval one. Major Carter had grounds for thinking that Hagn was concealing more and that he was making an attempt to communicate with the Germans by letter in code. The usual search of telegrams was undertaken but no wires to Pauline Hall and Synnoeve Braaton were traced. Pauline Hall was said to be receiving letters from Germany and to be both a paying guest in the house of Madssen of the Nord Announcen bureau and a worker in his office.

Synnoeve Braaton was said first to be an innocent young girl, whose letters to Laven had been intercepted by the Norwegian police; afterwards it was stated that Braaton was an assumed name. Synnoeve's family name was Oedarkvist and her father was a baker. Fru Julie Hagn was not dangerously ill as alleged by Synnoeve.

News of Hagn's arrest was communicated to the Norwegian minister and to Norway. Thereupon British agents in Norway protested that the Christiania police had lodged information against Hagn only on condition that he would be sent back to Norway where his evidence was required against two Germans, one of whom, Lawen, was believed to be the head of German spies against England. MI5G replied that the information given by the Christiania police only confirmed the suspicions already ascertained by the British authorities and that Hagn could not be released.

Several articles belonging to Hagn were sent for re-testing without further result but it was noted that the bottle of potassium iodide contained the usual number of tabloids although according to German instructions their agents were to use it to develop letters sent to them. On 5 June sentence was passed in Norway on ten persons mostly connected with shipping for espionage on behalf of the Germans and four other persons were acquitted, and the names of Dr Filchener, a well-known explorer; Rusk, a German–American well known to MI5 and one of the originators of the bureau; Wesedt, a German agent actively engaged in Bergen was brought into prominent notice, as well as the cover-address used for their correspondence: Thomson Fabriker, A/B Goteburg.

An effort was made to procure from Norway any letters written by Hagn, but the Norwegian government had intercepted only one letter written by Hagn to Lawen and required this piece of evidence for production in the trial of Erik Lawen (or Laven) alias Frits Lavendal. Laven, like Hagn an artist, had been arrested at Bergen and a German named Harthern, correspondent to the *Frankfurter Zeitung* was implicated in the same case. On their part, the Norwegian government asked for particulars of the means used to develop Hagn's secret ink and for permission to interrogate Hagn on his connection with Harthern and Lawen. Neither request could be granted by the British and the Norwegians declined to give any further assistance in the trial of Hagn. After forty-five different tests, the Norwegians succeeded in developing messages about the movements of ships in Hagn's letters to Synnoeve Braaten. As these, presumably, were the identical letters which our own chemist had tested in vain and as Hagn carried materials for an ink already known to us, it is to be supposed that the Germans had discovered some additional means of rendering the ink difficult to develop. Lawen, who was implicated in the destruction of Norwegian shipping by bombs, was sentenced to eight years' imprisonment, Schwarz to four years and Yhorsen to eight years. Harthern had to leave Norway.

After the first trial in Norway, on 5 June, MI5G obtained evidence that the *Ukens Hevy*, to which Hagn had contributed articles, was run by an editor influenced by Harthern and that Hagn himself had been an object of suspicion to respectable Norwegian journalists ever since September 1916.

On 3 July, contrary to the usual practice, MI5G had decided to publish the news of Hagn's arrest on the grounds that it was already well known to many persons, and that the pending trials in Norway would infallibly lead to its publication there and the British press would have a grievance if the news appeared first in a neutral country. The summary of evidence was completed on 13 July and the trial took place on the 27 and 28 August. Hagn was charged under DRR 48, 18A, and 22A on four counts, of having committed a preparatory act in coming to England on 11 April, of having been in communication and of having attempted to communicate with a spy address, and of being in unlawful possession of a medium for secret writing. He was found guilty on all counts and sentenced to death. The sentence was confirmed.

The Norwegian minister petitioned for mercy on the grounds that there was medical evidence of Hagn's 'reduced mentality'. A statement as to Hagn's mental condition had been accepted by the court and considered before passing sentence; it was therefore decided that there were no military grounds for commuting the sentence, but for diplomatic reasons and as an act of friendship to the Norwegian government that the sentence should be commuted to one of imprisonment for life.

A notice of the sentence and its commutation was issued to the press on the grounds that it would act as a deterrent and a warning to other neutrals, that it was an act of mercy and the trial was well known in Norway. When the news was received from Norway that secret writing had been found in Hagn's letters, he seems to have been informed of the fact. In a written statement he confessed that after his return from England in November 1916 Harthern had introduced him to Lawen who with Leifholt engaged him as a German agent. This took place at Harthern's flat in the presence of Synnoeve Braaten. By implication, Hagn's first visit to England was innocent; it is worth noting however that when he left England in November 1916 his ship was delayed and he stayed perforce for a night or two in North Shields where he met a certain Pastor Steen, who knew everything there was to be known about the Tyne Docks and shipping. There is little doubt that Hagn was of unsound mentality inclining to religious mania.

Through an unfortunate slip, Hagn was deported from England on 19 September 1919 without previous consultation of MI5.

★

Leon Francois van der Goten, a Belgian diamond-cutter, fled from Belgium with his family in September 1914. The party went to Breda, where for a time Leon lived on his mother's savings and after March 1916 became a waiter at the Cavalry Barracks moving subsequently to the Café de Pool in Breda.

Together with J. Ven he endeavoured to establish a courier service for smuggling news out of Belgium on behalf of A. Plus of the British Intelligence Service; they also helped young Belgians and Frenchmen to escape to Holland and conducted them to the Belgian consulate at Breda receiving £4 for each person safely brought across. Van der Goten secured four plans of strategic points in Belgium, those he sold to Plus having previously made copies for his own future use. Dissatisfied with his remuneration van der Goten procured from Mr Gradon, Belgian consul at Rotterdam, an introduction to the Uranium Hotel which was the centre of the Allied Secret Services, and there offered the services of himself and Ven to the British. After an interval of sixteen days the offer was declined. It would appear that since January 1917 Theunissen of the French Secret Service had been keeping van der Goten under observation. While van der Goten was awaiting the result of his overtures to the British he quarrelled with Ven whose share of profits he had retained. As a result the Belgian consul refused to pay him some 200 francs owing for the latest batch of Belgian refugees. Then came the refusal of the British to employ him. In a rage van der Goten vowed that as soon as the Belgian consul paid him he would betray the Allied Services to the Germans. Theunissen learned of the quarrel with Ven and of the threat, reported it and thence forward took every step under direct instructions from his employers.

Through a second intervention of Mr Gradon, van der Goten, had, it would seem got in touch with a Mr Robinson of the British Service and had proposed and been commissioned to organise a service of information on the Belgian railways. Theunissen, who had wormed himself into van der Goten's confidence and become his partner, learned of the scheme and of van der Goten's intention to betray the Belgians taking part in it. He informed the French, and Robinson, who had never really trusted van der Goten, cast the man off.

Van der Goten then announced that the time had come to go over to the Germans and soon after he asked Theunissen to give to the Germans certain definite information against Belgian couriers. Theunissen then stated that the Germans were already in possession of the facts and that he himself was a German agent, whereupon van der Goten said they would share the profits. Finally, at van der Goten's request, Theunissen undertook to introduce him to a German Secret Service agent. An agent of the French Service named Gremling, who spoke German well, was put up to play the part under the alias Lieutenant Kriohel. At the meeting van der Goten produced a plan of the flying camp at St Denys, Belgium, stating that it was the copy of an original which he had obtained from a courier working for the British; he gave other information and accepted six weeks, pay and a season ticket for a month usable on the Dutch railways in order that he might visit the various British agents. A trap was laid for him by the Ukranian Bureau into which he fell. Between 6 and 18 May he sent in four reports giving correct information about the Allied Services. Having found out all van der Goten knew and seeing that he was dangerous, the French determined to get him out of Holland. Greed was his dominating passion and he hated the British. By playing on these motives he was induced to ask for work in England. After some apparent demur Krichel accepted him to go to England as a courier on condition the first journey was made with Theunissen. Van de Goten then went to the Ukrainian Bureau with a vague report that German agents were going to England; he was told to find out more. A passport and British visa were secured and once safely on board the *Kirktiam Abbey*, van de Goten was told that he was to go to Folkestone and collect German reports about a possible German bombardment of the British coast. Van de Goten accepted the mission but afterwards took fright and wished to leave the vessel; Theunissen reassured him.

The two men were arrested at Hull and sent up to London van der Goten was interrogated at Scotland Yard and asked to see a British Secret Service official. He had recourse to the usual excuses namely, that he had come to unearth and traduce a nest of spies In England.

According to English law, van der Goten could not be tried for any offence committed in Holland; there remained the fact that on the boat he had accepted a definite mission for a person whom he believed to be a German agent.

Through the courtesy of the French Intelligence Service, Gremling and Theunissen were brought over to give evidence at the seminary of evidence taken on 10 and 11 September and also at the court martial which was held on 24 September. The exhibits included the four reports which van der Goten had furnished during May and the interrogation of 18 June, the passport showing that he had come over as a railway official and a piece of paper giving the approximate size of the plan which van der Goten had shown to Krichel. The Belgian Auditeur-General was represented at the trial.

Van der Goten was tried under DRR 48 and found guilty of committing an act preparatory to a contravention of DRR 16 with intent to assist the enemy. He was sentenced to be shot but at the prayer of the Belgian government the sentence was commuted to life imprisonment.

Van der Goten's wife cast him off and eventually went to live with Theunissen. This circumstance, possibly coupled with van der Goten's reiterated appeals for justice, induced the Belgian government to take up his case and ask that he should be handed over to the Belgian military on the grounds that the sentence inflicted was somewhat severe and put out of date by the ending of hostilities. It was decided that the Army Council had no power to hand over the prisoner but only to remit the remainder of the sentence. The Belgian minister therefore appealed for this act of clemency but the Army Council considered the crime committed by van de Goten to be a particularly heinous form of espionage and that a remission of the sentence was not only in itself undesirable but impolitic as it would be used as a precedent and encourage the making of other appeals on behalf of other criminals.

★

Jose do Patrocinio, journalist, was the son of a Brazilian journalist who had achieved fame by procuring the abolition of slavery in Brazil and had also evidenced sympathy for Great Britain during the Boer War. In 1912 when at Santos, Jose do Patrocinio made the acquaintance of a French dressmaker named Josephine Antoinette Conqui, and she became his mistress. The couple came to France in 1913 and lived in Paris and at Nice. In 1914 Patrocinio was given a post in the Brazilian consulate at Antwerp, where he acted chiefly as courier, Conqui returned to Nice. In September he was sent to Liege to pick up Brazilian subjects, and subsequently carried official documents between Le Havre and The Hague via Southampton. He returned to Brazil early in 1915 and was subsequently posted to Amsterdam, where Conqui joined him on 19 July. In 1917 the Brazilian government reduced the pay of all its officials and Patrocinio's was reduced to £10.7s.9d a month. Finding it difficult to live he applied repeatedly for an increase of pay or for funds to enable him to return to Brazil.

Patrocinio was in debt for some £60. At the end of July he applied to the Brazilian minister for passports for himself and Conqui with a view to going home. The minister, who had wired asking that Patrocinio's salary should be raised, urged him to wait some months but could give no guarantee of a rise of pay. Patrocinio determined to go home and proposed to travel via England and France where he intended to marry Miss Conqui. The event brought to light Patrocinio's real motive for the journey. Through the introduction of a pro-German Brazilian journalist, Patrocinio had known a certain Loebel intimately since 1916. Loebel, hearing of his straits, suggested there was an easy way of making money and introduced him to a German agent named Ben Levy. Levy offered Patrocinio first £1,000 to procure for him a false Brazilian passport and afterwards, shifting his ground, he engaged Patrocinio to go to England and France to ascertain when the next military offensive would take place. Patrocinio was instructed by Loebel in the use of secret ink, was given a long list of addresses in various countries to which to send his reports and one address at Frankfurt-am-Main. He was to spend six or seven weeks in France, to collect there military information only, and then to go to Switzerland and to write thence to Frankfurt for his pay.

On embarking at Rotterdam, Patrocinio and Conqui were seen by two witnesses taking affectionate leave of a suspect Belgian named Francois Albert Hertogs. They were thrown into utter confusion by a young Frenchwoman who innocently asked them whether they knew one Ben Levy; Patrocinio lost his head and mentioned Ben Levy to Roels, a Belgian courier, who already suspected him, and Roels then forced Patrocinio to confess.

After warning the captain of the vessel to look after Patrocinio, Roels went ashore and laid the information with the British vice-consul. In the evening he made Patrocinio write a signed statement concerning the affair with Levy and Loebol. Patrocinio then sought protection in apparent frankness and the usual story that he had accepted the mission in order to inform the British authorities and protect other young men.

When he landed at Gravesend he made a voluntary statement to the port officer but this declaration differed in some particulars from the written statement made under pressure from Roels. Meanwhile the British consulate had sent over a précis of the information lodged by Roels, and of a report from a Russian source that Patrocinio had received 1,000 francs on presenting his visa'd passport and 3,000 francs on embarking. It was supposed that Hertogs had brought him the money.

At the port 299 francs was found on him and Conqui. Patrocinio explained that this sum represented his savings which did not tally with the reason he had put forward for his journey to Brazil. Also, there was found among his papers a passport issued at Berlin in 1918 to a Brazilian journalist named Avila. This Avila had arrived in Holland from Brazil on 30 July 1916 in order to attend a prize court in connection with consignments of coffee made by La Companie Nacionale de Café de Santos to Malmo and Stockholm. Avila had landed at Gravesend on 21 September 1916 saying he had lost his papers in Holland. He had denied that he had visited Germany but was unable to explain satisfactorily how he had spent the interval between 30 July and 21 September. Subsequent search of Avila's effects had resulted in the discovery of a telegram from Johann Serte sent in Holland of La Companie Nacionale. The telegram referred to a remittance of £60 and a payment made to Patrocinio. Avila, who was reported to have carried documents for the Germans in a mirror, was allowed to go to New York with a no return permit. He turned up at Zurich in March 1917.

Patrocinio was interrogated as to his possession of Avila's passport and the meaning of this telegram. He explained that it referred to a payment he had received for acting as interpreter to Avila; with regard to the passport, he could give no satisfactory explanation of having it in his possession. With regard to the Belgian Hertogs, Patrocinio stated he had met the man only the day before embarking at Rotterdam and Conqui admitted knowing Hertogs the man, but denied that she knew his name. Enquiry however showed that from 21 to 31 August Patrocinio had frequented Hertogs' company in Coomans Hotel, and Hertogs was reported to have said that he knew Conqui was a German spy. Hertogs was the son of a coffee planter, domiciled at Antwerp but resident in America during the war; Hertogs had remained at Antwerp during the German occupation and had escaped into Holland on about 30 August 1917. Enquiry made by the Belgian Secret Service elicited no proof that the man was a German agent but certain facts showing that he had had suspicious dealings with German officers.

Besides Loebel and Levy, Patrocinio had admitted to the Belgians that he had been on friendly terms with a German agent named Lieber (possibly a figment of his brain) and with Delaraye, a Brazilian engaged in illicit trading in rubber.

Patrocinio had also stated that he had left collars etc. impregnated with secret ink and his list of spy addresses in Coomans Hotel, but no trace was found of them. On the other hand, Tinsley succeeded in procuring a mass of correspondence which Patrocinio had left behind in his rooms at Amsterdam. This showed that with the connivance of the Brazilian consulate in Amsterdam and of the Brazilian legation in Berlin he had acted at one time as intermediary for correspondence passing between Berlin and Brazil, and had probably employed stewards of one of the Dutch liners to carry the letters. Besides, it established his contact with many suspects of whom the most interesting are the following: Suzanne van Damme, a known German agent, of van Gelder & Son, Bingel 230, who supplied him with funds, and Eugen Nobel, an American consul, had been in close touch with Charles Hastings. Subsequently Tinsley discovered that Felix V. Versaille a suspect, Frederick Lambertus Falck, suspect; Maringer, a well-known German agent of many years' standing; and Madame Schory, daughter of Aime Moll interned in England, and herself a deportee of July 1916, had all been in touch with Patrocinio.

The fact that the man was in debt, which he strenuously denied, was also proved. Patrocinio had been interrogated on 7 and 10 September and on the 11th he was confronted with Mr Roels. He was again interrogated on 10 October. His statements varied in some particulars but the fact remained that he had admitted the spy connection voluntarily, and that the only evidence showing that he might have intended to use secret ink were three ball-pointed pens found in a lacquer case. One of these had been used but the test did not reveal the presence of secret ink. There remained only a letter from Suzanne van Damme from which it was dear that he both knew her and made appointments to meet her. Regarding this woman it would seem that there was no clear evidence that she had ever received spy letters from England.

Lieutenant Henry Curtis-Bennett was instructed to prepare a case against Patrocinio under regulations 18, 48 and 18A. Sir Archibald Bodkin then wrote that these regulations applied only to offences committed in England or 'perhaps on board British ships on the high seas' and that even 'preparatory' acts, acts 'not sufficiently proximate to the substantive offence as to amount in law to an attempt to commit such offence,' committed abroad were chargeable here only in so far as they were relevant to and explanatory of actions committed in this country.

In point of fact Patrocinio had committed no offence in any place within British jurisdiction, and there was no evidence that he had come over with intent to spy. Even the possession of Suzanne van Damme's address was not incriminating since he had made no attempt while in England to communicate with her. Moreover, it was a question whether van Damme was a spy within the definition of DRR 18A, since her activities were confined to countries other than Great Britain.

In addition, the circumstances in which the address was found gave no reasonable ground for suspecting Patrocinio of communication or attempted communication with a spy.

Sir Archibald Bodkin pointed out that the regulation required simplification so as to include as offenders persons who before their arrival in this country had been visiting or in communication with an enemy agent abroad unless they could prove that they came to this country on legitimate business and did not know or suspect that the agent was a spy. He suggested also an enlargement of the definition of spy to include a person reasonably suspected of acting as an enemy agent, thus abolishing the need for proving actual or attempted communications. Legal action was taken in the sense indicated. Patrocinio was recommended for internment under DRR 14B on the grounds of his hostile associations and of the suspicion that he was a German agent; the order was made on 29 November.

Repeated attempts to procure his release or transfer to the Brazilian authorities broke down the first time on the opposition of MI5 and the second time presumably on that of the Foreign Office. Patrocinio had appealed to the Advisory Court which decided that if the Foreign Office saw fit, on grounds of policy, he should be sent back to Brazil provided the Brazilian minister would pay for his journey and undertake that he should stay in Brazil till the end of the war, and that until such arrangements were made Patrocinio should remain in custody. A deportation order was served on Patrocinio on 23 January 1919.

Conqui, about whom there was considerable doubt and who was too stupid to be dangerous, had been released on 16 September 1917 and had left for Brazil with a no return permit on 23 February 1918.

After the case of Patrocinio, an undoubted enemy agent against whom no offence could be charged, DRR 18A was redrafted so as to include as an offence, communication with an enemy agent within or without the United Kingdom; previous to coming to this Kingdom; the definitions of 'communication' and 'address' were enlarged to cover activities and places within and without the United Kingdom, and the definition of 'spy' was altered so the expression 'enemy agent' would include any person who is, or has been, or is reasonably suspected of being or having been employed by the enemy either directly or indirectly for the purpose of committing an act either within or without the United Kingdom which if done within the United Kingdom would be a contravention of these regulations, or who has, or is reasonably suspected of having, either within or without the United Kingdom, committed or attempted to commit such an act with the intention of assisting the enemy.

★

Mrs Luise Mathilde Smith, nee von Zastrow, was born at Nieder Heidesdorf Schleslen, Germany in 1867. She went to live on the Riviera in 1896 and later on moved to Venlo where she kept a house described varyingly as a boarding-house and a charitable institution. Once also she mentioned having a boarding-house at Lugano. She returned only once to Germany and that was on the occasion on her father's death in 1913. In February 1915, Luise von Zastrow married Dr John Henry Smith at the British consulate.

Dr Smith was a photographic chemist, a man of parts and highly respected by those who knew him, a native of Kirkcaldy, Fifeshire, who had been educated at the Dublin College of Science and then at Zurich where he graduated as a Doctor of Philosophy. He worked on chemical research in Milan, and at Gateshead married a Swiss lady in 1886 and a year or two later returned to Switzerland for his health. Driven out of business by German competition he moved to Paris in 1907. He is stated to have remained there until the outbreak of war, when his business closed down. Dr Smith's first wife died in 1908. Of their large family three daughters played some part in the second Mrs Smith's story. Kelly, an imbecile, who was in an institute at Lausanne; Clara, who was in a situation at Zurich; Florrie, aged twenty-three, who for four years had earned her living in Spain, first as a companion in the south, and then in a German firm in Barcelona. Clara and Florrie were born in Switzerland, their native language was German. In marrying Dr Smith, Luise von Zastrow displeased her family; the marriage however was a happy one. She never regretted it and there is evidence to show that up to the time of her sentence she was on good terms with Florrie and even after continued to do her duty by the sick daughter, and was treated with affection by Clara.

After the outbreak of war, Mrs Smith and her husband were reported to have stayed at Venice until Italy joined the Allies. Then they moved to Switzerland and returned to England in October 1916, leaving some trunks and furniture at Lausanne. They settled for a time at Romiley in Cheshire and later on moved to Manchester where Dr Smith occupied some small post as a lecturer and research worker.

On her arrival in England, Mrs Smith's German origin was reported to the Chief Constable of Cheshire, who verified her passport, directed that observation should be kept upon her and informed MI5. The address was put on check. An intercepted letter from Florrie Smith at Barcelona caused the branch to procure further particulars about the family and later on it was known that Mrs Smith and her mother were corresponding through the intermediary of a lady at Neuchâtel, Switzerland. Various harmless letters passed and as the police observation brought no result; the check was cancelled in May 1916. The following year Florrie Smith returned from Barcelona to take up war work and be with her father. The port officer drew attention to the fact that she spoke English and French imperfectly and had corresponded for years with her father in German.

She applied for a post in the Cheshire Censorship and MI5 supplied the few particulars known to them about the girl. It does not appear that she obtained her post but later on she was at work for the War Office in London and filled the duties of a typist and translator of Spanish.

Letters of March, May and August from the Chief Censor at Cape Town showed that Mrs Smith had attempted to smuggle cuttings of pro-German Swiss newspapers excluded from South Africa to von Zastrow at Grootfontein. The cuttings were concealed in parcels of tea and calico, and in balls of fancy cotton and worsted. The first two letters arrived in June when the existing legislation had made no provision for dealing with such cases, but Mrs Smith's correspondence was put on check.

But by July 1917 regulations 24, 24A and 24B had been to a great extent redrafted and these were issued in their new form on 17 July. Under DRR 4E (3) it was made an offence to transmit through the post any written or printed matter by any indirect route or method involving evasion of the censorship. Mrs Smith despatched the third parcel on 20 July; notice of its despatch was received by MI5G on 30 September. The bureau, having ascertained that Mrs Smith had contravened the order decided on prosecution and consulted the Censor as to procedure. As however it was the first offence brought to notice under the new regulation, the Censor could give no help, but acting on the order of the DSI wrote to Mrs Smith warning her that she had committed an offence. Mrs Smith received this letter and composed one in return inquiring what the nature of her offense might be but this she did not post. The letter was afterwards found among her effects.

While action against her under DRR 24B was being considered a letter which she wrote to her mother from Hampstead on 6 October was submitted to the bureau. The context, which was in a simple arbitrary code about fishing and pheasant shooting, showed clearly that it was written in answer to a question put by 'Hildchen' as to the results of the U-boats and airship campaign. Mrs Smith expressed the view that the Germans must not expect too much of the submarines, a certain number of ships were sunk but the ships were cleverly handled and people were restraining their appetite. Still, the results of the campaign were beginning to make themselves more felt and many more boats were at work than earlier in the year. As for the Zeppelins, the losses were greater than the results and the campaign made bad blood needlessly but the U-boats she wished every success. Hampstead was not worth a visit.

Later Mrs Smith wrote describing the aerodrome at Hendon; she said that she had fulfilled Hildegard's wish and hoped soon to find to find a situation at the seaside. With this letter an obscure card to 'Rita' was enclosed.

Other letters showed that Mrs Smith had a hope of getting her marriage declared illegal, recovering her German nationality and returning to Germany, but she was in close touch with her step-daughters. The police interviewed her and perhaps from loyalty to Florrie and Clara, Mrs Smith mentioned only the imbecile, Nelly. Dr Smith had died in March 1917, and after spending some weeks in hospital, Mrs Smith had stayed six to eight weeks at Blackpool, then four weeks at Manchester and early in August had come to Hampstead. As she did not wish to touch her capital invested abroad, she was earning her living as a cook. She was somewhat embarrassed in answering questions about the letters.

Arrangements were made to interrogate Mrs Smith at Scotland Yard. She came on 17 August and admitted the code in the letters but declared that her intention was to discourage the Germans. She also admitted having sent the parcels to South Africa. She was arrested on suspicion of having conveyed information to the enemy. Her papers contained a number of addresses mostly on the coasts and evidence of her pro-German sympathies, also a letter dated 9 September 1917 signed Hildegard and asking for her opinion on the fish-breeding in which Werner was so deeply interested. While in prison, Mrs Smith wrote to Manchester to a solicitor named John Crofton, asking him to act for her; he refused and at the same time informed the authorities that she had been in his service as cook in July and early August, and during that time had asked him about birds and sport.

The bureau suggested, and Sir Archibald concurred, that on the evidence afforded by the parcels and letters, charges could be framed against Luise Smith under DRR 24B, 18 and 48.

As a British subject she would have the right to claim trial in the civil court and this would have necessitated obtaining the consent of the Attorney-General. In order to simplify proceedings, and as the case at first sight did not appear very grave, there were some questions as to whether it might not be dealt with in a summary court. The summary court could inflict merely a penalty of six months' imprisonment, or a fine, or imprisonment coupled with a fine. The competent military authority of London decided that a summary court was not adequate to try the case.

The original parcels which had to be produced in evidence arrived on 3 January, by and on 10 January; Mrs Smith was served with a generally worded notice of the charges which would be preferred against her, and at the same time with a notice that she could claim to be tried in the civil court. She signed her claim on 12 January. Following the usual practice in these spy cases, the bureau arranged to take a summary of evidence as though the case were to be tried by court martial. This no doubt enabled the branch to keep a firmer hold on the preparation of the case. While in prison, Mrs Smith admitted to C. Gallagher that she had communicated with her brother Werner, captain of a submarine stationed at Kiel, through Madame Pasquier; also that she had visited Rhyl while troops were in training there; Colwyn Bay, Cornwall, Devon and Bournemouth; also that she had conveyed news to Switzerland concealed in her husband's clothes and that the parcels were sent to her brother at Grootfontein. She also stated that her youngest step-daughter, Florrie, was a Spanish translator at the War Office. It would also appear that at some time a message had been sent to her by submarine. Reference to a German peerage showed that Mrs Smith was related to Werner von Zastrow, her brother, married to a Countess Moltke; Max Rudolf von Zastrow, brother, staff officer in the German Army; Mathilde Asta, sister, wife of Count Alfred Eugen Bethusy Hue, imperial vice-consul at Copenhagen; Hildegard, wife of Hans Bareuther-Nitze, a civil servant in Saxony. Her family had been well-known to King Edward.

Intercepted letters showed that Smith would continue her foreign correspondence through Clara Smith and even possibly extend it. She had in Lugano a great friend, named Baroness Blum, who it was thought might be the wife of Baron Blum, the German agent. To the original indictment, further graver charges were added and it was decided to try the case in camera.

On 4 March, Smith was sentenced to ten years' imprisonment. Florrie Smith then treated her step-mother with coldness and pretended to have been driven from home by her, which was untrue. Clara, on the other hand, kept up friendly communications with Luise Smith through Florrie. On 7 March she sent a message to the effect that 200 francs had been received for Kelly. Florrie thereupon wrote 'to open her sister's eyes' Madame Pasquier also wrote to Florrie Smith, saying she knew where Mrs Smith was housed and was not surprised. While in prison,

Mrs Smith declared that she had a brother named Werner, a captain of a submarine stationed at Kiel, and that she wrote to a brother in South Africa.

In May Axel Damn, a Danish advocate, cabled to ask about the charges on which Luise Smith had been committed and the length of the sentence, and he offered every help 'whether legal or economic'. Other attempts to elicit information about the case came from Weuchatel, Germany and an Enquiry Bureau in Berlin.

★

In reviewing the foregoing account of German centres in Holland and the spy cases of 1917 from the point of view of MI5, it is evident that British counter-espionage had broken the German military and naval organisation. During 1917, the consequence of the revelations in New York made themselves felt; in Norway also a great spy centre was destroyed. On the other hand, the weight of the German attack was transferred to attacks upon the political and social fabric of the British Empire. Peace, propaganda, strikes, addition and revolution take the first place in their effort.

Those spies who were caught by MI5 appear to be isolated individuals, except where they travel in couples. The cases however are of great interest from the legal point of view. Towards the end of December, the case of a Belgian deserter travelling under a false name and smuggling rubber for the German Bureau at Antwerp, caused a reconsideration of DRR 18A. The man admitted part of his connection with the Germans, but stated truly that he had furnished reports to the Belgians concerning his dealings with the Antwerp Bureau. The experience of MI5 showed that communication of information by word of mouth was on the increase; the Germans had always made use of reporters on board ships, and after the discovery of their latent secret writing, when it became too dangerous to use that method, spies were sent out carrying addresses and instructions in their heads, and returned similarly without recording a syllable of the information they had acquired. There was no provision to meet this state of affairs, therefore DRR 18A was redrafted so as to make it an offence to visit the address of or to consort with a spy under suspicious circumstances.

A further difficulty arose in the case of Patrocinio who, after accepting a mission against this country, changed his mind, confessed on board ship to a Belgian agent, and was arrested on landing. The only wrong he had committed had taken place outside British jurisdiction, which made it difficult to bring charges under DRR 18, 18A and 48. Moreover, amplification of proof was required in cases where persons were sent over to collect information and transmit it by word of mouth, DRR 1BA was therefore amended so as to include as an offence certain actions that had taken place outside the United Kingdom in its altered form the alteration runs.

For the purposes of this regulation but without prejudice to the generality of the foregoing provision:

> 1(a) A person shall unless he proves the contrary be deemed to have been in communication with an enemy agent if (i) he has either within or without the United Kingdom visited the address of an enemy agent or consorted with an enemy agent, or (ii) either within or without the United Kingdom the name or address or any other information regarding an enemy agent has been found in his possession or has been supplied by him to any other person or has been obtained by him from any other person.

The remaining clauses were altered in the same sense, and address was made to Luise von Zastrow's case too is interesting as furnishing an illustration of certain gaps in the defence against evasion of the Censorship, and the flooding of this Kingdom with peace and other propaganda.

Details of defence worth mentioning are the value of getting a signed declaration that a man will not desire or attempt to leave the country; if the man breaks that pledge, there is presumptive evidence against him.

From the counter-espionage point of view it is worth noting that a legation recommendation is procured somewhat easily and affords but little guarantee of character. Also that as soon as the Christiania police began to move, the Germans tried to recall their spy, Alfred Hagn.

★

In 1916 to 1917 the German centres of espionage directed against England and France were summed up by the French Intelligence Service:

1.  The Antwerp Bureau collects and co-ordinates the work of the agents recruited in occupied territory and intended to operate in France and England. In Holland it also recruited agents for maritime espionage for the naval base at Zeebrugge and also in exceptional cases, when the opportunity offers but without in any way seeking it, to act the part of spies in Allied countries.
2.  The Sammelstelle Nord at Wesel and its offshoot at Dusseldorf, with the help of the Kommandatur at Cologne, co-ordinates espionage against Holland, France and England, with the help of mobile agents recruited in the Netherlands. It also sends spies to Italy and finally undertakes the collecting of maritime news.
3.  Above these two organisations there is a directing authority whose headquarters is at Berlin, at least for purely military questions, and thither intelligent agents are sent at the end of their course of training.

At this time, Antwerp was said to be recruiting principally natives of occupied territories and taking care to compromise them up to the hilt before sending them to the Allied countries. Such persons were recruited by the police at Brussels which kept touch with the bureau at Antwerp and Villa Arcadia in Scheveningen. Agents for sea espionage in the Dutch ports were recruited on the spot. The German consulate at Amsterdam sent out two couriers daily, who exchanged papers with persons belonging to the German legation, and then went on to Koosendaal by train, and thence by motor to Antwerp.

The Wesel branch directed its activity against Holland and England mainly. It had sub-offices at Cologne, Munster and Dusseldorf. Its activities included sea espionage on ships leaving the Dutch ports and the corruption of Dutch officials in the army, police and on the staff of various ministers. The agents were denoted by the letter 'L' followed by a number of thee figures. Its recruits were sent to Dusseldorf for training. The work in Holland was under the direction of Paul Daelen, ex-captain of the Hamburg-Amerika line, living at Stadhouderstraat, Amsterdam, a very active individual. Connection between Wesel and the German counter-espionage service in Holland was maintained by Dr Hagn who had an office at Villa Arcadia, 106 Badhuisweg, Scheveningen. Reports coming from Rotterdam were carried through to Wesel via Cleves, by a woman; other reports were collected at Arnhem. Pressing information collected by Dutch marine officers in German pay was telegraphed to the railway station on the Elk frontier and telephoned on to Wesel. Vollrath, arrested at Rotterdam in 1916, had permission to telephone direct to Wesel night and day, on the grounds that he was a correspondent of the *Hamburger Fremdanblatt*.

Active work in Holland was conducted from offices in the German legation itself and in June 1917 from passport inspection offices of the German legation established at 106 Badhuisweg, Scheveningen, where von Behr was then head of the counter-espionage section.

The Berlin branch exercised control at Antwerp and Wesel. It trained Wesel recruits and awarded special recompense to Antwerp agents. Captain Bodenheimer was at the head of the service at 37 Grollmannstrasse in Berlin, where agents were trained. He had a delegate, Lieutenant Wouter at The Hague who received the reports of women agents when they returned to Holland.

It was the Villa Arcadia which seems to have supplanted the Antwerp Bureau to a great extent. In May, Frans Schmidt, first secretary of legation at The Hague, and Gleichmann, were working for this office and Schmidt was recruiting spies to act against England, France and Russia. Tinsley wrote from Holland that Schmidt was most anxious to get men over to England and that at least twelve had passed through his hands recently. He was most anxious to keep in touch with these men and to pump them but MI5G refused to send information to be transmitted to men whom they had never seen. At that time, the Germans had very few men in England.

Schmidt was wanting especially news about the political situation and the food supply in England, and to guide him on these points he asked for cuttings from obscure provincial newspapers. The reports and cuttings were to be conveyed across by a sailor as the English were on the watch for secret ink, and they were to be delivered by hand at 13 Snellinkstraat at a price of 100 marks per letter.

There was besides an important centre in the Warmoestraat, Amsterdam. One of its sections was under the direction of a Boer, L. van Ryn, a British subject who had repeatedly tried to get in touch with the Admiralty. He posed as head of the passport office of the German legation but his real task was to control the counter-espionage service and watch the commercial relations of England, Holland and France. He travelled frequently in Germany and employed his nephew, Eskens, to collect information for him. Eskens also kept touch with Max Josephson.

Max Josephson, designated A-87, was a German reserve officer who, since November 1915, had been suspected of recruiting spies destined for England. He recruited and trained spies in Holland. In July 1917 he was said to have an office, full of British shipping journals and statistics, of ship-building in England. He was said to photograph the documents which were required in a hurry.

Johann Jacobus Verbrugge, formerly a pilot in England who afterwards worked at Antwerp and Flushing, was employed to collect reports from officers and seamen of Dutch ships and received letters under his wife's maiden name. Between 16 December 1916 and 22 January 1917 a number of commercial letters and wires addressed to Verbrugge were submitted to the bureau but only one or two coming from a suspected person were stopped. Instructions issued to the German Intelligence Service in Scandinavia state that the only method by which reliable information can be obtained is by means of persons travelling from enemy countries on enemy or neutral ships arriving in Scandinavia. Knowledge of minefields, mine-free channels, the waters where sea marks have been allowed lo required for U-boats operating enemy waters. Through shipping alone can knowledge be obtained of the enemy guard service for the protection of their shores and commercial routes.

The personnel of merchant ships and especially the captain, to whom more liberty of action is accorded in an enemy country than to others, are the most valuable givers of information. Next come the mates, and lastly, stokers, freight-agents and provision agents. Five hundred kroner a month is paid to captains and mates of enemy merchantmen, 300 to the same class of officer on neutral passenger ships to England, 100–110 kroner to mates on neutral merchantmen trading uninterruptedly in English and French ports, or else 25 to 50 kronor for every piece of news. Fifty kroner a month was the lowest rate of pay to the humbler members of a ship's crew.

Information inaccessible to seamen but of great importance was obtained through pumping travellers returning from enemy countries. Harmless conversation with educated travellers was invaluable in this respect. Personal relations with representatives of the neutral press also gave excellent results.

The above recommendations form an instructive commentary on the evidence afforded by the Antwerp roll of spies and by the American journalists' affair. But even more interesting from the point of view of counter-espionage is the following:

> Reliable persons were needed to go to enemy countries on special intelligence missions, and of these the best were educated persons who had already travelled abroad for their firms. All agents sent to the enemy countries were of course obliged to do real business and it was desirable that the neutral firms who were willing to engage 'our commercial representation' should be informed of the principal motive for his trip. In selecting a firm thus willing, the point to observe was that the sending of such a commercial representative should appear natural. Agents should be able to justify a prolonged stay in the country. Waiters, barbers, nurses, metal-workers for shipyards and munitions factories were the classes of agent most required for work in England. Intelligent women were in urgent request for experience

showed that where men were suspected a woman would arouse little
suspicion. The great danger for all such agents was the transmission of
news, but German chemical science had reduced that to a minimum
and chemical means had been developed to arouse no suspicion.

It is worth noting that most of the information contained in this authentic
document was already known to MI5 by deduction from the evidence
supplied by the cases, or from notices sent in by MI-1(c).

At the end of the summary for 1916 mention was made of certain
measures taken to detect the payments made to spies through the banks.
Other measures were mentioned in the first half of this report (1917). A
fourth check on incoming remittances was added in 1917.

Early in 1917 it was suspected that agents were being paid from America
and the Censor was asked to keep special watch on sums coming from
American sources. The following month the Censor was asked to note
advices of any remittances of £50 and upwards which might occur in the
correspondence of neutral banks with their agents here. At that time some
system of forwarding money to persons here through the German consul at
Rotterdam seems to have been discovered by Tinsley. The Censor sent in
his lists and G2 prosecuted enquiries about the recipients, through the police
when the remittance was made directly by post to the individual concerned,
through the Bankers' Clearing House when it was paid through a bank.

The lower and higher limits of the sums on which particulars were
asked for were £9 (afterwards lowered to £5) to £160.

In July 1917 the Censor protested against the practice of the American
Express Company which forwarded lists of PoWs receiving remittances
from abroad and placed on the same lists the names of uninterned
persons, also in receipt of regular payments, so as to make them appear
to be PoWs. The Censor proposed that all incoming remittances to
persons other than enemy subjects should also be referred for enquiry.
Accordingly, in February 1918, the Censor was asked to send in weekly
returns of all remittances of £10 and upwards for which no satisfactory
reason or an unsatisfactory reason had been given.

Shortly after, the bureau rejected proposals for controlling by legislation remittances from enemy countries to uninterned aliens here on the grounds that the evidence pointed to there being few enemy agents in receipt of pay from abroad and that the proposals made were unworkable.

Meanwhile, since December 1917, a retrospective investigation of cases of remittances made from August 1914 onwards had been in progress without much result. Many of the recipients could not be traced, others seem to have come here on flimsy pretexts and for suspiciously short intervals and the drawback was specially noted that, in the early days of the war, letters could be kept at the post office and handed over the counter to the person who might call for them without his being required to give his address.

As regards the investigations made on the statistics supplied by the Deutsche Bank, Major Anson stated that they had merely resulted in the compilation of useful records, and that so far as he recollected, no case had been brought to light of money having been sent for improper purposes.

It was agreed that remittances to enemy agents would hardly be made through German banks and the tracing of agents through remittances from hostile countries via neutral banks was impossible; nevertheless, when definite suspicion existed against an individual it was of interest to know that payment had been made. Therefore this class of remittance was to be treated as a money order, and the names of the recipients of £10 and upwards to £100 were to be carded on the same index. This index was kept by G3(b). In a memorandum on the payment of German agents drawn up in October 1918, when the possible use of British notes was being considered, the following instances are given of how some of these payments were camouflaged:

– A Dutch workman in munitions received irregular payments of £8 to £15, the pretext being that they were the product of a legacy from an aunt.
– A traveller for a commercial house received £150 a month which was paid into a bank in Holland. He was informed of such payments

by his father who referred to them as business connected with the coal trade. Occasionally the father drew money from the account and telegraphed it over to a bank in London.

–   An agent received his salary in payments of irregular amounts made to the Zurich branch of a Swiss Bank. The head office of the bank would send notice of such payments having been made by Mr So-and-So of Zurich. The agent would draw a cheque and give it to a relation living in France: this man would cross the frontier to Switzerland, cash the cheque, and forward the proceeds in Swiss notes.

In each case an intermediary was involved and the system was so complicated that tracking through mere records was impossible. Nevertheless, as a preventive, the checking of such records had great value.

★

Many times the head of G Branch had called attention to the difficulty in dealing adequately with undesirables who could not be convicted of hostile origin or association. In April a new regulation was issued empowering the Admiralty, Army Council or Minister of Munitions to make rules for securing and preserving order and good behaviour in areas where bodies of HM Forces were located or munitions being manufactured. Under the regulation, persons convicted of any contravention of DRR etc. could be prohibited from residing or remaining in or entering such areas. Another regulation was drafted giving power to close premises altogether or impose restrictions on the use of premises suspected of being used for purposes prejudicial to the safety of the United Kingdom by persons of hostile origin or association or by fomenters of disaffection etc. among the troops and the civilian population.

In May it was known that the Germans were making great efforts to obtain information about the sailings of ships to and from this country. MI5 got the Home Office to send a circular to the Chief Constables calling for special watchfulness on the part of the police with regard to unauthorised persons who might be watching the movements of ships or making enquiries on that topic. A warning also issued as to the use of a special incendiary bomb made to look like a brand of corned beef.

In October 1917 it was known that the Russians were issuing diplomatic passports to unsuitable persons and it was suggested that visas in Petrograd should be refused to all persons not belonging to one of the following categories recognised by the French as persons to whom diplomatic privileges should be accorded:

1. Diplomatic and consular officials and attachés and their families.
2. Members of the government travelling on duty and their wives.
3. Persons on government missions.
4. Diplomatic couriers.

The question of curtailment of these categories, especially No. 3 was mooted by the Army Council.

The following table shows to a certain extent the work which chiefly affected the G Branch during 1917.

| Statistics for 1917 | | | | | |
|---|---|---|---|---|---|
| | Jan | Dec | Jan–June | Totals June–Dec | Year |
| Personal dossiers made | 785 | 2,071 | 5,288 | 11,529 | 16,817 |
| Telegrams submitted by Censor | 494 | 1,167 | 5,415 | 5,996 | 9,411 |
| Letters submitted by Censor | 5,334 | 2,376 | 17,926 | 13,805 | 31,731 |
| Peace letters | 277 | 283 | 1,979 | 1822 | 3,801 |
| Anti–military cases | 270 | 640 | 1,818 | 3,461 | 5,379 |
| Suspects circulated | 279 | 293 | 1,781 | 1,747 | 3,529 |
| Internments recommended | 22 | 6 | 43 | 14 | 61 |
| Internments sanctioned | 17 | 5 | 32 | 11 | 43 |
| Permit applications examined | 2,709 | 1,557 | 11,719 | 12,409 | 24,188 |
| Passport applications examined | 1,836 | 706 | 6,760 | 7,324 | 14,084 |
| Inland passes | 12 | 13 | 104 | 130 | 234 |

| Credentials examined | | | | | |
|---|---|---|---|---|---|
| Postal Censor | 363 | 233 | 1,212 | 1,786 | 2,998 |
| | Jan | Dec | Jan–June | Totals June–Dec. | Year |
| Red Cross and St John of Jerusalem | 175 | 60 | 1,475 | 1,034 | 2,509 |
| Anglo-French Hospitals | 104 | 32 | 488 | 384 | 872 |
| Ministry of Munitions | 785 | 197 | 4,973 | 13,057 | 8,030 |
| Intelligence Department | 145 | 170 | 842 | 939 | 1,781 |
| For licence to post parcels | – | – | – | – | 662 |
| Aliens previously employed in munitions allowed to leave UK | | 94 | 72 | – | 384 |
| Missing aliens | 576 | 153 | 1,451 | 708 | 2,159 |
| Persons seen at Scotland Yard on behalf of MI 5, the Home Office and the ports | | | | | 232 |

# CHAPTER V

# 1918

BY the New Year of 1918, MI5 had been responsible for the arrest and trial of twenty-one male spies, and two women. Of these twenty-three individuals, thirteen men had been executed, and seven had been imprisoned. Of the women, both had been convicted and imprisoned. One man, Anton Küpferle, had committed suicide while on trial. In addition, 136 men had been interned under DRR 14B, as had twenty-one women.

In 1918, G Branch underwent a further major reorganisation. Captain Radcliffe of G3 was made responsible for maintaining liaison between MI5 and Allied military missions, including military attachés, in the United Kingdom. To G3 also was entrusted the examination of Special Censorship documents which were passed to them from H3.

The collecting of ciphers and codes (D5) was handed over to D Branch as also the co-ordination of British Special Intelligence Missions in Allied countries (D4). In November 1918, a further sub-division of the branch took place. The duties assigned to MI5G, which were divided among nine sub-divisions, were defined as follows:

(i)     Control of investigation of all cases of enemy espionage and sabotage in the United Kingdom.

(ii)    Detection, arrest and bringing to justice of offenders.

(iii)   Counter-espionage and classification of the methods employed by enemy espionage and sabotage agents.

(iv)    Co-operation with government departments, naval and military authorities and police for the above purposes.

(v)      Control of intelligence police at headquarters.

(vi)     Surveillance of suspicious characters.

(vii)    Preparation of cases against persons arrested for prosecution by military and civil authorities in connection with espionage.

(viii)   Examination of suspicious letters and cables as referred.

(ix)     Investigation into evasions of censorship.

(x)      Registration and records of Home Office Warrants and special Censorship checks as imposed.

(xi)     Correspondence and communication with Allied military missions in the United Kingdom on matters affecting counter-espionage services.

(xii)    Investigation into the activities, where detrimental to national interests, of persons of Russian, Finnish, Polish and Czechoslovak nationalities.

(xiii)   Investigation of seditious and pacifist propaganda prejudicial to military security.

Certain restrictions due to the Armistice are noticeable in these clauses: on the other hand the progress of Bolshevism and the urgency of checking its propaganda is marked in the clauses relating both to persons of Russian nationality and to the censorship and Home Office Warrants. This is specially brought out in the very detailed instructions as to Distribution of Duties, which is quoted in full below.

## G1

Investigations into cases of espionage and sabotage by foreign agency in the United Kingdom, also counter-espionage and classification of methods of espionage and sabotage.

## G2

(i) General duties connected with enquiries into the bona-fides of persons in the United Kingdom (as previously).

(ii) Co-operation with government departments, naval and military authorities and police for above purposes.

*G2(a)*

(i) Examination of suspicious letters and cables referred by Postal and Cable Censors, commandants of PoW camps, or other government departments, for enquiry; and investigation connected therewith.

(ii) Investigation into irregular methods of correspondence and evasion of censorship.

(iii) Executive duties connected with enquiries into the bona-fides of persons in the United Kingdom.

(iv) Preliminary investigations into cases of suspected persons.

(v) Correspondence with police forces of the United Kingdom on the above subjects.

*G3*

(i) Correspondence and communication with Allied military missions in the United Kingdom affecting counter-espionage services, and the suitable distribution of information from these sources.

(ii) Special investigation into the cases of suspected persons in diplomatic, financial, and political circles.

*G3(b)*

(i) Liaison officer with Postal and Cable Censors.

(ii) Registration and control of records showing all bank and postal remittances sent to individuals in the United Kingdom from neutral European countries, and investigation in connection therewith.

(iii) Registration and records of Home Office Warrants and Postal and Cable Censorship checks as imposed.

*G4*

(i) Russian, Finish, Polish and Czechoslovak affairs.

(ii) Investigation of cases of the above nationalities and their activities in connection with Bolshevism, espionage, strikes, pacifism, etc. in the United Kingdom.

(iii) Investigation into the bona-fides of persons of the above nationalities entering or leaving the United Kingdom, or applying for permits

to work on munitions; and of all persons travelling to or from
Russia, together with those recommended by MIR for employment
in Russia.

(iv) Investigation of cases of sedition and dissemination of peace
propaganda, and of offences committed against DRR 27 and 42,
otherwise than through the press.

(v) Collection of evidence and transmission to the Home and Scottish
Offices of cases not directly affecting military security or arising from
enemy activities.

(vi) Examination and preparation of reports and articles on sedition and
peace propaganda as affecting military security.

## GL

(i) Preparation of cases against persons arrested for prosecution by
military and civil authorities in connection with espionage.

(ii) Investigation of reports on enemy agents in Allied and neutral
countries, as referred.

## GP

(i) Control of intelligence police at headquarters.

(ii) Surveillance of suspicious characters.

(iii) Special enquiries where secrecy and rapidity are desirable.

★

In April 1915, when various instances had occurred of the use of
telegraphic business code for purposes of espionage, MI5 drafted
an order for the competent military authority to seize and deposit
with the Chief Censor the private code books of the Deutsche Bank and
the Dresdner Bank. Two years after the Deutsche Bank was raided by
order of the War Trade Intelligence Department and MI5G asked that
any documents suggestive of espionage should be handed over to the
bureau. The examination of the documents had not been completed by
September and there is no record of the transfer of any papers to MI5.

In February 1918, in connection with the Bolo revelations, arrangements were made for the officers of MI5 to see the deed-boxes and confidential matter belonging to the Deutsche Bank, the visit being carried out under an order from the competent military authority. The visit was made, but the task of going through the papers would have been so enormous and the result of such doubtful value that the matter was dropped. But a couple of months later, during the preparations for moving the Deutsche Bank to other premises, three codebooks were discovered. An order to seize them was made out on behalf of the bureau, which had meanwhile become possessed of circulars purporting to be of German origin and dealing with measures to be taken by German banks, firms, clubs, etc., for collecting information which would be of use to the Imperial Government.

| Statistics for 1918 | | | | | |
|---|---|---|---|---|---|
| | Jan | Nov | Jan/June | June/Nov | Total 11 months |
| Personal dossiers | 2,290 | 1,867 | 10,107 | 10,998 | 21,189 |
| Telegrams | 1,034 | 1,147 | 6,742 | 5,941 | 12,693 |
| Letters (note: the statistics no longer differentiate between different types of letter) | 3,085 | 2,409 | 18,784 | 15,257 | 34,041 |
| Anti-British cases | 626 | 131 | 2,512 | 1,853 | 4,365 |
| Suspects circulated | 274 | 140 | 1,359 | 932 | 2,291 |
| Internments under 14B | 1 | 1 | 7 | 10 | 17 |
| Permit and passport applications | 2,862 | 2,107 | 16,911 | 12,305 | 20,216 |
| Credentials examined | 729 | 1,820 | 4,105 | 11,599 | 15,704 |
| License to post parcels | | | | | 1,491 |
| For munitions work | 278 | 250 | 1,716 | 1,440 | 3,156 |
| Missing aliens | | | | | 4,057 |

In 1918 it was suggested that Germans might try to use the passes and railway warrants of officers and men who had lost than on the retreat and so gain access to the United Kingdom. Germans were reported to be landing spies from aeroplanes behind the lines in France. The immense extension of munitions factories and dearth of native labour, and consequent importation of foreign labour, offered opportunities which the Germans did not neglect. Rasmussen, who was employed by Vickers, complained of the very inferior mechanics who had been engaged in Denmark for that firm and stated that, in order to gain admission into England, a man who was no mechanic at all had sought to pass as one and had offered him a bribe for his help. Lastly, through MI-1(c) news was received that six Swedish Reserve Fleet officers were to be placed as mates on vessels trading to England and America, and that Berlin looked upon this step as a sure coup.

All the ports were circularised and instructions issued to keep a lookout for these men; the port officer was to detain them and report their arrival by telephone.

One such person was detained and interviewed at Scotland Yard; his answers were unsatisfactory in some ways, but there was no evidence against him. He was not allowed to land in the United Kingdom, as he was found on board the *Mongolia*, on which he was making three trips to France; the French ports were notified. The following ways of carrying messages were reported: in cigarettes, which were lit while the police were conducting the search; in cabochon rings and plaster bandages (seventeen circulars issued to ports, capitals of various organisations); concealed in bread, meat, etc. by a ship's steward named Johan van Bystervelde; written on the paper rolled into rope, with which the Germans were replacing string; and tied round packages. (Ports, capitals, WTID, Home Office, etc., in all eighteen circularised.)

So, early as May 1916 a warrant had been obtained for censoring incoming mails from the French Departments adjoining the Swiss frontier, and a test censorship had been carried out with little result. In September 1916, MI5 had reason to believe that German agents were passing information to Germany via French towns on the Swiss border but, as the French were said to have organised a very careful censorship along their frontier, no action was taken by the British. At the end of 1917 three German agents caught in France confessed that their reports were to be sent to addresses (possibly postboxes only) in towns on the French border, where agents would collect them and convey them into Switzerland. MI5 was able to quote an instance in which a harmless Briton was communicating with the wife of a known German agent at Geneva.

The remedies suggested were the tightening of the frontier controls and the creation of a postal zone of some depth on the frontier with vigorous censorship of all letters sent to that zone and of all letters despatched from it to Switzerland. A test censorship carried out in April by the British Censorship was fruitless.

Special chemical tests were carried out without result on the Swiss, Dutch, Scandinavian and Spanish mails, and all applications for trade and technical publications were to be submitted to MI5G. The Censor proposed passing through all printed matter to persons on the General Black List but MI5G objected.

The question of reducing the number of checks and work of the Censor loomed very large in 1918. The practice had been to photograph all letters submitted to testing on behalf of MI5G; the Censor now limited the practice to those letters of which MI5G expressly asked for a photograph.

All correspondence was divided into three categories end submitted as follows:

-   Category A. All letters in original.
-   Category B. Photographs only of the letters and envelopes together with the Censor's comment.
-   Category C. The Censor's comment only.

In imposing a check reasons as full as possible were to be given. The existing list was to be revised in the light of these instructions but MI9 was to continue testing categories B and C for secret ink at suitable intervals.

If MI9 could vouch that business correspondence emanated from wholly British and reputable firms, such letters need be submitted only in photograph. Eventually it was arranged that letters in B category should be tested unless instructions to the contrary were issued by G officers.

In July cablegrams had been divided into three somewhat similar categories. In October it was arranged that reasons for cancelling any check should be given to the Postal and Cable Censors.

Certain persons whose correspondence was being censored under a HOW had become aware of the fact and it was necessary to try to obviate this. In a general discussion, the point was made that some delay was inevitable in London and still more in the country, therefore, the fewer letters dealt with the better; also that delay with regard to London letters might be diminished if they were dealt with at the place of posting. It was decided that only a proportion of letters should be stopped on one check, that Lieutenant Booth should exercise his discretion on the proportion in each case, and that, in order to help him, the officer putting on the check was to state as far as possible:

(a)  What class of letter was to be dealt with.
(b)  The place where a suspicious letter might be posted.
(c)  When a man had been, or was about to be, directly questioned.

The vast scale of the work done by the GPO appears from the returns of the first week in June 1918 when 1,458 letters were intercepted on 131 HOWs in operation at thirty-one sorting offices. The record of all checks was kept by G3(b). In June G officers were instructed each to keep the record of his own checks in addition to the central record and to overhaul it frequently with a view to reducing the number to the lowest possible.

Repeatedly throughout the war, the transmission of news through gramophone records etc, was reported and measures of protection debated, in 1915 MI5G had some examination of records made but without result. During 1916 the discussion continued but projected measures broke down under the difficulty of administration. In 1917 Arabic records were submitted for examination by the Oriental School of Languages.

The question was raised again in 1918 when a Dane asked for a dictaphone record of a speech. It appeared that the manager of the London Dictaphone Company had in 1914 suggested that all these instruments should be examined by the Censor, but this was not considered necessary. Many Germans, however, had bought dictaphones in the earlier stages of the war and the records could be smuggled. A circular was issued to the ports that, all gramophone and dictaphone records were to be detained unless the traveller had a permit. This was afterwards corrected and orders issued that all dictaphone records but only suspicious gramophone records were to be sent to MI5G for examination.

★

It was reported in February 1917 that Russian banknotes were being sent from England to Switzerland to be disposed of at a premium to the German and Austrian banks. In April, Italian notes were being bought up at Lugano, the notes being despatched from England instead of Italy even though Lugano was only ten miles from the Italian frontier.

Copenhagen was applying for American notes at a high premium, the rate of exchange on notes being six francs to the dollar, whereas for cheques it was only five francs. Traffic in English banknotes began quietly in Switzerland towards the end of November 1917. Messrs Thomas Cook received a request for £200 in £10 notes and, on their enquiring as to the purpose for which these notes were required, the request was withdrawn. But early in 1918 the demand began again and on 8 March 1919 the Treasury informed the DSI of a report received from Messrs Thomas Cook's branch at Zurich to the effect that Swiss bankers were making large demands for British banknotes ('uncut'), on the pretext that they were required for the payment of large purchases of British goods. On the same day the consul-general at Rotterdam reported similar transactions in Holland. Afterwards it was said that repatriated German PoWs were carrying abroad quantities of notes and that notes were also being imported into Holland by the crews of Belgian Relief Commission steamers.

As regards the PoWs, the report was false; such persons were allowed to carry only £10 and this they took usually in the form of Treasury notes. Next came the news that both British and American notes were in great demand in Switzerland. Applications for American and British notes were also coming in from Spain and Sweden. Spain had begun to apply for American notes in February 1918. The purpose for which these notes were required was not clearly established; about eleven different explanations were given of which the most interesting are:

1.  Payment of enemy agents.
2.  Propaganda and fomenting of trouble in India and Egypt (one of the principal buyers was a man named Leu, whose account was kept by the ex-Khedive).
3.  Bribery on the Western Front as formerly on the Russian and Italian Front.
4.  Investment by German anti-Austrian private individuals.
5.  Payment to peasants of the Ukraine in return for food supplies.

Finally, the Trade branch of the Censorship reduced the case to two questions necessitating alternative policies, stating that if enemy governments were buying the notes to pay for food or for any purpose, political or economic, action must be taken at once, but if the notes were being bought by Russians or Ukrainians as a reliable form of currency no action was needed. Meanwhile various measures had been taken to get behind the facts. The Treasury considered the large buying of British notes as on the whole favourable to the country's interests, therefore the Treasury proposed to let matters alone.

The Deputy Governor of the Bank of England thought the buying of notes had not taken place on a large enough scale to make drastic action necessary, but the movement should be watched and, if action should become desirable, the Bank and the War Office should confer and agree upon a plan before approaching the Treasury. The Deputy-Governor was anxious to know whether the demand was for cut or uncut notes.

The policy of observation was carried out as follows: MI5 arranged with Messrs Thomas Cook to forward to Zurich twenty notes of £100 and to watch and report on their sale. As it was supposed the notes would be returned to the bank to be cashed, the numbers were put on check at the bank and also at the Censorship. Mr Maxse, the consul-general, was asked to place some British notes in Holland and to watch their course there.

The Censor made arrangements to record the numbers of all notes entering and leaving the United Kingdom. A careful record was kept at the ports of all British and American notes of £5 and upwards carried abroad by passengers. Treasury notes, however, were not to be recorded. Further action was not possible since, although Messrs Thomas Cook considered that passengers had no need to carry more than £10 in notes, restriction of the amount carried by passengers could be imposed only by an order under DRR and to this the Treasury had objected. Certain definite information was obtained by the measures adopted:

1.  The notes sent to Switzerland were sold at a rate of 25 francs, while the proceeds remitted to London were at 20 francs 76. In April the exchange on notes rose to 27 francs, and in the first week of May to 32 francs, but by the end of the month it had dropped to 22 francs; the notes were being bought by German and Austrian speculators.
2.  In Holland the prices during March and April were 11 francs 80 and 13 fl, as against cheque rates of 10 fl 60 and 10 fl 8; the notes were being bought by Galician Jews and were destined, it was supposed, for South Russia.
3.  Censorship returns showed the following totals of exported notes:

| Dates | Total in £ | Countries |
|---|---|---|
| 20 March 1918 to 20 April 1919 | £74,002 | Switzerland, Holland and Norway |
| 28 April 1918 to 11 June 1918 | £47,003 | Switzerland, Holland and Norway |
| Week ending 18 May 1918 | £76,270 | Switzerland, Holland and Norway |
| Week ending 25 May 1918 | £61,416 | Six countries |
| Week ending 1 June 1918 | £110,961 | Nine countries |

Switzerland and Holland remained the chief importers of banknotes. From 13 May all notes leaving the United Kingdom were marked in the Censorship in such a way that they could be identified on return. Then came a report from Christiania that higher prices were being obtained for larger suns and that clean notes were wanted. It was then arranged that outgoing Treasury notes as well as bank notes were to be marked and MI5's officers at the ports were to keep watch for such notes coming in.

In September 1918 it was reported that an employee of Hannevigts Bank of 56 Old Broad Street in the City of London, was doing a large trade in exporting British notes to banks in Christiania and Amsterdam, where the notes were sold to German customers at a considerable profit. A man named Bauman was reported to be making a fortune by sending banknotes per registered post.

The Censor denied this. The check on these notes was given up in November 1918. During the time of its running only one enemy agent had been detected who had been paid in banknotes and those notes had not been marked.

★

As early as January 1916 a report had been received and circulated to the ports and Scotland Yard to the effect that 500,000 notes in English currency had been despatched from Berlin to Switzerland and Holland for anti-recruiting propaganda in England. In February 1917 the *Daily Express* published a note to the effect that there was 'abundant evidence' that German Secret Service money was pouring into the country. This was traced back to the editor of the *Liverpool Courier*, who had heard from a Member of Parliament that the funds of various pacifist societies in this country were replenished by monies paid into Oriental banks, specifically the Imperial Bank of Persia, and that an elaborate system of bills of exchange was in use to disguise from the societies the source of these funds. The editor could not, however, remember the name of the MP, the Imperial Bank of Persia was supposed to be above suspicion, it was in any case difficult to approach except through the Foreign

Office, and the bureau decided that the information was imaginary. But Major Drake requested the management of the Bank of Persia to notify any curious remittances, a wise precaution, for in October of the same year the bank reported that telegraphic instructions had been received from the Swiss bank to remit £5,000 on behalf of Schiff Manovitch, Petrograd, to D. Datavoff of Meshed, Persia. G Branch referred the matter to D.

Eventually the transfer of monies amounted to £75,000, and proof was obtained that the agents of a certain Persian firm were purchasing German goods in Moscow and remitting large sums from Russia to Persia via London. This agent, Vahaboff, was afterwards stated to be working for the Bolsheviks. The one clue followed up resulted in procuring some evidence of Bolshevik propaganda in the east.

In November 1918, on the advice of G4, the bureau, having ascertained that a Russian Jew named Axelrod, an Internationalist belonging to the Russian Socialist Revolutionary Party and possibly also a Bolshevik, was receiving money through Mr Arthur Henderson, asked that early information (if possible before the money had been released) should be given to the bureau of all remittances from Russian subjects in neutral countries, and stated that remittances made in the Bolshevik interest would probably be for small sums so as not to attract attention. Sir Adam Block for the Treasury pointed out that such payments would very likely not be made by Russian subjects, and that under DRR 41DD no such payment could be made by Russian subjects resident anywhere or persons residing for the time-being in Russia to persons or to the credit of persons residing in the United Kingdom without previous reference to the Trading with the Enemy Branch, which was the authority administering the regulation. Therefore it was decided that MI5 should continue to watch the monthly returns and to warn the Treasury if payments were being made to undesirable persons, and the Trading with the Enemy Branch was to report to MI5 any suspicious case occurring under Regulation 41DD.

In connection with Axelrod, Colonel Sealy Clarke made strong representations to the effect that the Foreign Office should get rid of this dangerous party of Russians as soon as possible and should no longer sanction the issue of visas to Russians of the type. The DMI ordered that where strong military reasons (and Bolshevism was one) existed for refusing a visa, MI5 was to take a firm stand with the Foreign Office and, if necessary, the Foreign Secretary himself was to be seen. G Branch had advised strongly against the admittance of Axelrod's party but had been overruled by the DMI. The practice of G Branch was to refer all cases of refusal of visa to Colonel Kell.

★

This case is illustrative of G Branch's work and co-operation with the French services. Enquiry came from French counter-espionage, 18 Bedford Square, as to Cesar Vital, a Belgian engineer, who had travelled much between England and Lisbon via France and was suspected. MI5's G3 dealt with this case. Information was sent to M. Noiriel that Vital was a man with an unusual knowledge of mining and metallurgy and German methods, besides knowledge of aircraft, electrical matters and many other matters connected with war methods. He had cane to England from Paris in January 1916 and got in touch with engineers here. He asserted that he had escaped from Belgium since the German occupation and that someone was impersonating him there.

He was engaged in various negotiations of importance which misfired strangely when apparently on the point of success. He went to Spain in May 1916 and during his absence information was laid against him. The rigorous search of his person and baggage on his return from Spain called forth a protest from M. Hymans, the Belgian minister, and Vickers' directors, for when Vital was working in the electrical department, asserted that he possessed their confidence. Vital returned to Spain in November 1916. Subsequently the opinion of the directors changed, Vital was dismissed from Vickers in June 1917 and went to live in France at the end of August 1917. The BCI informed the British authorities that Vital had left a box at an address in Bloomsbury and was claiming it from the landlady.

Authority to search under DRR 51 was given by G2. The box had been there since May 1916. The contents were examined by Lieutenant Bremer in the presence of M. Noiriel. The trunk was sent to Paris; MI-1(c) had been asked to trace Vital; he turned up in Madrid in November.

Enquiries had been made of the Belgian minister in Lisbon; he thought Vital reliable and an employee of the Belgian government. The French authorities were satisfied as to Vital's bona-fides and asked that his property might be returned to him, and there was no objection from G3 as Vital had been in the Belgian Secret Service. The hamper was despatched from Paris on 26 May 1919 and it reached Richborough on 3 July 1919. It arrived in London on 21 July 1919 and was sent to the Belgian authorities to be forwarded.

# German Espionage Suspects Investigated by MI5

| Name | Conclusion |
|---|---|
| Nicholas Ahlers | Arrested, 5 August 1914 |
| Ramona Amondarain | Deported, September |
| W. E. Andrews | No record |
| Fredrik Apel | Arrested, 4 August 1914 |
| George Vaux Bacon | Sentenced to life imprisonment, 28 February 1917 |
| Richard Berger | Left the country in 1913 |
| Robert Blackburn | Imprisoned for two years, October 1914 |
| Alexander Blok | German intelligence officer in Amsterdam |
| Blonden | No record |
| Eva de Bournonville | Sentenced to life imprisonment, January 1916 |
| Cornelis den Braben | Arrested, June 1915 |
| George Breckow | Shot, Tower of London, 26 October 1915 |
| William F. Brown | Arrested, 14 August 1914 |
| Emil Brugman | Deported, 1915 |
| Franz Bubenheim | Left the country |
| Oscar Buchwaldt | Arrested, 4 August 1914 |
| Fernando Buschman | Shot, Tower of London, 19 September 1915 |
| Johan Jakob Calkoen | Left the country, June 1915 |
| Barnet Carlishe | Arrested, June 1915 |
| Vittorio Corini | Scheduled for arrest, 1917 |
| John Couttes | No record |
| Wilhelm Croner | Committed suicide, 23 January 1913 |
| Francis Deacon | No record |
| Fredereich von Diederichs | Arrested, 4 August 1914 |

| | |
|---|---|
| Hilmar Dierks | German intelligence officer in Rotterdam (alias Richard Sanderson) |
| Adolphe Dittmar | Arrested and deported, April 1915 |
| Charles Dittmar | Arrested and deported, April 1915 |
| Max Dressler | German intelligence officer in Ostend |
| Suzanne Dupont | Deported, August 1916 |
| Edward Durkin | Arrested, 6 August 1914 |
| Hans Eils | German intelligence officer in Antwerp |
| Abraham Eisner | Excluded from Porstmouth, August 1914 |
| John Emery | No record |
| Johann Engel | Arrested, 4 August 1914 |
| Edward Evans | No record |
| Friedel Fels | German intelligence officer |
| Heinrich Flores | German intelligence officer in Rotterdam |
| Madame Fontaine | Arrested and deported, April 1915 |
| Fowler, Frederick | Arrested, 4 August 1914 |
| Arthur Glanville | Disappeared, March 1914 |
| Heddy Glauer | Escaped to Ireland, 1911 |
| Leon van der Goten | Life imprisonment, September 1917 |
| Frederick Graff | Enrolled as a double agent, 1916 |
| Armgaard Graves | Imprisoned, April 1912 |
| James Gray | Placed under surveillance, December 1915 |
| Frank Greite | Ten years' imprisonment, July 1916 |
| Heinrich Grosse | Imprisoned, February 1912 |
| Adolpho Guerrero | Ten years' imprisonment, July 1916 |
| Alfred Hagn | Life imprisonment, August 1917 |
| John Hahn | Imprisoned for seven years, June 1917 |
| Joseph Hallmeyer | No record |
| Charles Hastings | Interviewed at Scotland Yard, March 1016 |
| John Hattrick | Arrested, May 1912 |
| Thomas Hegnauer | Arrested, 4 August 1914 |
| Line Heine | Arrested, 4 August 1914 |
| Siegfried Helm | Arrested, September 1910 |
| Carl Hemlar | Arrested, 4 August 1914 |
| Carl Hensel (alias Irving Ries) | Shot, Tower of London, 27 October 1915 |

| Karl Hentschel | Confessed, April 1913 |
| Baron von Hettlebadt | Interned, September 1914 |
| May Higgs | Interned, December 1916 |
| Francis Holstein | Scheduled for arrest, August 1914 |
| Marius Hoogendyk | Arrested, June 1915 |
| George Hopley | Arrested, November 1914 |
| Stephen Horvath | Implicated, July 1915 |
| Ludovico Hurwitz y Zender | Shot, Tower of London, 11 April 1916. |
| Frederick Ireland | Arrested, February 1912 |
| Aladdin bin Issel | Left the country, December 1913 |
| Haicke Janssen | Shot, Tower of London, 30 July 1915 |
| Abdon Jappe | Three years' imprisonment, November 1915 |
| H. F. P. Kinzler | Deported, April 1916 |
| William Klare | Imprisoned for five years, June 1913 |
| August Klunder | Arrested, 4 August 1914 |
| E. J. Knight | No record |
| Hans von Krohn | German naval attaché in Madrid |
| Marie Kronauer | Arrested, 4 August 1914 |
| Otto Kruger | Arrested, 4 August 1914 |
| Johann Kuhr | Arrested, 4 August 1914 |
| Johann Lassen | Deported, January 1916 |
| Max Laurons | Arrested, 4 August 1914 |
| Anna Liebfreund (nee Stad) | Arrested, June 1915 |
| Lewis Liebfreund | Arrested, June 1915 |
| Ignatius Trebitsch Lincoln | Confessed, January 1915 |
| Carl Lody (alias Charles Inglis) | Committed suicide, November 1914 |
| Franz Lozel | Arrested, 4 August 1914 |
| Fred Manasse | Arrested, October 1915 |
| Josef Marks | Imprisoned for five years, September 1915 |
| Ernest Melin | Shot, Tower of London, 10 September 1915 |
| Albert Meyer | Shot, Tower of London, 2 December 1915 |
| Carl Meyer | Arrested, 4 August 1914 |
| Gerty Moore | No record |
| Carl Muller | Shot, Tower of London, 23 June 1915 |
| Hugo Munscheid | German intelligence officer in Antwerp |

| | |
|---|---|
| Ahmed Nedjib | Left the country in 1913 |
| Gustav Neumann | Witness at the Schule trial, November 1913 |
| Robert Nichol | Discharged from the Royal Navy, November 1912 |
| Gosta Olai | Left the country, November 1912 |
| George Parrott | Imprisoned for four years, August 1913 |
| August Patrocinio | Arrested, September 1917 |
| George Pelling | Scheduled for arrest, August 1914 |
| Philip Penrose | Resigned from Chatham, August 1914 |
| William Power | No record |
| Walter Reimann | Left the country, August 1914 |
| Carl Reimers | German intelligence officer in Potsdam |
| Hilda Reynolds | No action taken, October 1915 |
| Edith Riley (Mrs Penrose) | No record |
| Mrs Emily Riley | Arrested, 4 August 1914 |
| Emily Riley (Mrs Pelling) | No record |
| Nellie Riley | No record |
| Patricia Riley (Mrs Hentschel) | No record |
| Celso Rodriguez | Arrested, 4 August 1914 |
| Augusto Roggen | Shot, Tower of London, 17 September 1915 |
| R. Roland (or Ronald) | No record |
| Willem Roos | Shot, Tower of London, 30 July 1915 |
| Robert Rosenthal | Hanged, Wormwood Scrubs, 15 July 1915 |
| Pierre Rotheudt | Sentenced to ten years at Fresnes, December 1916 |
| Roxroy | No record |
| Antonius Rummenie | Arrested, 4 August 1914 |
| Kenneth de Rysbach | Life imprisonment, June 1915 |
| William Sagar | Interned upon his release from imprisonment. |
| Harry Sampson | Imprisoned for twenty-eight days, April 1914 |
| Frederick Scherer | Deported to Belgium, April 1915 |
| Otto Scherer | Deported to Belgium, April 1915 |
| Heinrich (Hugo) Schmidt | Detained as a PoW, 12 August 1914 |
| Adolf Schneider | Arrested, 4 August 1914 |
| Adolf Schroeder (alias Frederick Gould) | Imprisoned for six years, April 1914 |
| Max Schule | Sentenced to twenty-one months, August 1911 |
| Heinrich Schutte | Arrested, 4 August 1914 |

| Pauline Slager | Left the county, August 1915 |
| Maria Slager | Banned from entry, 1917 |
| Wilhelm Slager | Banned from exit, 1917 |
| Sopher | Interned, May 1916 |
| Kurt Sparr | No record |
| David Stad | Arrested, June 1915 |
| W. Stamm | Arrested, 5 August 1914 |
| George Stammer | German intelligence officer in Berlin |
| Albertine Stanaway | Arrested, March 1917 |
| Gustav Steinhauer | Chief of German Secret Service |
| Peter Steunebrink | Banned from re-entry, November 1915 |
| Karl Stubenwoll | Arrested, 4 August 1914 |
| Fred Sukowski | Arrested, 4 August 1914 |
| Robert Tornow | German intelligence officer in Rotterdam (alias Pierre Theisen) |
| Kenneth Triest | Arrested, 1915 |
| Georgine Ulrich | Arrested, August 1915 |
| Leopoldo Vieyra | Life imprisonment, 11 November 1916 |
| Charles Wagener | Arrested, September 1914 |
| Karl von Wilier | Arrested, 4 August 1914 |
| George Wittstruck | Excluded from Sheerness, August 1914 |
| Chalres Wunnenburg | Arrested in New York in February 1917 |
| Jacobus van Zurk | Deported, March 1917 |

# G Branch Personnel

## G Branch Personnel, February 1917

### G
- Major J. F. C. Carter
- Major V. Ferguson
- Major H. B. Matthews

### G2
- Major E. St. G. Anson

### G2(a)
- Mr P. W. Marsh
- Commander F. B. Henderson CMG DSO
- Major C. A. M. Dunlop MC
- Captain A. F. Hordern
- Captain G. Cookson

### G2(b)
- Major S. C. Welchman
- Major G. Lubbock

### G2(c)
- Captain S. J. Sassoon
- Lieut. W. F. Fielding

## G2(d)

- Mr H. B. Clayton
- Mr G. Streatfield
- Lieut. F. H. Lawes
- Mr H. B. Goad

## G3

- Major E. St. G. Anson
- Miss B. Beddome
- Miss B. A. Balance
- Miss O. Beddome
- Miss L. M. Jackson
- Miss G. Thorburn

## G4

- Major Baron W. G. Bentinck CMG DSO

## G5

- Lieut. M. Bremer

## G6

- Lieut. S. Taylor
- Mr B. Westell
- Lieut. S. R. Cooke
- Lieut. Henry Curtis-Bennett

# G Branch Personnel, June 1917

## G

- Major J. F. C. Carter
- Mr M. M. Cousins
- Mr B. E. Boulter Esq.
- Miss G. Holmes

- Miss N. Borrett
- Miss K. Lee

*G1*

- Major V. Ferguson
- Major H. B. Matthews
- N. W. Bray Esq.
- W. N. Parker Esq.
- Miss M. C. Robson
- Miss G. K. B. Crick
- Miss H. W. Neal

*G2(a)*

- Commander F. B. Henderson CMG DSO
- P. W. Marsh Esq.
- Major C. A. Dunlop MC
- Lieut. S. M. Cookson
- G. H. Streatfield Esq.
- Miss Y. M. Adair
- Miss S. M. Humble
- Miss M. Piper
- Miss E. Williams

*G2(b)*

- Lieut. Colonel G. M. Ormerod DSO
- Major S. C. Welchman
- Captain S. J. Sassoon
- Lieut. F. H. Lawes
- Miss E. E. Tunningley
- Miss M. D. Gibbons

*G3*

- Mrs B. Brooke
- Miss D. Dallas

## G4
- Major Baron W. G. Bentinck CMG DSO
- Miss L. Gracey
- Miss M. Harris

## G5
- Lieut. M. Bremer

## G6
- Lieut. H. H. Curtis-Bennett
- Captain S. R. Cooke
- Lieut. S. Taylor
- S. Westell Esq.

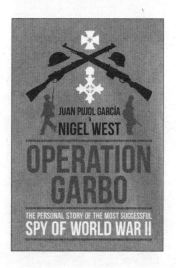

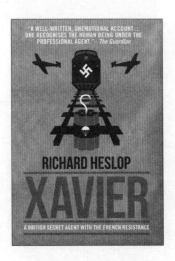

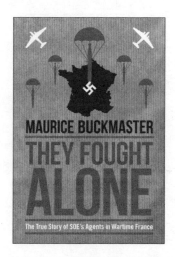